PUSHKIN

PUSHKIN
A Biography

Elaine Feinstein

THE ECCO PRESS

THE ECCO PRESS
100 West Broad Street
Hopewell, New Jersey 08525

Printed in the United States of America

Library of Congress Cataloging-in-Publication Data
Feinstein, Elaine.
Pushkin / by Elaine Feinstein. — 1st ed.
p.   cm.
Includes bibliographical references.
ISBN 0-88001-674-4
1. Pushkin, Aleksandr Sergeevich, 1799–1837.   2. Poets,
Russian—19th century—Biography.   I. Title
PG3350.F45   1999
891.71'3—dc21   98-38981
[B]   CIP

9 8 7 6 5 4 3 2 1

FIRST ECCO EDITION 1999

CONTENTS

ACKNOWLEDGEMENTS

The author gratefully acknowledges permission to quote from Gillon Aitken, trans., *The Complete Prose Tales of Alexander Pushkin* (Vintage, 1993); A. D. P. Briggs, *Selected Poems of Pushkin* (Everyman, 1997); Robin Edmonds, *Pushkin* (Macmillan, 1994); Professor James E. Falen, *Eugene Onegin* (Oxford University Press); Kluwer Academic and Lippincott Raven Publishers Inc., for raising no objection to the use of material from Magarshack, *Pushkin: A Biography* (London, 1967), and D. S. Mirsky, *Pushkin* (Routledge, London, 1926); to Weidenfeld & Nicolson for permission to quote from Alan Palmer, *Alexander I* (London 1974); to Harvard University Press for lines from Ernest Simmons, *Pushkin* (1927; also published by O.U.P., London 1937); Secker and Warburg Ltd for lines quoted from *The Bronze Horseman and Other Poems* by Alexander Pushkin, translation copyright D. M. Thomas; to the Athlone Press, London, for permission to quote from Tatiana Wolff, *Pushkin on Literature*; and to Antony Wood for permission to quote from an unpublished MS and from *Mozart and Salieri: The Little Tragedies of Alexander Pushkin* (Angel Press, 1982). I am particularly grateful to Professor J. Thomas Shaw for permission to quote from his three volume *Letters of Alexander Pushkin* (University of Pennsylvania Press and Indiana University Press, 1963). In that and subsequent editions, Professor Shaw punctiliously uses first letters followed by dashes for words whose meaning the context makes clear, since these have never been spelled out in any Russian edition of Pushkin's works. It is very generous of him to allow me on my own responsibility to spell out these words according to contemporary English usage.

I am particularly indebted to Tatyana Bulanina of the Dmitrij Bulanin publishing house, whose help made it possible for me to quote material from the following books first published in Russia: P. K. Guber, *Don-Zhuansky Spisok Pushkina* (1990); A. P. Kern, *Vospominanya o Pushkine* (Sovetskaya Rossiya, Moscow 1988); Yuri Lotman, *Pushkin: Biograpfyia pisatelya stat'i i zametki 1850–1990 Yevgeny Onegin, Kormmentariy* (St Petersburg, 1995); P. Obodovskaya and M. Dementyev, *Natalya Pushkina po epistolarnym materialam,* second edition (Sovetskaya Rossiya, Moscow 1987); I. I. Pushchin, *Zapiski o Pushkine* (Moscow, 1925); P. E. Shchegolev, *Duel i smert' Pushkina: issledovanyia materialy* fourth edition (Kniga, 1987); Serena Vitale, V. P. Stark, M. I. Pisareva, S. V. Slivinskaya, *Letters of George Heeckeren 1835–1836* (Zvezda, St Petersburg, no 9, 1997); and Serena Vitale, V. P. Stark, M. I. Pisareva, S. V. Slivinskaya, *Letters of Georges d'Anthes to Ekaterina Goncharova 1836–1837* (Petersburg, 1995, no 8).

ILLUSTRATIONS

INTRODUCTION

Alexander Sergeevich Pushkin is Russia's greatest poet and the foun-
tainhead of literature in the Russian language. The novelists and poets
who followed him, through the two centuries since his death, have all
acknowledged their debt to his genius. He is so much a part of the
Russian sensibility that his name can be used in common domestic
speech: a child, for instance, might be scolded, 'Who do you think will
close the door after you ... Pushkin?' The shape of his tragic life has the
resonance of a legend. Yet even the outline of that life is unfamiliar to
the general reader in the rest of the world.

It was a life of poignant brevity. Pushkin was the child of a feckless
Russian aristocrat and a descendant of the African slave who became a
favourite of Peter the Great. His poems aroused the suspicion of two
tsars, and were found among the papers of all the Decembrist conspirators. He was a man of reckless ebullience and ready wit, a profligate
who had affairs with some of the most beautiful women of his time yet
chose a cold young beauty for his wife. At 37, he was killed in a duel
fought to defend her honour.

In the English-speaking world, all the classic biographies written in
the West are out of print as I write.[1] Since the publication of the most
recent biography, much important new material has thrown light on the
events of Pushkin's last year, particularly the character of Baron Georges
d'Anthès, whose pursuit of Natalya Nikolaevna, Pushkin's wife, led to
the fatal duel. An archive of letters from d'Anthès to his protector, the
Dutch Ambassador Baron van Heeckeren, was discovered and deci-
phered by Professor Serena Vitale of the University of Pavia, and published in 1995. Since then, the work of Vadim Stark of Pushkinsky Dom
in St Petersburg, alongside other evidence unearthed by the Dutch scholar
Frans Suasso[2] in the Netherlands State archives, and the work of I.
Lefkovich of Pushkinsky Dom, have established not only the duplicity
of Heeckeren and d'Anthès in presenting their relationship as that of

father and adopted son but fresh evidence which accounts for d'Anthès's sudden and unexpected marriage to Ekaterina, Natalya's sister.

Equally significant is the publication of the magnificent facsimile edition of Pushkin's working notebooks, edited by Professor Sergey A. Fomichev and Professor I. Ligachev of Pushkinsky Dom. This, together with a monograph by Fomichev,[3] turns out to be an invaluable entry into the contradictions of Pushkin's inner world.

For almost everything in Pushkin's personality was paradoxical. To take one example, which seems to go to the heart of the man, even though Pushkin's ancestry on both sides was always important to him, he went out of his way to stress the pride he took in his African inheritance. In a stanza of *Evgeny Onegin*, written in Odessa in 1823, he indulges in a fantasy of escape by boat to the warm sky of 'my Africa'.[4] He delighted in his friend Nashchokin's gift of an inkwell with a statuette of a black man leaning on an anchor in front of two bales of cotton, offered in honour of both Pushkin's literary genius and the origins of his illustrious forebear.

As a child, however, his looks, combined with his mother's mockery, made him uneasy about his appearance. Many caricatures of his profile in his working notebooks exaggerate his features, and in a poem, 'To Yurev', written in 1820,[5] he links his sense of ugliness to his African inheritance with impudent panache:

> While I, always an idle rake
> Ugly descendant of a Black
> Reared in a wilderness, can take
> No pleasure in the pains of love.
> Whenever I have won a beauty
> It is through shameless, hot desire
> That leads a nymph, still innocent
> To flush in an embarrassment
> She does not fully understand
> And stealthily observe a satyr.

His unfinished novel, *The Negro of Peter the Great* (1827–8), about his own great-grandfather, invents the inner world of a young black man who resents being treated as no more than an intriguing curiosity by white women. The doodles in the margin of the manuscripts betray how central such a thought was to Pushkin's own life, for all his own sexual successes.

The paradoxes of his character extend from his feelings about his blackness into every aspect of his relation to women. In his poetry he was the creator of heroines with a rare spirit and subtle intelligence, yet in his own life he preferred physical loveliness to any other quality, as Anna Kern, his 'vision of pure beauty', observed: 'and this explained his low opinion of them, which was, of course, completely in accord with the spirit of the age.'[6]

In 1829, when he was beginning to think of matrimony, Pushkin frivolously wrote the first names of all the women he had ever loved into the album of Elizaveta Ushakova, the younger sister of a woman he may have hoped to marry – this has come to be known as his Don Juan list. Yet he was no callous libertine, like Mozart's Don Giovanni, or as weary of the whole game as Don Juan in his own 'Little Tragedy', 'The Stone Guest'. Byron's pose of bored indifference to human affections impressed Pushkin for a time, but many of his loveliest lyrics reveal him suffering in a relationship which a woman is trying to end. The pattern of Pushkin's feelings about himself, occasioned by his numerous love affairs, is as important as the identities of the women to whom his lyrics were addressed, but has been far less extensively explored by former biographers.[7] One of his saddest lyrics, written in February 1824, has the key line, 'I understand, love was not made for me.'

Few people knew Pushkin intimately, though many were acquainted with the man who was both gregarious and an exhilarating companion. Aside from schoolfriends such as Ivan Pushchin, who was sent into Siberian exile, and Baron Anton Delvig, from whom Pushkin was separated for many years while himself exiled in southern Russia, Pushkin revealed his inner self to few of his admirers. Still less did he expect to share his uncertainties with the women he loved. For all the lively wit that earned him the nickname of 'Cricket', he must have often been a lonely man.

The inconsistencies of Pushkin's political position have made it possible for almost all factions to enlist his poetry as an endorsement – even Slavophils such as Dostoevsky have been able to claim this most urbanely European of poets as their own. Pushkin's close friendships among the Decembrists, and his affection for the folk tales of the common people, made it easy for the former Soviet government to present him as an early Revolutionary poet. On the other hand, since the Tsar exercised a close censorship over everything Pushkin wrote, those living under Soviet tyranny could recognise in him a martyr figure comparable to the writers suppressed by the Communist regime. This is partly because Pushkin's political thought evolved during his lifetime. However, Alexander Kushner, since Joseph Brodsky's death the most distinguished St Petersburg poet of our own day, put the matter to me wryly in October 1997: 'Like every good poet, Pushkin had one opinion in one poem and another in another. It depends on the mood and the context which prompted the poem ... a poet never says "yes" or "no", but "yes" and "no" at the same time.'

Pushkin's working notebooks throw light on some of the contradictions of his political beliefs. He might well have been on Senate Square with his Decembrist friends in 1825 if he had not been exiled to Mikhaylovskoe. Loyalty to friends was a matter of honour, and he was no coward. But he was no unequivocal Revolutionary either. Sketches in the early notebooks show him trying on the wigs of figures from the French Revolution with some irony, and by the end of his life he had come to distrust the opinion of the mob as profoundly as Shakespeare. Nevertheless, the execution of his Decembrist friends rose to his mind whenever he wrote of cruelty, and sketches of their hanging haunt his manuscripts. For those who opposed the Tsar and those who opposed the Soviet regime alike, Pushkin's poetry 'accompanied Russian citizens into the darkest recesses of personal anguish, including persecution, the prison house and permanent exile'.[8] Now, in the confusion of a new capitalist Russia, as many Russians are turning back either to the Church or to alternative forms of spirituality, there is an insistent pressure to see Pushkin, too, as having become a convinced believer toward the end of his life.

In Russia this deference to Pushkin's exemplary status can be overpowering; it lies behind several unpleasant attacks on Andrey Sinyavsky's charming and light-hearted *Strolls with Pushkin*. I am indebted to Sir Rodric Braithwaite for an account of the deliberations of the Writers' Union in the autumn of 1989, 'in which one writer saw a direct connection between Sinyavsky's book and a recent desecration of a Pushkin monument in one of the non-Russian Republics of the Union and another said that "socialism and the fatherland are in danger" ... in this context the fatherland and Pushkin are the same thing.'

There is no doubt that so much solemnity would have amused Pushkin. In one of his 'Little Tragedies' Pushkin tells the story of Mozart's poisoning, and in a few brilliant pages suggests both Salieri's envy of genius and the unworldly frankness of Mozart's generous spirit. Alexander

Kushner thought Pushkin looked at Mozart 'as if into a mirror'. There Pushkin made out a human being who was as happy in a tavern as at dinner with his equals, and whose intelligence went as finely into his poetry as Mozart's went into his music. His posthumous triumph over the courtiers who patronised him has been as triumphant as that of the composer.

The clarity and simplicity of Pushkin's language, alongside his extraordinary felicity of form, have made his poetry peculiarly resistant to translation, though there have been two excellent versions of his masterpiece, *Evgeny Onegin*. Aside from the intoxication of Pushkin's verse, *Onegin* has a subtlety of human understanding and a tragic shapeliness which make the poem instantly enjoyable, and readers will perceive how it prepares the way for the nineteenth-century Russian novel. His magical lyric gift is another matter. To imagine his qualities as a poet, a reader of English literature would have to invent a writer with the facility of Byron, the sensuous richness of Keats and a bawdy wit reminiscent of Chaucer.

Where no translator is mentioned in this book the translations of poems quoted are my own, but I have also gratefully used translations by James E. Falen, A. D. P. Briggs, Antony Wood, Jill Higgs and D. M. Thomas and their authorship is credited in the footnotes. Pushkin's personal letters have a particular vigour. For these, I have used J. Thomas Shaw's three-volume edition (Indiana University Press, 1963). Quotations from Pushkin's unpublished articles have been taken from Tatyana Wolff's invaluable *Pushkin on Literature* (1971).

I should like to thank those who have made translations of prose texts from the Russian – Cathy Porter, Seryozha Zakin, Claire Farrimond and Alla Gelich. I should also like to thank Sir Rodric Braithwaite; Professor Sergey Fomichev and Vadim Stark of Pushkinsky Dom; Dr Sergey Nekrassov and his curators at the Pushkin Museum in St Petersburg; Professor Mikhailova in the Pushkin Museum in Moscow; Megan Dixon, research assistant of Professor David Bethea, and contributors to the Proceedings of the Wisconsin Pushkin Conference who allowed me to see their articles in MS, notably S. L. Davydov, Caryl Emerson and William Mills Todd III; Professor Anthony Briggs, who very kindly allowed me to see in MS some of the essays which will form part of his book *Why Pushkin?*, and who read this book in proof; those friends such as Antony Wood and Anthony Rudolf who have helped me with the loan of books and advice; Simon Franklin and Jana Howlett of the University of Cambridge; Richard Cohen; Phil Cavendish of the School of Slavonic Studies; and Tatyana Wolff, for recording a number of Pushkin poems on tape for me. I should like to thank Antony Wood and Tatyana Wolff for reading this book in MS, Alla Gelich who read the chapter on d'Anthès, and Tatyana Bulanina for her generous help in clearing permissions with writers and editors in Russia. I should also like to thank my invaluable secretary Jane Wynborne, and finally my husband Dr Arnold Feinstein, for his scrupulous collation of drawings in Fomichev's monograph and Tsyavlavskaya's *Risunki Pushkina*.[9]

Elaine Feinstein
December 1997

CHAPTER ONE

Imperial Russia

The visible symbol of Imperial Russia was St Petersburg itself, built on marshy, frozen wastes at the edge of the Baltic in the early eighteenth century. It was the location chosen by Peter the Great as his window on to Europe, mainly because Peter hated Moscow, the ancient Russian capital, for its backwardness, crooked streets and murderous rebellions. He intended his city to have architecture of classical proportions, with broad streets, open, clean and eminently easy to police. The lives of innumerable peasants, soldiers, convicts and prisoners of war were sacrificed to that ambition. In sunshine, St Petersburg is one of the most glittering cities on the face of the earth, yet even at the time of its creation Peter's first wife put a curse upon it, and it remains at the mercy of floods to this day. As Nikolay Karamzin, the great historian whose life was in part contemporary to Pushkin, remarked, 'Petersburg is founded on tears and corpses.'

The Court in St Petersburg, however, with its brocade coats from France, lace ruffles from the Netherlands and buckled shoes from England, was as splendid as any in Europe. The splendour concealed the violence that held the autocracy in place. Peter had declared his intention to break with the Asiatic barbarism of Moscow, but he used torture to impose his will, and sometimes even took part in person. Offenders were burned with hot irons, broken on the rack and had their tongues torn out. Peter had his own son, Alexis, tortured to death for alleged treason. The man whose 'will founded the city beneath the sea' unquestionably wanted to make Russia great. He founded an Academy of Sciences, a

Russian public museum, a library and the first newspaper. He was physically inexhaustible and immensely gifted. However, the bulk of the population of his empire lived in poverty and illiteracy. Most of his people were peasants, and throughout the eighteenth century almost all of these were either serfs of private landowners or in bondage to the state. There was no bourgeoisie of a Western European kind. Very few Russians lived in towns, and of those who did most were desperately poor. Merchants depended on the patronage of the nobility, and had little opportunity for enterprise of their own. Bureaucrats were either of noble origin or ennobled on gaining high position, and there were very few intellectuals. All power lay in the Tsar, and the noblest officers of the land gained their power only from the confidence of the Emperor.

Tyranny was easy to justify by the danger of rebellion, which was real enough. Weak rulers, such as those who succeeded Peter the Great, were murderously deposed in a series of palace coups, usually instigated by favourites with the support of the Guards regiments. Even Catherine II (r. 1762–96) who had come to power with the intention of reforming the condition of the peasants, gave up all idea of radical reform after the great peasant uprising (1773–5) under the Don Cossack Emelyan Pugachev. In any case, Catherine was less liberal than Western admirers, who knew of her correspondence with Voltaire, liked to believe. Not only did she extend Russia's Imperial rule over several neighbouring peoples, she enacted a system of laws which put well over half the population of Russia in bondage to their owners. In Western Europe there had been no serfdom since the Middle Ages, and by the last quarter of the eighteenth century ideals of self-government and individual freedom had led to the establishment of the United States, a revolution in France and constitutional monarchy in Great Britain. Catherine wanted no such ideas to gain currency inside her own empire. In 1790 Aleksander Radishchev, who denounced the moral evils of serfdom in 'A Journey from St Petersburg to Moscow' was sent to Siberia in chains for beliefs Catherine might once have praised for their compassion. Pushkin knew the skills she used and wrote of her: 'If ruling means knowing human weakness and using it, then Catherine deserves the awe of posterity.' Neither then nor in Pushkin's time were her sexual appetites, any more than those of later rulers, regarded other than indulgently by her Russian subjects.

The power of Imperial Russia was at its height when Alexander Sergeevich Pushkin was born in the last year of the eighteenth century, three years after Catherine's reign ended, during the short rule (1796–1801) of her son Paul I. As a Grand Duke, Paul had run his own estate with a private army dressed in Prussian uniform. As a Tsar, Paul became dangerously capricious. His closest advisors, even his wife and the mistress who adored him, all fell under Paul's suspicion. Some idea of his need to impose formal respect can be gained from Pushkin's story that when Paul met him as a year-old child in his pram, the Tsar reproached his nurse for not seeing that his cap was doffed in respect. It was said Paul peered anxiously at sentinels to make certain the guards had not been changed without his instructions. It was in this mood that he fortified the Mikhaylovsky Palace in St Petersburg and took up residence there on 13 February 1801, but his fears did not preserve him. Count Peter von Pahlen joined with several other officers to remove Paul forcibly from the throne and install his son, Alexander, who was thought to have liberal sympathies. Alexander was forewarned of the conspirators' intentions and assured that no harm would come to his father, but in the event Paul was strangled during the attempt to put him under arrest.

Born under Paul I, Pushkin lived more than the first half of his life under the rule of Tsar Alexander I, an altogether more complex character than his father. Alexander's accession to the throne was greeted with tears of joy and people embracing in the streets of the capital. Nor was their enthusiasm altogether misplaced. The early years of Alexander's reign were relatively liberal; he was a dreamer with blue eyes, whose principal tutor as a child had been the Swiss Cesar Laharpe. Alexander began his rule with a genuine hatred of despotism, and at first turned for advice to Mikhail Speransky, a thinker dedicated to removing social injustices.

Internal affairs, however, were not Alexander's only problem. After a series of military defeats he had to sue for peace with Napoleon on a raft on the river Niemen at Tilsit in 1807. The French invasion of 1812 aroused a great wave of patriotic indignation among the Russian people, though Westernisers among the aristocratic elite had been very sympathetic to French political aspirations. The invasion led to slaughter without parallel in the history of warfare. As seen by Tolstoy in *War and Peace*, the military commander Kutuzov encouraged the French army to advance far into Russia, and even allowed Moscow to burn so that winter would destroy Napoleon's troops. Certainly Alexander made little contribution to such military decisions – throughout the war he sought comfort in reading the Scriptures, praying the while to be forgiven for his own complicity in the deposition of his father.

After the victory against Napoleon there was a brief upsurge of hope for some improvement of Russian society, but Alexander had by this time turned away from any concern with temporal change towards the Church and reactionary clerical mystics. He brought Count Aleksey Arakcheev, whom he had met while still a child on his father's estate at Gatchina, back into power. Arakcheev was a man described by Pushkin as 'without wit, without feelings, without honour'.[1] Arakcheev had small, cold eyes, a reputation for cruelty and a belief that Russia needed to be controlled with brutality. Another man of extremely conservative views, Admiral Shishkov, was made both Minister of Education and head of the Censorship Department. It was in response to this disappointing reversal of policy that secret societies began to be formed to work for some measure of reform, and it was Alexander's unexpected death at Taganrog that gave an opportunity for an uprising in favour of constitutional government on 14 December 1826. It was an uprising which had been dreamed about for a decade, but in the event was both spontaneous and ill organised. The rebels on Senate Square were put down with great ruthlessness by Alexander's brother, Nicholas I, who set up the notoriously oppressive Third Department under General Alexander Benckendorf to control any other stirrings of revolt among the intelligentsia. The rising of those who came to be called Decembrists was the single most important political event in Pushkin's short life, though accident prevented him taking any part in it.

In Pushkin's lifetime St Petersburg was pre-eminently a city of balls, display and pride in rank. It took little account of artists of any kind, or even ancient lineage unless accompanied by wealth. When, some twenty years after Pushkin's death, the composer Glinka left St Petersburg for ever in 1856, he got out of his carriage and spat on the ground that had never given him his due. It was not a rejection Pushkin was ever privileged to make.

CHAPTER TWO

Childhood

The character of Alexander Sergeevich Pushkin was formed in a childhood of such neglect and disorder that in later life he described the experience as 'intolerable'.[1] It was an upbringing that shaped his reckless temperament, his conflicts with authority, his vision of women and his precocity as a poet. His parents were feckless, charming and disorganised, although well enough suited as both aspired to the glittering *haut monde* which Tolstoy describes in the opening chapters of *War and Peace*. Unfortunately, this style of living was altogether beyond their means.

The poet's father, Sergey L'vovich Pushkin, was descended from Russia's ancient nobility. Not since the seventeenth century, however, had the Pushkin family enjoyed wealth or influence in the power structure of Russia. Sergey had been enrolled at birth in the Izmaylovsky Regiment, but he found military service irksome. When he was transferred to a regiment where officers were expected to carry canes, he complained that the custom made it awkward to sit playing cards with his friends.[2] He also disliked wearing gloves and often either left them at home or lost them. A year after his marriage he resigned his commission and the Tsar, Alexander I, found him some minor administrative work for which he was paid a minimal salary. Sergey never visited his family estate, Boldino, in Nizhny Novgorod province, and left the administration of that property and his twelve hundred serfs to a steward.

What Sergey L'vovich enjoyed most were glittering social occasions in the houses of wealthier friends. There he was valued as a wit and a brilliant performer in amateur theatricals. He had a highly polished command of the French language and the exquisite manners of a marquis.[3] Sergey L'vovich also had a passion for literature and a facility for writing well-turned verses in ladies' albums.

Inside the family, particularly with his three children, he was less charming. 'Pushkin's father, Sergey L'vovich, had a fiery temperament and was excessively irritable, losing his temper at the lightest complaint from a tutor or governess, so that the children were more afraid than fond of him.'[4] He behaved as if his own financial extravagance were a matter of no consequence. He once exploded in fury, however, when his younger son broke a glass at dinner, and when asked by his friend Prince Pyotr Andreevich Vyazemsky why he made such a fuss about a glass that only cost twenty kopecks, corrected him angrily, 'Excuse me, sir, not twenty kopecks but thirty five kopecks!'[5]

The poet's mother, Nadezhda Osipovna, was a grandchild of Abram Petrovich Gannibal, the African slave who became godson, ward and favourite of Peter the Great. Some biographers have liked to stress that Abyssinians are not so much African as Arab. Pushkin himself used the word 'negr' without embarrassment and found his exotic ancestry a matter of great excitement. Nadezhda herself was known as 'the beautiful Creole' and displayed a lively, carefree nature in society. Nevertheless, she had endured an unhappy and difficult childhood. Her father Osip, who held the rank of Major in the artillery, had, strangely enough, made the first marriage between the Gannibal family and the Pushkins, and it proved a disastrous match: Osip was constantly unfaithful and Maria Alexeevna miserably jealous. Only two years after their wedding she was rejected altogether by her husband, who ordered her to pack her things and leave the house, refusing even to allow her to take her young daughter Nadezhda with her. Then he secretly and bigamously married a rich widow, Ustina Ermolayevna Tolstaya. Maria Alexeevna, the poet's grandmother, was left in complete poverty, from which she was only rescued by her brother-in-law, Ivan Abramovitch Gannibal, who was Admiral of the Fleet and had been responsible for the victory of Navarino in 1773. Ivan Abramovich, an altogether kinder man than his brother Osip, took legal action on his sister-in-law's behalf and so brought his brother's bigamous marriage to the attention of the Empress. As a result, Osip himself was banished to the village of Mikhaylovskoe where he remained until his death. The illegal marriage was dissolved, mother and child reunited, and Osip forced to give Pushkin's mother a quarter of his estate, which included the village of Korbino. For all the melodrama of her life, however, Maria Alexeevna retained a warmth and affection markedly in contrast to that of her daughter Nadezhda.

Maria Alexeevna had very much indulged her daughter Nadezhda in the hope that her attractive figure and handsome features would bring her a good marriage, even though she had only a small dowry. This contributed to Nadezhda's vanity and to her overweening emphasis on manners and appearance. She had a great deal of energy, and after her marriage coped with a house move every year from 1799 to 1807. Unfortunately she had little common sense. She enjoyed moving furniture about from one room to another and there was a sense of camping out within the family home each time she changed the arrangement. Baron Modest Korff, a schoolfellow if not a friend of Pushkin, once remarked of Nadezhda's domestic skills that she had to send out for crockery if more than two people were invited to dinner and declared in his memoirs – which are, it should be noted, generally hostile to Pushkin –

> There was something eccentric about the whole Pushkin family. His father was an affable chatterer in the manner of the old French school, with his anecdotes and riddles, but he was essentially an empty, useless, idle man in silent subjugation to his wife. The latter was neither stupid nor ugly, but she had a multitude of peculiarities, including irascibility and eternal absent-mindedness. Her bad housekeeping was particularly noteworthy. Her home was always upside down. In one room was rich antique furniture, in another bare walls or a straw chair ... there were numerous drunken, dishevelled servants and legendary disorder : old and dilapidated carriages, skinny nags and never enough of anything, from money to the last glass.[6]

Though the description of Sergey L'vovich as 'silent' suggests little acquaintance with literary occasions in the Pushkin household, Korff's malicious description of the way Nadezhda ran her domestic affairs has the ring of accuracy. Korff based these observations on a period after he had left school and was living in an apartment in the same house as the Pushkins, on the Fontanka in St Petersburg.

Alexander Sergeevich Pushkin, Nadezhda's second child, was born on 26 May 1799 in a house on German Street, a fairly fashionable part of Moscow. Aside from the cupolas of the great churches and a few houses of wealthy noblemen, the city was rather like a large village of wooden huts, with geese and ducks swimming in pools of water on muddy roads. The rich noblemen in their grand houses led a life of fabulous luxury, with innumerable serfs to attend to their needs. They gave banquets and balls during a season which lasted from November to February, and to these grand social occasions poorer noblemen such as the Pushkins longed to be invited. These occasions were far less elegant than those of St Petersburg, Pushkin later observed:[7] 'imitating Petersburg fashion, the smart ladies outdid each other in the dresses they wore. Haughty Petersburg laughed from afar and did not interfere with old lady Moscow's fun.' For a year between 1802 and 1803 the Pushkins were invited to live in a wing of the Great Yusapov palace, a very grand house indeed, owned by Prince Nikolay Yusapov. The Prince had a winter garden full of exotic plants, parrots and golden pheasants and was a great lover of theatre and ballet. He enjoyed Sergey L'vovich's lively conversation, and was glad to help during his temporary financial difficulty. Pushkin mentions Yusapov Park briefly in a sketchy note about his first memories.

As a child, Alexander Sergeevich was something of an ugly duckling. His mother took against him quite early and always showed far more affection to his older sister, Olga, and his brother, Lev, who was six years younger. Until the age of six Alexander displayed no special talents, and his morose silence and plump, clumsy body exasperated his mother. He was awkward, even clumsy, often ill and had habits his mother disliked: she complained about the way he rubbed his hands together and his habit of losing his handkerchiefs. To cure him of the nervous hand-rubbing she punished him by tying his hands behind his back for a whole day, and to remind him not to lose his handkerchiefs she had one sewn to his jacket. She was seemingly indifferent to the humiliation the boy suffered at being introduced in this way to her guests. At children's parties she nagged him to join in the dancing, even though his awkwardness provoked unkind laughter. Nadezhda would have preferred an athletic young man and to this end forced the child to run about to improve his appearance. The child was far happier staying behind with his grandmother, Maria Alexeevna, who had come to live with her daughter. He particularly enjoyed exploring her room and workbasket to see how she did her needlework.

Nadezhda's apparent dislike for her second child needs some explanation. It may be relevant that another child, christened Nikolay, was born to Nadezhda in April 1801, and died on 30 July 1807.[8] Making due allowance for the sorrow of this loss, and the death of another son, christened Pavel, who lived for only six months in 1810, it still seems most likely that her hostility stemmed from his looks as, unlike her other children, Alexander had pronounced African features. Something in her traumatic experience of her own natural father may have lain behind her attitude to the son who most resembled him physically.

Although we cannot be altogether confident about Pushkin's childhood appearance, there are many descriptions of him, and throughout his life portraits show dark skin, thick lips and frizzy hair. Igor Geitman's well-known engraving made in 1822, for example, which his publisher Gnedich used as a frontispiece for *The Prisoner of the Caucasus*, emphasised Pushkin's African appearance, even though based on a school painting, probably by S. F. Chirikov, which shows a curly-haired young man with a pale skin and a rather European cast of features. A pencil drawing by V. A. Favorsky also emphasises the full lips and broad nose. In an oil painting by Inge, too, Pushkin has thick curly hair and skin markedly darker in tone than that of his school friends. P. K. Guber[9] even asserts that the majority of surviving portraits flatter him, and points out that Pushkin in his early French poem 'Mon Portrait' describes himself as having 'a proper monkey's face'.

Alexander certainly resembled neither parent. His father, to judge by a surviving portrait, had an oval, small-featured face, and his mother had a short face, almost without visible forehead, with a neatly turned, but rather mean mouth. Alexander's sense of 'otherness' gave him a particular interest in stories about his black ancestor told to him by his grandmother, Maria Alekseevna. At first, only Maria Alekseevna showed any awareness of Alexander's intelligence, and from her he learned to read and write Russian. (The language of the rest of the household, as was the custom in the Russian aristocracy of the time, was French.)

Maria Alekseevna could see the unhappiness beneath his often surly behaviour: 'Sometimes one cannot move him nor send him out to play with the children, and sometimes he gets agitated and excited and one does not know how to calm him down.'[10] Some time before his eighth year, however, the extraordinary precocity of his mind and imagination began to appear. In 1806, when asked why he was unable to sleep, the child replied, 'I am writing poems.'[11] Soon afterwards, when the family retreated from the heat of Moscow summers to Zakharovo, quite close by, where his grandmother had bought a ramshackle house surrounded by fir trees, the young boy began to take some pleasure in his life. He loved the woods, the little pond and the freedom from social constraints, and spent much time on his own in his personal fairyland.

Pushkin's other emotional support was his nanny, Arina Rodionovna, an illiterate, emancipated serf who had chosen to remain with the family and was very fond of him – she became the model for Tatyana's nanny in *Evgeny Onegin*. Not only did she tell the boy stories of ghosts and witches at bedtime, she gave him a loving tenderness he had not found in his mother, and he often called her 'Mama'. Pushkin's attachment to her is evident in many of his poems. In an unfinished poem, Pushkin wrote of her:

> Wearing a cap and old-fashioned clothes
> She made the sign of the cross as she whispered
> Stories of dead men to me; and under the blankets
> I held my breath, afraid to move.[12]

Aside from her skills as a teller of folk tales, Arina Rodionovna was a marvellous gossip and, even as she went on placidly knitting, could regale the enthralled child with news of those who had fallen in love, women who had cuckolded their husbands or men who had beaten their wives.

Alongside his new-found summer happiness in Zakharovo, Alexander Sergeevich was growing old enough to make use of the one advantage his unusual household could offer – an early, literary sophistication. Alexander enjoyed listening to his father reading French literature aloud, which Sergey L'vovich liked to do, though he otherwise gave his children little attention. In an unfinished romance, *A Russian Pelham*, Pushkin wrote of him:

> Father, of course, loved me but did not at all trouble himself about me and left me to the solicitude of Frenchmen who were continually being taken on and discharged. My first tutor turned out to be a drunkard; the second, not a stupid man and not without information, had such mad habits that once he almost murdered me because I spilled ink on his waistcoat; a third living with us for a whole year became insane.[13]

Pushkin learned little from these tutors. His education began in the evening after dinner when the ladies withdrew and his father retired to the library with his gentlemen guests for wine and cigars. His father might be a loafer but he genuinely loved French literature and his command of the language was perfect. Moreover, his social ambition and hospitality made his house something of a literary centre. Evenings at the Pushkin household drew many of the great literary figures of the day. Prince Vyazemsky, a wealthy nobleman and also a poet and man of letters, was a frequent visitor. Nikolay Karamzin, the celebrated historian, and the poets Vasily Zhukovsky and Konstantin Batyushkov were among the guests. Few of these writers are now widely known in the West. Konstantin Nikolaevich Batyushkov (1787–1855) was one of the outstanding poets of the generation preceding Pushkin. Vasily Alexandreevich Zhukovsky (1783–1852) was the founder of the Romantic movement in Russia. He was the illegitimate son of a nobleman and a Turkish slave girl, raised by his stepmother on his father's estate. He had gained influence at court through giving Russian lessons to the fiancée of the future Tsar Nicholas I. As a translator, he produced versions of Gray's 'Elegy on a Country Churchyard' and works by Walter Scott, Goethe and Schiller.

All of these men were to be important to Pushkin and came to be counted among his closest friends. They liked his father, who had the natural talents of a raconteur, and his uncle Vasily L'vovich, a well-known writer of light, mildly obscene verse, particularly famous for an unpublishable and risqué poem about a brawl in a brothel. Vasily L'vovich always had many intriguing stories to tell of life abroad. The eight-year-old Pushkin was allowed to sit quietly in a corner and listen to the conversation of these brilliant figures. Alongside literary discussion and the reading of poems, there was much salacious gossip, and the boy enjoyed the frivolous and cynical tone of many of the stories he overheard.

This experience prepared him for the erotic books of the French eighteenth century which he was allowed to devour freely. Sergey L'vovich had an exceptional library to which the child was allowed what access he wished, although there was a substantial collection of erotica. In such matters Alexander's father was far more permissive than his mother, who in 1810 ordered the boy to be sent from the room when he laughed at mildly risqué verses spoken by a sailor-poet at a friend's house. Gilet, the friend's family tutor, remarked, 'What a strange child! He is so young to understand such things.'[14]

Lev, who was six years younger, recalls his older brother spending whole nights in his father's library, reading without supervision. In this way he read Racine, Molière, Voltaire, 'The Iliad', 'The Odyssey' in French translation and many Latin classics. He was not always alone: his older sister Olga sometimes joined him and though she preferred sentimental literature – for instance, the romances of Mme de Genlis –

she also enjoyed the elegiac poetry of Gray and Thomson in translation. In the memoirs of his brother, Pushkin was said to know the whole of French literature by heart by the age of eleven.[15] He was particularly delighted by Voltaire.

Pushkin wrote verse himself by the time he was eight years old. This included a parody of Voltaire's epic 'Henriade' in six cantos, which told the story of a war of dwarves. He read the first four lines of this to his French tutor, M. Rousselot, who not only ridiculed the boy but complained to the poet's mother that her son was wasting his time on nonsense. Alexander was condemned and punished for what was seen as laziness, and in a moment of self-hatred burned his own manuscript in the stove. For all the misery of that gesture, Alexander's growing awareness of his own talents enabled him to overcome both his tutor's mockery and his mother's failure to protect him. He continued to make imitations of the French writers he loved, including Molière, whose work he had watched his father performing aloud. He also acted his own plays for his sister Olga who, after Pushkin's death, claimed to retain a memory of the opening quatrain of his burnt epic:

> Je chante le combat que Toly remporta,
> Ou maint guerrier perit, ou Paul se signala,
> Nicolas Mathurin, et la belle Nitouche
> Dont la main fût le prix d'une horrible escarmouche.[16]

(I sing the battle Toly won, in which many a warrior perished, and Paul distinguished himself, of Nicolas Maturin, and the beautiful Nitouche, whose hand was the prize of the terrible skirmish.)

She was not always enthusiastic, however, and once hissed a play of his, which prompted this neatly turned epigram:

> Dis moi: porquoi L'escamateur
> Fût-il sifflé par le parterre?
> Hélas, c'est que le pauvre auteur
> L'escamota de Molière.[17]

(Tell me: why was The conjuror hissed by the audience? Alas, it was because the poor author had filched his play from Molière.)

The neatness of these verses may owe something to the cleverness of Olga herself, as she recalled them after Pushkin had died. However, the few examples of French verse written at this very early period are marked by an amazing precocity. In the years between him first beginning to write and going to school he had the 'mind of a youth of twenty and the character of a child of twelve'.[18] As such, he was fascinated by the stories of his own family history.

Pushkin always took pride in the nobility of his Pushkin ancestry, which was older than that of the Romanovs themselves. The Pushkins had the right to the hereditary title of 'boyar', and their name was included in the Pedigree Book of Ivan the Terrible among the most noble families of Russia. Later in life, as Pushkin explored his family papers, he noted that in the seventeenth century some of his ancestors were court officials, governors of the provinces and ambassadors. He put two of these, Ostafy Mikhaylovich and Gavrila Pushkin, into his play *Boris Godunov* with particular pride and was very much to annoy the wealthier and more powerful aristocracy of his own day by impudently tagging them as newcomers in his poem 'My Genealogy', 1830.

Both the Pushkin and Gannibal families were marked with violence, particularly against women, and the violence was not confined to the remote past. A great-grandfather on the Pushkin side was said to have murdered his young wife in a fit of jealousy. His son, whom Pushkin described as a 'passionate and cruel man',[19] suspected his first wife of an affair with the French tutor hired for his son and imprisoned her in the house, where she died. The tutor was hanged on the gates of the family estate. His second wife was so afraid of her husband that she dared not refuse to accompany him on a visit, even when in the throes of labour, and so actually gave birth to a child on the road. Pushkin repeated these family legends with intrigued relish in later years, though after the poet's death his father took some trouble to deny them.

It was the life of the poet's great-grandfather, Abram Petrovich Gannibal, however, which most fascinated the boy, perhaps because he believed he could trace his own appearance back to him. Abram was born in Northern Abyssinia in the 1690s and may have been of noble stock; certainly he always claimed his father was a prince who lived a luxurious life and that he had nineteen brothers, of whom he was the youngest. Pushkin's own family traditions suggest Abram was abducted in his eighth year from the shores of Africa by 'a Frenchman collecting animals and other curiosities for Louis XIV'.[20] These trophies were taken from him by Turkish officials in Cairo, and Abram was then shipped to Istanbul to be placed in the Sultan's seraglio where he remained for a year. It was there the Russian ambassador found him, and sent him as a

present to Peter the Great. Very little else is known about the early years
of Pushkin's famous ancestor, and it is even difficult to be sure what he
looked like. While Russians have stressed the difference between '*Arap*',
meaning 'Arab', and '*negr*', meaning African, Pushkin himself uses the
words interchangeably.[21]

The portrait said to be that of Abram Gannibal is painted by an
unknown artist, and shows a handsome, black-skinned man with a blue
sash and several military honours. It may be, of course, that the artist
chose to flatter his sitter because of his importance. At any rate, neither
Gannibal nor his son, Ivan, painted in the 1890s, are shown with
particularly African features or curly hair, though their skins are certainly
dark. Russian critics have pointed out that Abyssinians were a very
mixed population which included Arabs, Turks and even Hebrews, but all
the evidence suggests that, whatever his race, he was at least sufficiently
African to pass on to his descendants a dark skin, full, thick lips and a
broad nose.

What is undisputed is that Abram was a precocious and intelligent
child, and that Peter the Great became so attached to him that he had
him baptised into the Orthodox Church at Vilno, with the Tsar himself
as his godfather and the Queen of Poland his godmother. When a brother,
who seemed to be of some standing in the African world, arrived to
claim Abram, the Tsar refused to part with him.

In 1716 Abram was sent by the Tsar to study in Paris, in particular
the skills of fortification and military mining. He fought with the French
army in the War of Spanish Succession and on his return to St Petersburg
in 1725 he was given a commission in the Tsar's own regiment. When
Peter's daughter, Elizabeth, came to the throne, after a period of some
instability, Abram was made Major General and granted the estate of
Mikhaylovskoe in the province of Pskov. Pushkin's unfinished novel *The
Negro of Peter the Great* (1827–8) gives a fictional account of those
Paris years. It is a tale sadly and significantly marked by the unhappiness
of a man who fears his black features make him little more than a
curiosity to women, but there is no evidence that such emotions troubled
Pushkin's great-grandfather.

Abram came back to Russia with French books that were to form the
basis of the Pushkin family library. During the reign of Elizabeth, Gannibal was made a General in Chief by the Empress and given the order
of St Alexander Nevsky. An eminent military engineer, he lived on well
into the reign of Catherine the Great and died surrounded with honours

and wealth in 1781, only 18 years before his great-grandson's birth. The man himself, according to Vladimir Nabokov,[22] differed 'in nothing from the typical career-minded, superficially educated, coarse, wife-flogging Russian of his day'. Abram's first marriage was to a Greek woman who seems to have disliked his colour. The violence of his response certainly bears out Nabokov's opinion: he succeeded in having her imprisoned for five years as an adulteress and she ended her days in a convent. His second wife he married bigamously. She was the daughter of an army captain and they had eleven children. It was her third son, Osip, who was Pushkin's grandfather.

Unlike Browning or Dumas, who might claim a similar strand of blackness in their genetic make-up, Pushkin referred to his own black forebear on many occasions. He drew attention to his African descent in a footnote to the first chapter of *Evgeny Onegin*, written in Odessa, where he explained, with some embellishments, the history of his great-grandfather's abduction and noble descent. The only male relative of the grandparental generation of Gannibals Pushkin knew personally was his great-uncle Peter Abramovich, whom he referred to cheerfully in his diary as an 'old negro'. Questions of colour and race are in themselves of little moment; it is only in the nature of their perception that character is given to the human mind. Pushkin, well aware of the strand of rashness and passion in his make-up, ascribed it often and proudly to his black ancestry. His friends came to do the same. It is often the gift of a poet to make advantage out of disadvantage, and turn a sense of difference into a source of strength. Pushkin had the genius to do so with defiance. So it was that, in the apartment on the Moyka canal in St Petersburg, where his flat has been preserved, the gift of a bronze inkstand with a statuette of a black man leaning on an anchor in front of two bales of cotton remained on his working desk to the end of his life.

CHAPTER THREE

School Days

In 1811, when Pushkin was twelve, his parents decided to send him away to school, and at first thought of sending him to a Jesuit college. Fortunately for Pushkin, a better opportunity presented itself before a final decision was made. That year Tsar Alexander I set up a lyceum in a wing of his own palace in Tsarskoe Selo near St Petersburg. This wing had been traditionally occupied by the Grand Princesses, but by 1811 only Princess Anna Pavlovna remained unmarried and she was moved out to make way for the new school. It was planned according to the ideas of Mikhail Speransky, the liberal political thinker largely responsible for the relatively tolerant political climate during the early years of Alexander's reign. The Tsar intended the *lycée* to educate young men from the best families who might thereafter be attracted into his civil and military service. To this end both pupils and teachers were carefully chosen. From the point of view of the Pushkin family there was an even greater advantage: the tuition was free.

The new school was modelled on the newly formed *lycées* of Napoleon, and drew on the traditional curriculum of English public schools in stressing languages, moral philosophy, simple mathematics, law, history and literature while encouraging the acquisition of fencing, riding and swimming. In other ways the atmosphere was very far from that of an English boarding school. Unlike the regime of Dr Keate of Eton, say, no corporal punishment was allowed and relations between staff and pupils were gentle and relaxed. A boy arriving at the school was greeted with genuine warmth, embraced and made to feel at home. At first the Tsar had planned that his two younger brothers (including Nicholas, the future Tsar) should attend the school, but his wife thought that was carrying liberalism too far. The *lycée* offered Alexander Sergeevich his first real taste of privilege. His earliest surviving letter, written in 1815 to Ivan Ivanovich Martynov, then Director of the Department of Public Education, perhaps in gratitude, contains a poem in praise of the Tsar.

V. Malinovsky, a graduate from Moscow University in Philosophy, whose radical views reflected those of Radishchev's banned 'Journey from Petersburg to Moscow', was appointed as Director. Malinovsky's own liberal opinions were well known as, in 1802, he had sent the government his 'Note on the Emancipation of Slaves' and in 1803 published an article arguing that 'conditions of permanent peace are inseparable from the true success of mankind'. The *lycée* was to be the special responsibility not of the Minister of Education but of the Chancellor, Count Rumyantsev, one of the most enlightened noblemen of his day.

Alexander Sergeevich was taken to St Petersburg on 20 July 1811 by his uncle Vasily, who was travelling with his young mistress, Anna Vorzhekin. Vasily wanted to stay at the oldest and most fashionable hotel in St Petersburg, Hotel Demuth. To this end, he shamelessly borrowed the hundred roubles given to Alexander by his grandmother. This left Alexander penniless and, as the money was never repaid, the incident permanently coloured the opinion he held of his frivolous uncle. When his uncle was out of the way, however, he soon made friends with Anna Vorzhekin.

In August 1811 Pushkin arrived at the school to take the entrance examination. He passed 14th out of 30. This was not a great tribute to the education he had so far enjoyed: the tests were not difficult and though he rated 'Very Good' in Russian, he was surprisingly only graded 'Good' in French. In Geography and History his examiners could only say that 'he had some information'. Probably his admission was due as much to his uncle Vasily's celebrity as a minor poet as to his own scholarly prowess.

During the weeks that preceded the opening of the lyceum Pushkin made a good friend in I. I. Pushchin, whose notes on their friendship are among the most valuable accounts we have of the poet as a schoolboy. Perhaps the similarity of their names drew them together, but for the benefit of an English reader I. I. Pushchin in these pages will be distinguished by his forename, Ivan. On their first meeting Ivan recalls Pushkin as 'a lively young boy, curly haired, quick-eyed and somewhat bewildered'.

Before the *lycée* opened that autumn the two boys took walks together in the palace's summer garden and met some of their fellow students. Ivan soon observed his friend's brilliance: 'Everyone could see that Pushkin was ahead of us and had read far more ... Pushkin's upbringing in the home of his father and grandfather, surrounded by a circle of writers, quite apart from his native talents, had speeded up his education.'[1] Rather in the spirit of Oxbridge at a later day, however, Pushkin and the other students affected to 'consider learning of no importance, wanting only to excel in running, jumping over chairs, throwing the ball and so on'.[2]

The *lycée* officially opened on 19 October 1811 in the presence of the Tsar and his court. There was a rehearsal for the occasion and much laughter and embarrassment as the boys practised their bows. On the day itself the Director, Malinovsky, was seen to be white-faced and shaking as he spoke because (as Ivan Pushchin discovered later) the speech he was to have given had been confiscated, presumably as too liberal. Professor Kunitsyn, an important influence on Pushkin's schooling, spoke boldly and without notes. The Tsar was so pleased by his speech about the duties of a citizen and a soldier that he immediately awarded him a Vladimir Cross. Afterwards the boys filed past the Tsar, who greeted each in turn gracefully. That evening the boys were allowed to eat as much pudding as they liked, take off their grand uniforms and play snowballs in the courtyard under the light of the illuminations.

On the whole, the boys lived well. The food was good: there was a lunch of three courses (four on Sundays) and a soft white roll with morning tea. Half a glass of port wine was allowed with dinner at first, though this was soon replaced by Russian kvass and water. There was no system of fagging. Several old men worked for the boys, tidying the rooms and making sure that their clothes and boots were clean. Among these, Ivan recalls Leontil Kemersky, who organised a corner where the boys could eat sweets, drink coffee and chocolate and even a glass of liqueur. Sometimes, when a boy was celebrating his nameday, there would be coffee in the morning or chocolate in the evening instead of the usual tea. The school had its own library, physics room and recreation hall as well as classrooms. The pupils' bedrooms were on the top floor and each contained an iron bed, a commode, a desk, a looking-glass, chair, washing table and night table. On each desk were an inkwell and a candle. It was a life which Pushkin recalled in later years as golden.

The outside world continued to impinge, however. It was in Pushkin's first year at the *lycée*, 1812, that Napoleon invaded Russia and the students watched in admiration and some envy as Russian soldiers rode past the school on their way to fight the French troops. The twentieth-century Russian scholar, Yury Lotman, speaks of Russian sacrifices in the battlefield being perceived by the young men of Pushkin's time as enviable since 'they led a man into History'.[3] When the news came that Moscow had been burnt in frustration of Napoleon's conquest, plans were made to evacuate the *lycée*. Napoleon's later defeat in the same year was greeted with wild enthusiasm.

In all the six years Pushkin was at the *lycée* he did not once return home, though his parents occasionally visited him at school, his father usually to scold him for some bad behaviour. He had left his parents with ease, not to say relief, though he must have missed his sister Olga and his indulgent grandmother and nanny. Nowhere in his poetry is there any reference to his mother and father.[4] Even his references to his uncle Vasily were exclusively ironic. It is striking that whenever Pushkin recalled his past he usually began with the *lycée*, as if he wanted to expunge any earlier memories. 'He was a man without a childhood.'[5] He was eager to make close friendships, and at the *lycée* he made friends who were to last him all his life, notably Ivan Pushchin, whose bedroom was next to his own.

Pushkin continued to suffer from that sense of his own ugliness which his mother's criticisms had exacerbated. 'The nickname of monkey was to remain with him a long time.'[6] Among his schoolfellows he was also dubbed 'the Frenchman', presumably because of his command of that language and also because he was felt to be 'a mixture of a monkey and a tiger'.[7] This was a phrase first coined by Voltaire to denote the qualities which made a Frenchman at once carefree and predatory, playful and fierce, a 'petit maître dandy' and a tyrant. His brother Lev points out in his memoirs, however, that although 'Pushkin was no beauty, his face was expressive and alive; and although short in stature (no more than five feet tall) he was slenderly built, unusually sturdy and well proportioned.'[8]

Some features of his character which were to put Pushkin at risk all through his life were already observed by his schoolfellows. 'He was from the start more quick-tempered than the rest of us . . . his inopportune jests and clumsy witticisms often placed him in some difficult position

from which he was then unable to extricate himself . . . He was a mixture
of excessive boldness and shyness. Both were often out of place and got
him into trouble.'[9]

His fellow pupils soon discovered the area in which Pushkin excelled
them all. One afternoon in 1811 one of their teachers suggested that the
boys describe a rose in verse. In no time Pushkin had read out two four-
line verses whose elegance and sophistication were marvelled at by
all his fellow students.[10] Soon he wrote for all the *lycée*'s magazines,
improvised epigrams and dashed off popular songs. 'We could all see
that Pushkin outstripped us, had already read a great deal we had not
even heard about, and that everything he read he remembered.'[11]

For all his astonishing memory, Pushkin was often in trouble with his
school work and was far from diligent. In reports at the end of the first
year, A. P. Kunitsyn, his professor in Moral Philosophy, remarked, 'He
is very intelligent, thinks and is witty, but is extremely unindustrious.'
He was rated 'Poor' in German, Logic, Ethics and Maths, 'Good' in
Russian and French literature. The only unqualified praise he received
was for drawing, fencing and calligraphy. A note on his behaviour
complained that he had 'little consistency and firmness, was loquacious,
witty and noticeably good natured, but very irascible and flippant'. His
supervisor reported, 'He has a talent more brilliant than well-grounded,
a mind more passionate and clever than profound. His diligence in study
is mediocre . . . His knowledge in general is superficial . . . A sensitive, hot,
passionate temper; giddiness, and especially a sharp disputatiousness, are
characteristic of him.'[12]

These comments, though far from flattering to the lively twelve-year-
old, are observant and already suggest some of the mature poet's character. The teachers knew their pupils well and the education was generally
excellent even though, by common account, the Professor of Russian
liked strong drink, women and fine clothes and the German teacher was
disliked because he chewed liquorice. Professor A. Galich was admired
by most of the other students, even though Pushkin called him 'true
friend of the cup'.[13] It was he, in 1814, who suggested Pushkin should
write the celebrated 'Recollections in Tsarskoe Selo' for the examination
at which the young poet so impressed the ageing Derzhavin and Pushkin
was grateful. A. P. Kunitsyn, the Professor of Moral Philosophy, was
also well liked and, as Pushkin recalled, 'formed us, and fed our flame'.[14]

With the unexpectedly sudden death of Director Malinovsky, however,
chaos overtook the *lycée* and for a time the teachers could not control

the students. There were night parties and practical jokes. Pushkin was often the ringleader in pranks that got both him and his friends into trouble. Once, he and Ivan Pushchin made egg-nog with rum, eggs and sugar, and a boy named Tyrkov was rather badly affected by the rum. 'Thanks to him,' Ivan records drily, 'the tutor on duty noticed an unusually animated atmosphere.' It was a matter finally referred to the Chancellor Razumovsky himself, who ordered the three main culprits to kneel at morning and evening prayers, be seated at the end of the table far from their friends and to have their names entered in a black book which would adversely affect their future lives after school. It was not an excessively severe punishment and the boys were soon allowed to move back up the table towards their fellows. Moreover, they were never entered in the black book. The true victim was an old man named Foma who had helped to procure the rum and was dismissed at once. 'We somehow remunerated him for the loss of his position,' says Ivan, who was in a rather better position to do so than his friend.

A schoolmate who shared in Pushkin's escapades and became his close friend was Baron Anton Delvig, a sensitive admirer of Pushkin's poetry and a poet himself. Another was V. Kyukhelbecker, whose height and thinness earned him the name of Tapeworm. (Sadly, Pushkin was among his tormentors.) Kyukhelbecker was an inoffensive, kindly boy with a German accent. Although his own verse won little admiration, he went on to become one of the best critics of his day, before becoming involved with the Decembrists.

Among Pushkin's other friends were Yakovlev, who became a dilettante composer, and A. Illichevsky, who edited some of the school's literary magazines. Pushkin continued to contribute to these, but his fame soon began to spread outside the school gates. In June 1814, when Pushkin was only 15, a poem of his appeared in the most influential literary magazine of the day, *Messenger of Europe*. It was a poem advising a friend not to consider the life of a poet, which was 'one misery after another, with even the roar of fame no more than a dream'.[15]

In January 1815 the boy received extraordinary recognition from Derzhavin himself, the greatest poet of the preceding generation. Invited to hear recitations of the pupils at the *lycée*, Derzhavin had fallen asleep but was suddenly galvanised into attention when Pushkin began to read his poem 'Recollections in Tsarskoe Selo'. It is a moment caught in 1911 in a celebrated oil painting by Ilya Repin (1844–1930), though the artist surely exaggerates the Hussar-like panache of Pushkin's gesture at his adolescent reading.[16] After hearing Pushkin's poem, the older poet said, 'I live on. He is the one who will replace Derzhavin.' The idea of such recognition, a mantle of greatness passed down from one generation to the next, appealed to the Russian imagination so strongly that it was even represented in a similarly histrionic fashion in a Russian silent film made in the first decade of the twentieth century.

Overwhelmed as he was by the experience, Pushkin gave an altogether less romantic account of it in his own 1835 'Reminiscences'. He remembered his friend Delvig going out on the stairs to wait for Derzhavin so that he might kiss the divine hand of the man who wrote 'The Waterfall'. There, Delvig was shocked to overhear the old poet ask the doorman, 'I say, my good man, where is the privy here?' a commonplace human grossness which Pushkin records with some relish. Nevertheless, Pushkin confessed he was unbearably excited at reading before the great poet and ran away with his heart pounding when the reading ended.

For all his flight, such recognition was a transforming experience. In *Evgeny Onegin* Pushkin recalled his sensation of triumph:

> And with a smile the world caressed us:
> What wings our first successes gave!
> Aged Derzhavin saw and blessed us
> As he descended to the grave.[17]

The poem, which so impressed Derzhavin, included a startling picture of Moscow ruined by fire:

> Moscow of a hundred domes,
> The jewel of our fatherland,
> What has become of you? Where once
> Was majesty, now ruins stand.
> Your sightless face hurts Russian eyes,
> The palaces of Tsars and nobles
> With all their towers consumed by fire.

No doubt some part of the ease with which Pushkin established himself among the leading literary figures of the day can be attributed to memories of hospitality in the Pushkin household. Pushkin's father certainly liked to think so. Remembering events some time after his son's death, Sergey L'vovich claimed that Derzhavin and he were once dining with Count Razumovsky, then still Minister of Education under Alexander I, and that while Razumovsky hoped to see Pushkin turn to prose,

Derzhavin passionately wished him to remain a poet.[18] Pushkin's father declares that he echoed the same opinion but, like many things in that memoir, his comments reflect later experience and thought. In any case, Pushkin was to excel in every genre he touched, and the great Russian nineteenth-century novel could hardly have existed without his tales in prose.

While he was still at school Pushkin was elected to the Arzamas Society, set up in 1815 to promote new literature, in opposition to the more pompous nationalist and traditional club, the Beseda (meaning 'Conversation'), headed by Admiral Shishkov. The Arzamas had Karamzin at its head, and included Vyazemsky and Zhukovsky amongst its members, and Alexander Ivanovich Turgenev (1784–1845), who was not primarily a writer but one of the most enlightened and intelligent men of the day. For a schoolboy it was an amazing honour to be included among such an elite, even though their gatherings were far from solemn. The older poets gave Pushkin the nickname of 'Cricket'. In a schoolboy letter to Prince Vyazemsky, after his election to the Society, Pushkin professes particular delight in a new sociable life: 'I assure you that solitude is indeed a very stupid thing, in spite of all the philosophers and poets who pretend that they have lived in the country and are in love with silence and quiet.'[19]

Not all his fellow pupils liked this precociously successful literary figure among them. Modest Korff, the rather priggish German schoolfellow who went on to become an important figure in the Imperial administration and hence a Count, claimed that students and teachers alike were afraid of Pushkin's 'evil tongue and poisonous epigrams'. Pushkin's quick repartee, however, was sometimes relished by his fellows. When the Tsar visited the school he asked the class, 'Who is first here?' Pushkin promptly replied, 'There is no first here, your Imperial Majesty; all are second.'

E. A. Engelhardt was appointed as Director of the *lycée* in March 1816. The new Director was a kindly man who was convinced that the boys must be brought into contact with ordinary society. Under his care they were allowed far more time outside the school walls than before and some families in the town were encouraged to invite them to social occasions. In summer the Director took the boys on hiking trips, and in winter he went skating and sledging with them. Most of the students liked Engelhardt very much, but Pushkin soon ran foul of him.

It was Engelhardt's habit to invite boys to his house for evenings where they were entertained by his daughters and other friends. There were parlour games and songs in which Pushkin joined. A young and pretty widow, Maria Smith, kept house for the Engelhardts at the time and, with some impudence, Pushkin not only flirted with her but gave her a verse epistle called 'To A Young Widow'. In this, written in 1817, he begs her not to moan softly in her sleep when she feels pleasure, and hints that her tears are not only for her husband. The poem opens thus:

> O Lydia, my love forever,
> Through my gentle slumber, why
> Spent with passion's joyful fever
> Do I hear you softly sigh?

This alone suggests a shared bed; and the poem concludes by advising the young widow not to be afraid of her husband's ghost:

> Trust in love, no guilt is ours
> No one, jealous, on our pillow
> From eternal darkness lours.
> Brawling breaks not tranquil night
> Nor will envious shadows stay
> Here poor lover to affright,
> Or to rouse the sleeping day.[20]

Maria was offended by the frankness of the language and showed the poem to the Director. As a result, Pushkin became a less frequent visitor to the Director's house. In a poem written in 1817, 'Letter to Leda', perhaps directed at Maria Smith, Pushkin declares he will come to her bedroom and that she will recognise him by his 'fearless, trembling hands, passionate breath and hot lips'. This hardly establishes that any such encounter occurred outside the young man's feverish imagination and Maria Smith does not figure on Pushkin's list of early loves.[21]

Another incident further distanced Engelhardt and his precocious pupil. The regimental band played every evening in the Court quarters of the Guards before sunset and the students liked to attend these performances. A corridor connected the lyceum with the wing of the palace where the Guards performed and the boys used the passageway as a short cut. The main attraction of this corridor lay in the possibility of meeting a pretty servant of Princess Volkonskaya called Natalya, who was willing to allow the boys to kiss and fondle her.

One evening Pushkin was going through the corridor alone in the dark and heard the sound of feminine skirts. Thinking it was Natalya, he seized the passing figure playfully. Unfortunately, it was the Princess Volkonskaya herself. Horrified by his own impoliteness, Pushkin told Ivan Pushchin about this incident and Ivan advised him to throw himself on Engelhardt's mercy at once. Instead, Pushkin wrote a letter of apology to the Princess, but she had unfortunately already complained to her brother and he had taken the matter up with the Tsar.

The Tsar paid a visit to the Director himself to discuss the matter, alongside a number of other minor complaints about students climbing his fences and stealing apples. Engelhardt, for all his own reservations about this particular student, pleaded Pushkin's case, and it is said that after hearing his defence Alexander whispered smilingly to Engelhardt, 'Between ourselves, the old lady is no doubt enchanted with the young man's mistake.'[22] Even though Pushkin learned of this, he refused to see Engelhardt's defence of him as an act of kindness and maintained that the Director was only protecting his own interests.

Engelhardt, who was far from stupid, observed Pushkin's continuing unfriendliness and was concerned. Engelhardt's puzzlement is understandable as he had always treated Pushkin well. It is hard to resist the explanation that Pushkin had an instinctive dislike of even the most kindly authority.

Hoping to remedy the situation, Engelhardt approached Pushkin directly one day while he was sitting alone at his desk, and asked the reason for his hostility. Pushkin was embarrassed and confused, apologised and at length broke down in tears, which Engelhardt sentimentally shared. The reconciliation did not last long. When Engelhardt returned unexpectedly a little while later, he found Pushkin hastily concealing some papers in his desk. Engelhardt pressed Pushkin to show them to him in spite of Pushkin's obvious reluctance, imagining the boy was too shy to show his verses. Opening the desk, Engelhardt found an unkind caricature of himself and several vicious epigrams, and is said to have remarked, 'Now I see why you do not wish to come to my home. However, I don't know what I have done to deserve your dislike.'[23] Pushkin probably could not have explained it himself.

Both earlier clashes with Engelhardt had originated with Pushkin's pursuit of women. 'Pushkin was so fond of women,' a contemporary acquaintance, S. V. Komovsky, writes, 'that even the touch of a hand while dancing at a school ball aged 15 or 16 was enough to make his eyes blaze, and he would redden and snort like an ardent stallion in a young herd.'[24] Although S. V. Komovsky ascribes this to the 'sensuality of his African nature', Pushkin's burgeoning eroticism owed rather more to the French poets he had always studied. 'It isn't nature that teaches us about love, it's the first dirty novel,' Pushkin noted gloomily,[25] having already as a child avidly read his father's collection of French pornographic literature. In seeing attractive women as sexual prey, Pushkin was not markedly different from other gallants of the time, particularly the wild young officers stationed in the barracks at Tsarskoe Selo, whose evening parties of drinking bouts and ribald stories he liked to join. His earliest sexual education would have come from their chatter and perhaps the caresses of young female serfs in his parents' house.

Pushkin's adolescent feelings towards women, however, were unusually violent. In stanzas which Pushkin later expunged from chapter four of *Evgeny Onegin*, he describes the effect of pretty women upon him. In their presence he first melted into silence, then began to tremble and hate the object of his desire, and soon began to see them as poisonously filled with malice and treachery. One would not have to be a twentieth-century Kleinian to guess such intense confusion rose from the troubled inner world of a young man whose mother had failed to establish a warm relationship with him. While it was customary in most aristocratic families for mothers to see relatively little of their children, Pushkin's mother was unusual in coming close enough to find fault.

In the Upper Grade of the *lycée*, where supervision was less strict, pupils had frequent permissions to go into town, and Pushkin joined in the pleasures enjoyed by the local hussars, which included visits to local prostitutes with pastoral pseudonyms. He became so close a friend of one of the most confirmed rakes, Captain Kaverin, that he even considered joining the regiment. He enjoyed the affectation of worldly cynicism worn by many of the aristocratic officers, but some had their own idealism and were interested in constitutional reform. The young Hussar who most affected Pushkin in this respect was Colonel P. Chaadaev, a distinguished thinker who was only 23 when Pushkin met him in 1817 but whose influence was to be important.

Among the poems Pushkin wrote at the age of 15 is an erotic '*jeu d'esprit*' in which he imagines becoming a pinch of snuff in order to slip beneath the clothes of a lady he admired:

> My dear Lucille, how changeable you are...
> It used to be the morning bloom you bowed to –

> But now the weed
> That fashion's need
> Has artfully transformed to fine grey powder! ...
> Let some old beauty, sixty if she's a day
> Retired from love, forsaken by the graces,
> Her body quite without unwrinkled places –
> Let her pray, and yawn, and huff
> And find, in one good pinch, unfailing respite
> But if, my beauty, *you* are so fond of it
> And if I – the power of fancy! – *were* the stuff,
> And your snuff-box closed on me
> And you took a pinch of me
> In those soft fingers – rapture! Down I'd spill
> Inside your silken dress
> Over your smooth white breast,
> I'd spill and spill until –
> But no, an empty dream. That happiness
> Isn't for me. Fate isn't kind. Enough!
> Oh if only I *could* be that snuff![26]

For all the precocity of his sexual imagination, Pushkin was in love with love itself mainly as a source of literary emotion. In 1815 he wrote a poem recalling a childhood love experienced when he was barely nine. In his Don Juan list (written much later in life) the first name he notes is Natalie, but there is a good deal of disagreement about which of the three pretty young girls of that name Pushkin had in mind. One was the maid he had confused with Princess Volkonskaya. There was also the daughter of Count Kochubey, who lived for a time in Tsarskoe Selo and visited the *lycée*. However, the most likely contender was an actress seen on stage in St Petersburg while Pushkin was in his last year at the *lycée*; she was seemingly very beautiful though not particularly talented. It was a love which did not even take Pushkin backstage.

The mood he evokes with most confidence is the adolescent yearning for physical love, as in the opening of 'Moon':

> Out of the clouds why do you venture
> O solitary moon, and on
> The pillow where I lie alone
> Squander your melancholy splendour?
> You, with your gloomy visitation

> Awaken dreams of love, the pain
> Of hopeless passion, and the vain
> Longings of lovers' aspiration...[27]

He did form a bashful, adolescent attachment to Ekaterina Pavlovna Bakunina, the sister of a school friend, which lasted all winter, spring and most of the summer of 1816. This involved little more than brief meetings on the steps or in the park, but drew from Pushkin a cryptic journal entry, in which on 19 November 1815 he wrote,

> I was happy, I enjoyed myself
> As though drunk with quiet joy and pleasure.

Whatever caused this happiness, his description of it is followed by an account of staring out of the window for hours in the hope of seeing Ekaterina and his delight when she appeared in a black dress which clung to her figure. Ekaterina may have given Pushkin some encouragement, and when the family left St Petersburg Pushkin was for a time inconsolable. In some poems written between 1816 and 1817 Ekaterina figures under the names of Lila and Lida, but these are humorous rather than melancholy poems and he seems to have forgotten her rapidly.

In the first of Pushkin's working notebooks held by Pushkinsky Dom can be found fair copies of early poems written while at the *lycée*, many in the handwriting of Anton Delvig and Ivan Pushchin. Pushkin must at some time have intended them for publication. The critic D. S. Mirsky is right to point out that, for all the cleverness of Pushkin's lyceum verses, the genius which marks his later work was not yet present. Nevertheless, his friend Delvig saluted him memorably:

> Pushkin! Not even the forests will conceal him!
> His song and lyre betray his presence,
> And Apollo will steal him from other mortals
> To live for ever on triumphant Olympus.

Just over a year before the first class was to graduate, the Tsar summoned Engelhardt and asked if any of the boys wished to enter military service. He must have been disappointed to hear that only ten wished to do so. (Pushkin was undecided at the time, but his parents were against it.) A class of military science was established, however, on a voluntary basis. The Tsar also wanted the boys to be sent as pages to the Empress Elizabeth during her summer visits to Tsarskoe Selo to accustom them to court duties, but Engelhardt refused on the grounds that the boys would lose time from their studies. Horse-riding lessons with General Levashov, however, Engelhardt did approve, though many of his pupils proved such incompetent riders that the general was reduced to despair.[28]

The first class to enter the *lycée* graduated in June 1817 in a quiet ceremony which the Tsar attended: all the pupils passed before the Tsar in order of age and announced their ranks and awards. Pushkin was graded ninth in the class (14th was the lowest). He had been an indifferent scholar and the only subjects in which he excelled remained Russian and French literature and fencing.

Engelhardt's judgement on him at the end of his schooldays was severe:

> The highest and final purpose of Pushkin was to shine, and in poetry alone, having neither penetration nor depth and an entirely superficial and French mind ... His heart is cold and empty; there is neither love nor religion in him; perhaps no young heart was ever quite so empty as his. Tender and youthful feelings are debased in his imagination, profaned by all the erotic productions of French literature which, before entering the Lyceum, he knew almost by heart...'[29]

The most interesting of these comments of Engelhardt's concerns the coldness and emptiness he saw in Pushkin. In part the Director must have been reflecting his own frustration in failing to make an affectionate relationship with his pupil; in part he had a genuine dislike of French culture. But he had identified something important in the boy's character at this period – underneath the wildness, hot temper and pranks, which produced quarrels with friends as well as enemies, there remained a bewildered and unloved child.

For Pushkin, his school was more important than home had ever been. The first class to enter the *lycée* was united into something like a family and met every year on 19 October at the house of Baron Anton Delvig long after leaving school to mark the anniversary of the foundation of the *lycée*. Pushkin has left several poems inscribed with that date, which are among his best.

CHAPTER FOUR

Dissipations 1817–20

A fter his graduation on 9 June 1817, Pushkin returned briefly to
his family home in Mikhaylovskoe in the province of Pskov. He
had seen nothing of simple village life for six years and enjoyed
what he found there – country baths, strawberry-picking and dancing
with village girls.[1] He also relished a meeting with Peter Gannibal, the
last surviving son of the famous Abram. They shared home-made vodka
and got on exceedingly well, though they quarrelled briefly over a girl at
one of the country dances and Pushkin hot-temperedly challenged the
old man to a duel.

After a month, Pushkin returned to St Petersburg, where his parents
now lived in a modest apartment on the Fontanka. He was eighteen
years old and eager to enjoy whatever life could offer. The six years
Pushkin had spent away from home, however, had not improved his
relations with either parent. The poor state of the family finances did
not prevent his mother and father from keeping up as grand a show as
they could, but they were reluctant to spend money on their son. Sergey
maintained his habit of calling on the higher aristocracy, using a dil-
apidated carriage and an ill-fed horse, yet he refused to pay for a pair of
dancing pumps for his son and offered him instead an old pair of his
own which dated back to the Court of the late Tsar. Once, when Pushkin
returned home ill in a cab, his father was forced to pay the horseman
eighty kopecks and for some time afterwards nagged his son about this
expenditure.

His mother was now irritable with everyone, and ran the household with alarming whimsicality. Her domestic serfs were usually drunk and surly, but her main concern was to prevent them wearing beards and she refused to allow them – or even her husband – to smoke a pipe. Neither parent had much time for their son. All graduates of the *lycée* were required to enter either military or civil service, and Pushkin had taken up a lowly and undemanding position at the Ministry of Foreign Affairs. For this he only received seven hundred roubles a year, which could not possibly finance the kind of life he wanted to lead. There was bound to be friction over money – Pushkin's father grew meaner as his own circumstances worsened, and his mother always preferred to spend money on Olga and Lev.

The doors of Petersburg society were open to Pushkin, not only through his father's contacts but through his own friendships formed at the *lycée*. He was soon part of a glittering world of young men much richer than himself, some of them officers in the Guards. As Silvio remarks in 'The Duel' in Pushkin's *Tales of Belkin*, 'Wild behaviour was the fashion in our day.' Pushkin enjoyed the leisure of a dandy as his position at the Foreign Office was purely nominal, and spent the next three years in the world he describes with such brilliance in chapter one of 'Evgeny Onegin': drowsing in bed all morning, strolling at leisure along the Nevsky Prospect in the afternoons, and invited to grand soirées at night. He, too, liked to take a sleigh in the evening to Talons, a well-known French restaurant, where he could enjoy wine, English roast beef with truffles, Strasbourg pie and Limburg cheese before going on to the theatre. At the same time, he continued to frequent officers and friends in the barracks on Million Street and through Pavel Katenin, a poet and translator of Corneille, was introduced to the men and women of the theatre.

At eighteen, Pushkin was short (though not as short as John Keats). He was sturdy and athletic and particularly enjoyed swimming, horse-riding and fencing. His face, with blue eyes in his mulatto complexion, was extraordinarily vivacious, and his ebullience brought him the nick-name 'Spark' to add to his Arzamas 'Cricket'. Nothing pleased him more than flirting with women. His brother Lev observed that he could be both half-hearted and rude when he was uninterested in the subject of the conversation, but, though Pushkin was not good-looking, Lev insisted, 'Women liked him: he was extremely entertaining in their company.'[2]

Pushkin lived in a tiny room on the floor above his parents' apartment. A friend, Vasily Ertel, describes him lying on his narrow bed in a striped

Bokharan dressing-gown: 'Beside the bed, on a table, were papers and books. Objects appropriate to the rooms of a worldly young man about town were juxtaposed with the poetic disorder of a scholar.'[3]

Pushkin's adolescence was a period of wild behaviour and some affectation. He grew long fingernails and behaved rowdily in the theatre. He gave himself up to debauchery of all sorts, spending days and nights in an endless round of drunkenness and orgies. It is astonishing that his health and his talent survived such a lifestyle, accompanied as it was by the usual diseases. A. I. Turgenev writes of one sad episode, 'Pushkin is very ill. He caught a cold while waiting at the door of a certain whore, who would not let him in out of the rain, in order not to infect him with her own illness.' Most of Turgenev's observations were less considerate, however, and he was soon to remark, 'Venus has nailed Pushkin to his bed.'[4] Venereal disease was rife among all the young gallants of the time, many of whom were quite as lecherous as Pushkin. 'Two elements reigned supreme in him: satisfaction of physical passions and poetry; he gave free rein to both.'[5] Nevertheless, even Korff – a most hostile witness – recognised that Pushkin continued to write poetry during these years of dissipation; it was what distinguished him from most of the young men in whose company he caroused. Even in 1818 his poetry had 'a purity and flexibility, ease and elegance', as D. S. Mirsky puts it, unequalled by anything in Russian. Where Zhukovsky had been influenced by German literature, to which Pushkin was almost indifferent, Pushkin had been under the influence of Voltaire since a child, and was always attracted to the clarity of the French poet, E. D. Parny. In Pushkin's hands the trifles, or *bezdelki*, favoured by friends like Delvig were given a more personal, often grosser twist – as in his poem 'To Yurev', quoted in the introduction, which revealed so much he usually kept hidden. This is the poem of which the poet Batyushkov exclaimed, 'How this rascal has learned to write.'

Pushkin's undiscriminating sexual energy was both expected and acceptable among his officer friends. As he scribbled later in his first Kishinev notebook: 'More or less I have been in love with all the pretty women I have ever known,'[6] adding sadly, however, 'They all scorned me handsomely; they all, with one exception, flirted with me.' He fell equally in love with the actress Semenova or a pretty ticket-seller, and was unashamed of his acquaintance among the ladies of the brothels, writing even to his friend and literary mentor Zhukovsky without fear of reproach that he 'does not sleep for whole nights on end, visits brothels all day and sometimes plays at Bank in the evening'. He was hardly flouting the social code of the times in going to prostitutes. Lev Tolstoy is said to have been taken to a brothel by his brother when he was only fourteen years old. Unlike Tolstoy, however, after he had 'accomplished the act'[7] Pushkin suffered little shame or guilt. For all his superstition, Pushkin had little fear of divine retribution; religion was not, at this stage of his life at least, a matter of great consequence either to him or his fellows. As D. S. Mirsky remarks drily, 'It is natural in a society where vice and French philosophy were equally fashionable, that religion should be held in little esteem. The generation on the whole was fundamentally irreligious, and the exceptions were few.'[8]

The Imperial Theatre was the centre of an elegant social life which Pushkin and his friends much enjoyed. Pushkin has left his own account of his and his friends' behaviour:[9] 'Just before the start of an opera, a tragedy or a ballet, the young man saunters up and down the first ten rows of seats, steps on everybody's feet and converses with all his acquaintances and strangers ... She is acting today. She is dancing. Let's clap her. Let's call her out. She is so sweet. What eyes she has, what tiny feet!'

For all his later passionate love of theatre, Pushkin behaved childishly there, even allowing for the fact that he was the age of a modern undergraduate. Sometimes he acted the role of a bored fop, yawning ostentatiously. One evening he entered the box of some friends in the Grand Theatre wearing a periwig, which made him very hot. He made jokes during the performance and, taking off his wig to reveal a head shaved after a recent illness, fanned himself with it during a particularly dramatic scene. He was probably drunk, as he slid off his chair to the floor soon afterwards. Another report has him pounding on the head of a bald man in front of him by way of applause.

He was quick to take offence if anyone criticised his behaviour. 'Pushkin has a duel almost every day,' lamented the wife of the historian Karamzin in a letter to Vyazemsky.[10] In this, she exaggerated. However, there were some encounters which almost led to duels. His behaviour in the theatre, for instance, provoked a Guards Major, who at first refused to fight with an unknown youth. There is also a charming account of a duel with his old schoolfellow Kyukhelbecker, who called him out after Pushkin had written an unkind epigram about him. Kyukhelbecker shot first and missed, and Pushkin then dropped his weapon and wished to embrace his friend. Kyukhelbecker insisted that Pushkin take his shot, but Pushkin claimed that snow had got into his weapon.

Pushkin probably drank rather less than his rakish friends, but as little as Pierre does at the opening of *War and Peace* did he feel drunkenness as a disgrace. Pushkin once laid a wager that he could drink a whole bottle of rum without losing consciousness and, though he apparently passed out, he continued to move the fingers of one hand so the consensus was that he had won his bet.

Writing on 27 October 1819 to Pavel Borisovich Mansurov, when his friend had left St Petersburg for Novgorod,[11] Pushkin playfully describes the way he and several friends habitually looked out of the windows of the apartment of Nikita Vsevolozhsky, a student of history and a translator of comedies, to watch a young girl run by every morning: 'As before, telescopes rise towards her, pricks too.'

In 1819 Pushkin wrote an elegant erotic tribute to Olga Masson, a well-known courtesan at whose door he once found himself knocking, only to hear the grumbles of a maid and the cunning whispers of her mistress. The poem concludes with an appeal:

> Olga, dear priestess of pleasure,
> Listen to our lecherous pleading
> In the name of dissipation,
> Sexual bliss, licentious fun,
> Showing off or earning money
> Please select a night for us,
> For rapture and oblivion.

Quite apart from this riotous life, Pushkin's noble descent gave him entry to the salons of the titled intelligentsia, including that of Princess Golitsyna, whose beauty and cleverness attracted many to her gatherings, which often lasted until three or four in the morning. A gypsy fortune-teller had foretold she would die at night so she never went to bed before daybreak. Separated from her husband, and living with much gaiety, she had many admirers and, although she was twenty years older than Pushkin, according to the historian Karamzin, 'he fell mortally in love with her'.

Pushkin, along with several of his most intimate friends of this period, including both Ivan Pushchin and Baron Delvig, belonged to 'The Society of the Green Lamp'. This was a group of young friends, including several Guards officers, who met in a room (with a large lamp) at the house of Nikita Vsevolodovich Vsevolozhsky. In some ways, for Pushkin, 'The

Green Lamp' replaced Arzamas, which had been dissolved in 1818. At 'The Green Lamp', too, friends gathered to read original literary productions and exchange witty talk and epigrams. There was wine to be drunk, cards to be played and sexually uninhibited female company.

Many of the members of 'The Green Lamp', including Delvig and Ivan Pushchin, had serious political concerns, however, and to these meetings Pushkin was never admitted, even though he shared their liberal point of view. There were heated discussions on ways to reform the Russian aristocracy. Among those who took part in them were some who also belonged to the Union of Welfare, a precursor to the Decembrist Movement – this Pushkin was never invited to join. It seems likely his wild and thoughtless behaviour is one explanation for the caution his friends felt about admitting him to the inner circles of a conspiracy against the government, ripening at this very period. Professor Fomichev, to whom I spoke at Pushkinsky Dom in 1997, suggested an additional reason: Pushkin had very different circles of friends and some were officers loyal to the Imperial hierarchy, to whom a casual remark might have been dangerous.

Many ideals of the Decembrists were drawn from those of the first Director of the *lycée*, Malinowsky, and those of Pushkin's favourite teacher, Kunitsyn – Pushkin shared most of those ideals. That he did not join any of the conspiracies at this time is unlikely to have been a matter of his own reluctance. The most likely explanation is that he was felt to be too volatile in temperament for secrets to be confided in him. Pushkin's friends felt they could not rely on him. They did not doubt his courage, but his discretion.

His lack of self-discipline was unmistakable. His wit, gaiety, even precocious intelligence, were not in themselves likely to recommend him as a trustworthy fellow conspirator. His letters had a colloquial freedom which make them a delight to read but hardly suggest common sense or caution. Writing to a friend in Novgorod, Pushkin regales him with an account of an evening spent enjoying champagne and the company of actresses: 'The former gets drunk and the latter get fucked.' It is a comment of more exuberance than grace. 'Gaiety be our true companion to the grave and let us die clinking glasses,' he wrote on 4 May 1815 in his 'Epistle' to his friend Ivan.

At the same time, it must be observed that Pushkin would hardly have continued to enjoy the friendship of mentors such as Karamzin, whose history of the Russian State he much admired, the sad poet Zhukovsky, whose role as tutor to the Grand Duke Alexander gave him close connections with the Empress, and Vyazemsky, who was not only a poet but a wealthy nobleman in government service, if he had been only the feckless playboy his friends feared.

Was Pushkin's frivolity a disguise for a serious political thinker, whose humanity was already engaged in imagining some reform of Russia in which so many lived as slaves? In Ivan Turgenev's speech at the unveiling of the monument to Pushkin in Moscow in 1880, he quoted Evgeny Baratynsky, an enormously gifted poet, who had sorted through the papers of his dead friend, including *The Bronze Horseman*, and remarked, 'Can you imagine what astonishes me about these poems more than anything else? The abundance of thought. Pushkin was a profound thinker. Who would have expected it?' Next to Pushkin, Evgeny Abramovich Baratynsky (1800–1844) was the greatest poet of his generation. The two might have been closer friends but, as Alexander Kushner observed to me in St Petersburg in 1997, 'Neither of them wanted that.'

Pushkin was not careless in all matters. He polished even his lightest and most licentious lyrics. After nights of debauchery he could still work every morning at *Ruslan and Lyudmila*, a 3,000-line fairy tale. His friends observed his growing body of work with wonder. There is a letter from Zhukovsky to Vyazemsky in 1818 which records, 'Marvellous talents! What wonderful verses! He is haunting me through his poetic gift like a ghost!' Yet on one occasion he foolishly staked one thousand roubles, that is more than one year's salary, at a sitting. (He was obliged to settle the debt with a manuscript of his verse, then ready for publication.) As Vyazemsky recorded, 'Until his death Pushkin was a child at gambling and in the last days of his life he lost to men from whom everyone but himself used to win.'[12] Pushkin continued to love gambling, though poor luck and exceedingly bad judgement were to pursue him as a gambler all his life. Korff's observation, if not his disapproval, is worth some credit: 'Always without a penny, everlastingly in debt, with constant scandals, frequent duels, intimately acquainted with tavern keepers, bawdy houses and Petersburg harlots.'

His younger brother, Lev, suggests in his memoirs that Pushkin had some hesitation about joining the conspirators. It was at this period that his fortune was told by a German palmist named Kirghof, and Lev was very taken with the accuracy of several of her predictions, claiming that 'Mme Kirghof predicted Pushkin's Northern and Southern exiles, his marriage and untimely end, and warned him that he would meet his death at the hands of a tall, fair man.'[13] It is entirely possible that Pushkin believed in her prophetic powers as he was more than usually prone to superstition. Yet, even if he did, his credulity never prevented him challenging any fair-haired man to a duel, and there is something oddly implausible about the explanation that he refused to join any secret society because 'they were directed by a certain Adam Weisshaupt and Weisskopf and Weisshaupt are one and the same'.[14] It is much more significant that neither Ivan Pushchin, Delvig nor Kyukhelbecker, all of whom joined the Union of Welfare, urged him to any such commitment.

Ivan Pushchin, his closest friend, declared, 'He always agreed with me about the common cause, communicating our ideas in his own way, both in his talk and in his poems and prose,' but 'the unpredictability of his passionate nature and his association with unreliable people alarmed me'.[15] He had ample reason to be wary of trusting a friend who once shouted in the theatre so that everyone could hear: 'Now is the safest time to be in St Petersburg ... there's ice on the Neva.' By this everyone in the audience would have guessed Pushkin to mean that in winter you could escape from the Peter and Paul fortress. 'Of course, such talk was nonsense: but for all Pushkin's liberal views, he had the wretched habit of betraying his noble character and he often angered me, and indeed all of us.'[16]

Whatever else he may have been, Pushkin was not a fool, and the behaviour described above by Ivan needs some explanation. He might have been simply drunk, but alcohol was not a serious problem for Pushkin – he enjoyed his iced champagne, but when he worked for long hours at a stretch he preferred iced water or lemonade. His rash behaviour in the theatre probably sprang from his awareness that poverty made it impossible for him to compete on equal terms with the young gallants of St Petersburg society. He was engaged in adolescent showing off. Ivan Pushchin remarked sadly, 'What a strange mixture this magnificent creature was. Never did I stop loving him, and I know that he reciprocated my feelings. But sometimes, out of my deep friendship for him, I longed for him to look at himself truthfully and understand his behaviour.'[17]

Although he did not join the conspirators, who were to be among the leaders of the Decembrist Revolt in 1825, Pushkin did write a number of poems which became rallying cries for that movement. These were only circulated in manuscript, but as the Decembrist Ivan Yakushkin said; 'There was not at that time a literate ensign in the army who did not know them by heart.' Among the most famous of these poems was 'Ode to Freedom'. 'Volnost', Freedom, was the title of a famous work by Radishchev, whose revolutionary ideals had been an influence both among teachers at the *lycée* and among some of the hussars Pushkin admired during his schooldays. Pushkin's own poem was to that extent derivative. Its power, however, was unmistakable, particularly in the context of an autocracy that was unequalled in Europe. To suggest that tyrants of the world should shiver was political dynamite, even if Pushkin had not gone on to recommend insurrection to the oppressed:

> Fallen slaves, take heart like men.
> Listen to these words and rise.

The poem describes the weapons of torture still in use, and reminds kings that where scourges and leg irons exist monarchs, too, are in danger. As witness to this, he dares to remind his readers of Louis of France, who only a generation earlier had lost his head on the scaffold of the French Revolution. Although Pushkin calls the axe that struck off the royal head 'criminal', he openly enjoys the downfall of tyranny. The most offensive verse from the point of view of Alexander I was the one that gave an ominously quiet picture of St Petersburg itself:

> When the star of midnight glints
> On the darkly flowing Neva
> And a quiet sleep weighs down
> A head without anxiety
> The thoughtful singer looks towards
> A certain desolate monument
> A palace now forgotten, once
> Belonging to another tyrant,
> And hears the voice of history.

The Mikhaylovsky Palace had stood empty since the assassination of Paul I, Alexander's father. This verse was a particularly dangerous one as it refers not only to the tyranny of Paul I, but hints obliquely at Alexander's involvement in his assassination since it was at Alexander's order the palace was kept desolate. Alexander I continued to feel a guilty sense of complicity, even though he had only agreed to the deposition of his father, and he was likely to respond angrily to such a casual reference to the crime. A. I. Turgenev, himself a liberal, whose own brother was a member of the Union of Welfare, was afraid to send a copy of 'Freedom' to Prince Vyazemsky, saying, 'Walls may have eyes and even ears,'[18] while Karamzin wrote of the situation, 'Over the poet Pushkin at the moment there is not simply a cloud, but a thunderbearing cloud.'

Another poem was written in 1818 to Petr Yakovlevich Chaadaev, the philosopher whom Pushkin had known as a young officer at Tsarskoe Selo and who had now begun to circulate some of his thoughts in French manuscript. In this Pushkin speaks of yearning for 'the moment of sacred liberty' and ends the poem,

> There will rise, believe me, comrade
> A star of captivating bliss, when
> Russia wakes up from her sleep
> And when our names will both be written
> On the ruins of despotism.

Those last lines could be read as an invitation to an uprising comparable to the French Revolution, though it may be Pushkin hoped for no more than a decisive move to a constitutional government.

There were other dangerous poems. In 1818, Pushkin wrote 'Noelles' which is light-hearted in tone and tells how Mary in heaven is soothing the tearful infant Christ by threatening him with the arrival of the Russian Tsar. The Tsar, however, promises to send Lavrov, the head of the Ministry of Police, to a lunatic asylum and grant human rights to all his people. At this the Holy Infant weeps for joy though uncertain whether the Tsar is joking or not. Mary tells him to go to sleep unless he wants to hear more fairy tales. 'Noelles' includes a reference to the Tsar's broken promise, made in a speech before the Polish Diet in 1818, about establishing a constitution.

'The Village' (1819) contains more specific criticism of the injustice of an autocratic system. The poem opens with a lyrical description of Mikhaylovskoe, with its hayricks, cornfields, windmills and opportunity for peaceful contemplation. This section of the poem was submitted for publication and received the blessing of the censor. In the second section, which only circulated in manuscript, Pushkin turns his attention to the realities behind the landscape, particularly the horrors of serfdom where landlords whip haggard serfs over ploughs they will never own. As if to make certain that his behaviour would from this time forward be under police surveillance, Pushkin also wrote a satirical squib about the Tsar's chief minister, Arakcheev, in which he was said to be 'full of malice and without wit, feeling or honour'.

Even if Pushkin had in mind no more than reform, preferably administered at the behest of the Tsar, not even the mildest move towards reform would, by this stage of Alexander's reign, have been regarded tolerantly. Alexander I had once been a close friend of the Czartoryskis, an enlightened Polish aristocratic family, and had declared to Czartoryski that 'he hated despotism, no matter what way it was exercised; that he loved liberty, to which all men had a right; that he had taken the strongest interest in the French revolution, and while condemning its terrible excesses, wished the French Republic success.'[19] Alexander had been rightly perceived as a liberal when a group of Paul's courtiers determined to rid the country of their mad Tsar, but he was only a few weeks short of his twenty-fourth birthday at his coronation in 1801. At first, well aware of the need for educational reform, he had gladly accepted advice from Mikhail Speransky. Two decades later, he was happy to take counsel from Arakcheev, whom he knew to be a ruthless reactionary.

Alexander was also a devout man, whose sense of his own sins preyed heavily upon his mind. During the war with Napoleon he had not only sought comfort constantly in a reading of the scriptures, but also experienced moments of religious ecstasy as the battle swung in Russia's favour. Misfortunes, particularly the death of his sister's favourite child, Catherina, brought him quite naturally into the hands of reactionary clerical mystics. They frowned on reform, and under their influence so did Alexander.

In the same Pushkin notebook where his friends had written their lyceum verses there are drafts of new work and several drawings. Although there are no traces of seditious verses, a large number of pages have been torn out. In the first careful draft of his long poem *Ruslan and Lyudmila*, on which he had been working, for example, on folio 53,[20] the drawings give some sign of what may have been in his mind. The seemingly innocent line 'Dneiper's rebellious billows stirred' appears to have triggered thoughts of rebellion in general. There is an image of a young Triton, and a sketch of Professor Kochansky, Pushkin's teacher of classics, but also, and crucially, Alexander I caricatured as a cherub with puffy cheeks and very little hair, blowing a horn. There is also a list of dates, beginning with the year in which the Tsar signed a peace treaty with Napoleon at Tilsit, which Pushkin considered a shameful act.

Pushkin jocularly complained to his friend Vyazemsky on 21 April

1820, 'The circle of poets is becoming tighter by the hour – soon we shall be forced, for lack of listeners, to read our verses aloud to each other.' He was, however, mistaken.

His most reckless verses were already only too widely known, including a stanza which suggested the Tsar had been cowardly at the battle of Austerlitz. A government detective had already tried to obtain Pushkin manuscripts from his servant, Nikita Kozlov, who was offered a bribe of 50 roubles but refused to hand them over. When Pushkin heard from his servant about the police inquiry, he took the precaution of burning all his papers. Soon afterwards he was summoned to appear before Count Miloradovich, the Governor General of St Petersburg.

A vivid account of Pushkin's appearance before Miloradovich is given by F. N. Glinka, a friend who knew the Count well. The Count told Glinka that he had been ordered to seize both Pushkin and his papers, but thought it was more delicate to invite the poet to send for the papers himself. 'He appeared very quiet, with a bright face, and when I asked about his papers he answered, "Count, all my verses have been burnt. You will find nothing in my room. But if it is agreeable to you, everything may be found here," and Pushkin pointed to his head. "Order paper to be brought. I will write everything that has been composed by me." '[21]

Pushkin then wrote the whole of his work out again from memory, a piece of behaviour that charmed the Count with its frankness and suggests that Pushkin must have known how widely his verse had been copied and learned by heart and was not prepared to disown it. Ivan Pushchin remarked, 'After this daring exploit, Pushkin was allowed to go home and told to wait for instructions.'

For all his recklessness, Pushkin probably conveniently forgot some of his most dangerous work. He had every reason to worry. The Tsar, who liked to think of himself as a liberator of Europe from the tyranny of Napoleon, had come to fear irreligious and seditious verse. Arakcheev was in control of Russia and must have read Pushkin's insulting epigram. Pushkin risked being sent to Siberia or, even worse, to the Solovetsky Monastery on the White Sea.

It was fortunate that Pushkin continued to enjoy the favour of established writers of an older generation.[22] The historian Karamzin offered to help after extracting a promise from the poet that he would write nothing against the government for two years. Vyazemsky and Zhukovsky also came to his assistance. Somewhat younger than Karamzin,

Zhukovsky's relationship to Pushkin was that of a seven-years-older brother. Pushkin had been a frequent visitor at his house and Zhukovsky thought his talent miraculous, even though he disapproved of his life of dissolute idleness. He, Glinka and A. I. Turgenev all attempted to use their influence to prevent Pushkin being sent to the north-east.

Before deciding what to do, the Emperor called on Pushkin's old lyceum Director, Engelhardt, to complain that his former pupil was flooding Russia with seditious verse. Engelhardt, who had no reason to remember Pushkin with particular affection, nevertheless pleaded his youth as an excuse, predicted his talent would bring glory to Russia and asked the Emperor to treat the young man with leniency.

The Emperor, however, was determined to inflict some punishment and at length acted on Karamzin's suggestion that Pushkin be sent not to Siberia or the Solovetsky Monastery on the White Sea but to Southern Russia, where he was to serve under Lieutenant General Inzov. When this was conveyed to Pushkin, he was relieved of his worst fears. Nor was he altogether sorry to leave Petersburg since, like Evgeny Onegin, he was becoming 'wearied with the noise of balls and with turning morning into midnight'.

Several biographers have suggested that Pushkin's departure from St Petersburg also marked the chance to escape the scene of a deep but unrequited love, a theory first advanced by A. I. Nezelenov, a nineteenth-century Pushkin expert, and developed by M. O. Gershenzon. It was Gershenzon who noted that Pushkin, when first sent out of the capital, spoke of 'bonds in which he had been struggling in captivity', and suggested that this must refer to a passion which had not yet stopped giving him pain, even though the object of it had been left behind in the north. There are references in his letters not only of 1819 but as late as 1828 to such an unhappy attachment. And there is some evidence to support Gershenzon's theory in the so-called 'Don Juan list' which Pushkin wrote in the album of Elizaveta Ushakova in 1829.

This celebrated list gave the initials of the forenames of all the women Pushkin had ever loved. It was a list divided into two parts – in the first part were serious loves, in the second lighter attachments. The first part included the initials 'N.N.' and with the exception of these all the other names in the list of serious loves have been identified. Many investigators have supposed these initials to refer to Pushkin's lost Petersburg love. A poem 'Dorida', written in Petersburg at the beginning of 1820, speaks of thinking of the woman he really loved while lying in the arms of another, though this is far from conclusive proof that he was thinking about the mysterious N.N.

Other evidence comes from poems of Pushkin written around this period, and the fact that he felt he was suffering a loss of creative powers. An inability to write was often connected to unhappy love, and even when he reached the Caucasus later in the year all Pushkin had written was the short epilogue to the recently completed 'Ruslan and Lyudmila' and in that he laments,

> The flame of poetry is dead
> And I search in vain for responses.

This early unhappy love is unlikely to be identified. Although he did meet the 19-year-old Anna Kern before leaving St Petersburg, and he was to have a passionate love affair with her later in life, there is nothing to suggest he did any more than admire her at this stage. He may have been saddened by his infatuation with Princess Golitsyna. There are other contenders for the role of a woman, not even aware of his love, of whom he thought obsessively. What is most important is that in 1820 Pushkin could look back on a life which had been more than usually filled with sexual excitement and illicit pleasure, but held little evidence of shared love with any woman. Perhaps he did not expect it, or even altogether desire it. His strongest emotional attachments were to his boyhood friends.

On 6 May 1820 he set out for Ekaterinoslav on the Dnieper river. He had a thousand roubles in his purse as travelling expenses from the Ministry, which was rather in excess of his usual yearly salary, and a sealed letter for Inzov. Two lyceum friends, Delvig and Yakovlev, saw him to the outskirts of St Petersburg. Pushkin was dressed jauntily in a red shirt with a girdle and a felt hat. He expected to return in a few months to St Petersburg. He had completed *Ruslan and Lyudmila*, a long and lyrical poem already begun at the *lycée*, on 26 March 1820. When Zhukovsky received a copy of this, he sent Pushkin a portrait of himself with the dedication: 'To the victorious pupil from the defeated master.' Pushkin was delighted with Zhukovsky's response. When the decree of exile forced him to leave St Petersburg three weeks before publication, the praise became particularly precious. His feelings must have been confused as he travelled. A scandal had begun circulating in St Petersburg just before he left about a whipping he was supposed to have suffered at the hands of Miloradovich which, though false, he had been unable to counter. The humiliation of this may have worn off in the welter of new impressions, however, as he left behind the only world he knew. He was just three weeks short of twenty-one and, even though he was travelling into exile, he was not altogether despondent.

CHAPTER FIVE

To the South

Pushkin set out on a journey of two weeks to Ekaterinoslav, a thousand miles south, and arrived there about the middle of May. It was a small town on the Dneiper river, in which many of the inhabitants lived in little more than huts. He duly presented himself to General Inzov, with his letter of recommendation. The contents were unknown to Pushkin, but parts are worth some attention. The letter had been written by Kapodistria, the Minister for Foreign Affairs, and makes clear that, although Pushkin was not to be considered as an exile, but as a civil servant transferred to another post within the Imperial Service, the official judgement on his behaviour remained harsh.

'Permit me to report certain facts about him,' wrote Kapodistria:

Filled with bitterness during the course of his whole childhood, young Pushkin left his parental home without feeling any regrets. His heart, destitute of any filial attachments, could feel only a passionate desire for independence ... He entered the world endowed with a flaming imagination, but weak in the complete absence of principles ... There are no extremes into which this unfortunate young man has not fallen, just as there is no perfection which he might not have achieved by the excellence of his talents ... Certain poems, especially 'An Ode on Freedom', have brought Mr Pushkin to the attention of the government ... along with the highest beauties of design and execution, this poem reveals dangerous principles ... Mr Pushkin, it appears, will reform if only we believe his tears and promises. In any case, his patrons suppose that his penitence is sincere and that, removed for some time from St Petersburg, provided with an occupation and surrounded with good examples, one may make of him a fine servant of the government, or at least a writer of the first rank.

Kapodistria emphasises Pushkin's lack of filial respect and lack of principles; no doubt his friends stressed his feelings of childhood neglect.

Whatever General Inzov made of this appraisal, he received Pushkin with great kindness. Inzov had been brought up by Prince Nikita Trubetskoy and was rumoured to be of illegitimate royal descent. He may have been particularly sympathetic to a young man embittered by an unhappy family background. He himself was a bachelor of fifty-one, and his whole life had been spent in the army. He was a Freemason – masonic lodges were not yet regarded with suspicion – and well read: he collected manuscripts and enjoyed books of history. He was at this time the head of the Committee for the Protection of Russian Colonists of the Southern Region of Russia. When he was appointed Viceroy of Bessarabia shortly after Pushkin's arrival, he moved his headquarters to Kishinev in that province.

In June 1820, Pushkin still knew nothing of his literary success in the north. *Ruslan and Lyudmila* had been ready for the printer on 6 May 1820, just before Pushkin had been summoned before Miloradovich. In his absence, *Ruslan* had received so enthusiastic a reception that Pushkin now enjoyed a popularity no Russian poet had had before him.

An English reader, meeting an outline of the tale, may find it difficult to understand the excitement it aroused. A Russian contemporary of Pushkin, however, familiar with Zhukovsky's attempts to write folkloric poetry, would have encountered the deft, even impudent ease of Pushkin's verse as altogether new. The originality lies at once in the colloquial voice and the adroit irony. The poet is present in his poem to comment on the fairy story:

> Every day I wake and praise
> The good Lord gratefully: there are
> So few magicians nowadays.
> Our marriages, therefore, all honour
> To them, are in no such danger.

Ruslan and Lyudmila is a tale of magical transformations, swords and monsters. Lyudmila is abducted on her wedding night by the invisible magician Chernomor. Her bridegroom, Prince Ruslan, along with two of her disappointed suitors, sets out in pursuit of her. One of these suitors, Ratmir, is easily distracted by a castle filled with delicious naked women, but Prince Ruslan has to confront the huge severed head of the enchanter's brother, kept monstrously alive by villainous magic. Though his trunk rots in the desert, his spirit longs for death. The sad and grotesque moment when the giant severed head at last wins the release of sleep is both moving and surreal. When Ruslan happens on Ratmir, however, the former rivals gossip like two young men about town, and Ratmir's decision to remain in the agreeable company of his harem of pretty women comes in for no moral condemnation. There are other unheroic human insights. Although she first rejects a feast offered by her captor, Lyudmila begins to eat when she finds she is hungry. She knocks the magician's cap to the floor but, once alone, cannot resist trying it on:

> She put the cap upon her head
> Straight at first, and then askew.
> Then back to front. What happens next?
> Miraculous days, all magic new.
> Her image vanished from the mirror.

Ruslan is a poem with obvious debts to Ariosto, and in some ways resembling Spenser, though without any of Spenser's moralising. The Russian public found it altogether delightful. Pushkin added an epilogue while he was travelling in the Caucasus, and several years later a Prologue, learnt by every Russian child, in which the whole story is put into the mouth of a learned cat:

> A green oak on a curving bay
> A golden chain about the oak:
> By day and night a learned cat
> Walks round and round upon that chain.
> And to the right, it sings a song,
> And to the left, it tells a tale.

Those who have enjoyed the first film of Maxim Gorky's trilogy will remember the way those lines affect the young Gorky as he first learns to read.

Throughout their relationship, Inzov treated Pushkin with great indulgence and gave him little work to do. But Pushkin did not take to Ekaterinoslav, nor did he much enjoy discovering that his reputation had preceded him. A group of local notables visited him in his hut and found him with a piece of bread spread with caviare, and a glass of red wine. When Pushkin asked them what they wanted and was told that they had come to see the famous poet, he responded grumpily, 'Well, now you have seen him. Goodbye.'[1] He also offended ladies at a banquet given by the Governor of the province by wearing transparent muslin trousers without underwear in hot weather.

Soon after his arrival he caught a chill swimming in the river Dnieper and it was in his hut, as he lay in bed trying to recover – 'delirious, without a doctor, with a pitcher of iced lemonade' – that he was visited by General Raevsky, his son Nikolay – a young officer whom Pushkin had known in St Petersburg – and two of his daughters.

Pushkin was lying on a bench, unshaven, pale and thin, when Nikolay brought the family doctor Evstati Rudykovsky, who was travelling south with the Raevskys. Rudykovsky's own account suggests Pushkin was seriously ill, though he stubbornly refused to take the medicine Rudykovsky prescribed.[2] It was Nikolay's suggestion that Pushkin might like to join the family, who were travelling into the Caucasus to take the waters of the spa towns there. Seeing how ill the poet was, Inzov gave his blessing to the journey, the more readily since General Raevsky made himself personally responsible for Pushkin's behaviour. In his official explanation for allowing Pushkin's departure, Inzov remarked, 'I hope I shall not be blamed for this or be called over-indulgent. In truth, he is a good lad, unfortunate only that he ended his course of studies too soon; a learned shell remains forever a shell.'[3]

For his part, Pushkin was ecstatic at his change of circumstances, though it was not an easy journey and he lay ill in a carriage for a further week. The roads were rough, and the latter part of the journey demanded a military escort as the local tribes were far from willing to accept Russian rule. The Caucasus was the 'sultry frontier of Asia'[4] and Pushkin was overwhelmed by his experience of it.

> I lived in the Caucasus for two months. I needed the waters very badly, and they helped me exceedingly ... These medicinal springs are all located not very far apart in the last spurs of the Caucasus mountains. I am sorry, my friend, that you could not see this magnificent range of mountains, with their icy summits which from afar in the clear twilight look like strange, many-coloured and motionless cards.'[5]

In Pyatigorsk Pushkin recovered sufficiently to play a rather silly joke on

Rudykovsky. The doctor held a senior rank in the army and Pushkin wrote his name down in the local Commandant's visitors' book as 'a physician in ordinary'. Against his own name, as if in excuse, he wrote 'adolescent'.[6] For all this continuing evidence of childish mischief, as a poet Pushkin was maturing quickly. The Caucasus profoundly impressed itself on his writing for the next four years. In Pushkin's working notebooks, nearly three years later, there is a sketch of a rock appearing from the sea which looks like the gate of Karadag in the Crimea, though by this time Pushkin is at work on stanza 46 of the first chapter of *Onegin*, written in October 1823.[7]

By 1 August, with Pushkin's health restored, the party set out on the return journey, pausing for a visit to the little town of Kerch to look at the ruins of the supposed tomb of Mithridates. Pushkin plucked a flower there as a memento, but he lost it the next day without much regret. From Theodosia they set off by sea to Gurzuf in the Crimea. In the same letter to his brother, Pushkin recalls with equal delight the landscape of poplars, grapes, laurels and cypresses, and the sight of Tatar settlements. In Gurzuf, he spent three weeks and these he speaks of to his brother as the happiest in his life.

It was Pushkin's first experience of family life without grudging and quarrelling. It was, as he tells his brother, 'a free and untroubled time in the circle of a pleasant family ... a happy, southern sky; a marvellous region; scenery which delights the imagination; mountains, orchards, the sea.' He admired the lucid mind of General Raevsky, a kindly, affable man who treated Pushkin with all the affection he might have hoped to receive from his own father and never did. Raevsky was a hero of the war with Napoleon and commanded the Fourth Corps of the Second Army, which was stationed in Kiev. He was a man who loved literature, and had brought up his family to do the same. Pushkin's St Petersburg friend Nikolay wrote poetry and read it avidly. All three daughters were charming; they ranged in age from the thirteen-year-old Sofya to the twenty-three-year-old Ekaterina.

In a poem beginning 'The daytime candle has gone out', composed on a ship at night on the journey to Gurzuf, Pushkin writes of the moment when 'love faded and the Muse appeared', which suggests that by the time Pushkin arrived in the Crimea whatever pain of lost love he was suffering had become duller, since he could write again.

It was in Gurzuf that Pushkin was given the second of the 18 working notebooks that are in the possession of Pushkinsky Dom in St Petersburg, probably by one of the Raevsky daughters. On the first page there is a dedication and a pencil sketch of a woman's profile, perhaps the donor. It contains the epilogue to *Ruslan and Lyudmila*, dated Caucasus 26 July 1820.

The Raevsky family had a large house overlooking the sea at Gurzuf, and Pushkin spent his three weeks there walking, talking and swimming. He also fell in love with one, or perhaps all, of the charming daughters of the Raevsky family, then travelling with the party – Mariya, Elena and Ekaterina. The three sisters loved the poetry of Byron, which they could read in the original; indeed, they embarked on teaching Pushkin to read him in English.[8] Byron's poetry had been read in Russia with great enthusiasm in French translation as early as 1815, notably by Pushkin's mentors A. I. Turgenev, Vyazemsky and Zhukovsky. Whether or not Pushkin had learned to read English well enough to cope with the original language earlier, it was certainly in Gurzuf that he fell under Byron's spell. *Childe Harolde* in particular took Pushkin's imagination by storm, as a man saying a sad farewell to his native land. In his short stay in Gurzuf, a matter of only a few weeks, Pushkin wrote his first draft of *The Prisoner of the Caucasus*.

Pushkin was to have many reservations about Byron in later years, but he was still young and impressionable in Gurzuf. The saturnine Colonel Alexander Raevsky, Nikolay's brother, who had joined the party, also much impressed Pushkin with his world-weary pose of a Byronic hero and his claims to have nothing but scornful contempt for human virtues. His small eyes gleaming behind spectacles reminded Pushkin of Voltaire. Alexander Raevsky was four years older than Pushkin, and the cynicism of his views exerted an enormous fascination on the young poet already under the spell of the 'mad, bad' English author of *Childe Harolde*. Later in Pushkin's life he was to speak of Raevsky as his 'evil genius' and to describe the charming young man as someone who 'poured cold poison into my soul'. Raevsky played an underhand and despicable role in one of the most important love affairs of Pushkin's life. On this journey he seemed a witty companion, though he may have provided the model for some of the characteristics of Evgeny Onegin.

Meanwhile, there were the Raevsky daughters. The youngest girl with the family at the time, Mariya, was fifteen, with small features, bright eyes, a turned-up nose and particularly small feet. In her journals, written much later, she remembers running down from her carriage to the sea and beginning to paddle there:

It was an open stretch of water and, not suspecting that the poet was following us, I began to amuse myself by running after the waves, and when they rolled up I fled from them. I ended by getting my feet wet. Of course I said nothing about this and returned to the carriage. Pushkin found this a very graceful picture ... and wrote some charming verses about this childish prank.[9]

She was referring to the famous stanzas in *Evgeny Onegin*, often dubbed the 'pedal digression':

> I longed to join the waves in pressing
> Upon those feet these lips ... caressing ...

In Soviet times, Pushkin's love for Mariya was stressed because she went on to marry the Decembrist hero, Prince Sergey Volkonsky, and when the Prince was exiled to Siberia Mariya followed him loyally there. Whatever Pushkin's feelings, Mariya herself seems to have been very little affected at the time. It is possible that the dedication to Pushkin's poem 'Poltava' refers to her.

The eldest of the Raevsky daughters, Ekaterina, attracted Pushkin's more mature interest, though he characterised her as 'power-loving, proud, cunning and harsh'[10] and probably had in mind no more than a holiday romance. He enjoyed a light-hearted flirtation with the other sister, Elena, as well. All this generated a great deal of jealousy on every side and perhaps for that reason the passion of female jealousy forms an important part of Pushkin's poem *The Fountain of Bakhchisaray*, which draws on life in the Crimea, to which in later years Pushkin dreamed of returning, 'having forgotten about love'.

The days at Gurzuf came to an end when General Raevsky, who had made himself responsible for Pushkin, returned to Kiev. Pushkin had to put himself back into the service of Inzov, who had by this time moved his headquarters to Kishinev. With the General's party, which included his son Nikolay, Pushkin travelled on horseback over the Crimean mountains to Bakhchisaray, arriving there with a fever and little interest in his surroundings. Bakhchisaray had been the centre of empire for many khans, and the palace there had a fountain of tears at its heart. Of this palace he wrote to Delvig,

On entering the palace I saw a ruined fountain; water fell in drops from a rusty iron spout. I roamed about the palace indignant at the carelessness with which it had been allowed to decay ... Almost by force N.N. [Raevsky]

led me up the rickety staircase to the ruins of the harem and to the Khan's graveyard ... I was racked with fever.[11]

These are scenes which returned to Pushkin when he wrote *The Fountain of Bakhchisaray*, though they made little impression on him at the time. He later dedicated that poem to Nikolay, in gratitude for his affection. The party also visited the famous Monastery of St George and the ruins of the Temple of Diana, where Iphigenia was reputedly sacrificed.

Then Pushkin took his leave of the Raevskys and travelled into Bessarabia to what he was to call the 'accursed city of Kishinev'.

CHAPTER SIX

Kishinev

Kishinev is a small town on the river Byk in Bessarabia, then a recent Russian conquest which had changed hands several times in struggles with the Ottoman Empire. Inzov had the task of administering the territory according to the laws and customs of the country under a council of indigenous boyars. The town's narrow, crooked streets were crammed with many cultures – Moldavian peasants, Greeks, Turks, Jewish merchants and the adventurers of many nations. Some people were dressed in the fez of Islam, others in caftans or Turkish pantaloons; some, who affected to be part of French culture, wore lace sleeves.

Kishinev was a frontier town, as exotic in its own way as the Caucasus. It was also a city where more than ten per cent of the population were Jews, who had moved to Kishinev when the city became a commercial centre in the eighteenth century. Tyrannous restrictions were imposed on them, and a great many of them were extremely poor. Pushkin observed their 'hovels' and wrote of 'the dirty little shops of the Jews' to his friend Vigel, but he showed remarkably little of the characteristic Russian suspicion of them. Indeed, perhaps his own exotic ancestry and sense of difference enabled him to sympathise with their vulnerable situation: in a poem written in 1826 he wrote of the terror of a whole family in a Jewish cottage. An old man sits reading the Bible and his wife is setting a table for a skimpy supper when there is a night-time knock on the door:

In that cottage full of sorrow
Granny sets the supper table.
Having closed the Holy Book
The old man pressed the metal clasps.
Granny lays the meagre supper
And calls the family to eat.[1]

Pushkin arrived on 20 or 21 September 1820 and was invited to live in Inzov's own house, which lay on the outskirts of town and was surrounded by vineyards. It was Inzov's responsibility to report on Pushkin's behaviour to St Petersburg, which he did generously while remaining benevolent and protective in other ways. Pushkin was given little work to do apart from translating into Russian Moldavian laws originally written in French. At first he enjoyed finding his way into Kishinev society and making friends among the officers stationed there. He joined them at theatres, balls and gambling and in exploring the disreputable life of the town. Moreover, Inzov gave him as much leave of absence as he liked, and Pushkin was able to visit the Davydov Estate in Kamenka in the Ukraine (Raevsky's mother had married a Davydov as her second husband).

In Kamenka Pushkin was given the billiard room for a study and finished 'The Prisoner of the Caucasus' in February 1821. Indeed, he prolonged his leave for several weeks to enjoy the company of the Davydov brothers, both half-brothers of General Raevsky. Pushkin described the elder as 'Falstaff, for his girth rather than his wit', and wrote to his friend N. I. Gnedich on 4 December to report his enjoyment: 'My time is spent between aristocratic dinners and demagogic discussions ... There are few women, much champagne, many clever words, lots of books and a few verses.'[2]

Among the few women was Aglaya, the wife of the elder Davydov brother, whose charm and coquetry Pushkin responded to at once. In a short poem to her he mocks her readiness to yield her favours to other lovers:

One man I know had my Aglaya
For his moustache and uniform,
Money won her for another.
Any Frenchman roused her warmth.
Cleon's mind excited her,
And Damis, with his tender song.

> Tell me, though, my dear Aglaya,
> How did your spouse win your desire?

Pushkin may himself have enjoyed her favours for a time, but he was hardly involved emotionally and he also flirted outrageously with her daughter, Adele, who was only twelve, making strange faces at her over the dinner table and writing a poem for her recommending that she seize the first possible opportunity to enjoy the pleasures of love.

All this made Kamenka so enjoyable that Pushkin stayed on far longer than he had leave, and after a month a letter had to be written to Inzov on his behalf to make the excuse of a severe cold. Inzov replied indulgently that he was most relieved to hear Pushkin had not lost his way on the wintry steppes, and hoped that Davydov would not allow him to return until he had recovered his strength.

Later Pushkin visited Ekaterina Raevskaya in Kiev, where she had become engaged to a Commander of the 16th Division, Major General Orlov. Of him Pushkin remarked that he was the only man he had ever seen to be made happy only through his own vanity. It was of quite another friend called Orlov, news of whose marriage astonished everyone, that Pushkin wrote his famous epigram.

> In abject nakedness, Orlov
> With his Istomina lay in bed.
> The general had once again
> Failed to achieve the least success.
> So, with a magnifying glass
> And without wish to cause offence,
> Laisa said, 'Now let me see
> With what you try to penetrate me.'

Soviet editors totally emasculated this poem by removing the last line of the epigram, just as in Pushkin's adolescent and charming poem about snuff Russian editors removed '*mezhdu nog*' – 'between her legs' – and replaced them by '*mozhet byt*' (meaning 'perhaps'). Dots run through Soviet editions for words which seemed to them unacceptably obscene.[3]

There was far more to Ekaterina's fiancé, Major General Orlov, than Pushkin observed in Kamenka, however. Orlov was part of a growing revolutionary movement, which involved many officers in southern Russia. Once again, as with friends who belonged to 'The Green Lamp', Pushkin was never admitted to their most heartfelt concerns.

Orlov himself was to be a future Decembrist, though not the most important of the conspirators. The authorities had long had him under observation. Several leading members of the southern branch of the revolutionary movement also called in at Kamenka during Pushkin's stay there. At no time was he admitted into their serious discussions. One evening, in the presence of General Raevsky, who was not privy to the conspiracy either, there was a rather disingenuous discussion about the possible existence of a secret society against the government. One young man laughingly dismissed the idea as a joke. At this, 'Pushkin arose, red in the face and said with tears in his eyes, "I have never been so unhappy as now; I had already seen my life in the future ennobled with a lofty purpose, yet all this was only a vile joke!" '[4]

It may be that awareness of Pushkin's genius had led his schoolfriend Ivan Pushchin to preserve Pushkin from danger by keeping him in ignorance of secrets, but it seems more likely that in Southern Russia the conspirators saw the young man as altogether too irresponsible, too impulsive and too dissipated to be reliable. One of the conspirators even disliked him and thought him 'something of a bully. He is conceited and has a desire to ridicule and sting others.'[5] Even to those who loved him, Pushkin appeared too lightweight, too ebullient, too like the cricket of his adolescent nickname to be serious. Professor Fomichev suggested an additional and rather plausible reason for the reluctance of conspirators in the south to admit Pushkin into their secrets. Pushkin was known to be under surveillance by the police and, as a marked man, any associates were likely to attract unwelcome scrutiny.

Pushkin returned to Kishinev in March 1821. In April 1821, asked by Kapodistria for a report on Pushkin, Inzov replied that, 'The years and time will teach him reason' and that 'he was taking no part in the present troubled circumstances'.[6] Political events were, however, brewing up all round him. The liberal views of Orlov's division were well known in St Petersburg, though Orlov himself was protected by powerful family connections. Orlov was conveniently away from Kiev when the police took their first action against the spread of liberal sentiment.

Once again, Pushkin was perilously close to the action. On 16 February 1822 the principal scapegoat was a 27-year-old major of artillery. His name was Raevsky, though he had no family connections to General Raevsky. He was a brilliant young man, with some poems to his name, who had protested against the cruelties of army life, particularly the flogging of soldiers. He and Pushkin were personal friends – indeed,

Pushkin was able to warn Raevsky about his impending arrest after overhearing a conversation about it at Inzov's house. This gave Raevsky a chance to burn his papers, though even so his fate was harsh. After his arrest he was tried several times over the course of the next five years' imprisonment, once before the Grand Duke Konstantin. In 1827, when Raevsky hoped he might at last be set free, the new Tsar Nicholas I intervened personally to order his exile to Siberia and there he was forced to remain until his death in 1872. Raevsky was a Mason as well as a member of the Union of Welfare. Partly as a result of his trial, membership of masonic lodges was banned by the Russian government in August 1822.

Pushkin was personally acquainted with many of the most serious conspirators in the area, including P. I. Pestel, one of the leaders of the movement for social change and of all the rebels probably the one with the sharpest mind. He is described by the Decembrist Lorer as of Napoleonic appearance – that is, short, swarthy and with dark lively eyes. On 9 April 1821 Pushkin made an entry in his diary: 'This morning I spent with Pestel, an intelligent man in every sense of the word. "At heart I am a materialist," he says, "but my reason was opposed to it." We discussed with him metaphysical, political and moral subjects etc. He is one of the most original minds that I know.'[7]

Pushkin's first portrait of Pestel is just a profile, an early attempt to fix an interesting face. Pushkin was searching for the line between Pestel's forehead, the bridge of his nose, lips and chin, but did not attempt to draw either the eyes or the head itself. His second attempt to draw Pestel can be found in a manuscript of 1823. There is still no eye, though Pushkin seems more at ease with the line of the profile. At his third attempt Pestel's silhouette has a military collar. This drawing is among drafts of the 21st stanza of the second chapter of Evgeny Onegin. It was made at the beginning of November 1823, perhaps still under the strong impression of meeting Pestel in person. The next Pestel portrait is an accomplished drawing with a firm hand. It is on the margins of the draft text of Onegin's monologue from the fourth chapter of the poem, dated 8–10 October 1824, Mikhaylovskoe. In this drawing we can make out a man's head and a silhouette of his military uniform. The high forehead, elongated eyes and straight nose are all sharply observed, as are the small distance between Pestel's nose and full lips, and the firm, though not heavy, chin. His hair is brushed back, and Pushkin has given us a hint of Pestel's slightly protruding ears.[8]

Although the cast of Pestel's political opinion was clear, Pushkin was never told of his central position in a conspiracy. Indeed, he was so far from guessing at it that he did not think to burn two sketches he had made of Pestel when he was destroying other incriminating material at the time of the Decembrist Revolt. Some five years later Pestel was one of the five conspirators hanged for his part in the Decembrist plot.

Pushkin then lived on the very edge of a major conspiracy without being involved in it. This is not to say that he kept out of trouble. On his return from Kamenka and Kiev he threw himself energetically into a life of frivolity. Some of it was innocent enough. He loved gypsy music and dancing, and sometimes joined in with native street performers. He lay in bed late, tracing patterns on the walls of his room by shooting wax pellets from a pistol. He walked around the town without a hat as he had pawned his own to purchase some wine. Sometimes he adopted bizarre clothing, masquerading as a Turk, a Serb or a Moldavian on his walks through public gardens. Poverty had something to do with his strange clothing – for some time Pushkin's salary of 700 roubles had not been paid by the government and his father had refused to send him any money. The gaming tables became a habit with him. Unfortunately he had less luck and as little skill with cards in Kishinev as he had shown in St Petersburg.

It must be remembered that Pushkin continued to feel as much an exile from St Petersburg as the Roman poet Ovid had from Rome – also, as it happened, in Southern Bessarabia. On his trip to Akkerman with Colonel Liprandi, Pushkin sought out the supposed grave of Ovid. There is an anecdote which tells us that he spent the night in an old tower opposite the town of Ovidople, meditating on the Roman poet's misfortunes. Pushkin thought more highly of his poem 'To Ovid' than he did of either *Ruslan and Lyudmila* or *The Prisoner of the Caucasus*, as he confessed to his brother in a letter of 30 January 1823. And in one of the most beautiful passages of *The Gypsies*, too, the old man recalls the tradition of an exiled bard who had the holy gift of song and was much loved by the Gypsy people. 'To Ovid', a poem of more than a hundred lines, written in hexameters, was finished on 16 December 1821. In the last lines Pushkin speaks of being,

> Your equal, not in fame, but having the same fate,
> My lyre fills the northern desert, where
> I wander, lonely, on the banks of Danube,

Without a friend in all the world to listen; among
These alien hills, these sleepy fields and forests
Only the peaceful muses show me kindness.

Many of the poems in the first Kishinev notebook reflect his identification with other exiles, including Napoleon now that he had been safely defeated and imprisoned on Elba.

Pushkin was lonely for those he loved: friendship was a passion with him and he particularly missed his younger brother Lev, whom he was afraid would be urged by his parents to forget him. In a letter to Delvig on 23 March 1821 he wrote, 'I know they will try to erase me from his heart – they will think that is beneficial. But I feel we shall be friends and brothers, and not only in our African blood.'

Most of all he missed his fellow poets. Letters were now his only means of staying in touch with the literary world. When he heard from Nikolay Ivanovich Gnedich, a poet who not only acted as Pushkin's publisher but was also to be a noted translator of the Iliad, Pushkin speaks of the letter 'finding him in the wilds of Moldavia'. Writing to A. I. Turgenev on 7 May 1821 Pushkin pleaded, 'You haven't forgotten me, have you? ... Without the Karamzins, without you two and also without certain other selected ones, one would be bored even in a place other than Kishinev.' His exile in 'the wilds of Bessarabia' meant he was cut off from journals and new books as well as friends. On 21 September 1821 he wrote to Nikolay Ivanovich Grech, 'I have tried writing to Delvig and Gnedich, but they don't give a hang. What might this mean? If I have simply been forgotten, then I do not reproach them: to be forgotten is the natural lot of the absent ... but if they are angry with me or have come to the conclusion that I have no need of their letters – then that is bad.'[9]

To read these letters is to listen directly to the voice of Pushkin. They are casual and brilliant by turns, honest about his own feelings yet often ribald and gay. Commenting on the fact that his friend M. F. Orlov (perhaps the Orlov in his obscene epigram) had recently married, Pushkin pretends not to understand how that could have happened, 'unless he mixed up his head and the head of his penis and fucked his wife with the wrong one'.

Despite this characteristic playfulness, in Kishinev Pushkin was reading and writing more seriously than he had during the whole of his hectic life in St Petersburg. That he was able to do this alongside so public a dissipation is a mark of his remarkable physical stamina. He wrote copiously. However wild his nights, he rose at dawn and wrote cross-legged, sitting in bed, often forgetting breakfast and even lunch and breaking into fury if he was disturbed. When the weather was fine he worked outside, either in Inzov's gardens or in the fields beyond. On his travels in Southern Bessarabia with Liprandi, Liprandi recalls finding him sitting unclothed on his divan with scraps of paper all around him. It was poetry that was to save his spirit from desolation, not political commitment, though his sympathies remained liberal and in 1821 he wrote 'The Dagger'.

'The Dagger' was in some ways as dangerous a poem to write as 'Freedom'. It celebrates the assassination in 1819 of a reactionary German playwright and Russian official, August Friedrich von Kotzebue, at the hands of the German nationalist student, Karl Ludwig Sand. The poem opens grandly, invoking Hephaistos, the god of Lemnos, as the maker of the weapon – Pushkin claims a dagger – as always a defender of freedom since it might be anywhere, even beneath the glittering clothes of those near the throne. The poem threatens that an unexpected blow will always find a man who is the enemy of freedom, even though he is 'Hidden behind locked doors / Or asleep, among his family'.

In naming Sand and in calling him 'righteous', Pushkin was certainly making a gesture of some bravura. He himself called 1821 'the last delirious expression of my liberalism'. There is a sketch of Sand in Pushkin's working notebook of the period, along with sketches of the French revolutionary Marat and the Greek prince Ypsilanti, and aide de campe to the Tsar, who wanted Russia to support an uprising of the Greeks against their Turkish oppressor. Above Marat's head Pushkin has placed the triangular blade of the guillotine. Even in this 'delirious year' he had not forgotten the Terror that followed the French people's struggle for freedom.

The first Kishinev notebook also contains a number of doodles which reveal Pushkin's observation of the rich ethnic mix of peoples around him and his personal acquaintance, including the officer Deguilly who had once refused Pushkin's challenge to a duel. Even though in a letter to Delvig in March 1821 he complains, 'My muse is pining away from continence, and I rarely sin with her,' nevertheless he reported that he had finished his new poem, *The Prisoner of the Caucasus*.

The Prisoner of the Caucasus was modelled on one of Byron's eastern tales, with the difference that Pushkin was actually living in the region rather than relating to it as a tourist. Under the influence of *Childe Harolde*, however, Pushkin was able to see and present his involuntary exile from St Petersburg in a new light – that of someone leaving behind the superficial world of society for the chosen freedom of an outcast. In thinking intelligently about the psychology of such a choice, Pushkin had become not only an imitator of Byron but a commentator upon the Byronic ethos, though he was to do so with more subtlety later. The influence of Byron's poems such as *The Corsair, The Giaour* and *The Prisoner of Chillon* is evident throughout the poems of Pushkin's Kishinev period.

The Prisoner of the Caucasus opens with a marvellous description of life in a Circassian encampment. A Russian captive is dragged, lassoed and half dead, into the midst of these tribesmen. The Russian is a poet, a dreamer, a lover soured by some unexplained experience, who has abandoned society in pursuit of liberty. Now he has been taken captive. At night a beautiful Circassian girl brings him a drink of mare's milk, and seems moved by his condition. The days pass and she brings him wine and nurses him until he begins to recover. As he takes an interest in the simple courage and hospitality of his captors, admiring – as Pushkin had on his journey through the mountains – both the horsemanship and the weapons of the Circassian warriors, she falls in love with him. When the Circassian girl confesses her love, he cannot return her affection and refuses to pretend.

> 'But who is she, your beautiful sweetheart?
> Do you love her? Are you loved?'

she asks, unable to understand his reluctance. Nevertheless, she releases him and they run away from her tribe together. The prisoner does not love her, and possibly could not love anyone – certainly he makes no attempt to save the girl who has rescued him when she falls into a freezing mountain river. The coldness with which the prisoner responds needs some explanation. Pushkin's emotionally deprived childhood may have left him, for all his gaiety and exuberance, with a splinter of ice in the heart which made it difficult for him to feel sympathy, however easy he found it to fall in love and be aroused to sexual desire. Pushkin describes as altogether admirable the stoic indifference Circassian tribesmen show towards their own fate, but the unheroic behaviour of his prisoner excited disapproval among his friends, even in those who praised the verse. Pushkin sent the poem to Nikolay Ivanovich Gnedich on 29 April 1822, giving him the 'boring cares of publication' and by 27 June

1822 was glad to receive the news that publication was assured.

In an early letter to Gnedich, Pushkin wrote that in *The Prisoner* he wanted to show 'the indifference to life and its joys, the premature senility of the soul, which is so characteristic of our younger generation'. Pushkin himself was only 23, and we have to ask whether this description of the prisoner's character resembles Pushkin's adopted manner or his inner being. To Vladimir Petrovich Gorchakov, who wondered why the hero did not drown himself after the girl had done so, Pushkin declared boldly in October 1822: 'The character of the prisoner is unsuccessful; this proves I am no good as a hero of a romantic poem. In him I wanted to depict the indifference toward life and its pleasures and the premature old age of the soul which have become the distinctive features of the youth of the nineteenth century.'[10]

It is perfectly possible that up to this point Pushkin had felt only the 'vehement desires' of which he wrote in 'To Yurev' but little *affection* for the women he pursued, and that this is what he intended by 'indifference'. Even so, his description of his feelings at this juncture suggests an acolyte of Byron, particularly the Byronic figure of *Childe Harolde*, to whose worldly melancholy Pushkin was attracted during his time in the Caucasus. The mood of this poem, together with an Eastern influence in poems such as *The Fountain of Bakhchisaray*, led to his characterisation by enthusiastic critics as a Russian Byron.

Writing of the poem to Vyazemsky on 6 February 1823, Pushkin remarked with less affectation: 'You say my dear fellow that he is a son of a bitch for not mourning for the Circassian girl. But what should he say? "He understood everything" expresses everything ... Others are vexed that the Prisoner did not throw himself into the river to drag my Circassian girl out. Yes, jump right in; I have swum in Circassian rivers. In them you yourself will drown, and not a devil of a thing will you find. My prisoner is an angelic fellow, not in love with the Circassian girl. He is right in not drowning himself.'[11] Whether or not the vivacity of this defence persuaded his friends, his other readers had no such reservations and his readership was increasing prodigiously. The majority of the population were altogether unschooled, but literacy was spreading, and enthusiasm for Pushkin spread far outside the cultured elite. Indeed, the widening public for books and journals led both to the commercialisation of literature, hitherto impossible to imagine, and even more anxious interference by censorship.

Alongside this romantic tale of a disillusioned young rake in *The*

Prisoner of the Caucasus, Pushkin had already begun to write his masterpiece, *Evgeny Onegin*. Once again Pushkin's doodles in his working notebooks provide a clue to his state of mind as he sketches a group of figures in a bordello and roughs out his plan for a 'Tale of a demon in love'.

The bordello drawing is a complicated composition, in which a demon is shown escorting a young man into a brothel. There are many objects which relate only ambiguously to such a scene, notably a skeleton, a fencing sword and a skull. These objects were drawn in later, and relate to Pushkin's intention to write a poem about a demon who falls in love, an idea conceived in his southern exile but which never materialised, at least in its original form. The idea of a cold-hearted but non-supernatural devil, leading a young man to his destruction in this world, bears some resemblance to the plot of *Evgeny Onegin*. There are two other related drawings – one, of an elegant demon sitting next to a roasting spit, and another with a demon above the apparition of a half-naked woman.[12]

Pushkin remained – with good reason – worried about the reactions of censorship to whatever he wrote. In a letter to Bestuzhev, a critic who was to become an editor, with Ryleev, of the *Northern Star*, on 21 June 1822 he wrote with some irony, 'Give my greetings to the censorship, my ancient girlfriend; the dear creature seems to have grown still more intelligent. I do not understand what in my elegiac fragments should have troubled her chastity ... I foresee problems in publishing my poem "To Ovid". One may and must deceive the old woman, for she is very stupid ... apparently they have frightened her with my name.'[13]

For all his fear of the moral snooping of censorship, Pushkin wrote two of his most outrageous poems while he was in Kishinev, *The Gabrieliad* and *Tsar Nikita and His Forty Daughters*. Humour and Jewishness seem to have gone together in Pushkin's mind. In 1820 he wrote a little poem to a Jewish friend, Rebecca, called 'Christ is Risen', in which he wishes her a happy Easter, sends her a kiss and even promises to take up her faith if she will return his embrace. He ends bawdily,

> I'm ready to put into your hands the one thing
> Which distinguishes a true Jew from an Orthodox Christian.[14]

The Gabrieliad, written at the end of Lent 1821, opens with Pushkin in the bed of a young Jewess, reading her a poem:

> There is a young Jewess whom I adore
> Both for her earthly beauty and her soul.
> Sixteen, dark brows, two supple girlish mounds
> Rising and falling beneath her linen dress.
> A leg for love, a jewelled row of teeth...
> Jewess, why are you smiling? Why that blush
> Spreading over your face? Darling, I'm sorry.
> I don't mean you, it's Mary I'm describing.[15]

Pushkin proceeds to give an earthy, blasphemous account of the Annunciation. At the centre is Mary, a lovely young Jewish girl neglected by her ageing old carpenter of a husband, who sees that she is fed but otherwise takes no notice of her. The Lord sees her beauty and, touched with divine lust, summons her to heaven in a dream. There she is distracted by the raffish good looks of the Angel Gabriel. Unaware of any danger, the Lord picks Gabriel as his go-between. Meanwhile, the Devil, hearing a Jewish girl is about to be given a child destined to save mankind, takes a hand and appears before Mary in the form of a snake. When she recognises him he excuses his own behaviour towards Adam and Eve. The story had been unfairly told, he explains. Eve was mooning about in a garden,

> Quietly and innocently living;
> If you can call it life. Monotonous days
> And tedious years.

There was no sexual love between Adam and Eve, the Devil explains, because the Lord wanted Eve for himself. It was the Devil who introduced Adam and Eve to the delights of love, and these he describes to Mary in a passage of erotic lyricism intended to excite the young girl's libidinous feelings. Once convinced his verbal seduction is having an effect, he turns himself into a handsome young man, puts a hand under Mary's clothes and feels beneath them for what he wants. The mundane realism of that fumbling is peculiarly shocking. Gabriel disturbs the Devil and drives him off but, rather than defending her purity, soon falls to the enjoyment of Mary himself. Later the Lord appears in the form of a white dove and settles on Mary's most intimate parts:

> he pecks it, crawls around
> And twirls about, his little feet and beak
> hard at it.[16]

Mary is both exhausted and voluptuously gratified by the enjoyment of three lovers in one day, and the poem concludes with a charming picture of Joseph as a complacent cuckold. The poet prays that if he is under the same threat he may show infinite patience to his wife.

The Gabrieliad is written in elegantly rhymed iambic pentameters, whose ease and simplicity bear the unmistakable mark of Pushkin's verse. The poem circulated only in manuscript copies and Pushkin would never have considered publication as it would have appalled Alexander's fanatically religious advisors. Indeed, Pushkin was to deny his own authorship a few years later when a copy was brought to the attention of Tsar Nicholas I. Nevertheless, even his most respectable fellow poets were quick to enjoy it. On 1 September 1822 Pushkin sent Vyazemsky a copy, and Vyazemsky described it in a letter to A. I. Turgenev on 10 December on 10 December 1822 as 'a splendid frivolity'.

Tsar Nikita and His Forty Daughters, also written in 1822 in Kishinev, has a similar humour and gaiety. Far from pornographic in the sense of titillating, it is as assuredly and magnificently obscene as Chaucer. The poem is written in a jaunty rhythm:

> Tsar Nikita once ruled widely
> Richly, cheerfully and idly.

The subject is the forty daughters of the Tsar, who lack their female parts. The Tsar makes it a criminal offence to speak to his daughters of what is missing and threatens severe punishment for any subject who is rash enough to do so.

> Women have their tongues pulled out,
> Men will lose more precious members.

The girls grow up, still deprived, until a counsellor remembers a procuress, reputed to be a witch, who might be able to help them. This proves to be the case. The witch gives the Tsar's messenger a little casket filled with all sizes and colours of the missing parts. Riding back, however, the messenger is overcome by curiosity to know what he is carrying. He finds the casket locked, can't hear anything inside and then, sniffing at it, he 'smells a familiar scent'. Astonished and intrigued, he can't help opening it, and out of the casket fly the forty parts, like little birds, and settle on the branches of nearby trees. The messenger is terrified at the thought of arriving back at Court with the casket empty, but nothing he says or does will persuade his precious cargo to fly back into their prison.

He is saved by the advice of an old woman, plodding along the road, who advises him simply to show his penis – 'Just you show them ... and they'll come down on their own,' she suggests. This is what happens – the female parts are all safely secured in their casket and the messenger rides back to the Tsar and his reward. The poem concludes impudently in Pushkin's voice as he recognises that people may be puzzled to make out his intentions.

> And why tell such a silly story?
> What's it to them? I wanted to.

Shortly after completing *The Prisoner of the Caucasus* Pushkin began 'The Robber Brothers', a narrative poem based on the true story of two robbers who escaped their guards and were trying to swim the river Dneiper in their chains. Only part of the poem remains, however, because Pushkin disliked and burned the second part of it. The merits lie in the lurid descriptions of the robbers' 'underworld', though there are echoes of *The Prisoner of Chillon*.

In 1822 Pushkin began work on a poem less frivolous than these and far more extraordinary than *The Prisoner of the Caucasus*. Some time in December 1821 he had visited nomadic communities living on the Bessarabian steppes and collected impressions of them. There is even a legend that he spent some time living with a community of Gypsies. The whole area was filled with Gypsies, much distrusted, as indeed they still are, by the present local Romanian populace, and loved by Pushkin for their independence, music and vivacity. Hence *The Gypsies* was far outside the scope of the Byronic poems he was imitating. He had seen the encampment he describes at the opening of the poem.

> Their camp at night is gay as freedom.
> They sleep at peace under the skies.
> Between the wheels of van and wagon
> Old carpets hang; their supper fries
> Upon an open fire; their horses
> Graze the bare field; behind the tent,
> A tame bear sprawls at ease.

The first draft of the poem was not written until later in Odessa, and revised in Mikhaylovskoe.

The Fountain of Bakhchisaray is also in the first Kishinev notebook – it is a poem set in the ruined harem Pushkin had visited with Nikolay

Raevsky in the same palace of the Khans which had impressed Pushkin so little at the time. Now reflecting on the fountain, Pushkin invented the tale of a Crimean khan who falls in love with Mariya, a beautiful Polish girl in his harem who longs for her freedom. When she dies in mysterious circumstances the Khan suspects his former favourite Zarema of killing her and has Zarema thrown into the sea. The fountain of tears is erected to commemorate Mariya when the Khan returns from the wars.

For all the pleasure Pushkin must have taken in creating the music of this poem, he was soon dismissive of its merits. Writing to Vyazemsky, he declared it trash. Nevertheless, *The Fountain* was published in 1823 with an introduction by Vyazemsky, who named Pushkin as being at the forefront of Russian poets. The poem was very successful, earning Pushkin 3,000 roubles, whereas *The Prisoner of the Caucasus* had only earned about 500. With its publication, Pushkin was able to contemplate a future in which he would be able to live on his writing. He was the very first Russian poet to think of doing so. Nor did he give himself any airs about writing for money. As he wrote later to Vyazemsky in March 1823, he was happy to have his poetry looked upon as a trade: 'Aristocratic prejudices are suitable for you but not for me ... I look at a finished poem of mine as a cobbler looks at a pair of boots: I sell for profit.'[17]

It would be hard to overstress the central paradox of Pushkin's character in these years: mature and sophisticated in all literary matters, his observable behaviour remained outrageously childish. A letter of A. I. Turgenev in 1822 reports that he 'struck a certain noble in the face, and fought a Colonel with a pistol, but without any bloodshed'.[18] He had a quarrel which nearly led to a duel in a billiard hall where he had gone with three Russian officers, one of them a brother of Orlov, Ekaterina's fiancé. There, Pushkin amused himself by scrambling the billiard balls of two of these friends, and in response one of the officers called him a schoolboy. This insult led Pushkin to challenge him to a duel and invite the other to be his second. Only the officer's good humour prevented this coming to something serious the following day when Pushkin allowed himself to be placated.

Pushkin's behaviour provoked a number of duels in Kishinev which he seems to have relished. In the face of danger he had an admirably icy courage. Once at a card game where he was losing steadily to an officer of the General Staff called Zubov, he implied that the officer had cheated.

This led to a duel, and legend[19] has it that Pushkin brought cherries to the field outside the city where the duel was to take place. He ate these while his opponent took aim. Zubov shot and missed. At once Zubov ran to embrace his cool enemy, who refused to take his own shot and left the field. He met another, and far more formidable opponent, Colonel S. N. Starov, after a quarrel with a young officer of the Egersky regiment over whether an orchestra played a quadrille rather than Pushkin's preference, a mazurka. That duel was fought out in a blizzard so ferocious that the opponents could barely see one another. Both fired twice and missed before the duel was called off by their seconds. Mutual friends managed to prevent the meeting being reconvened and at the usual meal of reconciliation Starov is said to have remarked, 'To tell the truth, you stand up under bullets as well as you write.'

On the duelling ground Pushkin always comported himself with dignity, even if the story about eating cherries under fire is an invention. There were less admirable pieces of behaviour, notably towards the Moldavians, who were a timid people for the most part. In one dispute, over a card game, he took off his shoe and struck a Moldavian in the face. (He was only punished mildly by Inzov for this.) Pushkin thrust a pear in the face of another Moldavian, and his irritability was such that he once challenged a Greek to a duel merely for expressing surprise that Pushkin had not read a particular book.

Another quarrel arose with Todor Balsh, a Moldavian merchant with whose wife Pushkin was on intimate terms. Perhaps to annoy Mme Balsh, Pushkin began to pay court to her thirteen-year-old daughter. In an insulting exchange of words one evening with Mme Balsh in the casino, Pushkin threw doubt on the manhood of Moldavian men and had his own courage called into question by her. In response, Pushkin went directly to where Balsh was playing and challenged him to a duel. According to the account of P. I. Bartenev[20] the mystified Balsh asked his wife what had happened to provoke such a challenge and, on being told that Pushkin had been offensive, asked, 'Why do you demand satisfaction from me when you have allowed yourself to offend my wife?'[21] This he said so loudly that Pushkin lost his temper and would have hit Balsh over the head with a candlestick if a friend had not caught his arm. The next day Balsh was brought to ask pardon from Pushkin, though it is not clear what the poor man had done wrong. Asked what kind of pardon he wanted, Pushkin slapped Balsh's face and left the room. A duel would have certainly followed if Inzov had not put Pushkin under house arrest for two weeks and removed his boots as an additional precaution.

Pushkin's childishness at this period resembled that of his most dissipated days in St Petersburg, but as he had no close friends in Kishinev to share his serious moments he was painfully lonely underneath his wildness. He was fortunate that Inzov continued to feel real affection for him and even provided him with money, food and sometimes clothes, in spite of his inexcusable behaviour. It was Inzov who arranged for his allowance to be renewed.[22] Nor was Pushkin ungrateful, observing with some compunction that Inzov 'puts his trust in nobility of feeling because he himself has noble feelings'.

Another army officer, V. P. Gorchakov, writes of seeing Pushkin in a Kishinev theatre, 'a young man of short stature, but quite robust and powerful ... often laughing with an abundance of unnecessary hilarity, and then suddenly becoming so meditative as to arouse interest. The features of his face were irregular and plain.'[23]

Gorchakov also reported that, meeting Pushkin the following day, he asked him to recite a verse or two of a song he had written, and that Pushkin had suddenly seized a rapier and begun to play with it. Another friend, Druganov, appeared.

> Like a naughty child he began to make passes at him with the rapier. Druganov avoided the rapier with his hand. But Pushkin did not desist, and Druganov began to get angry ... To avoid a quarrel I again asked Pushkin to recite the Moldavian song. He willingly agreed, threw the rapier aside and began to recite with great spirit.[24]

Other scrapes led Inzov to confine Pushkin to the house as a punishment, on one occasion for three weeks.

Much of Pushkin's behaviour was not only immature but edged with malice. Despite his regard for Inzov, he took a particular pleasure in offending the man, who had remained consistently his chief benefactor. Knowing Inzov had a simple religious faith, Pushkin delighted in asking sacrilegious questions at mealtimes and he taught his parrot a Moldavian oath, which the bird repeated to a local cleric. In church he made faces and put a thumb to his nose behind Inzov's back. Nor were men his only butt. He wrote flattering verses in a young lady's album to her great delight, as if in admiration of her beauty, and then dated the poem 1 April. At a party another young lady hid her shoes under a divan because her feet hurt. Pushkin stole them and the embarrassed woman had to walk to the door in her stockinged feet. Some of his behaviour was not only ill-mannered but rash. He made a joking remark about the Bible in the presence of the rector of a local seminary and was threatened with a summons from the Holy Synod.

The majority of Pushkin's relations with women in Kishinev left him without any recollection. His passions may have been aroused, but not his emotions. Two women, however, deserve mention. The first of these was Kalypso Polychroni, the daughter of a Greek fortune-teller, who had reportedly been the mistress of Lord Byron during his first spell in Turkey. Pushkin, so much under the spell of the English poet, found the thought of a relationship with her exciting for this reason. Kalypso had left Turkey for Odessa when there were attacks against Greeks in Constantinople. Her attractions lay in her tempestuous nature, rather than her physical beauty. Guber quotes F. F. Vigel, who knew her well. 'She was ugly, small, with an almost imperceptible bust, a long dry face, always flushed, with a long nose and huge fiery eyes ... Her voice was tender and alluring, not only when she was speaking but when she was singing dreadful, gloomy Turkish songs, one of these was rendered into Russian under the name "Black Shawl" ... Besides Turkish and Greek, Kalypso knew Arabic, Moldavian, Italian and French ... had she lived in the time of Pericles, history would surely have preserved her name.'[25]

Kalypso met the poet halfway through 1821, but by the beginning of 1822 Pushkin was already losing interest in her. There are unreliable but romantic tales of her later fate. The Romanian writer Negrucci writes of her departing for Moldavia to a monastery where she attended all the services with pious ardour and where nobody suspected her of being a woman until her death.

Pushkin's other Kishinev involvement was his attraction towards the listless and languid Romanian Pulkheria, in every way the opposite of the fiery Kalypso. She was the daughter of the boyar Barfolemey and Pushkin was only one of many admirers. A. F. Veltman, who lived in Kishinev at the same time as Pushkin, sketched her in the following way:

She was an inexplicable phenomenon of nature. Several times I tried to tell myself that she was a perfect work of art, not of nature. Her movements could have been the mechanical movements of a machine. Her face and hands were so fine they reminded me of stretched parchment. Pulkheritsa was a round, plump, fresh girl; she liked to speak with a smile, but this was

not the smile of coquetry; it was simply the smile of a healthy, carefree heart
... Many wanted her hand in marriage; her father would give his agreement;
but as soon as the would-be betrothed began to seek her heart, Pulkheritsa
would interrupt his declaration of feeling with '*Quel vous êtes?*'[26]

Pushkin supposedly valued her simple-hearted beauty and 'her dumb
heart which never knew desire or envy'. It seems unlikely he came any
closer to this object of his affections.

The same need for drama which led Pushkin into foolish duels was
more nobly excited by the first stirrings of the Greek War of Independence. Bessarabia already had many refugees from Turkish atrocities,
of whom Kalypso Polychroni was one. The thought of noble Greeks
struggling against their oppressors was a natural cause for a young and
volatile spirit. Like Byron, Pushkin imagined the Greeks as heirs of a
great ancient civilisation. In the first half of March 1821 Pushkin wrote
joyfully to Vasily Lvovich Davydov,

> Greece has revolted and proclaimed her freedom ... On February 21, Prince
> Alexander Ypsilanti ... published proclamations which quickly spread
> everywhere ... that the hour of Turkey's downfall has come, and that a
> *great power approved of the great souled feat!*[27]

By this 'great power' Pushkin understood, as most would have done,
that Russia herself gave support to Ypsilanti's movement. The situation
was far more complex. The original Greek plan had been to launch their
rising in December 1820.[28] An emissary had arrived in St Petersburg early
in 1820 with the hope of persuading the Foreign Minister, Kapodistria, to
accept the leadership of the secret organisers of the Greek revolt. This
he had refused. Prince Alexander Ypsilanti, however, responded favourably to a similar invitation and travelled to Kishinev where he had his
family estates. He there proclaimed that the insurgents would see 'a
mighty Power defend their rights' and Ypsilanti and his troops crossed
the frontier at the River Prut.

In the same letter to Davydov, Pushkin speaks rashly and excitedly of
a secret society which had been organised as early as thirty years before
with the aim of achieving the liberation of the Greeks. Pushkin made no
attempt to throw in his lot with the rebels, either then or later, as Byron
was to do, although one of his motives in joining a masonic lodge was
to plan support for the Greeks, and this was duly reported back to St
Petersburg. On 2 April Pushkin recorded in his diary, 'I'm absolutely

sure that Greece will triumph and the 25,000,000 Turks will leave the flourishing country of Hellas to the lawful heirs of Homer and Themistocles.'[29]

In fact, the Turks soon reoccupied the principalities of Moldavia and Wallachia and by June the brave but mistaken Ypsilanti had fled to Austria. The involvement of the government of Russia is not clear but Pushkin hoped that if Russia did become involved he would be allowed to join in the fighting, as he said in a letter he wrote to A. I. Turgenev, then visiting Odessa, whom Pushkin was not allowed to visit. 'If there is any hope of war, for Christ's sake leave me in Bessarabia.'

No support was forthcoming from Russian troops and the revolt was soon quenched. Two years later, shortly before leaving Southern Russia, Pushkin wrote to Vyazemsky of his mistake in imagining that 'a nasty people, consisting of bandits and shopkeepers, were by birth the legitimate descendants and heirs of their fame in schoolbooks'. Robin Edmonds claims that neither Pushkin's first enthusiasm nor his later withdrawal of support from the Greek cause were well thought out, and it is hard to rebut this assertion. On the other hand, Pushkin had closer political issues to confront.

He was beginning to understand how closely his own fate was bound into the history of Russia, which had developed so differently from that of any other European country. It was at this period in Kishinev that Pushkin began to develop his own formidable investigations of that development. He began by making notes on recent Russian history, particularly on the period of Catherine the Great. In these notes he shows his exasperation with contemporary foreign writers who had showered excessive praise on Catherine, while failing to observe that, even as she abolished the nomenclature of slavery, she imposed serfdom in Belorus, then free, and in the Polish provinces. She might have notionally abolished torture, but she nevertheless encouraged the secret police to flourish. Western writers, who knew Catherine through her correspondence with Voltaire, should at least, Pushkin thought, have been dismayed to learn that she sentenced Nikolay Ivanovich Novikov, who did so much to spread the ideas of the enlightenment, to confinement for 15 years in the fortress of Schlusselberg. While thoroughly investigating Russian history, Pushkin also took great interest in the languages and folklore of the peoples of Bessarabia, the Caucasus and the Crimea.

In his letters, Pushkin shows clearly how he was beginning to reject the omnipresent influence of French literature on Russian poetry, basing his opposition on 'its stupid versification – timid pale language – always on leading strings'.[30] To Gnedich, on 27 June 1822, he rejoiced that 'English literature is beginning to have an influence on the Russian. I think it will be more advantageous than the influence of timid, affected French poetry.' Pushkin's admiration for English literature was discriminating and far wider than for the poems of Byron. He already loved Laurence Sterne, who was to be an influence on *Evgeny Onegin*, and wrote of Zhukovsky's translation of Moore's *Lalla Rookh*, 'The whole of *Lalla Rookh* is not worth ten lines of *Tristram Shandy*.' In the same letter to Gnedich, Pushkin showed some impatience with Zhukovsky's intention to translate Southey's *Roderick*.

Although understandably distant towards his father, whose help at this period ran to little more than the offer of a few old clothes, Pushkin wrote with affection and concern to his brother and sister on 21 July 1822', 'I miss you – what are you doing?' He urged his brother not to follow his own example and become a poet. 'Tell me – have you grown up? When I left you were a child.' To his sister Olga he added in a postscript, 'Have a good time and get married.'[31] In a letter to Lev on 4 September 1822 he expounded his plan for Lev's career in the services, recommending a place in Raevsky's regiment where he might soon become an officer. This advice he developed more fully in another letter written between 4 September and 5 October, this time in French – presumably to give it maximum accessibility as Lev preferred not to write letters in Russian. Some of this moral advice has a Roman stoicism. 'Never accept favours. A favour most of the time is an act of treachery. Avoid patronage completely, because it enslaves and degrades,' he writes. It was not hypocrisy, however, but miserable personal experience that led Pushkin to add the Polonius-like advice, 'Never borrow; rather suffer destitution. Believe me, it is less terrible than people imagine, and especially less so than the imminent certainty of being dishonest or of being so considered.'[32]

Pushkin's advice about women has a different tang.

> I will point out to you only that the less one loves a woman, the surer one is of possessing her. But this pleasure is worthy of an old eighteenth century monkey. As for the one you will love, I hope with all my heart that you will possess her.[33]

He relied on his brother Lev to bring him news of the literary doings in St Petersburg and encouraged him to seek out his own old friends and colleagues. This Lev was only too happy to do. Yet Pushkin hardly knew his brother, as he began to recognise in a letter on August 1823 to Vyazemsky. 'What kind of person is he? ... They say he is a fine fellow and a Moscow dandy – is it true?'[34]

Lev had a genial personality and had been much pampered by both his parents. He had a marvellous memory and knew most of his brother's verse by heart. Unfortunately, he also had a garrulous tongue, gossiped about what Pushkin was up to in Kishinev and was certainly responsible for a quarrel with Pushkin's publisher, Pletnev, which arose from Lev repeating some unkind remarks Pushkin had made in a letter about Pletnev's verse. Pushkin's response to discovering this piece of foolish behaviour was indulgent enough, though he was irritated by his brother's carelessness. In his draft of a letter to Pletnev in an attempt to ameliorate the situation in November/December 1822 he comments, 'You would, without doubt, forgive my thoughtless lines if you knew how often I am prey to what they call spleen.'[35]

The last thing he wanted was to have his brother become a poet.

> Thank you for the verses; but I would have thanked you more for prose. For God's sake regard poetry as a kind, wise granny on whom one can drop in sometimes to forget for a moment all the cares and bothers of life, and to be diverted by her charming chatter and fairytales; but it is rash to fall in love with her.[36]

Pushkin had himself begun to think seriously about prose and an article, drafted in 1822 and unpublished in his lifetime, is evidence of his growing literary maturity:

> Precision and brevity – these are the two virtues of prose. It demands more and more matter – without it brilliant expressions serve no purpose. (But actually it would not harm our poets to have a considerably larger stock of ideas than it is usual to find among them. Our literature will not go far on memories of departed youth.)[37]

In Kishinev, Pushkin's spirits were often low and he sometimes feared he had been completely abandoned. Most of his autobiographical notes of the period were later destroyed by his own hand, but he wrote many letters begging friends to help him to return to St Petersburg. His childhood may have predisposed him to feelings of neglect, but his fear of abandonment in the south had a solid basis.

Count Kapodistria, who had formerly shown some concern for

Pushkin, had now not only left government service but Russia itself. The Tsar could hardly be expected to remember a poor secretary dumped in a far-off southern province of his Empire. Zhukovsky had gone abroad. In 1823 Pushkin took the risk of writing himself to the new Head of the Ministry of Foreign Affairs, Count Nesselrode. His petition to return was referred to the Tsar but rejected. Pushkin began to fear his exile was going to be permanent, and his depression deepened.

In March 1823 he wrote to Vyazemsky with a certain irritation, not to say rudeness, 'I thank you for the letter, but not for the poem: I had no need of it – I read your "First Snow" as long ago as 1820 and know it by heart. Haven't you anything new?' But his friends had not forgotten him. Turgenev and Vyazemsky wrote to one another about the possibility of Pushkin's transfer to the service of Count Vorontsov in Odessa. 'Get busy, kind people!' wrote Vyazemsky. 'All the more so in that Pushkin really desires to steady himself, but boredom and vexation are bad counsellors.'

For all the vexations of Kishinev it was there on 28 May 1823 that Pushkin began *Evgeny Onegin*. In its inception the poem resembled Byron's *Don Juan*, but it was a poem far to surpass the model and Pushkin was to grow in maturity and emotional understanding throughout the eight years of its composition. Crucial early scenes of *Evgeny Onegin* are written in his second Masonic ledger, where his drawings speak of many other preoccupations, especially the French Revolution.

Perhaps, indeed, it was in Kishinev that Pushkin began to throw off the affectations of Romanticism. At the end of May he spent a month in Odessa and liked what he saw there. At the beginning of July he left Kishinev for Odessa and entered the service of Count M. S. Vorontsov.

CHAPTER SEVEN

Odessa: July 1823–July 1824

O dessa was the administrative centre of Southern Russia, a thriving port on the shores of the Black Sea, with fine private houses, and much that was European in style. The city attracted tourists from several Western European nations. There were hardly any paved streets and no reliable supply of drinking water but, as Pushkin recollected many years later when he wrote of Onegin's travels, there were compensations. Wine was imported free. There was a good French restaurant and an opera house at which it was possible to watch the latest Rossini opera. For a while Pushkin was delighted with the change from Kishinev.

He was appointed to the service of Count Vorontsov, the Governor General, whose father had been Ambassador in England and whose household was the pinnacle of Odessa society at the time. Vorontsov was a very different figure from Inzov – a man always impeccably dressed, formal in manner and punctilious in every part of his life. Pushkin stayed at first at the Hôtel du Nord, then moved to a house on one of the main streets, from which he could see the sea. Nevertheless, on 19 August, a month after his arrival, he was writing to Vyazemsky of his boredom.

Some explanation of this can be deduced from the memoirs of F. F. Vigel, who first met Pushkin in Odessa. Vigel was an older man of considerable ability who went on to become Vice Governor of Bessarabia. He had also been a member of Arzamas and was still in touch with several of Pushkin's friends. These are his impressions of Pushkin that August:

In the room next to me lived Pushkin, the exiled poet. In Odessa, where he had just settled, he had not yet succeeded in finding any lively company ... for me, the conversation of Pushkin was like electricity making contact with the black preoccupations inside me; it suddenly produced a thousand lively happy and youthful thoughts, so that we suddenly seemed almost the same age. Often, in the midst of some idle, amusing conversation, a bright new idea flew from his soul which astonished me with the wide range of his intelligence. ... Little by little I discovered a whole buried treasure of sound reasoning and noble ideas, which he concealed under a soiled cloak of cynicism.[1]

That discovery of 'noble ideas' hidden beneath outward frivolity was one many closer friends of Pushkin markedly failed to uncover. It may be that, in his first Odessa loneliness, Pushkin let Vigel enter his thoughts more intimately than he usually would, or it may be that Vigel, like many writers of memoirs, was displaying the easier wisdom of hindsight. Certainly, the absence of 'lively company' was something Pushkin found hard to bear. He could see the superiority of Odessa to the 'accursed city of Kishinev where you won't find attractive ladies, nor a madam, nor a bookseller', but when Vigel left for Kishinev soon after this, Pushkin betrayed some homesickness for that 'accursed city' in a letter to him (11 October–4 November). He asked his friend to tell Pulkheria that he was still head over heels in love with her, and reflected rather glumly that although he drank as much as Lot ever did in Odessa there was no daughter in sight. He lacked friends of like mind rather than drinking companions or sexual favours, however. In the same letter he remarked, 'Not long ago we had a fine day here. I was president of the drinking bout; everybody got drunk, and we made the rounds of the whore houses.'[2]

There were other reasons for his loneliness. Odessa was much more expensive to live in than Kishinev. Always short of money, Pushkin found his 700 roubles a year insufficient even for basic necessities now that he no longer enjoyed the free board and lodging provided by Inzov. The presence of an opera house and good restaurants meant little if he lacked the money to enjoy these pleasures. In November he wrote to his brother for help. 'Make it clear to my father,' he wrote, 'that without some money from him I cannot live ... I am sick of seeing the indifference of my father to my situation – although his letters are very pleasant.'[3]

Pushkin's complaint against his father, who was always so short of money himself, might seem unfair, but Sergey did have access to capital in the form of land and estates, and Pushkin remembered with some bitterness that his father had often grudged expenditure on him that he would not have refused Lev. In the same letter to his brother, Pushkin recalls unhappily, 'This reminds me of St Petersburg, when sick, in the autumn mud or hard frosts, I used to take a cab from Annichkov Bridge, and he would always scold about the eighty kopecks (which surely neither you nor I would have begrudged a servant).'[4]

Pushkin began to write of himself as 'the Odessa hermit'. What he needed most was to be in love. By this, Pushkin meant a state of excitement aroused by a particular woman, linked directly to his creative life as a poet. It is possible to doubt, as Yunna Morits (a Moscow poet of our day) did in conversation with me in 1997, whether Pushkin loved *any* of the many women he pursued sexually. Henri Troyat, an early biographer, observed, 'Love and poetry were for him divergent manifestations of a single force ... his ... pure African sensuality.'[5] Nevertheless, in Odessa he fell in love with two women simultaneously, though with very different parts of himself. The initials of Amalia Riznich and Elizaveta Vorontsova stand, as Guber puts it, 'peaceably side by side' in the Don Juan list. Amalia Riznich was the wife of a rich Odessa businessman, Elizaveta the wife of the Governor General Vorontsov himself.

Pushkin met Amalia Riznich in the summer of 1823, probably at the Operatic Theatre in Odessa. Her husband, Ivan Riznich, a Serbian grain merchant, was a hospitable and charming man, with one of the finest houses in Odessa. He married Amalia in 1822 in Vienna and brought her to Russia in 1823. She was the daughter of the Austrian banker Ripp, and was of German, Italian and probably Jewish descent. Eye witnesses remember her as tall and slender with fiery eyes, an astonishingly white neck and a black plait of hair more than four feet in length. Guber notes that 'her feet were very large, and for this reason she always wore long dresses which trailed on the ground'.[6] Pushkin had a special weakness for beautiful and slender female feet, 'but we must suppose that his enchantment with the lovely Amalia was such that he did not notice this failing.' A Professor K. P. Zelenetsky, who wrote about Pushkin's time in Odessa when many eye-witnesses were still alive, gives an excellent portrait of the beautiful Amalia, describing the marked originality of her costume and manner, 'and it appears *other circumstances*,'[7] as he remarks enigmatically, which accounted for Vorontsov's unwillingness to invite her to his house. Amalia usually wore a man's hat and riding costume and it was probably her reputation as an immoral woman to which Zelenetsky alludes.

Almost all men of the upper social circles in Odessa, both young and old, however, were guests at the Riznich house. There were constant dinners, gatherings and picnics, and Amalia was much admired as the hostess on such occasions, while her husband remained in the background. She loved to dance and play cards, and flirted outrageously with her admirers. Pushkin relished her company and his charm soon won him Amalia's interest. His fame as a poet perhaps had some part in that, though, as his brother Lev wrote in his memoirs, 'he generally disliked talking about poetry and literature, and never touched on the subject with women. Many women, especially at this time, never suspected he was a poet.'[8] Anyone who read poetry knew his name well, however. Simmons tells a story of Pushkin pausing to look over a field battery in Southern Russia and being asked for his name. Once identified as the famous poet, he was then carried in triumph to the officer's tent. A gun was even sounded in his honour. It seems likely that Amalia Riznich was well aware of his celebrity.

The nature of the attachment between Pushkin and Amalia has been disputed. Ivan Riznich, many yeas later, insisted that he always 'kept a concerned eye on his wife's behaviour, carefully protecting her from a fall. She was attended by a faithful servant, who knew every step taken by his master's wife and reported everything back to him.' Although Pushkin fell passionately in love with Amalia and, according to Riznich, 'hung round her like a kitten', his love was unrequited. Amalia was indifferent to him.[9]

It may be so, though Riznich's assurance that his wife remained completely unresponsive to Pushkin need not be believed. 'It is well known that in such cases the husband is the last to find out and, even when he does at last find out, is liable to deny the obvious in conversations with strangers.'[10] The later course of Amalia's life, in any case, suggests that Riznich's attempts to protect her virtue were a total failure. Moreover, though such evidence ought always to be treated with caution, Pushkin's extremely frank poetry supports the physical nature of his relations with Amalia, though not all commentators agree about which poems arise out of their relationship. One, at least, suggests Pushkin's own emotional involvement as well as a sexual relationship, and is one of the finest lyrics Pushkin wrote at this time:

> One single candle throws a melancholy light
> Beside my bed; these whispered verses flow
> Filled with my love for you, and your bright
> Eyes immense in darkness, glow
> As I listen to your voice repeating: love
> My love ... I love you ... I am yours.

Some commentators have eagerly attributed to this love affair all the love poems written while Pushkin was in Odessa, while others[11] limit the cycle of poems dedicated to Amalia to 'Will You Forgive My Jealous Dreams?' (1823) and 'Under The Blue Sky Of Her Native Land' (1826); alongside two stanzas from chapter six of 'Onegin', particularly stanza XVI, where he describes his own memories of the emotions roused in him by a voluptuous woman who died young. We know the stanza from its publication in Ya Grot's group of essays from Pushkin's friends in 1887.

Whatever Amalia's feelings for Pushkin, Pushkin's own feelings were seriously poisoned by jealousy. Indeed, when he came to describe Lensky's fit of jealousy in two excised stanzas from chapter six of 'Onegin' he was brought to remember how he felt about Amalia in Odessa.

Amalia Riznich brought a new and passionate simplicity to Pushkin's poetry. The poem which begins, 'Will You Forgive My Jealous Dreams?' ends with lines in that simple straightforward Russian Pushkin made his own, which have the unforced quality of ordinary speech, their rhymes in Russian as apparently effortless as the phrasing of Mozart.

> How can you receive him, in the reckless
> Hours before morning, half-dressed
> Without your mother or companion?
> I'm loved, aren't I? You are so tender
> When we are alone, your kisses are like fire.
> Beloved friend, please give up this torture.
> You don't know how very much I love you
> You don't know how thoroughly I suffer.

These bouts of jealousy had good cause for Pushkin was not Amalia's only admirer. His most serious rivals were a wealthy Polish landowner, Sobanski, and Prince Yabolonsky. In May 1824, rather more than six months after Pushkin's liaison with her had begun, Amalia was found to

have consumption and left for Italy with her small son. Prince Yabolonsky
followed her, and there they lived together for a time until Yabolonsky
abandoned her and she died soon afterwards. Her child from their
marriage also died – a terrifying end to the story. So much for her
husband's attempt to protect Amalia against 'a fall'. Zelenetsky's claim,
however, that her husband allowed Amalia to die of consumption in
Italy in the direst poverty, refusing her all support, is probably unjust.
Pushkin only heard of her death much later, at a time when his own
emotions were numbed by the horrifying news of his Decembrist friends'
executions. Pushkin allowed this stunned lack of emotion to permeate
his poem 'Under The Blue Sky Of Her Native Land'. Another of his
loveliest lyrics, written in 1830, may also hark back to his memories of
Amalia.

It was in Odessa that Pushkin's overwhelming need to be loved, as
well as sexually gratified, first began to show itself. This need could not be
assuaged by the conquests of promiscuous women like Amalia Riznich.
Hence, for all his jealousy of Amalia, Pushkin was emotionally engaged
in a quite different way with Countess Vorontsova. To judge by poems
written at this period, and from notes in his Odessa notebook, Pushkin
made Elizaveta's acquaintance in the summer or autumn of 1823. At this
time he was still involved with Amalia and a frequent visitor to
her drawing room. He remained obsessed with Amalia until October
1823 when he wrote 'Will You Forgive My Jealous Dreams?', already
quoted, and perhaps even for a little while after that. However, by
December he had transferred his most passionate longings to Elizaveta
Vorontsova.

It was an attachment that could hardly improve his relations with
Count Vorontsov, whose job it was to report on Pushkin's behaviour in
Odessa. Vorontsov had begun in any case to regard him with disapproval.
He had little admiration for poets, and though A. I. Turgenev had
persuaded him to rescue Pushkin from Kishinev, he always treated
Pushkin as an inferior in rank. Vorontsov once asked Vigel, who had
recently been appointed Vice Governor of Bessarabia, whether he
couldn't somehow persuade Pushkin to do something worthwhile. Vigel
suggested that men like Pushkin could only be great poets. The Count
indicated drily that he did not think this was good for much. His
underlings took their tone from him, and one of Vorontsov's secretaries
described Pushkin to I. P. Liprandi, a Russian officer who later became
Pushkin's friend, as 'vain, bad-tempered and spoilt by his con-

temporaries'.[12] At Vorontsov's house no attempt was made to conceal the fact that he was regarded as no more than a clerk in his department of the Chancellory.

Even if he had had no claims to aristocracy, the treatment Pushkin received from Vorontsov and from the minions who surrounded him would have nettled his pride. For Vorontsov's wife, however, he had an admiration bordering on reverence. Elizaveta was born Countess Branitskaya, the daughter of a Polish magnate and one of the nieces of the famous Prince Potemkin. This made her a relation of the Raevsky-Davydovs. In marrying Count Vorontsov, Elizaveta had made a brilliant match, not only because of his descent but because he occupied the powerful position of Commander of the Russian armies of occupation. It was, however, a marriage of calculation and her heart was not involved. Vorontsov, for his part, did not think it necessary to be faithful to his beautiful young wife. She was about thirty when Pushkin met her.

Vigel, who knew the Countess well, remarks 'she had every right to appear girlish. For a long time, when others were having their fill of society life, she lived in the country with her stern mother; when she was sent abroad for the first time, she married Vorontsov and suddenly all of life's pleasures appeared to surround her. She was young both in her heart and in her appearance. She did not have what they call beauty, but the swift tender glance of her sweet little eyes pierced you; the smile of her lips, the like of which I have never seen, seemed to invite kisses.'[13] Manuscript pages of Pushkin at this time show drawings of a woman's head, which are supposed to represent Countess Vorontsova.

The distinguished scholar Gershenson belittles the likelihood of there being a physical basis to the relationship between Pushkin and Elizaveta Vorontsova. 'I believe that it is possible, simply on the basis of the D. J. list, to say that P. was in love with Vorontsova, be that love long lived or fleeting ... the existence of intimate relations between them has to be rejected completely.' Even if her relationship to Pushkin was not a fully sexual one, however, this does not necessarily mean she failed to respond to his love. She gave him a ring, with a seal bearing a Hebrew inscription, which Pushkin regarded as his talisman. His sister tells that at Mikhaylovskoe Pushkin received letters bearing the same seal as that on the ring. On these occasions he locked himself in his room to read the letters which were presumably written by the Countess.

This was the ring Pushkin was remembering when, in 1827, he wrote his poem 'Talisman'. In it he speaks of a magic which would not prevent illness or bring wealth but would preserve him from deceitful lovers in the future:

> Whose eyes may trap you in their spell,
> And lips that have no love for you
> Kiss you in the night too well,
> Then, dear friend, to keep you from
> Forgetfulness and treachery:
> Here is a powerful talisman.

Pushkin also spent many hours in 1823 with a famous Polish beauty he had first encountered in Kiev – Carolina, the elder sister of Evelina Hansky who was to marry Balzac. Pushkin had met Carolina again briefly in Kishinev and then in Odessa where she lived as the mistress of Count de Witt. In Odessa Pushkin spent some time with her, reading Benjamin Constant's *Adolphe*. Much later, on 2 February 1830, Pushkin recalled their time in Odessa in a letter addressed to her as Ellenore, the heroine of *Adolphe*, and reminded her of their old friendship and 'your own life, so violent, so stormy and so different from what it ought to have been'. It was in Carolina's album on 5 January 1830 that he wrote the famous lyric, 'What Is My Name To You?' Their relationship was probably no more than sentimental. The poem opens sadly enough –

> What use is my name to you?
> It will die out, like the unhappy noise
> Of waves against a distant shore
> Or sounds at night within a quiet forest.

– but it closes with the suggestion that when she herself is miserable she may be glad to remember,

> There is at least one heart in which I live.

Pushkin's most famous lyric, 'I loved you once', of which the date is uncertain, may also have been written to her.

Pushkin's involvement with Countess Vorontsova was an altogether more dangerous matter, even when he had not yet broken off his love affair with Amalia. What made the affair entirely disastrous was the arrival of his old Byronic mentor, Alexander Raevsky.

Pushkin was touchingly delighted to meet his old friend, and had no reason to guess that Raevsky had himself come to Odessa primarily to renew his acquaintance with the Countess Vorontsova. Raevsky had met the Countess while an adjutant under Vorontsov in France and, for all his apparent cynicism, had fallen hopelessly in love with her. He did not confess this passion to Pushkin, however, and when Pushkin, who had no suspicion of Raevsky's involvement, admitted his own feelings Raevsky even teased him about their tenderness. For all his frankness, Pushkin did not gossip about any progress his suit to Vorontsova might be making. If there were secret meetings, Raevsky was never told of them and had to content himself with guesses and a watchful eye. Indeed, when Pushkin confided his distress about Vorontsova to Vyazemsky's wife, as she reported to her husband in a letter of 1 August 1824, she mentions his distress was about a love affair 'entirely chaste, and indeed only serious on his side'. What Raevsky guessed, however, was enough to warrant him trying to have Pushkin removed from Odessa.

Raevsky encouraged Pushkin the while in his pursuit of the Countess, a strategy with a disgusting motive. He could see that Pushkin's transparent attraction to the Countess was an excellent decoy to disguise his own interest in the Countess from Vorontsov. Raevsky was willing to be even more ruthless – he hinted to the Count that Pushkin's attachment was a matter of public gossip. It was not until some time in October 1824 that Pushkin discovered to his horror that Raevsky had been not only another admirer but perhaps even the lover of Countess Vorontsova for some time. The poem 'Demon', in which Pushkin writes of 'the evil genius that sought him out', was written in 1823 before Raevsky's treachery had been exposed. The poem concludes,

> And as we talked, his bitter smile
> And speeches filled my soul with bile.
> His slander tempted providence.
> Beauty he called an empty dream,
> And fancy drew his disbelief;
> Freedom and love were not for him;
> Ironically he looked on life –
> All matters and all creatures born
> Met with his devastating scorn.[14]

Vigel, in his memoirs, recalls joking with Pushkin that his African extraction made him resemble Othello, while Raevsky was like Iago.

Pushkin cannot have found it very easy to laugh at that. Raevsky's betrayal was immensely damaging.

It is hardly surprising that meanwhile Vorontsov became increasingly hostile in his reports on Pushkin to the authorities. On 6 March 1824 he wrote to General P. D. Kiselev, 'With Pushkin I have spoken only four words in fifteen days; he is afraid of me, since he knows very well that on the first bad report I will send him away from here, and nobody else wishes to be responsible for him ... On the whole, from what I hear about him from Gurev (a governor of Odessa) he is now very prudent and discreet; if he were otherwise I should ship him off, and personally I should be delighted, for I do not like his manner and I am not such an admirer of his talent – it is impossible to be a real poet without study and he studies nothing.'[15]

In response, Pushkin amused himself by writing insulting verse about his superior, of which the most famous example is probably the following epigram:

> Half Milord, half shopkeeper,
> Half erudite, half philistine:
> Half criminal. Now there's a chance
> For some integrity at last!

It is rather satisfying to discover from Vigel's memoirs that, ultimately, it was Raevsky's own life that was ruined by the depth of his attachment to Countess Vorontsova, whereas Pushkin's tender feelings found their expression in poetry. She may have been the occasion for one of his most original lyrics, in which Pushkin's tormenting jealousy is given a form which Pushkin invites us to hear as if spoken aloud by a character in a drama; his use of dots even indicates pauses in the actor's delivery. The poem opens in moonlight, by the sea, where a woman customarily sits to watch the waves:

> There she sits now sad and completely alone...
> Alone ... with no one begging for love from her
> Or kissing her knees in forgetfulness;
> She is surrendering her shoulders to no one
> Nor her moist lips, nor her white breasts.
> ...
> ...
> ...

No one is worthy of her heavenly love.
It's true, isn't it? You are alone. I am calm.
...
But if instead...

(The dots are Pushkin's own)

It hardly matters if it is, indeed, Vorontsova who aroused this passionate poem. It shows Pushkin possessed by longing and a vulnerability to the pains of love quite different from the cool indifference of his *The Prisoner of the Caucasus*. The emotions are not being used only to fire the poem – they appear to rise from some hitherto untouched part of his being. Whether or not she returned his love, Vorontsova has the distinction of being one of his models for the lovely Tatyana in *Evgeny Onegin*.

Pushkin's situation in Odessa had been much exacerbated by Raevsky's malicious insinuations. Vorontsov's dislike escalated until he was describing Pushkin as a 'feeble imitator of a disreputable eccentric called Lord Byron' to the Minister of Foreign Affairs on 27 March 1824. Getting Pushkin out of Odessa became an obsession with him. Even Kishinev was not far enough away, as he wrote to Count Karl Nesselrode, the Minister of Foreign Affairs and still Pushkin's chief, since officially the poet remained a member of the Foreign Office staff. Vigel reports that whenever he himself spoke of Pushkin to Vorontsov at this period, Vorontsov went pale and told him never to mention the scoundrel. When, by 2 May, his request to have Pushkin removed had still not received a satisfactory reply, Vorontsov reminded Nesselrode in an official state report: 'Apropos, I repeat my request, deliver me from Pushkin. He may be an excellent fellow and a fine poet, but I do not want to have him any longer, either in Odessa or Kishinev.'[16]

Vorontsov was so impatient for Pushkin to leave Odessa that when the Kherson district was attacked by a plague of locusts the same month Vorontsov ordered Pushkin, with some other members of his staff, to go and report on the situation. Pushkin was incensed by this, which he regarded as a deliberate attempt to humiliate him. Nor was he altogether unjustified. In the letter appointing Pushkin to Inzov in 1820 no duties had been specified and he had always been treated as a member of the Foreign Office on extended leave. In a letter to Kaznacheev, Vorontsov's first in command, Pushkin robustly countered the argument that since he was receiving 700 roubles a year he was obligated to do whatever he was told. He reminded Kaznacheev that he had been denied the possibility of conducting his own business of writing and publishing poetry for several years, since he needed to do so while living in Moscow or St Petersburg. 'I receive these 700 roubles, not as the salary of an official, but as the allowance of an exiled slave.' These arguments, alongside a rather pathetic offer of resignation on the grounds of ill health, were to no effect. So Pushkin travelled the 180 versts east with an ill grace, returning to Odessa, however, after only three days without taking much action.

It is possible that even before Vorontsov sent Pushkin on that mission, Pushkin and Elizaveta had broken off any intimate conversations, except for an exchange of letters. Their farewell meeting, according to Guber, was in a garden at night in the spring or summer of 1824. The only letter we have from Pushkin to Vorontsova, discovered in 1956, was written many years after that parting, on 4 March 1834, in response to Elizaveta's letter of 26 December 1833. In this she requested something from his pen for an almanac sponsored by her to relieve the poor of Odessa. It was signed with an almost illegible pseudonym – E. Wilbemans.

Pushkin recognised her handwriting and sent her a fragment which arrived too late for inclusion in her almanac. His reply is irreproachably correct, but he concludes, 'May I dare, Madame, to speak to you of the moment of happiness I experienced upon receiving your letter at the mere idea that you have not completely forgotten the most devoted of your slaves?'[17]

Pushkin's plea to his Ministerial superiors that he could only carry on the literary activity which had become his only source of necessary income in Moscow or St Petersburg was far from disingenuous. To live on the earnings of a poet he needed to be on the spot. *Ruslan and Lyudmila* had long since sold out and copies changed hands at twenty-five roubles each, but Pushkin felt that Gnedich had managed the publication badly. With the offer of two thousand roubles for *The Prisoner of the Caucasus*, Pushkin put his publishing into Pletnev's hands. For *The Fountain of Bakhchisaray*, which Pushkin entrusted to Vyazemsky, he received three thousand roubles, about five roubles a line. Vyazemsky made an energetic and punctilious editor, objecting, for instance, that 'wounding kisses' reminded him of the clap. Pushkin took the point and suggested 'piercing' as a substitution for 'wounding', adding gaily, 'That

will be something new. The point is that my Georgian girl bites, and this
absolutely must be known to the public.'

It was public taste that gave Pushkin the chance to live by his pen, but
he was intelligent enough to see this, too, could reduce his independence.
In 'Conversation Between a Bookseller and a Poet' (1825) he muses
sadly on the carefree days when he used to write for pleasure rather than
for money. There is something ineluctably modern in the bookseller's
advice:

> Our merchant age is pitiless;
> Money alone brings liberty.
> What is fame? Think nothing of it –
> A patch upon a poet's rags
> We need profit, profit, profit.[18]

Poverty, however, removed any inhibitions Pushkin might have felt as an
aristocrat selling his poetry for money. He claimed to feel no shame,
though he may have had some qualms, as he wrote in a letter to his
brother, 'I sing as the baker bakes, as the tailor sews, as Kozlov writes,
as the physician kills, for money, money, money.'[19]

Financial necessity was not the only reason Pushkin longed to leave
Odessa, if only for a short time. He felt excluded from the world he
wished to inhabit. A charming lyric of 1823, describing a caged bird set
free, gains an added poignancy from Pushkin's own sense of being
hopelessly trapped:

> In alien lands I still observe
> An ancient native custom:
> On this bright holiday of Spring
> I give a bird its freedom.
>
> Doing so brings me consolation:
> Why complain to God
> When I can give a single one
> Of his small creatures freedom?

All his own requests for release from his indefinite exile continued to be
refused by the Tsar's minister.

He missed the sophisticated conversation of his old literary world. As
early as 16 November 1823, for all his absorption in love affairs, Pushkin
was already lamenting in a letter to Delvig that he felt out of touch and

bored in Odessa. He writes of the imminent arrival of Italian opera as 'the envoys of paradise' and complained to A. I. Turgenev on 1 December, 'One has to spend three years in stuffy asiatic confinement to appreciate the true value of the air of Europe.' Opera, and particularly Rossini, whom he describes affectionately in Onegin's journey as 'always the same and always new, he pours out melodies, they flow and burn like young kisses, with everything sunk in voluptuousness ...', remained among the consolations of Odessa. His love of opera did not prevent him from ridiculing Vyazemsky's intention to write a libretto. The poet, he felt, should not be subservient to the musician. There is some irony in this since most of Pushkin's work first reached the West in the last two hundred years through the operas of Tchaikovsky, Rimsky Korsakov and Mussorgsky.

In his desperation Pushkin even thought of appealing directly to Alexander I. 'One thing remains – to write to him directly – to such-and-such, in the Winter Palace, opposite the fortress of Peter and Paul, or else on the quiet to take my cane and cap and go and have a look at Constantinople,' Pushkin wrote to his brother some time in January 1824.

Even so tiny a tourist adventure of a few days was refused. In his isolation the only happiness left to Pushkin was writing poetry. It might be argued that it always had been the centre of his life, and even that the pleasure he took in the women he loved was subordinate to that passion. On 8 March 1824 he said as much to Vyazemsky: 'I write for myself and publish for money, and not in the slightest for the smile of the fair sex.'[20] He was writing a great many poems which he did not expect to be published. These included *Evgeny Onegin* which he had already mentioned to Vyazemsky on 4 November 1823: 'There's no use even to think of publishing; I am writing it the way I feel like writing.' By December of that year two marvellous chapters were already finished and had been sent to a few friends. Not all of them approved the satirical portrait of St Petersburg life and his cynical hero dismayed his old friend Nikolay Raevsky, for instance (his demon's brother), who 'did not understand them very well'.[21]

The other great poem begun in Odessa was *The Gypsies*. The poem opens with the description of a gypsy encampment which Pushkin had observed in Kishinev, and continues as an old man waits by the fire for his daughter Zemfira to return. When she does she brings a lover with her, Aleko, a Russian who wants to join the tribe of Gypsies, a runaway from civilisation as the prisoner of the Caucasus had been. The old man welcomes Aleko courteously, without inquiring into his background, and the lovers go off to bed. In the early morning the Gypsies strike camp and a motley band of asses, men, children and a chained bear set out on their nomadic life. For a time Zemfira and Aleko live happily as lovers. When Zemfira questions him about what he has sacrificed to be with her, Aleko laughs at the idea of regretting stifling towns and city pleasures. None of the girls, for all their finery, is as beautiful as Zemfira. The old man, however, reminds Aleko that men used to a soft life usually don't relish freedom for long, and repeats the tale of a poet who lived on the banks of the Danube, charming the people with his stories, who could never get used to the life of an exile. Recognising the life of Ovid, Aleko reflects:

> Tell me then, what value glory?
> Doesn't the voice of praise sound hollow
> Passed down through generations
> Only to find some wild expression
> Here inside a smoky shelter?

Aleko learns to lead the dancing bear, and continues to live with the Gypsies for two years. But Zemfira, a defiant Carmen precursor, begins to find his love stale and taunts Aleko with the fact in a traditional Gypsy song.

> Old husband, gloomy man,
> Burn me or cut me:
> I don't care, I'm not afraid
> Of either fire or knife.

When Aleko asks her to stop singing such a barbarous song she shrugs and continues her song about a bold young lover:

> How I caressed him
> In the quiet night;
> We laughed as we thought
> Of your hair going white.

Aleko laments that Zemfira no longer loves him, and the old man explains that this is the nature of Gypsy freedom: women, too, are free to do as they like. Aleko is inconsolable. One night he follows Zemfira, finds her with her lover and kills him in front of her. Zemfira is altogether uncowed by Aleko's murderous rage.

> Enough of that. I'm not afraid
> Of you or your threats to me.
> I curse you as a murderer.

Infuriated by this, he kills her too, but her last words continue her defiance:

> How I loathe you.
> I despise you.
> I love another man,
> And die in love with him.

The two bodies are buried with traditional Gypsy ceremony. No attempt is made to punish Aleko, but the old man with great dignity asks him to go away.

> Now leave us, haughty man.
> We are a lawless nation,
> And use no rope or rack
> To punish those who damage us,
> But we don't live with murderers.
> The freedom that you have known,
> You want it for yourself alone.
> The sound of your voice hurts us.
> We are mild and meek of heart,
> You are fierce. So depart.
> Peacefully, but leave us.

Conscious as he was of an increasing richness and fluency in his writing, Pushkin realised the only obstacle in the way of retrieving his financial fortunes by literary success was Imperial censorship. Benckendorf and his minions scrutinised minutely every poem Pushkin wrote, and the process was cumbrous and slow. Pushkin's fame was spreading to the point where people were willing to listen to a reading of his *The Fountain of Bakhchisaray* even before it was published. Such celebrity would have once delighted him, but in Odessa he received news of one such reading with a little irritation. As he explained to his brother Lev, such public readings might well reduce the sales of his books. 'With the censorship in its present state, I cannot live by the pen.' Nevertheless, some time around 8 March 1824 he did manage to repay Inzov 350 roubles that he had borrowed from him. It was a generous acknow-ledgement of much past help, but Pushkin remained in urgent need of money. On 1 April 1824 he wrote to Lev, 'Here I am trying to avoid dying of starvation, and all they do is shout Fame ... Neither you nor father has written me a word in answer to my elegiac fragments – nor do you send me money.'[22]

For all his one-time wild and casual behaviour towards women, Pushkin was sensitive to exposing them to gossip by allowing verses about them to appear publicly which might embarrass them. In a letter to A. A. Bestuzhev, the literary editor, on 29 June 1824 from Odessa, Pushkin wrote blaming him for printing lines which might reveal his love for one of the Raevsky daughters:

> I happened once to be madly in love. In such a case I usually write elegies as another may soil his bed. But is it a friendly gesture to hang out my wet sheets in public? God forgive you, but you disgraced me by publishing the last three lines of my 'Elegy' ... Imagine my dismay when I saw them in print; the review might fall into her hands. What might she think? ... How is she to know that I did not mention her by name, that the letter was unsealed and published by Bulgarin, that the damned elegy was sent to you by devil knows whom, and that no one is to blame? I confess I value a single opinion of this woman more than those of all the reviews in the world and of all our readers combined.[23]

He had felt very much less nervously scrupulous about the exciting possibility, at the beginning of April 1824, that there were publishers eager to risk publishing the poem Pushkin had thought impossible for publication – *Evgeny Onegin* – as Pushkin wrote to Vyazemsky:

> Now let's talk of business, i.e. of money. Slonim offers to pay me what I want for Onegin ... The matter rests with the censorship, and I'm not joking, for this concerns my future and my independence, which I simply must have.[24]

Pushkin had every reason to be disturbed about the censorship as the Tsar's new Minister of Education and Head of Censorship was Admiral Shishkov. He was a man of conservative political views, with a rooted attachment to Church Slavonic and a distrust of the vernacular, who had once been at the head of the reactionary literary society which the Arzamas group had been set up to counter. Shishkov had clashed with several less vulnerable members of Arzamas and was unlikely to approve of Pushkin's satirical tone. For four years, between 1824 and 1828, Shishkov was both Minister of Education and Head of the Censorship Department.

By 1824 Pushkin had learned what he needed from Byron and in *Onegin* was altogether to surpass his mentor. His own involvement in both German and English literature during his years in the south had made its contribution. We know from a fragment of a letter to Kyuchelbecker that he devoured both Goethe (probably in French) and also, more importantly, Shakespeare. This reading gave him the assurance to judge his former idol. In a letter to Vyazemsky on 24/25 June 1824 he remarked: 'The first two cantos of *Don Juan* are superior to the rest ... everything about him (Byron) was back to front: there was nothing gradual about his development, he suddenly ripened and matured – sang and fell silent and he never recaptured his early notes. We no longer hear Byron after the fourth canto of *Childe Harold*; some other poet was singing, with great human talent.'[25]

When, in April 1824, Byron died at Missolonghi Pushkin was not moved to compose an elegy on his death, as so many European poets were. On 27 June 1824 Princess Vera Vyazemskaya, the wife of his friend, was visiting Odessa and reported to her husband, 'Pushkin absolutely refuses to write on Byron's death.' Pushkin's reluctance may be partly explained by his own emotional withdrawal from the cause for which Byron died. 'I am sick of Greece. One can discuss the fate of the Greeks as one can that of my brother Negroes ... but that all the enlightened people of Europe should rave about Greece is unforgivably childish.' Perhaps his reluctance lay in the distracted state of his own mind. Vyazemsky's wife reported, 'His brains are quite disorderly, no one can prevail on him ... I have never met such levity and such a tendency to malignant talk.' Such behaviour of Pushkin's helps us to understand how he so often gave the impression of a man too unpredictable and awkward to be taken seriously. When she had come to know Pushkin a little better she was able to modify her description. On 1 July she wrote, 'I believe that he is good, but his mind has been embittered by his misfortunes.'[26]

As so often, Pushkin's most whirling words disguised a thoughtfulness to which few friends were admitted. He had thought long and hard about revolutionary ideas while he was reading so industriously in Odessa. The poet had become a member of the Masonic lodge Ovid No.

25 in Kishinev on 4 May 1821, and when the lodge was closed down seven months later prudently removed their ledgers for his own use. On folio 7 of his Second Masonic Notebook, among several self-portraits, there are haunting images of himself in the costume and hairstyles of the French Revolutionary period.

The misfortunes of which Vyazemskaya spoke were real enough. Pushkin was unhappy in his position 'of depending on the good or bad digestion of such-and-such a superior; I am tired of being treated in my native land with less respect than the first English scamp who comes to parade his dullness and gibberish among us,' he wrote to Kaznacheev on 24 June in an attempt to retire from government service altogether. He was still waiting for an answer from the authorities a month later, as a letter to his friend A. I. Turgenev of 14 July makes clear.

On 8 June Pushkin, after receiving part of the 3,000 roubles due to him for *The Fountain of Bakhchisaray*, submitted a formal request that he be allowed to resign from Imperial service on the grounds of ill health. The illness of which he complained amounted to no more than a varicose vein in one leg, but this he described as 'an aneurysm'. His request was refused. In a letter to Vyazemsky on 24 June in which he explained that he had tendered his resignation from the Imperial service, Pushkin reported on the state of his quarrel with Vorontsov.

His attempts at escape had little effect and Pushkin was soon overtaken by events. A letter written either to Kyuchelbecker or Vyazemsky was intercepted by the police and in this he had remarked, light-heartedly but extremely rashly,

> I am writing a colourful stanza of a romantic poem and taking lessons in pure atheism. There is an Englishman here, a deaf Philosopher, the only intelligent Atheist I have ever met ... He has written a thousand pages to prove *qu'il ne peut exister d'être intelligent Createur et regulateur*, destroying in passing the feeble proofs for the immortality of the soul. This system, though not as comforting as is usually thought, is unfortunately most likely to be true.[27]

The Englishman in question was Dr Hutchinson, a physician for a time attached to the Vorontsov family. Some five years later Dr Hutchinson was to become a minister of the Church of England, which suggests that his views expressed in Odessa were no more than philosophical speculations, hardly revolutionary in English thought at the time. In Russia, however, an autocratic Tsar, brooding more and more gloomily on his own complicity in patricide, was coming to see the Church as his only hope of redemption. The words could hardly have been more dangerous. It was altogether reckless of Pushkin to commit such thoughts to paper. His friend Vyazemsky rebuked him, 'Do me a favour and be careful with your tongue and pen. Do not play with your future ... You have played enough of your page's jokes on the government; you have provoked it enough so have done with it.'[28]

Although the St Petersburg authorities had refused to allow Pushkin to retire gracefully from government service, they were glad to have a reason to dismiss him, and the discovery of his letter about 'lessons in atheism' gave them just such an opportunity. As a direct consequence, Pushkin had his name struck from the list of civil servants in the Ministry of Foreign Affairs, and with only 389 roubles as travelling expenses, was sent off to his parents' estate in Mikhaylovskoe in the Pskov district under the surveillance of the local police.

Pushkin's departure was not the end of Vorontsov's troubles with his charming wife, however. Raevsky continued to pursue the Countess for some time after Pushkin left Odessa; he was probably intimate with her until late 1824 when she abandoned him. He continued to harass her even then, and in 1828 stopped her carriage in the public highway and shouted, 'Take good care of our children.' A huge scandal resulted, and Vorontsov had Raevsky exiled.

Pushkin was far more in love with Elizaveta Vorontsova than he had been with any of the earlier figures to bewitch him, and in the autumn of 1824 she was the only woman who lived in his imagination. It is likely that her thoughtful innocence of manner went into his creation of Tatyana in *Evgeny Onegin*. Pushkin continued to treasure the ring she had given him as a talisman, even though he cut Raevsky out of his life completely.

A letter from Raevsky, who was staying with Elizaveta in Alexandria at the time, pleaded for their correspondence to be reopened, and confirms the identification of Elizaveta with Tatyana in Raevsky's mind at least: 'Now let me say a few words about Tatyana. She was sorry for the misfortunes that befell you.'[29]

Pushkin's poem 'To the Sea' was his farewell to Odessa. It was a poem that affected Marina Tsvetayeva, a great Russian poet of our own century, so powerfully that she could hardly bear the grey reality she found on holiday as a child in Nervi, when she had Pushkin's image of the ocean in her memory. Pushkin loved to look at the sea, and particularly enjoyed the terrace at the end of one of the two piers where the nobility went to enjoy the sea air in the evenings. He often used the bathing huts nearby, and wrote some stanzas in 'Onegin's Journey' of his pleasure in running down the steep shore to the sea. Then, sitting with a glowing pipe and revived by the salt waves, like a Muslim in his paradise, he enjoyed coffee with Oriental grounds.

'To The Sea' begins with a resounding 'Farewell, free element' and goes on to celebrate the sea's capricious power, sometimes preserving a fisherman's fragile boat, sometimes drowning a whole fleet of ships. In two verses of this poem Pushkin grieves for the death of Napoleon and says his farewell to Byron.

> He vanished, and left the world his laurel,
> All who love liberty now mourn for him.
> Let your storms well up and roar with them.
> He was your own singer, great ocean,
>
> The stamp of your image was upon him,
> He was made out of your own spirit:
> Like you, he was dark, deep and powerful;
> Like you, he was unafraid of anything.

As Pushkin set off for Mikhaylovskoe he took with him not only the first draft of *The Gypsies*, which he revised in Mikhaylovskoe, but the greatest achievement of his Odessa year – the first two chapters of *Evgeny Onegin* – the poem begun in Kishinev on 9 May 1823. He was not to add the final chapter until 1831 in Tsarskoe Selo. He was 24 when he began it, 32 when he brought it to a conclusion. The whole, even though written over eight years, has an amazing unity of style – a fizzing brilliance of seemingly effortless improvisation contained in eight chapters of intricately rhymed fourteen-line stanzas which flow as freely and openly as colloquial prose. Some sign that Pushkin understood the importance of *Evgeny Onegin*, even as he began his first light-hearted chapters, may be guessed from the absence of any scrawl interrupting their flow in the First Masonic Notebook. On folio 3 of that notebook, however, before *Onegin* begins, there is a whole gallery of key figures from his southern exile: Ekaterina Raevskaya from his time in the Crimea; Amalia Riznich, his Odessa love; Count Vorontsov himself, and also Dante. Pushkin grew up through the poem, and his conception of the characters in it grew and deepened as he did so. The outline of the story is easily told and seems slight enough, as the plot of a novel of Jane Austen or even George Eliot may seem slight, without the narrative intelligence of the commenting voice.

A young St Petersburg rake, Evgeny Onegin, takes up residence in the country, and there makes friends with a young and sentimental poet, Lensky. Partly out of boredom, and partly out of curiosity, Onegin allows himself to be taken to an evening at the Larins' to admire the charms of Olga, the daughter of the family, with whom Lensky is in love. The elder sister, Tatyana, falls in love with Onegin. Being open-hearted and without guile, she sends a letter to him declaring her love. Onegin refuses her offer on the grounds that he would be unable to make any woman a faithful husband. At a party for Tatyana's nameday Onegin amuses himself by flirting with Olga, in whom he has no great interest. This leads to a duel with Lensky in which the poet is killed. After some years of guilty wandering Onegin returns to St Petersburg to find that Tatyana has married a powerful and wealthy man and become a proud beauty. He falls madly in love with her and writes to say so, but she refuses to betray her husband.

It would be a mistake to identify Pushkin with his hero, and Pushkin himself takes some trouble to prevent his reader doing so. Indeed, there are three heroes: Onegin, the bored fop; Lensky, the minor poet; and the narrator, who is a stylised figure of Pushkin. One of Pushkin's sketches shows Onegin leaning to look on the Neva with the recognisably slouching figure of Pushkin at his side. Although Pushkin had something in common with his hero – he, too, had sauntered beside the Neva and had a father who ran up debts – Onegin is unable to tell a dactyl from an anapest, and begins to yawn as soon as he tries to write poetry.

Nevertheless, part of Pushkin's intoxication in writing the first chapter of *Onegin* at this time came from the opportunity it gave him to look back and evaluate his own St Petersburg adolescence. Pushkin impudently introduces one of his own friends, Kaverin, who had often dined at Talons restaurant with him, into his account of Onegin's St Petersburg life, and has Onegin enjoy one of his own favourite meals of roast beef, truffles, Strasbourg pie and Limburg cheese, before going off to the ballet or the theatre. Pushkin, too, had enjoyed invitations to several soirées in one evening, flattered his way into secret assignations and made a cuckold of many a complacent husband, who was

So pleased with all he had in life:
Himself, his dinner and his wife.

Nevertheless, Pushkin is not Onegin. The narrator and Onegin both claim to find their lives tedious, but for all his misfortunes Pushkin continued both in Kishinev and Odessa to relish, if not his situation, both life and the telling of stories about it. Like the Byronic Childe Harold, Onegin abandons both women and books with a bored disgust, which had never characterised Pushkin's relations to the women he slept with, even before the new tenderness he had discovered in Odessa. Nor is Pushkin overwhelmed with 'the emptiness that plagues Onegin's soul', though he had been touched with its chill in adolescence. Earlier heroes of his poems had *affected* such weariness of spirit and for a time Pushkin had been drawn to Alexander Raevsky for seeming to possess such a character, welcoming his company in his own exile and isolation for

The cold sharp mind that he possessed,
I was embittered, he depressed.

Looking back on his old Petersburg days and nights, they looked like an enchanted land to Pushkin as he conjured them up in his first chapter, describing,

The theatre's full, the boxes glitter
The restless, gallery claps, and roars
The stalls and pit are all ajitter,
The curtain rustles as it soars.[30]

He paints the delights of the ballet and the dancer, Istomina, whom he had once loved from a distance:

One foot upon the ground she places
And then the other slowly twirls
And now she leaps! And now she whirls!

Certainly Pushkin had once behaved with as much affected indifference to *manners* as Onegin, but in the poem he shows some dislike for the young fops who clap or jeer, while in the harsh St Petersburg winter outside,

And while the weary band of servants
Still sleeps on furs at carriage door ...
And while the horses, bored at tether

Still fidget freezing in the snow,
And coachmen by the fire's glow
Curse masters and beat palms together.

Onegin has a dressing room far more luxurious than anything Pushkin enjoyed:

Imported pipes of Turkish amber,
Fine china, bronzes ...

There is another key difference. If Pushkin spent three hours looking at himself in the glass as Onegin did, he did not like what he saw there. Never in Pushkin's life had a woman been drawn to him by his appearance alone, still less by his elegance as a dancer, though he admits that he once used to love the balls to which Onegin goes so eagerly.

Much in *Evgeny Onegin* oddly prefigures what was to happen to Pushkin himself, and it is worth noting that the tragic action of the poem was set in the countryside, and the verses which describe his hero travelling there were written before Pushkin himself was exiled to Mikhaylovskoe. The narrative opens with Onegin hurrying to the death-bed of his uncle, in great need of the estate he hopes to inherit but dreading the tedium of deathbed attendance. He finds his uncle already dead and himself the lord of woods, mills and streams. At first he is delighted to find something other than dissipation to occupy him – he reduces the rent of some of his serfs, which makes him unpopular among fellow landowners. For his neighbours he has nothing but contempt; rather like Alexander Raevsky, Onegin looks down on most of his fellow human beings. He does, however, become friendly with a young aspirant poet, Lensky, just returned from studies in Göttingen and filled with liberal sentiments and a romantic love for his childhood sweetheart, Olga Larina, a beautiful but completely ordinary girl. Onegin mocks his friend's attachment and presents himself as someone in whom 'passion's flame no longer rages'.

The lovely heroine, Tatyana, is Olga's sister. Her name has associations of 'humble roots and servants halls' for Pushkin, though for a reader of Shakespeare it recalls Oberon's Queen of the Fairies. Tatyana is portrayed as a pensive girl who likes to sit all day at the window, taking no pleasure in needlework, dolls or her sister's childish games. Countess Elizaveta Vorontsova's manner and her love of reading also went into the portrait. Tatyana particularly liked the novels of Richardson and Rousseau, and her parents saw no harm in this. Her mother read novels, too, and rather preferred Lovelace to Grandison herself, as indeed she'd preferred a more dashing suitor to the man she married. In a charmingly realistic and affectionate portrait of a fashionable girl giving up city ways and settling for life in the country, Pushkin describes Tatyana's mother whisked off to her husband's estates immediately after her wedding, and there making the energetic organisation of her household a substitute for the romantic love she had forfeited.

> She'd drive around to check the workers,
> She pickled mushrooms for the fall
> She made her weekly bathhouse call,
> She kept the books, she shaved the shirkers
> She beat the maids when she was cross...

Pushkin in Odessa was writing with the nostalgia of an exile as he recalls the glitter of ladies' gowns, the flirtations, the passing of secret notes. He digresses to reflect upon the pleasure he had always taken in small and tender feet, in helping an elegant foot into a stirrup, for instance, or watching the waves touch the feet of a girl (perhaps one of the Raevsky girls), but his mind is filled with St Petersburg, charming even in the morning after a ball. Evgeny drives back to bed just as –

> The merchant up, the milkmaid hurries
> Crackling the freshly fallen snow;
> The cabby plods the hackney row.
> In a pleasant hubbub morn's awaking
> The shutters open, smoke ascends
> In pale blue shafts from chimney ends.

Pushkin himself was about to discover the pleasures of the countryside in the province of Pskov.

CHAPTER EIGHT
Mikhaylovskoe 1824–6

Just before Pushkin left Odessa on 5 August, accompanied by his loyal valet Nikita, he unexpectedly won nine hundred roubles at a card game. This was just as well since his finances were in poor shape and he might not otherwise have been able to afford the hire of a carriage to take him to his parents' estate in Pskov province a thousand miles north. The estate lay in a hilly countryside of woods and meadows, rivers and beautiful lakes, and the village of Mikhaylovskoe was not far from the highway that connected Kiev to St Petersburg.

Pushkin travelled in wide Turkish trousers, a Moldavian cloak and a fez, with his thick curly hair falling to his shoulders. He had signed an undertaking before leaving Odessa[1] that he would make no stop on the way, and he was not even allowed to choose his own route: the authorities insisted his itinerary went through Vitebsk rather than Kiev or Kamenka. However, at Mogilev he was recognised by a nephew of Engelhardt, his old Director of the lyceum. Champagne was ordered immediately and Pushkin was able to enjoy the festivities until 4 a.m. when the revellers escorted him to his carriage.

He arrived in Mikhaylovskoe on 8 August 1824, to find his whole family, including Lev and Olga, were there for the summer. His parents were unusually pleased to see him. Their own social standing had been much reduced and the intervening years had aged them both; they were at first touchingly delighted at the arrival of their famous son. Once they heard why he came to be in Mikhaylovskoe, however, their attitude changed to a selfish terror that his behaviour would endanger their own safety. In their anxiety they showed more inclination to reproach their son than to commiserate with his troubles. Pushkin's father was already worried about subversive tendencies in the family since Lev had recently been expelled from his school and rumour had it this was because he had led a revolt in defence of his Russian master, Pushkin's school friend, the liberal idealist Wilhelm Kyukhelbecker.[2]

The family manor house, a one-storey wooden building, had deteriorated considerably since Pushkin's last visit seven years before. It was badly furnished and uncomfortable in winter and, although Pushkin got on well with Olga and Lev, his relations with his father and mother were soon put under great strain. Pushkin had been summoned by the Governor of Pskov and obliged to sign an undertaking of good conduct, and a local monk was made responsible for Pushkin's spiritual welfare. But it was Pushkin's father who was approached by Peshchurov, the local head of the nobility, to undertake the surveillance of Pushkin's daily behaviour. Had there been a history of good relations between father and son, this arrangement might have proved easygoing and even friendly.

In fact, it proved intolerable to Pushkin, who was particularly furious that his father had taken on himself the duty of opening his correspondence. There was little enough for his father to eavesdrop on, but to have letters opened was another matter. Pushkin was still obsessed with Elizaveta Vorontsova, and longed for letters sealed with a ring similar in design to the talisman she had given him. Whenever a letter arrived from Odessa with that seal Pushkin locked himself in his room to read it, and refused to let anyone in or out of his room while he did so. There is a note on the manuscript of the third chapter of *Onegin* after stanza XXXII which reads: '5th September 1824 *Une lettre de Elisa Worontsoff*'.

There were daily arguments about his father's interference, and on one occasion a quarrel so stormy that Sergey ran out of the room declaring that his son had threatened to strike him. For his part, Pushkin drafted, but did not send, a letter to the Governor of Pskov asking to be sent away, if necessary to one of his fortresses, rather than bear the situation in the family home. In a letter to Vyazemsky's wife at the end of October 1824 Pushkin wrote: 'You wish to know of this stupid existence ... My presence in the midst of my family has only redoubled my afflictions, already real enough. I have been reproached with my exile. They believe they are involved in my misfortune. They claim I am preaching atheism to my sister, who is a heavenly creature, and to my brother, who is very amusing and very young, who has been admiring my verses and whom I very assuredly bore.'³

To Zhukovsky he repeated the request he had made to the Governor of Pskov: 'Make haste; my father's charge has become known to all the house ... The neighbours are aware of it. I am not going to explain matters to them ... if it reaches the government, judge for yourself what will happen ... I was exiled for a stupid letter; what would have happened if the government should find out about my father's accusation? That smells of the hangman and the prison camp.'⁴

No sensible conversation was possible in so feverish and irrational a household and Pushkin even considered suing his father for libel. Fortunately, his father disliked the situation as much as Pushkin did and, speaking of his son as 'ce monstre, ce fils dénaturé', set off from Mikhaylovskoe taking Olga and Lev with him. Thereafter Pushkin settled down to live a quiet country life with his nurse, Arina Rodionovna, for company.

To reduce the cost of heating, Pushkin lived in a single room which served as bedroom, study and dining room. Across the corridor from that room slept Arina Rodionovna, whom he still called Mama. Pushkin woke early and usually swam in the river or took a cold bath before doing anything else. After his first cup of coffee he read or wrote all morning. Then he liked to walk or ride around the estate, wearing a red shirt belted with a sash, broad trousers, a white straw hat and a heavy cane. He also enjoyed exploring country fairs and markets. He liked to compose as he rode, and to read what he had written aloud to his nurse when he returned. In 'Winter Evening' Pushkin gives a charming picture of them sitting together in an ill-lit cottage with only the sound of his nanny's spindle whirring while storms rage outside. 'Before dinner, I write my memoirs, I dine late,' he wrote to his brother in November 1824. 'After dinner I go riding; in the evening I listen to fairy tales.'

The fairy tales were those told him by Arina Rodionovna. It was his chief evening amusement, but sometimes he practised pistol shooting and sometimes played billiards against himself. It might not have been the life he would have chosen, but it had its rewards, as Zhukovsky pointed out in a letter that first November. 'To everything that has happened to you, and to all you have brought on yourself, I have only one answer: poetry. You have not got talent; you have genius. You are rich, you have an inalienable means to transcend undeserved misfortune;

you can and must have moral dignity. You were born to be a great poet; be worthy of it.'[5]

There was little to distract him from that destiny, and he wrote to his brother, now back in St Petersburg, begging for books and once again, as he had in Odessa, Pushkin began to read intensively – history, memoirs, current literature and the classics of Germany, England and Italy. He was particularly taken with Shakespeare, Walter Scott and Schiller, and kept up a lively correspondence with his literary friends about his enthusiasms – his dislikes, too. Among his reading of the English classics was Richardson's *Clarissa*. Of that book's heroine he wrote, 'What an insufferably boring fool she is!'

He remained on good terms with his brother, whom he was trying, unsuccessfully, to use as his agent. It was Professor Pletnev, an amiable minor poet, to whom that role was soon to be entrusted. For the next eight years Pushkin was to live on the proceeds of his writing alone, but he was to write far more in the two years he spent in Mikhaylovskoe than in all his other four years in the south. This included revisions to *The Gypsies*, the greater part of *Evgeny Onegin* and some of the finest lyrics in the Russian language.

> Rose maiden, I am in your bondage
> Yet in your fetters feel no shame:
> A nightingale in a laurel bush
> Beside a proud and lovely rose,
> Might live a slave in such delight,
> And tenderly sing songs for her
> All through the dark, voluptuous night.

Writing to an Odessa friend on 9 December 1824, he reported: 'I have now been four months in the depth of the country ... it is dull, but what can one do about it? There is neither sea nor the blue southern sky, nor the Italian opera. But to make up for it there are neither locusts nor Milords Vorontsov either.'[6]

At first there was not much in the way of female diversion, although by November he had already discovered Olga, the pretty (serf) daughter of his estate steward, Kalashnikov, and taken her into his bed. Whether or not this young girl is the 'Olga' referred to on Pushkin's Don Juan list, as P. E. Shchegolev maintains, his relationship with her brought him physical contentment. She was soon pregnant with his child.

Such a relationship would not necessarily have aroused much compunction among Russian gentlemen of that era but Pushkin behaved with some solicitude. In May 1826 he wrote to Vyazemsky that he was sending him 'a very dear and good girl whom one of your friends has indiscreetly fattened up. I am counting on your philanthropy and friendship. Give her a refuge in Moscow and as much money as is necessary – and then direct her to Boldino (my patrimony, where chickens, roosters and bears wander about). ... I ask you to take care, with fatherly tenderness, of the baby, if it should be a boy. I do not want to send him into a foundling home – is it not possible to place him in some village or other, even in Ostafevo? [Vyazemsky's estate] My dear, I am conscience stricken as God is my judge, but it's a little late for that now.'[7]

Vyazemsky, however, refused to take Olga under his protection because as a serf she legally belonged to Pushkin's father. His advice was that Pushkin should confess the whole matter to the steward, Kalashnikov, remind him tactfully that he would one day be the steward's master and ask him to regularise affairs accordingly. To this Pushkin agreed in a letter of 27 May and on 1 July Olga gave birth to a son at Boldino. The child was christened Pavel but, whether or not he inherited his father's genius, nothing is known of him. Olga was married off to a small landowner who sadly turned out to be a drunkard.

Pushkin liked to walk around peasants' huts, both to talk with them and to listen to their jokes and songs. This was a matter of some concern to the Tsar's secret police and an account of their observations may be read in their official report on the summer of 1826. In all the accounts so painstakingly put together, it is Pushkin's dress which was the most frequent oddity reported. The information obtained from the innkeeper in the neighbouring town of Novorzhev is quoted by D. S. Mirsky:

1) That at the fair at the Svyatogorsky Monastery Pushkin was in a blouse with a pink ribbon for belt, in a broad-brimmed hat with an iron rod in his hand.

2) That at any rate he is discreet and circumspect, does not talk about the government and altogether there are no rumours circulating among the people concerning him.

3) That he does not seem to like company or to sing any seditious songs, and still less has he tried to raise the peasants.

Having gained entry to the house of the neighbouring squire, an agent was told,

1) That Pushkin is sometimes seen in a Russian blouse and broad-brimmed straw hat.

2) That Pushkin is friendly with the peasants and sometimes shakes hands with them when greeting them.

3) That he rides on horseback and, reaching the end of his journey, tells his man to let the horse alone, saying that every animal has a right to liberty.

A peasant of the monastery village said that 'Pushkin is an exceedingly kind gentleman who gives tips even to his own people (i.e. serfs), behaves himself simply and offends no one'.[8]

Mirsky also quotes from the diary of a merchant from Opochka. This reveals, among details about his dress, that Pushkin's name was already celebrated even among the uneducated middle classes:

> I had the happiness of seeing Alexander Sergeevich, Mr Pushkin, who in a way astonished me by his dress, namely he had on a straw hat, a crimson blouse, a blue ribbon around his waist, an iron rod in his hand, with exceedingly long black whiskers, looking more like a beard, also with exceedingly long nails with the ends of which he peeled oranges and ate them with great appetite, half a dozen of them I should say.[9]

For all the gaiety of his costume and the apparent ease of his manner, Pushkin knew he was being watched, and when he revisited Mikhaylovskoe ten years later spoke of his own sense of that surveillance.

> I saw a betrayer in every chance comrade ... everyone seemed to be a betrayer or an enemy ... I grew bitter ... tempests raged in my heart, and hate and dreams of pale places.[10]

Some of Pushkin's experience of country life went into *Evgeny Onegin*, chapter two, even if he did not avoid country society altogether as Onegin did at first.

> Once neighbours hear he keeps his stallion ready
> So he could quickly disappear
> The moment one of them was sighted
> Or heard approaching uninvited,
> They took offence and one and all
> They dropped him cold, and ceased to call.

Into his winter isolation on 11 January 1825 came Ivan Pushchin, Pushkin's closest friend from *lycée* days, braving the threat of official displeasure to visit Pushkin in Mikhaylovskoe. That there was some danger in him doing so is confirmed by the surprise of A. I. Turgenev when Ivan Pushchin told him of his intentions. Ivan had by this time left the army and taken a humble position in the Courts in the hope of giving assistance to poor litigants. In his memoirs Ivan gives a moving account of his arrival on a sledge at about eight in the morning. Pushkin was standing in the doorway in no more than a nightshirt, and Ivan jumped out of his sledge to embrace him.

> I grab hold of him and drag him into the room. It is bitterly cold outside, but in such moments a man does not catch cold. We look at one another, we kiss, we remain silent. He forgot that he should put something on, I did not think of my fur coat and hat covered in frost. It was about eight in the morning ... The old woman who had run up found us in each other's arms in the same condition as we were as we came into the house: one almost naked, the other covered in snow. Finally the tears broke (even now, after thirty five years, tears make it difficult to write in glasses) and we came to our senses.[11]

Ivan noticed Pushkin's poorly furnished, untidy bedroom, 'strewn with sheets and discarded paper, and the ends of quill pens' and remembered that at school, too, he had always written with the stubs of pens.[12]

Over coffee and pipes the two friends talked of Pushkin's life in Odessa and Vorontsov's jealousy, and what else might have led to his exile. They toasted an unnamed woman, probably Elizaveta. At one point Pushkin jumped up in agitated excitement at the thought of a society in which Ivan had a part working for the betterment of Russia, but he did not press his friend about it. 'Perhaps you are right in not trusting me. Truly, because of my many stupidities I am not worthy of such a confidence.'

Among these stupidities Pushkin might not have thought to include his relationship with the steward's daughter, Olga, who was already bearing his child. When Pushkin took his friend round the house they visited the room where she sat among the other peasant seamstresses, at work under the guidance of Arina Rodyonovna, and Ivan noticed a pretty girl whose figure and bearing stood out from the others. He at once suspected some relationship with Pushkin and, meeting his eyes, his friend confirmed as much with a wink.

Ivan had brought a manuscript copy of *Woe From Wit* by Griboedov, a contemporary writer they both admired, and Pushkin, after dinner and wine, was soon reading aloud from it with expressive gusto. When a monk (in reality a local investigator) turned up, Pushkin changed his reading matter to *Lives of the Saints* and poured out tea and rum for the monk. When he'd gone, Pushkin returned to *Woe From Wit*. The friends spent the whole day together, drinking several bottles of champagne with relish. Then Pushkin dictated the opening stanzas of *The Gypsies* for publication in *Polyarnaya Zvezda*.

At three in the morning they heard the bells of the waiting sledge and had to part. Even as they clinked glasses and made plans to meet in Moscow, they had premonitions that they were seeing each other for the last time. Ivan recalls his last memory of Pushkin on his snow-filled porch, holding a candle and calling after him, 'Goodbye, my friend.'

A year later Ivan had been exiled to Siberia for his part in the Decembrist conspiracy. Pushkin independently remembered the occasion sorrowfully in a short lyric after his friend's sentence:

> My first friend and my best companion,
> How much I blessed my fate on hearing
> As snows came drifting through my yard
> The tinkle of your sleighbell ring.
>
> Now I beg Providence, these lines
> May reach your spirit in its prison
> With something of the same comfort as
> The light of days at our Lyceum.

Pushkin's unhappiness at parting from his closest friend was assuaged by a group of neighbours, the Osipov family, who lived in the beautiful estate of Trigorskoe about two miles away from Mikhaylovskoe. Praskovya Alexandrovna Osipova was a distant relation of Pushkin's, a woman of about 43, twice widowed, with a large family. She had never been a beauty but she had a plump charm, silky chestnut hair, a love of poetry and an affection for Pushkin himself which continued long after he had left the district. How Pushkin felt towards her is not entirely clear, though he certainly respected her intelligence. She may, like his nanny Arina Rodyonovna and his grandmother, have given him the maternal tenderness he had so notably failed to find in his own mother. In any case, he continued a correspondence with her long after he had left Mikhaylovskoe. He may also have flirted with her, although there were many younger girls at Trigorskoe, including the Osipova daughters and a stepdaughter by her second marriage. In a letter to Vyazemsky's wife in October he spoke of listening to her conversations as 'his only expedient' and of the daughters, 'unappealing enough in all respects even though they play Rossini'. A letter to his sister in December spoke of all the inhabitants of Trigorskoe as 'insufferable fools except the mother'.

For all these criticisms, Pushkin began to visit these neighbours more and more often. In 1829, he recalled the loneliness of life in the winter countryside and his delight at the prospect of any neighbourly visit:

> While I sit playing draughts, tucked quietly away,
> Perhaps there should arrive a carriage, or a sleigh,
> Bringing chance visitors thrown suddenly amidst us,
> A mother and two girls (two blonde and shapely sisters)
> Then how the backwoods stir – what life this visit brings!
> The world, because of it, brims over with good things.[13]

Pushkin made a friend of the only other male in the Trigorskoe household, the twenty-year-old Alexey Vulf, a student at the University of Dorpat and a child from Praskovya's first marriage. This young man revered Pushkin as a poet and enjoyed pretending to treat him as Mephistopheles in sexual matters, though Vulf's own diary shows a coldness and calculation in relation to women which he could not be said to have learned from Pushkin.

Pushkin flirted with all the women in the Osipova household, however unappealing he had found them in October. He was most attracted to the fifteen-year-old Yevpraksia, who finds her place as Zizi in *Evgeny Onegin*, and no doubt the local gentry saw her as an ideal future wife for Pushkin, even though marriage was not on his mind. In a letter to Lev he describes how he measured the size of his own waist with Yevpraksia's girdle and claimed to find it the same size, which made her pout. Most of the pleasures he took in this household of charming young girls were harmless except perhaps for his relationship with Alexey's sister, Anna Vulf. She was at 25 already on the verge of being an old maid, and fell deeply in love with him. She was a plain girl and, although he accepted her affections and, indeed, entered her initials on the second part of his Don Juan list, he had no thought of a serious attachment. Her pleading letters suggest he treated her with less and less kindness as their relationship progressed through 1826.

On 21 July 1825, for instance, while 'gloomily drunk' and admittedly already in love with another woman, he wrote,

(1) In the name of heaven be scatter-brained only with your men friends; they will profit by it only for themselves whereas your girlfriends will do you harm; get it into your head that they are as vain and garrulous as yourself. (2) Wear short dresses, because you have pretty feet and do not fluff up your hair at the temples even when that may be the style since you have the misfortune to have a round face, (3) You have been very erudite of late, but do not act like it...'¹⁴

It is a little disturbing to realise that Pushkin probably made this unfortunate girl, whom he found both plain and insipid, his mistress. However, it was almost certainly at her own entreaty, and her letters to him at the beginning of March from Malinniki suggest that she had no objection to their new relationship as such. She speaks of having a cousin there passionately in love with her 'who does not wish anything better than to prove it to me, following your example ... He cannot reconcile himself to the idea that I spent some time with a terrible rake like you but, alas, I feel nothing at his approach.'¹⁵ A few days later she wrote that she had had a terrible scene with her mother. 'I really believe ... Mother wants to be the only one to possess you and leaves me here because she is jealous of me ... I am furious with mother. What a woman! After all, you are to blame for this too. Mother found you looked sad at the time of my departure. He seems to be sorry for you to go, she said. My wish to return fills her with suspicion and I am afraid to insist too much.'¹⁶

Pushkin must have chafed at the petulance of the conclusion of that letter – 'Goodbye, I hate you' – and regretted the involvement he had weakly allowed to form between them. Soon after the first letter she wrote to him again imploring him not to compromise her and blamed herself for being 'under a horrible spell'. By 20 April her tone had changed again and she was once more relating stories of another man eager to seduce her. 'He proceeds towards his goal with gigantic steps; I believe he excels even you in impudence ... However, do not be afraid. I do not feel anything towards him. He does not produce any *effect* on me, while one memory of you excites me ... I am very much afraid you do not love me at all. All you feel is a passing desire.'¹⁷ Though an eager and unfaithful lover, Pushkin was not a cold-hearted one: her letters filled him with dismay, even as he dealt with the crisis of Olga Kalashnikov's impending childbirth. And, quite aside from that affair, he was no longer heart-whole.

Anna Vulf's longstanding friend, Anna Petrovna Kern, was a woman Pushkin had met five years earlier at the Olenins', where Anna Petrovna and her husband were staying; Elizaveta Olenina being Anna Petrovna's aunt. Olenina's husband, Alexey, was President of the Academy of Arts and Director of the Public Library, and their house on the Fontanka was a meeting place for writers and artists. Staying with the Olenins was Anna Petrovna's first opportunity to meet people who thought and read. As she wrote in her memoirs, 'There were no cards, and no dancing either ... but there were charades.'[18]

It was at the Olenins' that Pushkin was first taken with her beauty, though Anna herself was too distracted by the game and another young man reading aloud as a forfeit to notice Pushkin at first. Anna Kern gives her own account of that meeting, in which Pushkin's exuberant adolescence is more apparent than his wit.

> During my next charade I was to act Cleopatra, and as I stood holding my basket of flowers Pushkin and my cousin Alexander approached me. Looking at the basket and pointing to my cousin he said, 'Et c'est sans doute monsieur qui fera l'aspic.' I found this remark impertinent and walked away saying nothing ... Dinner was at small tables, informally, without rank ... Pushkin sat behind me with my cousin, trying to attract my attention with such flattering remarks as 'Est il permit d'être aussi joli?' There followed more badinage, about who was a sinner and who not. Pushkin said, 'At any rate there will be plenty of pretty women in hell, and we can all play charades there. Ask Mme Kern if she would not like to go to hell.' I replied, seriously and somewhat curtly, that I would not. 'Well then, neither would I,' said Pushkin, 'even though there'll be plenty of pretty women there.'[19]

Anna Kern records in her memoir that Pushkin stood on the porch to watch her go, and quoted verses from chapter eight of 'Onegin', which she says refers to that early encounter. (The editors of the volume of her memoirs, however, favour Countess Natalya Viktorovna Stroganova instead.)

Anna Vulf had corresponded with Anna Petrovna Kern for some time, and Anna Petrovna had made sufficient impression on Pushkin in St Petersburg five years earlier for him to take a great deal of interest in that correspondence, guessing that she was the giddy wife of a very old husband. These letters included details of her enthusiasm for Pushkin's early poetry and Pushkin was intrigued to find how knowledgeable she was, having read not only *The Prisoner of the Caucasus* but also the first chapter of *Evgeny Onegin*, which had already been published in St Petersburg. Hearing that Anna was acquainted with his friend, the poet Rodzyanko, Pushkin wrote to him with some disrespect,

> Explain to me, my dear, just what Anna Petrovna Kern is like who has written a lot of kind things about me to her cousin? They say she is a charming thing ... In any case, knowing your amorousness and *unusual talents* in all respects, I suppose your business is done or half done. I congratulate you, my dear; write an elegy or even an epigram.[20]

To this, Rodzyanko made no reply until the middle of May, and then wrote a letter jointly with Anna Petrovna, in which they claimed that, even though she would have no legal children by her husband, she refused to accept Rodzyanko as a substitute.

Portraits of Anna Kern are said to be only approximations of her likeness, but she was clearly a beauty; biographers of Pushkin have been less generous about her character. D. S. Mirsky, for instance, remarks, after quoting the most famous of the lyrics Pushkin dedicated to her,

> Mme Kern was very far from being 'a genius of pure beauty'; she was a sensuous and light hearted woman of twenty five who was greatly disgusted with her unhappy husband. She does not seem to have any strong feeling for Pushkin, but she was ready to yield to every man she met. Pushkin was by no means repulsive. Besides, she was very sensitive to the honour of being loved by a famous poet. This last sentiment is very apparent in her memoirs.[21]

A modern reader would read Mme Kern's own account of her life more kindly. Though not sexually pure, she was far from a slut. Poets and musicians such as Delvig and Glinka testify to her lively mind, originality and strength of character. There are diaries, which she kept both before and after her meeting with Pushkin, and her memoirs, which she was brought to write in 1858, not only describe meetings with Pushkin but with Delvig, Glinka and the Tsar, who was much attracted to her.

Anna was born in 1800 in the province of Orel, where her maternal grandfather, I. P. Vulf, was the Governor. Her father was a Poltava landowner and Privy Councillor, an intelligent man, though with a frivolous spirit. Her mother was kind but sickly, and much under her husband's thumb. Her parents moved to the desolate Ukrainian town of

Abram Petrovich Gannibal,
Pushkin's maternal grandfather,
a Negro slave adopted by Peter
the Great, who rose to be a
general in the Russian army.

Nadezhda Osipovna
Pushkina, Pushkin's mother,
known as 'the beautiful
Creole'.

Sergei L'vovich Pushkin,
Pushkin's Father.

Moscow: View from
Lubyanka Street on the
Vladimirskie Gates (early
nineteenth century).

Ivan Pushchin (1817), a close friend of Pushkin's at the Lycée, later sentenced to exile as a Decembrist.

Pushkin's sketch of Kalypso Polychroni (1821), said to have been a mistress of Lord Byron.

Pushkin and Onegin together on the Neva Embankment: Pushkin's
drawing for *Evgeny Onegin* (1824).

Pushkin's sketch of Pavel Pestel
(1826), a leading Decembrist.

Mikhaylovskoe village, Pushkin's
mother's country estate (1837).

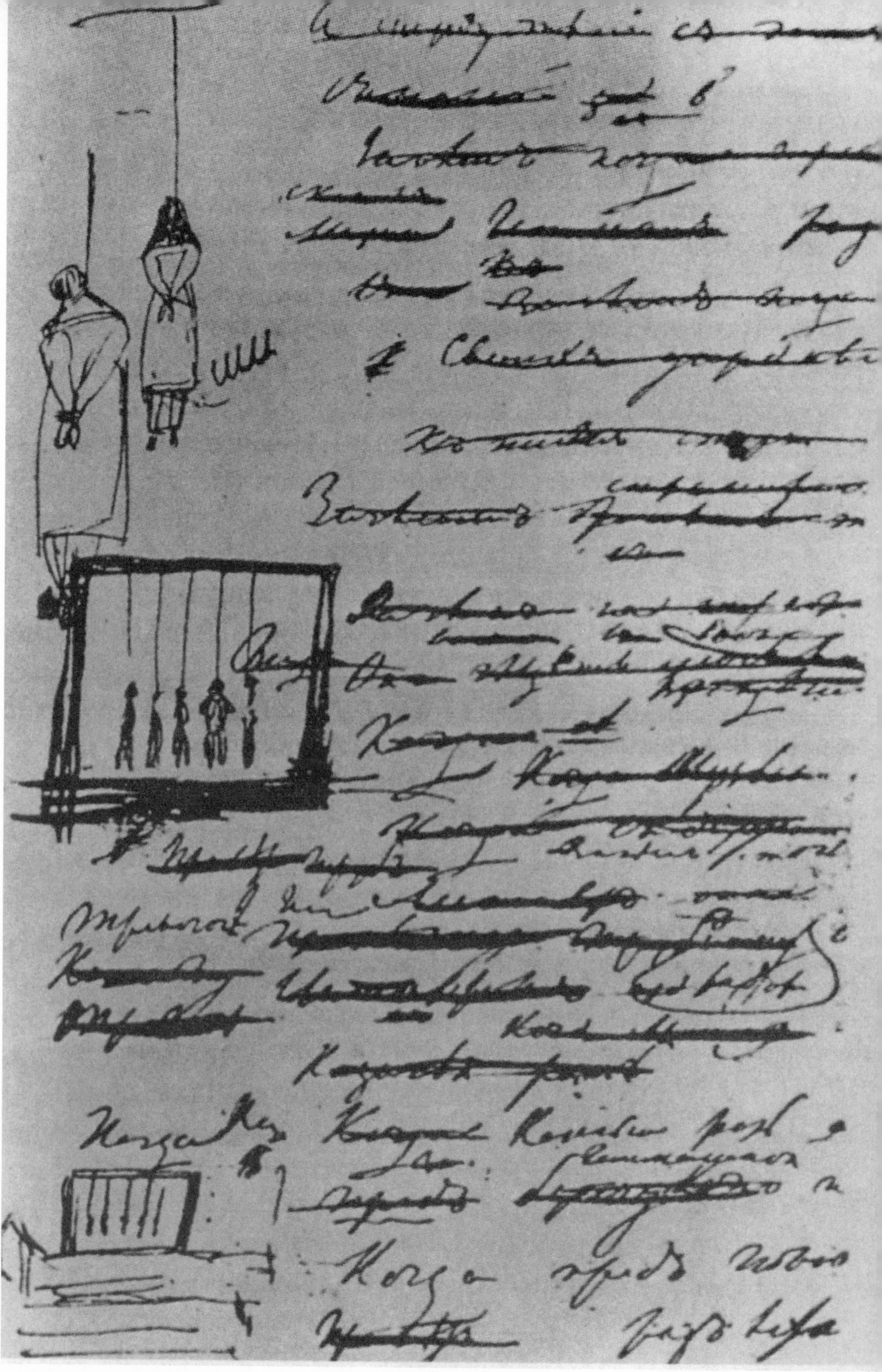

Two sketches of hanged men drawn by Pushkin in the margin of his manuscripts. Thoughts of the five Decembrist conspirators hanged in 1826 on the order of Nicholas I haunted Pushkin long after the revolt was suppressed.

Adam Mickiewicz, the great Polish poet, drawn by Pushkin.

Pushkin's sketch of Ekaterina Ushakova and her feet (1829).

A portrait of Natalya Nikolaevna Pushkina painted not long after she married Pushkin in February 1831.

Pushkin's sketch of his wife, Natalya.

Georges d'Anthès, whose pursuit of Natalya Nikolaevna led to the duel in 1837 in which Pushkin received the wound from which he died two days later.

Left Pushkin's last self-portrait (1836).

Opposite Thought to be the last portrait of Pushkin, possibly painted by A. L. Linev (1836–7).

The Pushkin Memorial Flat, 12 Moika Embankment. The study.

Portrait of Natalya Pushkina (1842–3).

The conditions of the duel between Pushkin and d'Anthès, drawn up by their seconds, Danzas and D'Archiac on 27 January 1837.

The Pushkin monument in front of the Russian museum. © Bridgeman Art Library, London/NY

Lubny when Anna was only a few months old, and then to Vulf's estate in Bernov, near Tversk.

Between the ages of eight and twelve Anna had a first-class education from a French governess, who encouraged her to read widely in her mother's library and to explore the fields and forests of the Tversk countryside. She lived at home until she was sixteen, sometimes dreaming in the woods with a book, sometimes dancing at balls and acting in amateur theatricals. A month before her seventeenth birthday she was married off against her will to a fifty-two-year-old District Army General, Ermolay Kern, who flattered her parents with the prospect of making their daughter a general's wife.

Kern was an old soldier who had come up through the ranks, a coarse, limited man who cared nothing for Anna's artistic aspirations and was interested only in parades, inspections and manoeuvres. As a man he disgusted her, so with marriage all her dreams of a happy life were shattered. For the following ten years she moved with him from town to town, living in army quarters and bearing him two daughters, born in 1818 and 1821. She had few friends as most of the other military wives envied her rank as the wife of a general. The high point in her early life was a meeting, during manoeuvres in Riga in 1817, with Tsar Alexander I, who invited her to visit him in St Petersburg. The young bride respectfully declined, explaining innocently that her husband had to remain at Lubny. With some naivety, but pertly, she suggested the Tsar might visit her in Lubny instead, and the Tsar laughingly promised to do so.

After returning home, life seemed even drearier and there were growing conflicts with her husband. She wrote in 1820:

> What boredom … I simply don't know what to do with myself. Imagine my situation … not a single soul to talk to, my head spins from reading. I finish the book and I am all alone in the world. My husband is either asleep, on manoeuvres or smoking.[22]

It was in 1824 that she returned to her parents' estate and met their neighbour Arkady Rodzyanko, a poet and friend of Pushkin, and it was he who gave her a copy of Pushkin's *Prisoner of the Caucasus*, *The Fountain of Bakhchisaray* and the first chapter of *Evgeny Onegin*, which had passed the censorship and been published in February 1825. So it was that Anna Petrovna was able to write about all these poems with such delight to Anna Vulf. When in June 1825 Anna Petrovna came for a visit to the Osipov family, she was well aware that Pushkin would be a close neighbour.

The Osipov family were having lunch when 'suddenly Pushkin entered the room, with a tall, stout stick in his hand. After this he often arrived during lunch, but never sat down at the table; he dined at home, much earlier, and ate very little. He always came with two great dogs, wolfhounds. Aunt, who was sitting next to me, introduced me, but (he) said nothing.'[23]

Soon Pushkin was visiting the Trigorskoe estate almost daily. Anna reports that he was unpredictable in his behaviour: 'at times noisily cheerful, at times sad, now shy, now impertinent, now boundlessly affable, now hauntingly depressed, and it was impossible to guess in what mood he would be the next minute ... Incapable of hiding his feelings, he always expressed them sincerely and was indescribably good when something pleasant excited him ... when he decided to be friendly, nothing could compare with the sparkle, the wit and attractiveness of his speech.'

In such a mood he told them the tale of a devil who travelled with a coachman to Vasilevsky Island, and on another occasion everyone gathered round to hear him read *The Gypsies* from a big black-bound book. Anna Kern, too, knew how to entertain. She sang a bacarolle, 'Venetian Night', based on verses by the blind poet, Kozlov. After that evening Pushkin wrote to his friend Pletnev, 'Tell Kozlov from me that a fair lady visited this land and sang his verses angelically. It is a pity he will not see her, but may God grant that he hears her.'[24]

In the next few weeks Pushkin saw Anna Kern every day, and the original impression of her that he had formed at his first meeting at the Olenins probably displaced the frivolous opinion his letters to Rodzyanko suggested.

The night before Anna Kern left Trigorskoe, her aunt suggested a visit to Mikhaylovskoe.

> The moonlit June night breathed the coolness and fragrance of the fields. We went in two carriages, my aunt and her son in one, my cousin Anna, Pushkin and I in the other. Never before or afterwards did I see him so kind and cheerful. He joked without sarcasm and sharpness, praising the moon without calling it stupid ... At Mikhaylovskoe we did not go into the house but went straight to the old, overgrown park ...[25]

Whatever was said or done on that magical occasion – and it may be that her watchful cousin Anna Vulf and the possibly jealous eye of Osipova herself made sure that little did – Pushkin remembered Anna's presence with tenderness. In a letter to Anna Vulf he wrote, 'every night I roam the park and repeat to myself "she was here". The stone on which she stumbled lies on my desk, beside a branch of fading heliotrope.'

Next day Anna Kern left for Riga with her cousin. That morning, before she left, Pushkin arrived and handed her a copy of chapter two of *Evgeny Onegin*. In its uncut pages she found a folded sheet of paper. On this he had written one of his loveliest lyrics which opens, recalling their first meeting in St Petersburg, with the verse:

> I remember the magical instant
> You first appeared to me
> Like a momentary vision,
> The genius of sheer beauty.

Over the passing years his imagination and dreams had continued to hold that memory, even though he thought he had forgotten her; now the sight of her had wakened his soul. The poem concludes:

> So once again the world excites
> My heart, to fresh awareness of
> Invention, godhead and delight:
> In life, and tears, and love.

Anna Petrovna reports, 'When I made to put away the poetic gift in my casket, he stared at me for a long time, then impulsively snatched it back and refused to return it to me.' Although from this account it does not seem that Anna would have had time to learn the poem by heart, she later repeated the verses to Baron Delvig, who published them in his magazine, *Northern Lights*, and to Glinka who set them to music.

From this holiday Anna Petrovna returned to Riga. A letter from Pushkin addressed to her aunt followed, with a character sketch of Anna Petrovna within it: '*elle est souple, elle comprend tout; elle s'afflige facilement et se console même; elle est timide dans les manières et hardie dans les actions; mais elle est bien attrayante.*'

In which particular actions she was bold is not entirely clear, but Pushkin was sure that she felt a secret tenderness for him. On 25 July he wrote to her directly in Riga asking if she would agree to correspond with him, which she did. He wrote her five letters which we have, though hers have been lost. It is hard to gauge from Pushkin's letters the seriousness of his feelings for her under their witty, flirtatious tone. The editors of Kern's memoir call her 'his partner in a literary game, his co-author of a romance in letters'. It was only later in Pushkin's life that this romance became a full sexual relationship.

In his first letter he writes, 'A correspondence leads to nothing, I know; but I do not have the strength to resist the desire to have a word from your pretty hand . . .'

In the second part of the letter, he writes,

> I take up my pen again because I am dying of boredom, and I can't get you off my mind. I hope you will read this letter in secret . . . will you hide it again in your bosom? If you fear my indiscretion . . . sign with a fictitious name, my heart will be able to recognise you.[26]

For all his declaration of boredom Pushkin was, in fact, passionately at work. Of Shakespeare, whom Pushkin had been reading in Letourneur's French translation, he wrote in 1825: 'I cannot get over him. Compared with him, how poor a tragedian Byron is. This Byron who only ever conceived one single character.' Alongside the plays themselves, Pushkin was also reading Schlegel's lectures on dramatic art, which were in the vanguard of Shakespearean criticism. *Boris Godunov* was particularly intended to bring the vitality of Shakespearean drama into the largely Racine-dominated Russian theatre. So importantly did he take this ambition that on 6 October he wrote to Zhukovsky, who had been urging him to seek medical advice, 'I shall not die; that is impossible. God would not want Godunov to perish with me.'

The play makes use of history largely unknown to a Western reader, who will have encountered what they do know of *Boris Godunov* from programme notes to the opera Mussorgsky based on Pushkin's play. Briefly, Boris was a boyar without a title, married to the daughter of Ivan the Terrible, whom Ivan took into his confidence. Ivan's son Dimitry died, supposedly as a result of stabbing himself in an epileptic fit. As Dimitry's death helped to ensure Boris's rule, historians have long suspected Boris of that crime, and Pushkin thought him guilty of it. After Ivan's death Feodor, the Angelic Tsar, became effective ruler in 1584, but Boris was elected Tsar in January 1598, where Pushkin's play starts.

Boris continued the policy of restricting the power of the boyars, though without Ivan's extreme cruelty. He had democratic ideas which on the one hand alienated the boyars and on the other failed to do enough for the peasantry, especially during the famine of 1601, to win popular support. In 1603 a rumour began to circulate that Dimitry, the murdered Tsarevitch, was still alive in Poland. Boris countered that rumour, but False Dimitry (so called because two other impostors followed him) rapidly made friends with Polish Jesuits and, with not more than 3,500 troops and the magic name of Dimitry drawing the superstitious mob towards him, marched towards Moscow. In 1605 Boris suddenly died, and thirteen months later Dimitry was crowned Tsar. Soviet Marxist historians saw Boris Godunov's attempt to strengthen the central authority of the government as sowing the seeds of the Peasant War of 1666–7. It certainly saw the first struggle of the Russian people against absolutism.

Pushkin's play is written in iambic blank verse, which is a sign of how deeply he accepted Shakespeare's influence at this time as the metre is not indigenous to Russia, and he used Karamzin's distinguished *History of Russia* as his source, not only for the line of the plot but also for significant details, rather as Shakespeare had used Holinshed. There are other resemblances. He mixes prose and poetry, as Shakespeare did in his history plays, and aspires to a similar depth of characterisation in his central figure. Boris combines Macbeth's guilt and despair, Richard III's cunning and Bolingbroke's shrewdness, and is a brilliant portrait of a weakened and despairing man.

There are wonderful scenes in the play – for instance, in an inn near the Lithuanian frontier. Police bearing the Tsar's ukase are searching for a man they wish to arrest. They seize an innocent, runaway monk, in no way resembling the man described in the warrant, who would have been taken off to be hanged had not his companion, also barely literate, examined the edict. As this man slowly makes out that there is no mention of hanging, he reads out a description of someone else in the room, whose reading suddenly improves wonderfully in response:

> Wait for it, you sons of bitches. Am I Grishka? What? Fifty years old, with a grey beard and a fat belly? ... It may be a long while since I tried to read, but I'll manage it if it's a hanging matter. *(He reads syllable by syllable)* Look here ... His age at his last birthday, twen-ty ... What, brother? Where does it say *fifty*? Look.

The colloquial prose writing in this scene was something quite new on the Russian stage.

Some debts to Shakespeare are very direct, for instance when Boris demands from a courtier whether the corpse they saw was that of Dimitry and finds their craven assent does not help him forget the danger the impostor presents to his own rule.

> Ugh, it is stifling ... Let me get my breath ...
> So this is why every night for the last
> Thirteen years I've dreamed of the dead child.
> Yes, yes, that's why. And now I understand.
> But who is he, my scary enemy?
> What's it to me, an empty name, a shadow?
> How can that tear away my purple robes?

Boris's dying speech closely resembles that of Henry IV. There is also a scene whose shape recalls that between Coriolanus and his mother, when the young patrician expects maternal approval for his arrogance and meets a rebuke instead. Dimitry, unwilling to believe that his Polish love, the beautiful Marina, might only be interested in his princely destiny, reveals himself to her as an impostor and meets her furious scorn rather than the reassurance for which he had hoped. Marina's ironic contempt for her lover's weakness is scathing.

> Who demanded any such confession?
> I marvel you have not yet told
> Your father out of friendship or the king
> In sheer high spirits ...

Unlike Coriolanus, however, who yields to his mother's common sense, Dimitry responds with equal pride, as if Ivan's ghost had adopted him as a son, and turns from Marina painfully, pointing out that the power of his name has made the whole country rise to follow him.

> I am the Tsar's heir. Shameful enough
> That I lower myself to love a Pole.
> Farewell for ever.

Pushkin always valued *Boris Godunov* very highly and on 7 November 1825 he wrote to Vyazemsky with unconcealed delight, 'What a Pushkin, what a son of a bitch! ... My Holy Fool is a comic fellow; Marina ... is a Pole, and is very beautiful ... Captain Margaret, who is continually swearing ... he won't be passed by the censorship.'

Now that Pushkin had left government service, and depended for his living on the money he earned from writing, the censorship had a force in his life unfelt by writers with other sources of income. Pushkin chafed at his situation. In a draft letter to Ryleev of June–August 1825 Pushkin contrasts Western writers who all wrote for money with the situation of poets in Russia where '(except for me) they write from vanity ... There if you have nothing to eat, you write a book; here if you have nothing to eat you enter government service and *don't* write.'

Pushkin's literary correspondence in his two years at Mikhaylovskoe expanded to take the place of all the conversation he might have enjoyed with friends, though in his loneliness he had come to rely on his own critical eye. On 25 January 1825 he revised his judgement of *The Gypsies*, which he had modestly made little of to Vyazemsky, and asserted jauntily, 'I think I told you that my poem *The Gypsies* is not at all good: don't you believe it. I lied!'

Far from showing any reverence to an older poet, Pushkin once more teased his friend for writing too little: 'Aren't there any poems by the late Vyazemsky?' In his isolation he had become assured in his own, often iconoclastic judgement of Russian literature. On 1 June 1825 he wrote to Delvig that he had been rereading Derzhavin and found 'he knew nothing of the spirit of the Russian language ... Reading him, one seems to be reading a bad, free translation of some wonderful original. I swear his Genius thought in Tatar ...'[27]

Most tellingly, and in a spirit which suggests our own time is less remote from his than we imagine, he wrote to Vyazemsky in November 1825,

Why do you regret the loss of Byron's notebooks ... Thank God they are lost ... Thank God they are lost! He confessed, unconsciously, in his poems, carried away by poetic rapture ... in the cold blood of prose he would have lied and dissembled ... We know Byron well enough ... Fancy wanting to see him on his chamber pot ... The crowd eagerly laps up confessions, memoirs etc, for in its baseness it delights in the degradation of the great, in the weaknesses of the powerful. It is overjoyed at the disclosure of any nastiness. *He is as petty as we are, he is as vile as we are.* You lie, you scoundrels: he may be petty and vile, but not in the way you are – in a different way.[28]

For all the speed and ease of his writing style, Pushkin drafted his letters carefully. All the more did he miss the spontaneity of conversation where he had the opportunity to be his own unpredictable and change-able self. All through 1825 he remained conscious of the distance that separated him from his close friends. When, on 25 January 1826, he wrote to Vyazemsky his joy was evident and what he revealed of his true emotional state suddenly unguarded: 'I am expecting my brother and Delvig in a day or two; for the moment I am absolutely alone.'

Pushkin awaited the arrival of his friend Delvig with particular anticipation. They had been exact contemporaries at the *lycée*, where, aside from editing magazines with Pushkin and paying tribute to his friend's genius in a poem, Delvig had excelled at storytelling games in which each of the other boys continued a tale started by one of his fellows. Pushkin had always valued his school friend's taste, and admired his poetry, and during 1815–16 Pushkin had written letters to Delvig's younger sister Masha.[29] Always a wit, Delvig had stamped the second issue of the manuscript journal 'Lycée Scholar' with the humorous inscription, 'Passed for publication by Censor Baron Delvig.'[30]

During Pushkin's dissipated years in St Petersburg Delvig was among his closest friends and the two of them, with Ivan Pushchin, had dressed up as 'rough people' in order to eat at a low tavern in Tolmazov Street. When Pushkin had his duel with another school friend, Kyukhelbecker, Delvig was Kyukhelbecker's second, and Pushkin incensed Kyukhelbecker by calling out, 'Delvig, stand with me. It's safer here.' Always an admirer of Pushkin's poetry, Delvig wrote to Pushkin in September 1824 that public opinion firmly supported him against Vorontsov, but advised him not to write 'anything careless' for a couple of years. For some time he had been promising Pushkin a visit. By 12 March 1824 he still had not done so, however, and Pushkin wrote to him in Vitebsk, only half-jokingly, 'Delvig, are you still alive?'

Delvig was famous not only for his wisdom and his kindness but also his laziness, which was the likeliest cause of his failure to respond to Pushkin's letters. He had, however, a technical mastery of many forms and was the first Russian poet to use the sonnet form gracefully in Russian. As Pushkin acknowledged in a moving tribute to him ten years after their schooldays came to an end, what he did well he did better than any. He was particularly gifted at epigrams and aphorisms, for instance:

> I have no fear of Death, and yet
> Will lose my body with regret.
> Who likes to think of throwing out
> Familiar clothes, although worn out?

Delvig was the editor of a yearly miscellany, and his house was the lively centre of witty and sophisticated friends.

When he did at last arrive, the young men spent days talking about literature and playing billiards, but Delvig stayed a disappointingly short while, and in a letter to Vyazemsky at the beginning of April 1825 Pushkin described how the young ladies of Trigorskoe had all fallen in love with him, while Delvig 'remained as indifferent as a block of wood ... since he was already engaged'.

With Delvig's departure, Pushkin was once again forced to return to correspondence and books for intellectual company. He was rarely solemn about his studies. On 14 March, writing to his brother to beg mustard, rum and pickles alongside the books he needed, he mentioned a collected edition of Russian verses, and commented, 'Seventy-five roubles is a lot. I wouldn't give that much for all Russia.' There were other visitors from his days at the lyceum, including the young poet Yazykov, in the summer of 1825. Yazykov's first poems had been encouraged by Delvig and he was a friend of Alexey Vulf. He went on to become a favourite poet of Nikolay Gogol.

In this period at Mikhaylovskoe, Pushkin was laying down the foundation of that great library of books from every important European language which can be seen to this day in his last apartment in St Petersburg. He had also begun to collect material on the rebellion of Emilyan Pugachev. This not only produced an excellent history of that period, but also formed the basis for Pushkin's remarkable novel *The Captain's Daughter*. It was fortunate that Pushkin had learned to trust his own literary judgement because not all his friends in St Petersburg saw *Evgeny Onegin* as an important poem. The literary editor Bestuzhev and the poet (and later Decembrist rebel) Ryleev found the early chapters altogether lacking in social awareness. Ryleev particularly urged Pushkin to resist the influence of Byron. It is sometimes forgotten, in the stress always given to Pushkin's pre-eminence, that there were other poets who could be regarded as his equals in some parts of the literary world, and there were those who took Ryleev very seriously, especially readers who admired the seriousness of his commitment to social improvement.

For his part, writing to his brother in February 1825, Pushkin had already suggested amusedly that Ryleev should include his grandfather Gannibal in the suite of Tsar Peter – 'His negro mug will have a curious effect on the whole picture of the battle of Poltava.' He wrote gently enough about Ryleev's poetry, saying he knew he was 'a poet at heart' and praising the originality of a bundle of poems Ryleev had sent to him, but he could not help remarking honestly, 'On the whole, they are weak in inventiveness and structure.' He ended his letter by saluting him as a fellow poet, but he was not diverted from his path by Ryleev's comments.

In response to Bestuzhev's criticism of *Onegin*, Pushkin wrote on 24 March 1825:

> Your letter is very intelligent, but all the same you are mistaken. All the same you are looking at *Onegin* from the wrong angle, all the same it is my best work. You compare the first chapter with *Don Juan*. Nobody esteems D.J. more than I do (the first five cantos, I haven't read the rest) but it has nothing in common with *Onegin*. You speak of the Englishman Byron's satire, and compare it to mine, and demand of mine the same qualities! No, my dear, you ask too much. Where is my *satire*? There isn't a trace of it in *Evgeny Onegin* ... Wait for the other cantos.[31]

It was at this period that Pushkin found the time to write down, in outline, a number of the folk tales he had heard from his nurse, Arina Rodionovna, whom he describes as his only real friend. He took particular delight in borrowing her peasant idiom and liked to repeat to his friends that she was the original of Tatyana's nurse. Most seriously of all, he continued to work at *Evgeny Onegin*.

For Pushkin was making use of his solitude in Mikhaylovskoe in a way not open to his hero, Evgeny, of whom Pushkin ironically observes that he was able to enjoy the beauties of lonely fields for no more than two days. Where Evgeny was bored by the lack of amusement in the country, Pushkin was turning all his experience there into poetry. He had already invented the flexibility and fluency of the Onegin stanza. Its fourteen lines, which resemble a sonnet in iambic tetrameter, have been brilliantly compared by Nabokov to a painted ball or top, 'its pattern visible at the start and finish but blurred in mid-spin'. In the first two chapters that form allowed Pushkin to play an ironic game in changes of stress and tone. Now that structure was to accommodate altogether darker material.

The four chapters of *Onegin* written in Mikhaylovskoe give the poem the force and economy of a novel rather than a picaresque romp held together only by the central character. *Onegin* becomes a psychological narrative in which the development of the action arises naturally from character. Pushkin has the social realism and subtle insights of a Jane

Austen. The dialogue continues to read as effortlessly as if a complex stanza were not being imposed upon it.

As chapter three opens Evgeny is bored, as he often is, and so, though he makes fun of the poet Lensky's enjoyment of simple family evenings at the Larins', agrees to visit the household as a diversion. There he observes the social rituals of the countryside – the dishes of preserves, the lingonberry wine, the unsophisticated conversation. Evgeny may be a snob but he is not without discrimination and, seeing Tatyana's silent wistfulness, is surprised at Lensky's preference for the far more ordinary Olga:

> Were I the poet, brother
> I'd choose the elder one instead.

The visit of such an eligible bachelor as Onegin inevitably causes a stir of gossip and speculation, and soon Tatyana has fallen in love with the handsome stranger. Once in love, Pushkin observes that her own dreams give Evgeny's face to the heroes of those favourite romances – often English novels – she loves so much. Pushkin pokes gentle fun at her admiration for the caprice, egotism and saturnine qualities of those heroes:

> It's now the British Muse's fables
> That lie on maidens' bedside tables.

For his part, he suggests, if he turned to prose he would prefer to write about an ordinary Russian life. Meanwhile, the details of the poem he is writing are marvellously sharp. The nurse, on her quilted cassock with a handkerchief on her head, mothers Tatyana in her sleeplessness, worries when she's feverish, makes the sign of the cross over her with a wrinkled hand and murmurs traditional blessings. She has the simple devotion of Arina Rodionovna, and something of the same sturdy common sense. When Tatyana begs her nurse to talk about her own experience of falling in love in days gone by, her nurse ridicules the idea:

> Oh come. Our world was quite another
> We'd never heard of it.

Tatyana's infatuation may be at first a creation of the books she has been reading, but what Pushkin makes his reader love in her is the absence of calculation. Once in love, she offers herself to Evgeny in a letter devoid of the least coquetry. Pushkin marvels at her innocent candour, contrasting it with the usual affectation of coldness and chastity adopted by social beauties only to lead their suitors on.

> The flirt will always reason coldly;
> Tatyana's love is deep and true:
> She yields without conditions, boldly –
> As sweet and trusting children do.

At first there is no reply to her letter. Pushkin paints a charming picture of Tatyana waiting at a window pane, breathing upon the chilly glass and tracing Evgeny's initials in the mist there, expecting him to appear whenever she hears the hoofbeats of a horse. In the event, she meets him by chance on a garden lane. Pushkin artfully closes the chapter without telling us how the meeting went.

Chapter four opens with an analysis of that deadness of the heart which characterises most Don Giovannis and particularly marks Evgeny's 'grumbling soul'. He is a jaded man, who no longer feels passionate even though he continues to pursue women:

> He sought them out with no elation
> And left them too without vexation
> Scarcely mindful of their love or spite
> Just so a casual guest at night
> Drops in for whist and joins routinely;
> And then upon the end of play,
> Just takes his leave and drives away.

Evgeny presents himself as so cynical and depraved a rake that he might well have been expected to take some casual advantage of the young girl whose attractions he had already noticed. He makes no attempt to do so. Rather, the tender simplicity of Tatyana's letter appeals to him just as it had affected Pushkin in writing it. When they meet in the garden he reacts to her candour with a confession of his own empty ability to feel deeply, albeit in a hurtfully patronising tone. Once in his stride he gives Tatyana a moral lecture on what marriage to a rake like himself was likely to involve. If he had ever thought to marry, Evgeny explains, she would have been his choice, but unfortunately he knows that marriage would destroy both of them because he would tire of her.

> In all the world what's more perverted
> Than homes in which the wretched wife

Bemoans her worthless mate, deserted
Alone, both day and night, through life.
Or where the husband, knowing truly
Her worth...
Is always angry, sullen, mute.

In his narrator's voice Pushkin reflects the while on the pleasure taken by friends in repeating the gossip of their intimates' misfortunes. It is a reflection he would have found time and again in the French *bons mots* of his adolescence. At this stage in his life nothing was further from Pushkin's own mind than matrimony, and he could hardly have been condemning Onegin for preserving his own bachelor freedom. Quite apart from Pushkin's involvement with the serf girl who was bearing his child, his own conduct towards Anna Vulf was rather less morally scrupulous than Onegin's. We may even be given an insight into Pushkin's own occasional feelings when he remarks,

But whom to love? To trust and treasure?
Who won't betray us in the end?
And who'll be kind enough to measure
Our words and deeds as we intend?
Who won't sow slander all about us?
To whom will all our faults be few?

When Pushkin concludes this passage by recommending to his reader a selfish cynicism, resembling Byron's, the irony is unmistakable.

Why spend your efforts all in vain:
Just love yourself and ease the pain ...
A worthy object! Never mind,
A truer love you'll never find.

Meanwhile, Evgeny falls into the life that Pushkin was living that very summer in Mikhaylovskoe – getting up at seven, swimming, then coming back to enjoy coffee over the latest reviews. When winter snows make such pleasures impossible Evgeny finds little to do but read Walter Scott, drink and play billiards. So it is that he accepts an invitation to Tatyana's nameday celebration, delivered by Lensky, by now only two weeks away from his marriage to Olga.

Chapter five opens like a fairy tale with a lovely description of a Russian winter: there is a child on a sledge, with his fingers freezing, and flashes of scarlet against winter trees. Tatyana, too much a prey to superstition to play at conjuring as village girls do on their nameday, nevertheless has a prophetic dream. Lost in some wintry landscape, a bear appears to help her cross a perilous bridge. Once on the other side of the bridge Tatyana flees, but finds the bear closely pursuing her and at last collapses in exhaustion. To her astonishment, the bear picks her up and carries her politely to his hut. She wakes to find herself surrounded by creatures as monstrous as any in Breughel's hell, guffawing and clapping. In the midst of this strange assembly of tusks and snouts she recognises Evgeny, who is evidently master of them all. Seeing Tatyana, he declares 'she's mine' and, as all the monsters leave the room, draws her gently to a makeshift bed. Before her dream can take this erotic suggestion further, Olga and Lensky appear, there is a furious argument and Evgeny snatches up a knife to stab Lensky.

Nothing in her book of dreams, which she turns to on waking, can give her reassurance. Her nameday begins ominously. At the feast Evgeny is placed opposite her at table. He sees her agitation but it makes him angry rather than compassionate and he gives her no more than a solemn bow when it is his turn to toast her. After the feast there is whist and dancing. With whimsical spite Evgeny invites Lensky's fiancée Olga to dance, and flirts with her when the dance ends. Olga blushes in appreciation of such flattering attentions, 'her prim conceited face alight'. Evgeny, in his boredom, is behaving with all the malice of Alexander Raevsky, finding some amusement in the ease of his conquest and seemingly indifferent to the pain of his friend's jealousy. When Lensky at last asks Olga for a dance, he is astonished to find she's promised yet another dance to Evgeny. Furious at her refusal, Lensky leaves the ball.

At the opening of chapter six Evgeny, once he observes that Lensky has left, grows bored with both his spiteful game and Olga, and leaves the ball himself. The next morning a note from Lensky brings a challenge to a duel. This Evgeny accepts, though he is by now a little ashamed of his own behaviour. Pushkin devises a situation which makes it impossible for him to patch up the quarrel with his friend by depicting the man who brings the challenge as a magnificent grotesque. Since this man is well known as a gossip, Evgeny is afraid he will spread slanderous tales about Evgeny's cowardice if he tries to call off the duel. Meanwhile, Lensky's anger with Olga cannot keep him from going to see her on the way to the appointed meeting place. When she greets him only with the simple query, 'Why did you leave last night so early?' he realises at once that she still loves him. This restores him to happiness, but not to forgiveness of Evgeny. The duel proceeds.

Pushkin gives a marvellous description of pistols being prepared, the balls going into place, streams of greyish powder settling inside the pans and flints screwed fast to metal. Then the steps are paced off and Evgeny fires first. With that single shot, Lensky falls dead. The heart that had been so full of passion and poetry only a few moments before is now silent 'as in a house deserted'.[32]

That single image of an abandoned house, a body once alive and now dead, echoes through the reader's mind. Reading these lines, with the knowledge of Pushkin's own death in a duel in the snow at 37, it is hard to avoid a shiver at so strange a prescience.

Evgeny is stricken at the sight of his friend's lifeless body, and Pushkin asks his readers to consider their own likely reactions:

> Well, tell me: what would you ... inside
> Be thinking of ... or merely feeling
> Were your good friend before you now,
> Stretched out with death upon his brow?

Pushkin chides them with too easy a lament for a poet who might have written great verse, pointing out he was equally likely to have dwindled into a bored, gout-ridden forty-year-old. For himself, he adds, bringing the chapter to an end before we can discover any more about the fate of the other characters, 'The years to solemn prose incline me.'

In the next verse he reflects,

> And is there no return of youth?
> Shall I be thirty soon, in truth?

Pushkin was no more than 26, yet this melancholy reflection suggests that the life of uncommitted flirtation had begun to pall. Certainly, in the exhilaration of his recent work, particularly *Onegin*, he was now impatient with his own earlier verse, which appeared in 1825 in an edition put together by Pletnev. Writing of this jocularly to his brother on 27 March 1825, Pushkin suggested a series of disclaimers which should have gone into the foreword: 'Many of these poems are rubbish and do not deserve the attention of the Russian public, but as they have been printed by God knows whom, and the devil knows under what titles, with the compositor's corrections and the publisher's mistakes ... here they are and gobble them up ...'

On 25 August Pushkin concluded the sixth chapter of *Evgeny Onegin* with the death of Lensky. However, he had not lost his pleasure in amusing verse. It is to this period that we owe the charming tale of *Count Nulin*, which was written very quickly – in two mornings, it is said. It is both a charming parody of Shakespeare's *The Rape of Lucrece* and a light-hearted account of the hidden immorality among the bored gentry of the countryside. The master of the house goes off with his hunting dogs in September, leaving his young wife alone to savour 'mud, sleet and the distant howl of wolves'. Pushkin lists what might be his heroine Natasha's occupations – salting mushrooms or feeding geese, for instance – then confesses that she entirely ignores her domestic duties, preferring to read novels.

Hearing the sound of an overturned coach, she senses a possible diversion and sends her servant to urge the unfortunate traveller in for dinner. Count Nulin, the visitor, is something of a dandy. He has a French valet but little money since he has squandered his inheritance on the hats, fans, waistcoats, cufflinks and other appurtenances of fashion which accompany him on his travels. Like his hostess, he reads romances and enjoys arias from Rossini. Once changed, he takes supper with Natasha. She asks solicitously about his wounds, and he explains how much he misses Paris, delighted the while by her charms. At twelve o'clock she wishes the Count goodnight, giving his hand a gentle squeeze when he bends over her. He is to be forgiven for imagining this as an invitation to further dalliance.

Natasha is undressed for bed by her maid Parasha, but the Count finds it difficult either to concentrate on Walter Scott or go to sleep. At length Nulin puts on his striped silk dressing-gown and goes off to find her bedroom. Pushkin explicitly and ironically compares Nulin to Tarquin and Natasha to Lucretia.

Natasha is either asleep or pretending to be so when Nulin falls to his knees at her side. In response to his protestations of love, however, Natasha lands him a good hard blow on the ear. Soon after this the noise of her maid Parasha's footsteps puts Natasha's would-be ravisher to flight. There is more than a hint that Nulin goes on to spend the rest of the night with Parasha instead.

Over breakfast next morning Natasha is sanguine and once again flirtatious with Nulin, but they are interrupted by the return of her husband. Count Nulin takes his leave. That might seem to be that, but the tale has a sting in its ending.

Away our hero's carriage rolled.
Natalya Pavlovna soon told
Her husband, neighbours, everyone
About his enterprise so bold.
But who laughed more than anyone
To hear Natalya Pavlovna?
No one will guess. How can that be?
Her husband surely? No, not he...
No, Lidin laughed most heartily
A neighbour aged but twenty three.
My friends, we may now truly say
That faithful wives are found today.[33]

For all this miraculous outpouring of poetry which his solitude had made possible, Pushkin continued to dream of escaping from his exile at Mikhaylovskoe. In spring 1825 he revived the idea of using his varicose veins, still referred to as an aneurysm, to help him do so and drafted a letter to the Tsar to ask for permission to travel abroad for treatment. He also circulated the rumour of his 'aneurysm' among as many of his friends as possible. In May 1825 Zhukovsky wrote anxiously to inquire about this illness, begging Pushkin to reply as seriously as possible.

I have heard from your mother and your brother that you are ill. Is it true? Is it true that in your legs you have something like an aneurysm, and that for ten years you have amused yourself with this guest without saying a word to anyone?[34]

Zhukovsky can hardly have failed to remember that the same illness had been mentioned by Pushkin when he wanted to leave Odessa. Pushkin replied to the letter with complete frankness. His varicose veins could easily wait for treatment, but Mikhaylovskoe was suffocating him and he longed for permission to go abroad. Both Zhukovsky and Karamzin encouraged Pushkin's mother to write an emotional letter to the Tsar on the poet's behalf, asking permission for Pushkin to travel to Riga to consult a specialist there. This request was refused, though he was graciously allowed to travel as far as Pskov.

Pushkin was furious at the prospect of treatment in Pskov.

I have checked about the Pskov doctors; they informed me that there is a certain Vsevolod there; a very clever vet and famous in the learned world for his book on the curing of horses.[35]

Several of his plans to escape from Mikhaylovskoe were little more than fantasy. In one elaborate scheme he planned to go abroad to Dorpat disguised as Alexey Vulf's servant and thereafter to join the revolutionary thinker Chaadaev wherever he might be staying in Europe. His brother knew of the plan, and probably talked about it unwisely in St Petersburg. Even if he had not, Pushkin's own letters to his brother, in which he speaks of his need for a travelling bag and a book on long-distance horseback riding, as well as a wish to avoid the usual routes, would have given the game away to any curious intercepting eye. These were hardly the requests of a man seriously in need of an operation.

In the event, Zhukovsky pre-empted Pushkin's plan by arranging for Dr Moier, who was a relation of his, to travel to Pskov in order to treat him. Hearing of this, Pushkin excused himself from the operation on the grounds that it was dangerous. 'It is all the same,' he mournfully concluded, 'to die from boredom or from an aneurysm, but the first is more infallible than the other.'

Pushkin continued to write impudent letters to Anna Kern, and though at this time she inspired him with a genuine passion he did not pretend that what he loved was her mind or her character.

> You tell me that I do not know your character. Of what import is your character to me? I do not deride it at all. Ought pretty women to have a character? The essentials are eyes, teeth, hands, feet. (I would add the heart, but your cousin Anna Vulf has overused this word ... I have behaved like a child of fourteen with you.)[36]

This emphasis on a woman's physical appearance above all other qualities markedly contrasts with Pushkin's concern for his heroine Tatyana's inner being in *Evgeny Onegin*. Pushkin was untouched by the least feminist sentiment, but he recognised qualities of soul in either sex. In the same letter Pushkin suggests a way in which Anna Petrovna might arrange a return to Trigorskoe, even as he betrays his own continuing jealousy of Alexey Vulf. 'I do not know why, but I do not like these students any more than I do Mr Kern.'

In a later letter he writes:

> Farewell. It is now night and your image appears to me, all sad and voluptuous; I see your glance, your mouth half-opened. Farewell, I believe myself at your feet. I press them, I feel your knees – I would give all my blood for one minute of reality.[37]

Anna Kern was at this time considering some way of separating from her husband, and Pushkin wrote,

> If monsieur your husband bores you too much, leave him; but do you know how? Leave the whole family, take the post to Ostrov and you will arrive – where? At Trigorskoe? Not at all. But at Mikhaylovskoe. This is the fine project which has plagued my imagination for the last quarter of an hour. Yet imagine what would be my happiness. You will say: 'But the explosion, the scandal?' What the devil! Upon leaving a husband the scandal is complete, the rest is of no consequence.[38]

It was not until October that Anna managed to visit Trigorskoe again, and she arrived most decorously with her husband. The occasion for her visit was as follows. Osipova had left Riga after discovering both the correspondence with Pushkin and her son Alexey's interest in Anna Petrovna. In September Pushkin pleaded with Anna Petrovna both to make peace with her aunt and to stop writing to Alexey Vulf. Anna persuaded her husband the General that only she could make peace between Osipova and herself, and so for a few days they visited Trigorskoe on a mission to do so. Notwithstanding the presence of the General, Pushkin saw Anna alone several times, according to her reminiscences, and in a letter written after that brief visit Pushkin writes of her as 'an angel fate sends to delight my solitude'. In a postscript he added,

> I take up my pen again to tell you that I am at your knees, that I love you always, that sometimes I detest you, as the day before yesterday when I said horrid things about you, that I kiss your beautiful hands, that I kiss them again in the hope of something better, that I can do no more...[39]

The ambivalence of this postscript is marked in the tone of all his letters to her – a mixture of tender desire and teasing which accords perfectly well with a casual letter to Alexey Vulf of 1826 in which Pushkin refers to Anna Petrovna without reverence as 'our whore of Babylon'. This letter to Anna was the last of a series, and coincided with the quite unexpected death of Alexander I.

All Pushkin's manoeuvrings to return to the capital were brought to an abrupt end by news of the Tsar's death at Taganrog, on the sea of Azov. This was a completely unlooked-for turn of events. The Tsar had travelled to Taganrog on account of his wife's health rather than his own. News of his death took until 27 November 1825 to reach St

Petersburg, and three more days to reach Mikhaylovskoe. When Pushkin heard that the ruler who had kept him away from St Petersburg for six years was dead, he was much agitated, at first simply with the hope of an end to his exile.

On 1 December Pushkin set out towards St Petersburg under the name of one of Osipova's servants. His motives are not entirely clear. Simmons suggests that Ivan Pushchin had summoned him to St Petersburg. Nothing in Ivan's earlier behaviour suggests this is at all likely, but there were many other possible reasons for Pushkin's excited departure. Moreover, the rapid change of mind – Pushkin returned to Mikhaylovskoe without finishing his journey, convinced that a brace of hares and a priest were unlucky omens – does not suggest he was honourably committed to some revolutionary enterprise. His letter on 4–6 December to his publisher, Pletnev, on receiving the news that Alexander I had died, suggests both his lack of awareness of the impending rebellion and the limits of his own expectation of change.

> For God's sake don't let them ask the Tsar to allow me to live in Opochka or Riga. What the devil's the good of them? *He must be asked for permission for me to go either to the capital or abroad.*[40]

For once Pushkin's superstitions were entirely well founded. Those hares running across his path saved his life. For both the southern society, of which Pushkin had lived ignorantly on the periphery, and the northern society, which included many of his close friends, saw their chance of revolution that December. The succession to the throne was uncertain – Alexander had no sons and his heir should have been his brother Constantine. Constantine, however, was married to a Polish Roman Catholic and had renounced the throne in favour of his younger brother Nicholas. His abdication remained secret. Both brothers were unpopular, but Nicholas was more feared.

Had Pushkin continued his journey he would have arrived in St Petersburg on the evening of 13 December and probably gone straight to his friend Ryleev's house. He would then have been present at the meeting of the Decembrists at which the rebels decided to set up a provisional government and declare the emancipation of the serfs. Instead, Pushkin was in Mikhaylovskoe when the news came of the revolt in St Petersburg.

The rebels had no real plan other than to take advantage of the confusion at the centre of power. A sentence, attributed to Ryleev, makes plain they had no conviction that they would succeed: 'Nevertheless we must make a beginning, something will come out of it.'[41]

The whole rising was badly co-ordinated. The conspirators had elected Prince Trubetskoy, the most senior army officer among them, as their commander. The 14th of December had been fixed as the day for the ceremony of an oath of allegiance to Nicholas. The Decembrists planned for all the regiments who supported them to come on to Senate Square, where they would shout for Constantine and a constitution. Of the sixteen regiments of guards stationed at St Petersburg, only one battalion and a few companies joined the rebels. Trubetskoy failed even to appear at the scene, and the rebel soldiers, given no leadership, took no action.

Once it was obvious that the rebels were not going to attack, Nicholas, who had been stricken with terror at first, plucked up his courage and ordered his supporters to open fire. The mutineers dispersed after the first few shots. Trubetskoy gave himself up to the police long before the day was lost. Within two hours all the rebels were arrested.

Nicholas's response to his easy victory was brutal. The interrogation of the conspirators themselves and of several others was extremely thorough, and lasted until June 1826. According to Mirsky, the Tsar handled some of the questioning himself with considerable charm and cunning and in this way produced several confessions and even apostasies, though no sentences were reduced as a result. By the end of that month the leaders of the conspiracy had been condemned to death by hanging, drawing and quartering. Nicholas later commuted that sentence to hanging alone. Those he sentenced to death included Colonel Pestel, whom Pushkin had met and liked in Odessa, and Ryleev, the poet with whom Pushkin had long been in correspondence. He also sentenced 120 of the conspirators, all members of the gentry, to hard labour with deportation. Among those who were sent to Siberia were some of Pushkin's closest friends, including Ivan Pushchin, his other school friend Kyukhelbecker, Alexander Bestuzhev, co-editor with Ryleev of the *Polar Star* and General Prince Sergey Volkonsky, who had so recently married Maria Raevskaya.

The executions were carried out on 13 July, and were bungled so horrendously that three of the rebels had to be hanged twice. On the same day over one hundred of the finest officers sentenced to penal servitude in Serbia began their journey, which itself lasted over a year, into exile. One hundred and twenty non-commissioned soldiers of the Chernigov Regiment were condemned to strokes of the birch that killed or maimed them, and a further 376 were stripped of medals and insignia and sent in carts to the Caucasus.

Pushkin knew all the most prominent of the conspirators, and had been in correspondence with them up to the very outbreak of the insurrection. When the news broke of their arrest and interrogation he had good reason to be alarmed. His own arrest seemed imminent and he burned his memoirs in case anything in them might implicate either his friends or himself.

Isolated as he was in Mikhaylovskoe, and now without many of his correspondents, Pushkin for several months had no clear idea of what was happening in St Petersburg. Nevertheless, sketches in both the Second and Third Masonic Notebooks show some of his thoughts and apprehensions. In the margins of the fifth chapter of *Onegin* in the Second Masonic Notebook there are self-portraits of Pushkin in Jacobin dress, portraits of Pestel and Ryleev, Ivan Pushchin and Kyukhelbecker. He was afraid to trust letters to the post since they might be intercepted, and waited until the second half of January before even getting in touch with Zhukovsky via someone travelling to St Petersburg. This letter was written at a time when he had not yet heard anything but rumours about the fate of his friends.

> It is difficult for me to ask you to intercede for me with the Emperor ... Probably the government are satisfied already that I did not belong to the conspiracy ... but it has published its ban on all those who, knowing anything of the conspiracy, did not report to the police. But just who except the police and the government did not know of it? The conspiracy was discussed at every street corner, and this is one of the reasons why I consider myself innocent ... It may easily happen that I shall be charged with political conversations with this or that one of the accused. Many of them were my friends. (n.b. Is it true that both the Raevskys are taken and are they really in the Fortress? Please write about this.)[42]

At that very moment the Commission of Inquiry had begun their examination of many of those under arrest, who were being asked how they had first been introduced to liberal ideas. Many of them, under questioning, named Pushkin's 'Ode to Freedom' as having influenced them. Baron Delvig, Zhukovsky and Vyazemsky were all anxious about Pushkin's new situation.

Pushkin wrote to Baron Delvig in February 1826:

Of course I am not implicated in anything, and if the government has time to think about me, it will be easily convinced on that score. But I somehow feel ashamed to petition, particularly at the present moment. My cast of mind is known. Having been persecuted for the last six years, disgraced by dismissal from the service, exiled into the depths of the country for two lines in an intercepted letter, I certainly couldn't feel kindly disposed to the late Tsar, though I fully acknowledge his true merits. But I never preached either rebellion or revolution – on the contrary.[43]

To Zhukovsky, Pushkin wrote straightforwardly, reminding him that his exile was due to no more than 'a thoughtless opinion, worthy, of course, of the disapprobation of anyone', but to this letter Zhukovsky replied on 12 April:

You have not been involved in anything – that is true. But in the papers of each of the active figures your verses have been discovered. This is a bad way to make friends with the government.[44]

Pushkin's emotions alternated between febrile suspense and stunned misery. He refused to allow his new publisher, Pletnev, to publish more of Onegin, still less *Boris Godunov* since, as Pushkin wrote on 7 March 1826, 'In my Boris they swear obscenely in all languages. It is not a tragedy suitable for the fair sex.' He was irritable and unhappy even before the news of the fate of his friends.

Pushkin's strongest wish was to escape from Russia, as he wrote to Vyazemsky on 27 May from Pskov. He could not understand how anyone who had any choice would wish to remain.

How can you, who are not on a leash, remain in Russia? If the Tsar grants me liberty, I won't stay a month. We live in a miserable age, but when I think of London, of railways, steamships, English journals or Paris theatres and brothels, then my remote Mikhaylovskoe fills me with melancholy fury. In the fourth canto of Onegin I have described my life; some time you will read it and will ask with a charming smile, 'And where is my poet? He has marked talent.' And, my dear, you will hear the reply: 'He has fled to Paris and will never return to accursed Russia – oh, the clever lad!'[45]

That charmingly imagined vision of freedom and the rich variety of life in Western Europe was never to be realised. Nicholas was victorious. The new Tsar proceeded to set up a Department of Secret Police, designed to be far more efficient than that of Alexander I, and set over it one of his most trusted advisors, Count Benckendorf, a formidable figure. It was he who had discovered the Decembrist conspiracy under Alexander I even before the revolt took place.

When the news of the Tsar's sentences reached Mikhaylovskoe, Pushkin was stricken with a horror which was never to leave him for the rest of his life. In the Third Masonic Notebook, which contains a fair copy of chapters five, six and seven of *Onegin*, even as the plot darkens towards the duel and death of Lensky, there on folio 37, under the scrawled line, 'And I, like a clown, might have hanged,'[46] is a sketch of a fortress gate, a scaffold and five swinging corpses. On the same folio are a dozen profiles including possibly one of Pushkin's father and his uncle Vasily, both of whom would, no doubt, have been implicated in Pushkin's own punishment.

By a curious coincidence, he heard of the execution of those sentenced to death and the deportation of close friends, including Ivan Pushchin, the day after he had learned of the death in Italy and in poverty of the tubercular Amalia Riznich, for whom he had felt such passionate jealousy in Odessa. The strange blunting of his feeling about the news of her death, which he describes in his elegy for her, is closely connected with the discovery of his friends' fate:

> Beneath the blue sky of her own country
>   She grew sick, and withered...
> Even now, perhaps, her young ghost
>   Above me still hovers.
> Yet now I feel only our separation.
>   I cannot rouse more feeling
> Than those lips, without the least emotion,
>   Which gave me news of her death.
> Yet she was someone I once loved with passion,
>   With daily tension and anxiety;
> For whom I felt tender unhappiness,
>   Pain and even madness.
> Where is that torment and affection? Sadly
>   For her too trusting spirit, see,
> The sweet memory of days gone by stirs
>   Neither tears nor reproach in me.

His own fate was about to be decided. Far from agreeing to let Russia's most celebrated poet escape abroad, the new Tsar summoned Pushkin to appear before him. On 3 September 1826 he received the following instructions:

Mr Pushkin may travel in his own equipage at freedom, not in the position of prisoner, and under the escort of the courier only; upon his arrival in Moscow he must present himself at once to the General of the day at the Staff Headquarters of his Imperial Majesty.[47]

CHAPTER NINE

Pushkin and the Tsar

Shortly after Pushkin left Mikhaylovskoe, Arina Rodionovna appeared at Trigorskoe, sobbing and out of breath, to tell the Osipov family about the messenger who had come to take the poet away to Moscow. Knowing the danger in which his writing had put him four years earlier, the family asked immediately if any papers had been confiscated. Arina Rodionovna was able to reassure them nothing had been taken away and no papers destroyed. She added without apology that she herself had destroyed the German cheese Pushkin loved as she found the smell so vile.[1]

Her distress was personal and unfeigned, and something of the love between her and the child she had always mothered is visible in a letter dictated and sent to Pushkin some time after this.

> My beloved friend Alexander Sergeevich, I received the letter and the money which you sent to me. For all your kindnesses, I thank you with all my heart. You are constantly in my heart and mind, and only when I sleep will I forget you and your kindnesses to me ... Come to us at Mikhaylovskoe, my angel, I will get all the horses ready for the road ... For your health I have prepared a wafer and said prayers – live well, little friend, let us love one another. I am in good health, thank God.[2]

Pushkin well knew how much Arina Rodionovna worried for him, as a little poem written in 1826 shows.

True friend in all my time of trouble,
Dear frail companion, all alone
You languish in your woodland hovel,
Watching, waiting for my return;
You worry, peering through the glass,
Always on edge you look and linger.
Your needles, as the minutes pass,
Stir slowly in your worn old fingers.[3]

For all the enormous danger he was in, Pushkin was sufficiently cheery
on the way to Pskov to scratch a scurrilous quatrain on the glass of the
tavern where he ate while waiting for his horses to be changed. But there
were five hundred miles between Pskov and Moscow and he had plenty
of time to wonder how the new Tsar was likely to behave towards
him. Unlike his brother Constantine, Nicholas had no reputation for
liberalism, nor had he shown any clemency to the rebels. He was well
aware of what the French revolution had done to Louis XVI and the
dangers any similar revolt might present to himself.

The previous six months had seen Pushkin change his mind often
about his own likely treatment. As late as August he still believed in a
possible amnesty for the conspirators sent to Siberia. He could hardly
fail, however, to ponder his own fate now alongside that of his Decembrist friends. He knew he had been named by many of those questioned –
along with Voltaire and Rousseau – as an inspiration of liberal thought.
He had already been punished for liberal opinions. The conspirators had
not indeed confided in him, but it would be hard to establish as much.

Such natural anxiety did not spring from any lack of courage, but he
had no wish for martyrdom. What he wrote in a letter of 7 March
remained his attitude: 'Whatever may have been the form of my thoughts,
political and religious, I will preserve in its integrity, but I have no desire
to oppose foolishly the generally accepted order and necessity.'

Pushkin arrived in Moscow on 8 September, having spent four days
on the journey. He was unshaven, dirty and tired when he appeared at
the office of the Chief of the General Staff, Baron Dibich, who ordered
him to present himself in his Imperial Majesty's study in the Chudov
Palace at four o'clock. Pushkin was still in his travelling clothes when he
and Nicholas I spent a famous hour alone together.

Pushkin was very much in the position of a supplicant. Moreover,
Nicholas I was an impressive figure of a man, taller than Pushkin by

nearly twelve inches. He had a handsome profile, with Germanic rather than Slav features, and a fine military air. Twenty years afterwards Queen Victoria noted the Tsar's appearance as 'magnificent still and very striking'. Pushkin, in contrast, was unkempt and 'an almost small man of medium build, restless, with long hair, rather curly at the ends', as an admirer, Mikhail Pogodin, the editor of the *Moscow Telegraph*, noted when meeting the poet two days later.[4]

The difference in physical stature, dress and authority, moreover, was in no way balanced by Nicholas's recognition of Pushkin's genius as a poet. Nicholas had little interest in literature, unlike his predecessor who had read widely. Nicholas, however, had been much impressed by the widespread influence of Pushkin's poetry among the conspirators and was well aware of Pushkin's popularity among the whole of the small educated class. The last thing he wanted was to take any action that would gratuitously antagonise those families which had already been traumatised by the severity of his response to the Decembrist revolt. The Tsar had his own inner uncertainties, too, in the autumn of 1826, for all his self-assured manner. He had immediate problems to face in the Balkans, the Caucasus and Poland. He had ascended the throne with blood on his hands and a memory he was never to forget of a hostile mob in Senate Square. He knew he was unpopular, 'that his coronation had been lack-lustre. Above all, he showed himself throughout his life to be an *actor*, and he had not yet found himself a role ... he was a Tsar who had begun his reign with executions and exiles. He craved popularity.'[5] For all these reasons, he might well have decided in advance to pardon a poet whom both Zhukovsky and Karamzin assured him could be an ornament to his reign as a gesture towards erasing his image as a cruel oppressor.

Of the favourable impression Pushkin made on the Tsar, the only evidence is that of D. Bludov, a Russian general, as retold by Bartenev.[6] The evening after his meeting with Pushkin, Nicholas met Bludov at a ball of the French Ambassador and said, 'Do you know that today I had a long talk with the most intelligent man in Russia?' The words were evidently spoken on the spur of the moment and, however genuinely meant at the time, Nicholas never repeated this opinion and remained indifferent both to Pushkin's poetry and his difficulties for the ten remaining years of the poet's life.

How did Pushkin conduct himself in the interview? He was not notably guarded in conversation. There is a tradition, Mirsky reports, that the

Tsar put Pushkin so much at ease that the poet forgot all etiquette, 'leant back against the table and continued conversing with the Monarch in this irreverent posture until he was gently rebuked by Nicholas'.[7]

In fact, there are at least 29 accounts of what happened when Pushkin met the Tsar on 8 September 1826.[8] What actually was said in the conversation cannot be certainly known since they spoke alone but there is surprising consensus on the main points covered – Pushkin's friendship with the Decembrists, Nicholas's future policy and his decision to act as the final arbiter of the poems Pushkin could publish.

What is most fascinating is to imagine how Pushkin made any favourable impression on the young Tsar. Pushkin's thoughts on the need for reform in Russia were not likely to impress, though Nicholas is supposed to have said to him,

> You hate me because I have crushed the party to which you belonged. But, believe me, I also love Russia, I am no enemy to the Russian people. I desire its freedom, but first it must be strengthened.[9]

One thing all commentators agree about is that Nicholas asked Pushkin if he were not a friend of many of the conspirators who had been sent to Siberia. To this, Pushkin bravely replied, 'It is true. I loved and esteemed many of them, and continue to nourish the same feelings.'[10]

At this point Nicholas is said to have asked the poet what he would have done if he had been in St Petersburg on 14 December, and Pushkin frankly admitted he would have been in the ranks of the rebels on Senate Square. He could have done no other. Friendship and loyalty were matters of patrician honour to Pushkin.[11]

Neither the Tsar nor the poet ever denied this exchange, and the very boldness and frankness of Pushkin's admission may have struck the Tsar favourably. Yuri Lotman suggests, however, that what so moved the Tsar with a sense of Pushkin's intelligence was that he intuited the very centre of Nicholas's anxiety.

> Wishing to urge the young Tsar towards the path of reform and to show him a lofty historical example, Pushkin turned his attention to the similarity of his position with that of Peter the Great in 1698, who also began his reign with great bloodshed and turmoil. In doing so he presented the Tsar with a role precisely at the moment when the Tsar did not have one formulated.[12]

It would have been an act of genius to present a mirror to Nicholas I in which he could read an image of himself in the likeness of Peter the Great. If Pushkin did so, however, he would have been reporting no more than what he wished to believe was possible. Yuri Lotman suggests Pushkin's hope arose naturally out of his own recent studies of Russian history.

At some point in the conversation the Tsar raised the question of what Pushkin was writing, and Pushkin said that he wrote little because the censorship was too severe and banned the most innocent works indiscriminately. Nicholas replied, 'You will send me everything you write and from now on I will be your censor.' This, which seemed to guarantee Pushkin the possibility of once again living by his writing, was one of the main reasons that Pushkin left the Imperial study in such euphoria.

The Tsar led Pushkin into an adjoining room and declared to those assembled there, 'Gentlemen, here is the new Pushkin for you, let us forget about the old.' Pushkin was apparently overcome with tears of relief and rushed to his uncle's house to tell him the joyful news.

The outcome of the interview, then, appeared at first altogether favourable. At the end of it Pushkin was free to go anywhere in the Empire he chose with the exception of St Petersburg and though he could only visit that city with special permission Pushkin had no sense that it would be unreasonably refused.

One thing which might even then have been completely undone Pushkin's hopes of forgiveness, however, was his celebrated poem on André Chenier, the French poet who died in 1794 on the guillotine. In part of this poem Pushkin speaks of the *'triste et captif'* lyre of the dead poet, and praises him rather than Byron, for whom the whole world is grieving:

> To me, another ghost calls out
> Too long unmourned, too long unwept,
> Who came down from the blood-stained block
> To find the shelter of the grave.
>
> A singer once of love and trees.
> I carry flowers for his tomb.
> He will not recognise my lyre.
> You and he both hear my song.

This had been published in a censored form in January 1826, long before the Decembrist revolt. There was an uncensored manuscript in circulation, however, to which copies of Ryleev's last letter to his wife had been added in some versions, and this might easily have made the poem seem to refer to the events of 14 December. This possibility might even have been in the Tsar's mind for the police would certainly have brought the matter to his attention in August. If the subject arose in conversation, Pushkin would have been able to prove the poem was written at the earlier date. If it did not arise, however, Nicholas might well have continued to suspect the poet even as he appeared to pardon him.

In any event, Pushkin's triumph was short-lived. He had come to Moscow with the new work that excited him more than any other, *Boris Godunov*. From this he gave a reading on 10 September at the house of Sobolevsky, who had been at school with his brother Lev, and on 12 October at the house of Dmitry Vladimirovich Venevitinov, whose collection of 'Articles about *Evgeny Onegin*' Pushkin had read in April 1825 in Mikhaylovskoe. When Pushkin returned from exile Venevitinov was only 21 years old, and Pushkin much wanted to meet him. The two men were distant cousins and took to each other immediately. There is a profile portrait which represents Venevitinov as a young man with a delicate face and the words 'Evgeny Onegin as Pushkin imagined him' beneath it.[13]

Pushkin's second *Boris Godunov* reading produced, as Pogodin records, a powerful effect on his listeners:

Some of us flushed; others shivered. It was impossible to contain oneself. One man would suddenly jump up from his chair, another would cry out.

When the reading came to an end, Pushkin was deluged with tears, congratulations and champagne and, fired by enthusiasm, continued the evening by reading other poems.

Boris Godunov had not, however, been submitted to the Tsar for approval, and when news of the readings came to the ears of the police, Benckendorf wrote to inquire why. Pushkin, who had either not realised that a reading in a friend's house was the same as publication, or had not yet grasped that even in a group of friends there was likely to be someone on the payroll of the secret police, was dumbfounded at how quickly he had managed to put himself in the wrong. Meekly, he submitted his manuscript for Imperial attention.

The Tsar then showed himself altogether incapable of grasping the literature he had offered to peruse. When Benckendorf returned the manuscript three weeks later on 14 December 1826 Nicholas had appended a note in his own hand. 'I consider that Mr Pushkin's aim would have been achieved if he had, with the *necessary expurgations*, changed his comedy into a historical narrative or novel in the manner of Walter Scott.' Since Pushkin's interest in the form of his play, with its Shakespearean mixture of prose and poetry and use of historical material, was paramount, he was much discomfited by this evidence of the Tsar's lack of literary sophistication. It augured ill for the benefits of Nicholas as censor. However, even without the Tsar's comments, *Godunov* was not destined to revolutionise the stage in Russia, as Pushkin had hoped, nor was it again to receive such another ecstatic reception in Pushkin's lifetime.

On 3 January 1827 Pushkin replied to Count Benckendorf respectfully, agreeing that 'as the Emperor thought fit to remark, it resembles a historical novel rather than a tragedy. I regret that it is beyond my powers to change what I have written.'[14]

Pushkin was open to the point of rashness. The Tsar, however, was not. Four months after the conversation with Pushkin the Tsar, for all his apparent benevolence, responded to Pushkin's mother, who had written to request a formal pardon, with a refusal. In a letter to the young poet Yazykov, Pushkin continued to repeat his belief that 'The Tsar has freed me from the censorship.' He had not yet fully realised how little would be changed for the better by having the Tsar as his censor. Everything he had sent to the censorship by the usual channels now had to be sent to the Tsar directly but this, in practice, meant the scrutiny of Count Benckendorf, head of the secret police.

CHAPTER TEN

Moscow

Pushkin's reputation was now at its height. He was, by common consent, the grandest literary lion of his day, and he revelled in the chance to talk to his friends once more, and add new ones. He was recognised wherever he went – audiences in the theatre pointed him out to one another and his presence was sought after by the most distinguished families.[1] The journalist V. V. Izmailov, too ill to witness Pushkin's triumph in person, wrote, 'I envy Moscow. It has crowned an emperor, now it crowns a poet.'[2]

Pushkin stayed in the Hotel Europa at first, then soon moved to the apartments of S. A. Sobolevsky, whom Pushkin nicknamed 'Falstaff' or 'Caliban'. Sobolevsky worked in the Department of Foreign Affairs, but as his nicknames suggest he enjoyed a rakish and frequently intoxicated life. He also loved poetry, and belonged to a set of intellectuals much influenced by German romanticism who called themselves 'Lovers of Wisdom'. Among these was the same Dmitry Venevitinov, at whose house Pushkin had read his *Boris Godunov*, and Pogodin, who had recorded his response to it. Pushkin's own mind was little inclined towards German metaphysics, though he relished one of Schelling's doctrines, which made the poet altogether independent from the judgements of the crowd.

Pushkin expressed to his many new friends the warmth of his gratitude to the Tsar, and at first the Third Section of His Majesty's Private Chancery, presided over by Count Benckendorf, inconvenienced him little. Moreover, whatever grief he felt for his exiled friends, the loyalty he now demonstrated to Nicholas was sincere. Given a test of his political trustworthiness in the shape of a report on possible reforms of the educational system, Pushkin carried the work out diligently, though in due course the Emperor objected that it laid too much stress on talent and knowledge and not enough on discipline and sound morality.

Nevertheless, Pushkin remained under careful scrutiny by Benckendorf's spies. It is chilling to reflect that even the Soviet system was hardly more efficient in finding people willing to act as informers. A police report to Benckendorf notes that 'the ladies spoil and flatter the young man'.[3] Fame was a potent aphrodisiac. All Pushkin's words were noted and reported back, and this was admitted in a note from Benckendorf to Pushkin after the *Boris Godunov* readings. Benckendorf complained that a letter of his had not been acknowledged and observed shamelessly that he knew Pushkin had received the letter 'for you have spoken about its contents to certain persons'.

Pushkin was at first too dizzy with Moscow festivities to be much oppressed by this. There were the balls of the nobility, with guests numbering a thousand, which required an immense riding school to be turned into a hall, and feasts which involved a mile of tables where, as he put it in a letter to Praskovya Osipova, still at Trigorskoe, 'meat pies have been provided like lumber'. Even more than these huge celebrations, he enjoyed the gatherings of the beautiful Princess Zinaida Volkonskaya, herself a poet and singer, whose salons attracted intellectuals and artists from many countries.

Princess Zinaida was a dazzlingly beautiful woman of considerable wealth, nicknamed 'La Corrinne du Nord'. Her house was decorated with painting and sculpture from all over the world. She wrote both prose and poetry, and had a passionate love of music. She arranged concerts at her house, and even played the part of Tancred in Rossini's opera, 'impressing everyone by her skilful acting and amazing voice.'[4] Operas were staged at her house all through the winter, and she gathered everyone who was brilliant in Moscow society to enjoy these performances. The young and talented poet, Venevitinov, loved her passionately and dedicated melancholy poems to her before his tragically early death.

Among her guests was the great Polish poet, Mickiewicz, and he and Pushkin became friends for a time. The Polish poet wrote home to a friend that he had become acquainted with Pushkin, and added, 'Pushkin is almost my equal ... In conversation he is very clever and ardent and knows contemporary literature well; his idea of poetry is pure and elevating.'⁵

In Princess Zinaida's salons no one played cards, but not all the entertainment there was cultural. There were charades, for instance, in which Pushkin took part with great enthusiasm. Once he was given the role of the rock in the desert during the migration of the Hebrews, which must have seemed an almost impossible task to represent. Pushkin covered himself with a red shawl, had someone touch him with a rod, then peeped out and poured water on the floor from a decanter – a piece of good-natured playfulness which confirms both his own relaxation and the gaiety of the company.

For this aristocratic salon to survive Nicholas's purges with such resilience was remarkable, the more so since the relationships between the Decembrist rebels and this section of the nobility were devastatingly close. It was at Princess Zinaida's house that Pushkin met Mariya, the daughter of General Raevsky, whose pretty feet he had so admired in the Caucasus. She was now Zinaida's sister-in-law and was going to join her husband, the Decembrist Prince Sergey Volkonsky, in Siberia. Pushkin intended to give Mariya a poem for Volkonsky and other friends but ultimately it was taken to them by the wife of another Decembrist. It was a rash gesture for the poem spoke of his own 'freedom loving voice' and concluded with a stanza:

> Your heavy chains will fall away,
> Your prison crumble, and with joy
> Freedom will greet you at the door
> And brothers give you back your sword.

Fortunately, this verse escaped the scrutiny of Count Benckendorf's Third Section. It must have heartened his exiled friends but in what spirit, one may wonder, was that sword offered to the prisoners by Pushkin? It is more likely that he had in mind a restoration of the right to wear a sword, rather than urging a weapon of further revolution into their hands.

In December 1826 he wrote the ambiguous poem 'Stanzas 1826' which gave wholehearted support to the government, while urging Nicholas to follow Peter's example in promoting enlightenment and being forgiving and merciful even though firm. 'Stanzas' has been read⁶ as an appeal for amnesty for the Siberian exiles. Other messages can be found in the poem, however. Even as Pushkin encourages Nicholas to become liberal, he seems to be reassuring friends who might suspect him of obsequiousness.[7]

The poem opens by reminding the reader that revolts and punishments also cast their gloom over the opening of Peter's reign so that the execution of the Decembrist rebels need not signal the beginning of a tyranny. These could have been matters already discussed with Nicholas. The second stanza distinguishes the reasoned opposition of Jakov Dolgoruky, who was noted for his sharp criticism of Peter's edicts, from the mindless opposition of the Streltsy – members of the Moscovite military corps who showed great savagery. George G. Gutsche[8] wonders whether Pushkin wanted to think of his own pardon as putting him in the same category as Dolgoruky. If that were so, the Decembrists, including his friends, would be implicitly criticised in contrast. It is quite possible that Pushkin *had* lost faith in the cause for which Ivan Pushchin had struggled, though his sadness at the thought of his friends' exile remained. The remaining stanzas are less controversial – the fourth stanza praises Peter and the last stanza instructs the Tsar to take pride in his ancestry and forgive without rancour.

Pushkin was in no way disposed to any action to safeguard his own life, as his willingness to accept any challenge to a duel makes clear. He was always ready. Even if he did not believe in what he was saying with much confidence, he was writing what he hoped was the case, rather than consciously trimming. As to the flattery of comparing Nicholas to Peter, Pushkin was well informed, not only about Peter the Great but about his own family's involvement in that far from idyllic period. On one side of his family was Gannibal, Peter's privileged advisor, but on the other was a Pushkin, hanged at the same Tsar's command at the end of the seventeenth century.[9]

Whatever might turn out to be the true nature of Nicholas, Pushkin's opinion at this juncture could only have been a guess. He put the public future out of his mind. There were many houses at which he was welcome, including that of Mariya Rimskaya-Korsakova and that of the Ushakovs, at both of which he fell mildly in love with the daughters. The Ushakovs were particularly close to him. He wrote poems to Ekaterina, the elder daughter, and it was in the younger sister Elizaveta's album that he wrote the notorious Don Juan list, which included Ekaterina's name but not Elizaveta's. There were rumours that the attachment between Pushkin and Ekaterina would lead to marriage. Ekaterina married another man but her husband remained so jealous of her affection for Pushkin that he destroyed a bracelet the poet had given her.

For all this Moscow excitement, the pleasures of flirtation and a visit to St Petersburg for which permission was readily given, Pushkin chose to return to Mikhaylovskoe for a while to give himself time to write. The country suited his mood, as he observed to Vyazemsky on 9 November 1826. 'There is a kind of poetic delight in coming back freely to an abandoned prison.' However, on 2 November he wrote a note to Zubkov, a friend of the exiled Ivan Pushchin, which suggests that some disappointment had contributed to his decision to leave Moscow. 'I am going to inter myself in the country until the 1st January – I leave with death in my heart.'

This dramatic description of his state of mind sprang from a disappointment in love of a new kind, a rejection not of illicit love but of a proposal of marriage. Pushkin had begun to contemplate settling down. The urgency aroused in him needs some explaining. He was no longer living either in exile or isolation, yet the element of desperation in his new pursuit of a wife is unmistakable. It is almost as if he were afraid of being alone for the rest of his life.[10]

As early as October, at the house of Vasily Zubkov, Pushkin met a young beauty, Sofya Pushkina, to whom he was distantly related. She was tall with black eyes and small, neat features,[11] and Pushkin immediately decided to marry her. She, however, was on the verge of an engagement to V. A. Panin, a Moscow gentleman who looked as if he were about to be successful in life, and declined to take Pushkin seriously.

His behaviour could hardly be taken as adequately considered. He was certainly enchanted by Sofya's youth and angelic innocence, but the proposal was made far too rapidly, almost as if he were afraid he might lose interest before committing himself. He made no attempt to get to know Sofya better and showed no wish for her to learn about him.

It was as if Pushkin had taken to heart Alexander Pope's dictum that 'most women have no characters at all'. Given youth and freshness, he imagined he could mould the character of any girl he seized upon as a suitable bride. What was important was that his Madonna should belong to an aristocratic family and have been trained in the social graces. Even his tender and natural Tatyana only became perfect in the eyes of Evgeny Onegin when perfected by her social life among the upper classes. The pattern of Pushkin falling in love with Sofya Pushkina was to be repeated in his suit later to Anna Olenina.

After his rejection by Sofya, Pushkin was back in Mikhaylovskoe by

9 November, after a journey of eight days in which his carriage broke two wheels. He found Arina Rodionovna had, with touching simplicity, learnt a new prayer for 'softening the heart of the Sovereign and the taming of his soul's ferocity'. Pushkin reported this with an ironic sense of its uselessness in a letter to Prince Vyazemsky in which he reflected that the prayer was probably composed under Ivan the Terrible.

Pushkin soon began to chafe, however, at the discovery that poetry was not flowing as he had hoped. His only diversions were those which had always brought him trouble. As he wrote to Vyazemsky on 1 December 1826 from Pskov, where he had paused to recover from a sore chest on his way to Moscow, he had in rage taken up gambling and was losing again so that 'instead of writing the seventh chapter of *Onegin*, I am losing the fourth at shtoss'. He began to plan a surprise return to Moscow, even though the roads were in poor condition.

Meantime, in a letter to his friend Zubkov of 1 December 1826, he was already reconsidering his choice of Sofya as a possible bride. Even if she consented, he was not sure it was fair to attach to himself so sweet and pretty a creature. 'My life up to the present, so wandering, so stormy; my character crotchety, jealous, touchy, violent and weak all at the same time.'[12]

In the few months following his return to Moscow for the second time Pushkin once again took to gambling, and he lost a great deal of money he could ill afford. Although he now commanded substantial sums for his poems, their publication was always a matter of delicate negotiation. The secret police watched his behaviour with sardonic objectivity: 'It seems he does not so much busy himself with poetry now as with gambling.'[13] Writing on 18 February 1827 to a friend in Borovsk, Pushkin remark of his Moscow life at this time, 'Spies, dragoons, whores and drunks loaf around at our place from morning till evening.' The delights of fame were wearing thin and he had begun to resent the way Moscow aristocrats treated him as a literary lion rather than a social equal. In February he rushed off to Tver to spend two weeks with Alexey Vulf, whom he had once dubbed Lovelace in Trigorskoe.

Meanwhile, Pushkin had made a new friend, Pavel V. Nashchokin, a man of whimsical charm and, at least for a time, of considerable wealth, who kept rooms in his house ready for Pushkin. Visitors to the Pushkin museum on the Moika in St Petersburg may be allowed to see some of the miniature objects Nashchokin once ordered to be made for his own doll's house, including a replica of a piano correctly strung, chandeliers,

tables and chairs whose perfection required the most skilled crafts-
manship. Pushkin took great delight in the details of these objects.

On Pushkin's second visit to Moscow, Nashchokin was living with a
gypsy girl, and Pushkin was able to indulge his love for gypsy music. He
was 27 and no longer relishing the life of a dissipated bachelor as
he once had. Nashchokin's generosity became a matter of increasing
importance to Pushkin. He had begun to feel the new constraints presented by his own dependence on the Tsar's whims, as he remarked in a
letter to Sobolevsky of 18 February. 'Here is the point: though freed
from the censorship, I must nevertheless, before I publish anything,
present it Higher, even though it is only a trifle.'

Pushkin had as yet no reason to complain of his treatment by Benckendorf, who wrote to him with reasonable courtesy and had reaffirmed
the Tsar's flattering promise to be his censor. However, Benckendorf had
as little interest in literature as the Tsar.

By 22 March 1827 Pushkin was writing anxiously to Benckendorf
about a group of poems which he thought Delvig had delivered to Count
Benckendorf prior to publication in his almanac *Northern Flowers*. The
Count's response to Pushkin's inquiry was not encouraging. He expressed
surprise that Baron Delvig – 'who I do not have the honour even to
know' – had behaved in such a way, intimating that Pushkin's use of
an intermediary was discourteous. Sobolevsky wrote an ominous and
prophetic epigram to mark the occasion, linking the Count with an old
school friend of Pushkin's, whose disapproval of the poet was well
known.

> Your first friend was Count Benckendorf;
> His only rival – Baron Korff.[14]

In April 1827 Pushkin asked for permission to visit his family in St
Petersburg. This was granted. No one was more delighted by the prospect
of Pushkin's triumphant return than his snobbish parents, who were well
aware of their son's literary success. Yet on the evening of his departure
Pushkin himself was moody and silent and stayed for only a short time
at the bachelor party set up to see him off in style.

His new need for some home of his own did not lead him to contemplate returning to his parents with any great satisfaction. What he
had wanted as a child had not been given to him, and he did not
anticipate finding it at 27 so he had no intention of staying with his
parents on the Fontanka, although he remained fond of his sister Olga

who was then living at home (his brother was in Tiflis). Instead of arranging to share his parents' apartment, therefore, in May 1827 Pushkin took a hotel room at Demuth's Inn. This was beyond his means but at least ensured his independence. His mother tried to tempt her son to stay at home by cooking roast potatoes, of which he was especially fond. Meals were usually sparse at her table as Pushkin's father had grown even more miserly as his income diminished and, though he sampled the potatoes, Pushkin had no intention of moving back as the son of the household.

It was Baron Delvig to whose house Pushkin was particularly drawn, and their friendship was increased by the discovery that Delvig's wife, Sofya, was both an admirer of Pushkin's poetry and ready to love him as a friend. It was also at Delvig's house that companions from their schooldays often gathered alongside literary lions such as Zhukovsky and Vyazemsky. Adam Mickiewicz, the only poet of equal stature Pushkin was ever to meet, also appeared at Delvig's gatherings when he was in St Petersburg. Mickiewicz wrote poetry in his native Polish, but he spoke both elegant French and also Russian, which was unusual in a Pole. He had already suffered for his political opinions, being arrested in 1823 and exiled to Russia in 1824. As a Pole, too, he still felt a great sense of betrayal. Alexander's speech in 1818 had advocated freedoms which came to nothing, and there was further bitterness as a legacy of the Polish revolt.

Pushkin was far more generous to Mickiewicz's genius than Mickiewicz was in describing Pushkin as 'almost an equal'. After listening to one of the Pole's improvisations for which he was celebrated, Pushkin said, 'Quel génie. Quel feu sacré. Que suis-je auprès de lui?' The two poets translated one another's poetry and Mickiewicz gave Pushkin an English copy of Byron, inscribed, 'Mickiewicz, an admirer of you both, presents Byron to Pushkin.'[15] The Polish poet left Russia for ever only two and a half years after they met for the first time, and their later relations were soured by Pushkin's attitude to Polish aspirations and Mickiewicz's reactions to Pushkin's The Bronze Horseman.

At Delvig's, Pushkin argued with a brilliance that neither Prince Vyazemsky nor Zhukovsky could match. Even the often grudging Mickiewicz observed that,

Pushkin captivated and amazed his listeners by the liveliness, acuteness and clarity of his mind ... When he spoke about European and native politics, one would think that one was listening to a man trained in governmental affairs, and saturated with daily readings of parliamentary debates.[16]

Delvig himself was 'one of Pushkin's greatest joys', as Mirsky puts it.[17] Delvig and his circle liked to tell stories of miracles, ghosts and the supernatural, rather as Shelley, Byron and their wives had done in Italy. Anna Kern was part of the same group and so intimate with Delvig that he sometimes addressed her as 'Darling wife' in his letters. Whatever their exact relationship, there was no jealousy between Pushkin and Delvig. Anna speaks touchingly of the affection Pushkin and Delvig had for one another, particularly on one occasion when Delvig returned from a visit to the Ukraine. 'Pushkin tore across the courtyard and threw himself into his arms. They kissed each other's hands and couldn't take their eyes off each other.'[18]

Anna Petrovna Kern was now definitely separated from her husband and lived with her father in the same house as Delvig; her apartment, too, became a meeting place for poets, including Pushkin's friend Dmitry Venevitinov, who had transferred his affections to her. Anna Petrovna became friendly with Pushkin's family, especially Pushkin's sister Olga, and she often visited them in their house on the Fontanka. Pushkin soon renewed acquaintance with his 'genius of pure beauty', with whom he had exchanged occasional letters over the intervening years.

In 1825 Anna had left Riga for St Petersburg, and from there sent Pushkin a volume of Byron he had been looking for. Their correspondence continued, though none of her letters survive other than the one written together with Anna Vulf on 16 September 1826. 'Anna Petrovna Kern orders me to tell you that she is selflessly delighted by your success ... and loves you sincerely, without guile.'[19]

When Pushkin celebrated his nameday with his family in 1827 he found Anna Kern visiting there. In her memoirs she gives a charming, if seemingly naive account of the occasion, describing how, after dinner, Pushkin's friend Abram Norov wondered why she had made no gift to Pushkin in return for so many fine poems. Anna at once took her mother's ring off her finger and Pushkin put it on his hand, promising to bring her one of his own the next day.

Next day Pushkin brought me the promised ring, with three diamonds, and asked if he could spend some hours with me. I had to visit Countess Ivelich, so I suggested that we go there by boat. He agreed, and I saw him once

again as friendly to me as he had been at Trigorskoe, joking with the
boatman, urging him to take care not to drown us.[20]

Pushkin's letters suggest their liaison continued into an intimacy well
beyond friendship. On 1 September 1827 he wrote to Anna Kern,
complaining that Anna Vulf had not kissed him on the eyes as Anna
Petrovna had commanded, and signing himself 'Apple Pie'.

At what precise point he and Anna Petrovna became lovers is not
clear, but that they did so is certain. Also, for all his courteous ways, he
had lost a great deal of the former respect he had for her. In the second
half of February 1828 he wrote to Sobolevsky, 'You don't write me
anything about the 2100 roubles I owe you, but you write me about
Mme Kern, whom with God's help a few days ago I fucked.'[21]

Nor was Anna Kern his only physical love in 1828. He was also seeing
a great deal of Countess Agrafena Zakraevskaya, who was 'famous for
her passionate nature and loose morals'.[22]

Agrafena, the wife of the Minister of Foreign Affairs, was nicknamed
the 'Bronze Venus' or 'Cleopatra of the Neva'. She liked to appear in
near-transparent gowns that showed off her magnificent figure against
the light. She may well have been in Pushkin's mind when he wrote of a
modern Cleopatra in his story 'Egyptian Nights', and she appears as
Nina Vronskaya in *Evgeny Onegin*, where Pushkin compares her marble
beauty with that of the transformed Tatyana. The poet Baratynsky was
in love with her, and Vyazemsky also courted her. In Pushkin she inspired
a number of fine lyrics, the best known of which is 'The Portrait':

> A soul of fire and southern passion
> Among cold women of the North
> She has no thought for your conventions
> But follows her impulsive path
> Indifferent to social bars:
> A comet without laws among
> The calculated round of stars.

Their love affair was brief, but she continued to confide in Pushkin the
most intimate details of her lovers for the rest of his life.

None of these affairs eased Pushkin's encroaching sense that bachelor
life was no longer satisfying and, for all his failure to win the hand of
Sofya Pushkina, he was determined to find a wife. For this reason, even
as he enjoyed the favours of Anna Kern and Countess Agrafena, he was

ardently pursuing Anna Olenina, the daughter of the President of the Academy of Arts and Director of the State Public Library. J. Thomas Shaw[23] argues that Pushkin had made a formal proposal and been rejected, and there are those who have attributed Pushkin's most famous lyric to her. The date of this poem is uncertain, and others, notably the Polish beauty Carolina Sobanskaya with whom Pushkin had spent some time in Kishinev and Odessa, have been suggested as the woman Pushkin had in mind. The greatness of the poem hardly depends on the attribution, and the blend of generous feelings and irony in the last line are altogether characteristic of the man.

> I loved you once, and even now, there may
> Remain a smouldering fire in my spirit;
> But I don't want you to be troubled by it,
> Or have your heart saddened in any way.
> I loved you silently and without hope then,
> Pained by my shyness and my jealousy,
> And yet with such an honest tenderness –
> God grant you may be loved as well again.

Anna Kern notes wryly that he never referred to Olenina with any particular tenderness, sharply observing Pushkin's indifference to anything but physical beauty in women and how little he expected from them in terms of appreciation of his work. She was also a little hurt, perhaps, to find her own sensitivity so misprized.

Whether or not he felt tenderness towards Anna Olenina, in 1828 Pushkin sketched her face in his notebooks, and there inscribed in French the name Annette Pouchkine, though he thereafter drew a line through those words. Marriage was still very much on his mind. Anna Olenina, however, did not find Pushkin particularly attractive, and noted in her diary,

Having given him a singular genius, God did not reward him with an attractive exterior. His face was expressive, of course, but a certain malice and sarcasm eclipsed the intelligence that could be seen in his blue, or rather glassy, eyes. The Negro profile that he inherited from his mother's line did not enhance his face. And add to that his terrible sidewhiskers, his dishevelled hair, his nails long as claws, his short stature...[24]

This unflattering portrait matches the most savage of Pushkin's own caricatures of himself, and is a direct confirmation of his worst fears about the way a young woman was likely to perceive him. It did not protect him, however, from continuing to think only of young and beautiful women as suitable for marriage.

Much about the same time that thoughts of his unsuccessful courtship of Anna Olenina were so preoccupying Pushkin, he dedicated a small poem to the English artist, Dawe, who wished to make a portrait of him. The portrait itself has not survived, and the poem is light-hearted enough in tone, but it is not without significance that he once again finds thoughts of his African appearance coming to his mind. He writes,

> Why should your miraculous pencil
> Waste time upon my African profile?
> Your skill may last for centuries,
> To be mocked by Mephistopheles.

In 1827 Pushkin had made a brief retreat to Mikhaylovskoe, complaining in letters from there that he had not been able to write much poetry and was, instead, turning to prose. There it was he began the unfinished novel, *The Negro of Peter the Great*, based on a highly fictionalised account of the life of his great-grandfather, which he took as far as he could in the first months of 1828.

Pushkin's Third Masonic ledger opens with a fair copy of *The Gypsies* in October 1824. On folio 22, alongside some work on *The Negro of Peter the Great*, are those sketches of an African face, with features Fomachev describes as recognisably Pushkin's own profile. In another album, with a simple black binding, is the fullest existing version we have of *The Negro of Peter the Great* in a fair copy as he wrote it in the summer of 1827.

In writing a tale of his ancestor Gannibal, Pushkin intended to centre the story on a Negro's wife who is unfaithful to her husband, gives birth to a white child and is punished by being shut up in a convent. The tale as it stands is unfinished, but it is masterly in its telling, and there are lively reflections throughout on the sexual situation of a black man in a white society.

The story opens in the licentious France of the Duc d'Orléans (Regent from 1715 to 1725) where Ibrahim, the black favourite of Tsar Peter, has been sent to learn the latest engineering skills of the West. This corresponds entirely to the knowledge Pushkin had of his own great-grandfather's life. The rest, however, is pursued as a novel. As a Negro, Ibrahim is a curiosity and, as such, is invited to the salons of women of high society. There he meets and falls in love with the first Countess who treats him with courtesy, having disliked the way most other women perceived him as 'a kind of rare animal, an alien, peculiar creature accidentally transported into their world ... He actually envied men who were in no way remarkable and considered them fortunate in their insignificance.'

There is much gossip about their liaison, but Ibrahim and the Countess manage to conceal the child their love engenders. When Peter summons Ibrahim back from France, the Duke advises him against returning on the grounds that Russia is not and will never be his native country. Nevertheless, Ibrahim determines to return and leaves a sad note for the Countess which includes the lines,

> Why strive to unite the destiny of so tender and beautiful a being as yourself with the unhappy lot of a negro, a pitiful creature whom people scarcely deign to recognize as human?

Once back in St Petersburg, Ibrahim begins to lead a useful and busy life, though when he remembers his Countess, 'jealousy began to set his African blood in ferment'. He is not miserable, however, until a tender letter from her arrives, reproaching him for his departure. Ibrahim – rather as Pushkin was often observed to do when missives reached him from women he loved – kissed the letter several times, but when Korsakov, his friend from Paris, appears and Ibrahim asks about the Countess, he soon discovers that though she grieved for his departure for a time she rapidly took a new lover. This leaves Ibrahim in the most profound unhappiness which Korsakov's cynicism does nothing to reduce. Ibrahim takes a certain delight in the rebuke Peter administers to the flirtatious Frenchman at a ball. Meanwhile, the wise Tsar (unambiguously wise in this tale) has seen Ibrahim's unhappiness. 'Listen,' he tells him, 'you are a lonely man, having neither kith nor kin, a stranger to everyone except myself ... If I were to die tomorrow, what would become of you, my poor African?' Ibrahim broods over the Tsar's advice, and decides that he should not be denied natural domestic happiness 'simply because I was born in the tropics ... I may not hope to be loved: a childish objection! as though one could believe in love. As though woman's frivolous heart were capable of love.'

The girl selected by the Tsar as a bride for Ibrahim was the beauty pursued by Korsakov at the Imperial ball. Her father, a prince, cannot help reflecting on Ibrahim's status as a 'bought Negro slave' when the

Tsar has issued his command, and is only a little mollified to learn that Ibrahim is, in fact, the son of a sultan. The bride's mother remains appalled by his 'dreadful visage'. Natasha, the chosen bride, herself swoons away at the news. His friend Korsakov gives him sensible, if cynical advice:

> Give up this idea. Don't marry ... There is no relying on any woman's fidelity. But you ... with your passionate, brooding nature, with your flat nose, thick lips and fuzzy hair, for *you* to rush into the dangers of matrimony...

That these are fictional thoughts attributed to his ancestor without evidence is manifest, but equally clearly it is Pushkin's imagination from which they spring, and as such have the force of its own preoccupations. If there were any doubt that these thoughts were part of his own brooding as he contemplated marriage, the caricatures on the manuscript of this working notebook, with their exaggeratedly simian profiles, spell out his obsession. The appearance of Gannibal himself remains conjectural, but in any case Pushkin had no military glory to counter the impression he made on pretty women to whom he presented himself as a suitor. *The Negro of Peter the Great* gives more insight into Pushkin's view of his black inheritance than events in his great-grandfather's life.

Members of the French court laugh at the Countess's choice of lover, and a sense of being an outsider is feelingly expressed. Even when Ibrahim is fêted by the Tsar in Russia, the colour of Ibrahim's skin continues to attract suspicious looks from other members of the Court, however much he throws himself into Peter's ambitious restructuring of Russia. Pushkin's plan for the rest of his novel was to have the young girl's infidelity produce a white child, just as Ibrahim's own adultery had led to the embarrassing birth of a black one. History records that Pushkin's great-grandfather Abram behaved with great savagery to his own wife once he suspected her of infidelity. Here Pushkin is analysing the forces that might have made him do so.

Some part of Pushkin's trouble, as he looked for a wife rather than a mistress, certainly sprang from his pursuit of beauty more than intelligence in women. In a note he observes, 'The fact is that women are the same the world over. Nature, having endowed them with acute minds and a most highly charged sensibility, well nigh denied them a sense of style. Poetry slides over them without touching their souls; they are insensitive to its harmony ... Listen to their literary judgements and you will be surprised by the distortion and even the crudeness of their understanding ... Exceptions are rare.'[25] He did not woo any of the exceptions as a wife.

Set alongside Pushkin's complex emotional life in 1827, it is hard not to find Anna Kern's sentimental account of their growing love a little saccharine. Certainly they spent many hours together, sometimes with his sister Olga, of whom Anna was a close friend, and sometimes in Delvig's apartment when he was away. Yet Pushkin also enjoyed a wide acquaintance with tavern keepers, prostitutes and young girls.[26] Pushkin's winter of 1827–8 was described by Vyazemsky in a letter to Turgenev as 'the most dissipated possible life', adding that 'St Petersburg may destroy him'.

Probably the richest hours Pushkin spent, aside from those spent writing, were in his friend Delvig's company. He once arrived at Delvig's apartment when a group of poet friends were there, bringing a skull given to him by Alexey Vulf and supposedly taken from the grave of one of Delvig's ancestors in Riga. In imitation of Byron, the skull was filled with wine and the company drank from it. The opening of the following well-known poem lightheartedly explains how he came by such an object which once held the brains of Delvig's hunting and drinking ancestor:

> Long since in parish register
> The Baron's death was certified;
> He slept with many an ancestor,
> There in Riga where he died...
> Some long-haired fellow, nature's pet –
> Poet with mathematic mind
> Contemplative and pompous bloke,
> Leech, lawyer, physiologist –
> In short for scholarship bespoke
> At Riga with his pipe appeared
> With cloak and cudgel and a beard...
> We know that for vain luxury
> The august thinker scorns to look;
> Mocks foolish bustle too, as he
> Whistles blithely in his nook.
> Yet in his life a crucial flow
> Our poor student soon descries
> His thought is an unusual one:
> He needs, it seems, a skeleton.[27]

Anna Petrovna reports that Pushkin visited her rooms, overflowing with images and harmonies from poems he was working on which he often repeated to her. 'He always did this when absorbed by some verse which had succeeded or which lay stored in his heart. In Trigorskoe, for example, he constantly repeated "She deceives, she does not come!"' (from *The Gypsies*).[28] Anna describes him as playful and joking and taking innocent pleasure in going through her album to improve others' contributions, insert humorous translations or in leaning over her while she was writing to her younger sister Elizaveta to add some romantic verses. She begged him for a copy of *The Gypsies* in memory of the time he had read the poem to her at Trigorskoe. 'He sent it over that day with its cover inscribed with the words "To her Highness A. P. Kern, from her devoted admirer Lord Pushkin".'[29]

Anna Kern admits, however, that for all their shared affection Pushkin was often wretchedly gloomy that winter. She and her friends were amused when 'In distracted moments he would hum some verse' or 'endlessly repeated the lines: "Inconsolable, you did not want to live."' His friends might choose to laugh but in writing to his old Trigorskoe friend, Praskovya Osipova, Pushkin confessed, 'This life is rather foolish ... the noise and tumult of St Petersburg have become completely alien to me.'

Pushkin and Anna Petrovna both helped his sister Olga when, very much against her parents' wishes, she eloped and married Nikolay Pavlishchev, a man with few prospects from an undistinguished family, in 1828. They received her in Delvig's flat after her secret wedding. It was not a very promising match since Pavlishchev was 'unimaginative, sour and unsuccessful', as Simmons puts it, and once he had become Olga's husband was to cause Pushkin many financial difficulties. However, Olga was over thirty, a spinsterly age in those days, and determined to have her way in spite of her parents' objections.

Perhaps Pushkin was becoming a little impatient with Anna Petrovna. On one occasion Pushkin accused Anna of causing the death of his friend Venevitinov by spurning his love. It may well be that Anna Kern is remembering accurately some such remark of Pushkin, but love was very far from the likely cause of Venevitinov's tragically early death. He had been arrested on suspicion of Decembrist connections in 1826 and, when interrogated, responded bravely that he had not been a Decembrist but might easily have been. He had to sit for thirty-six hours in solitary confinement before being finally released. His subsequent precarious psychological state is reflected in a final cycle of poems, and he died on 15 March 1827 of a 'nervous fever'. Delvig wrote to Pushkin from St Petersburg, 'My dear friend, you have probably been weeping for Venevitinov. I know how his death will shock you. What a combination of beautiful gifts with beautiful youth.'[30] The young poet's ashes were brought to Moscow and Mickiewicz and Pushkin carried them to his grave in the Donskoy Monastery.

Pushkin, if indeed he made the accusation Anna Kern attributes to him, was probably complaining that she had refused to Venevitinov favours he no longer thought of as any man's exclusive property since his attitude to the woman he had once called the 'genius of pure beauty' was no longer reverent.

Meanwhile, Pushkin may have decided to make a proposal to Anna Olenina's father, he must have been rejected, perhaps because he arrived insultingly late at a party at which the engagement was to be announced, perhaps because her father was privy to decisions taken about Pushkin by the Council of State, of which he was a member. Whether refused or simply disillusioned in his bid for a wife, Pushkin's depression deepened. There were other reasons to be miserable. In the second half of March or early April Pushkin was writing to Ivan Alexeevich Yaklov, a wealthy landowner with whom Pushkin often played cards, about debts still owed to him. 'My debtors do not pay me, and God grant that they not be completely bankrupt, but I (between ourselves) have already gambled away about 20,000 roubles.'

Pushkin was still very fond of cards, as Anna Kern reports in her memoirs. 'Like all gamblers, he was superstitious.' He remained recklessly generous, too. In the same passage she observes, 'once, when I asked him for money for a poor family, he gave me his last fifty roubles, saying it's as well for you that I won yesterday.'[31] On 15 July 1827 he sent Sobolevsky 2,500 roubles on hearing the news of the death of his mother.

Pushkin was also continuing to brood over the fate of his Decembrist friends and his own near miraculous escape. It seems probable that his poem 'Arion', in which he imagines himself, as in the ancient myth, the sole survivor of a shipwreck in which all his friends perished, refers to their tragedy. The poem concludes,

The helmsman perished, and the crew!
But the abating tempest threw
Me, the mysterious bard, ashore,
Of all that ship the only one;
I dry my wet robe in the sun
And sing the songs I sang before.[32]

Pushkin still had dreams of escaping abroad, but permission to do so was adamantly refused. He requested to join the army fighting the Persians in the Caucasus in any capacity. This, too, was refused – an Imperial refusal rather less personal than usual as Prince Vyazemsky also had a similar request rejected. In a letter of 21 April 1828 Pushkin wrote and asked the Tsar for permission to spend 'six or seven months in Paris', a request that probably never got beyond Benckendorf.

All this frustration and disappointment is reflected in the well-known lyric of 12 May 1828, in which he wonders why he has been given the gift of life when, as the last verse sombrely concludes,

There is no goal to aim at now.
With empty heart and idle brain,
Life is no more than a drab sound
That irritates me with its pain.

Money was his most serious material problem and it was impossible to ask his father for any because, for all his original delight in his son's reputation, Sergey remained a bitter man, convinced that his son had severely wronged him. Only a few weeks after Pushkin's successful interview with the Tsar, Sergey was writing to his brother Vasily, 'No, dear friend, do not think that Alexander Sergeevich will ever feel his injustice towards myself ... He is completely convinced that it is I who must ask his pardon ...' He concluded another letter, written on the same day, with the words, 'Finally, may he be happy, but let him leave me in peace.'

Pushkin wanted to see his father as little as his father wanted to see him, though on 18 May, writing to his brother Lev, he speaks of 'going to Petersburg to see our dearest parents, *comme on dit*, and to put my financial affairs in order'.

Unlike so many Russians, and perhaps because of his pride in his African blood, Pushkin was remarkably free from racial prejudice. However, a diary entry for 15 October 1827, written on his way from

Mikhaylovskoe to St Petersburg, describes how he was waiting at a station to change horses when four troikas drew up and he idly observed a group of people under arrest.

> One of the men under arrest was leaning up against a column. He was approached by a tall, pale, thin young man with a black beard, in a frieze overcoat, who looked a real Jew, and I took him for a Jew, and the close association of Jews and spies produced in me the usual reaction. I turned my back on him, thinking he had been summoned to Petersburg for information or explanations. Seeing me, he gave me a quick, lively glance. Involuntarily I turned towards him. We looked at each other intently ... and I recognised Kyuchelbecker.[33]

Pushkin naturally saw the world through Russian eyes. He had no compunction in describing the Cossack leader Bogdan Khmelnitsky as a 'heroic fighter for liberty' in his introduction to 'Poltava', even though Khmelnitsky was the author of one of the most horrifying massacres to afflict the Jewish people before the twentieth century. So, at the staging post, he saw the lank-haired, bent-over body of the convict as typically Jewish without realising that the posture came from malnutrition and ill-treatment until he recognised his poor friend. He and Kyukhelbecker fell into each other's arms. Kyukhelbecker was being moved from Schlusselburg fortress to the Dinaburg fortress. It was the last meeting Pushkin was to have with his old friend, who was kept in prison until 1835 when he was sent to a penal settlement in Siberia, where he died in 1845.

On one level Pushkin was hardly lonely in the first half of 1828. He still enjoyed the friendship of Prince Vyazemsky and Zhukovsky, who continued all his life to plead Pushkin's cause at Court, Pletnev, who acted as his literary agent and factotum, and the charming companionship of Pavel Nashchokin, a gifted and kind-hearted young man, always ready to spend money on Pushkin's amusement. There were attractive *grisettes* to solace him, society women to banter with him. Yet he sensed his youth running out, and with it the easy pleasure he had taken in being alive. In the following years that sense of encroaching time grew more and more menacing: 'No, no, is it possible that I shall soon be thirty years old? I await this fearful time, but I have not yet said farewell to youth.'[34] When his faithful nanny Arina Rodionovna died on 31 July 1828 he felt the grief of a son.

He made one important new friendship in St Petersburg – with Elizaveta Mikhailovna Khitrovo. She was sixteen years older than he, the daughter of Field Marshal Kutuzov who had fought at Borodino against Napoleon, and she proudly wore the watch that her father had carried in that famous battle. She had been married and widowed twice, and now took great pride in the intellectuals and writers who attended her salon, which was one of the most celebrated in St Petersburg.

Among the rough text of the story, 'The Guests Arrived at the Dacha', in Pushkin's working notebook for the year 1828 appears his pencil sketch of Khitrovo, a stout lady of pronounced middle age with whom Pushkin was never in love or sexually involved, though he enjoyed her celebrated 'mornings', which went on from one to four in the afternoon. 'There one could gather information about all the questions of the day – from a political pamphlet or parliamentary speech by some French or English orator to a novel or dramatic work by one of the literary favourites of the age.'[35]

Pushkin was always ready to receive maternal affection from women, but Khitrovo's interest in Pushkin was far more intimate. She wrote him many letters, to which he always replied politely, thanking her for her kindness and solicitude, though often offering excuses for not coming to hear further critical opinions of his work. 'I would hasten to come and collect others, if I didn't still limp a little and if I were not afraid of staircases.' Although he grew impatient with her persistence and sometimes ridiculed her among his friends for displaying her plump white shoulders with some vanity – there is a scurrilous epigram which mocks 'naked Lisa' – nevertheless, he often wrote to her with candour and clarity about himself.

Their friendship was closer than he liked to pretend. It was to Khitrovo that he spoke of his dislike of pursuing respectable women: 'Long live grisettes. With them it is much more direct and much easier ... Do you wish me to speak quite frankly? Perhaps I am elegant and genteel in my writings, but my heart is completely vulgar and my inclinations are all of the third estate ... I am surfeited with intrigues, feelings, correspondence etc etc.' Many of his letters, however, are entirely taken up with excuses for failing to come and see her and as late as the second half of 1830 he wrote to Vyazemsky, 'If you can make Elizaveta Khitrovo fall in love with you, then do me this divine favour.'

To Khitrovo's daughter, Countess Dolly Fikelmon, the wife of the Austrian Ambassador, however, Pushkin was very much attracted. To his friend Nashchokin he confided a story about Dolly which closely

resembles an incident in *The Queen of Spades*. Pushkin claimed he had
hidden himself under a sofa until it was safe for the two lovers to go off
to her bedroom. Unfortunately, it was daylight when they woke and
Pushkin was only able to escape unnoticed by bribing a servant to let
him out. Pushkin and Dolly had no further relations as lovers, and she
harboured some malice towards him, perhaps because she learned this
tale had been repeated as gossip.

It was at the opening of 1828 that Pushkin wrote a poem in praise of
the Tsar, which immensely pleased Nicholas but antagonised many
liberals among his friends and brought no reward to the poet. There
must be some doubt as to whether Pushkin genuinely believed what he
wrote.

> I'm not flattering, when in free
> Praise of the Tsar I spend my art:
> All I do is speak my feelings
> In the language of the heart.

It was a poem in which Pushkin expressed the hope that Nicholas would
prove a liberal ruler of Russia. Sincere or not, such hopes were soon
extinguished.

In August 1828 a copy of Pushkin's *Gabrieliad*, written long ago in
Kishinev, had been found in the possession of a certain Captain Mitkov.
Pushkin emphatically denied authorship and claimed that he himself had
copied it from a source he had since forgotten, but the police found this
difficult to accept and the poet was only excused after a letter to the
Tsar, whose contents have not come down to us.

During the autumn of 1828 Pushkin shut himself up in his rooms to
work on *Poltava*, which he wrote with incredible speed – in a fortnight,
it is said, and without his usual revisions. It is by far the longest of his
narrative poems. The lines came to him even in his sleep and he sometimes
jumped out of his bed in the middle of the night to write them down in
the dark. Anna Akhmatova much admired the poem, and said of it,
'How did he know everything?' It may well have been the second chapter
which describes the torture and execution of steadfast heroes that felt
most pertinent. Perhaps it was the part that haunted Pushkin's nights,
too, for folios 40 and 44 of his working notebooks[36] show clearly images
of the hanged Decembrists. 'Peter's triumph at Poltava, not only over a
foreign invader but over internal separatism and revolt, was as stirring
a subject as the victory over Napoleon', as John Bayley points out.[37] For

Akhmatova, this might have been compared to the turning back of the Germans in the Second World War.

Nevertheless, I am inclined to agree with A. D. P. Briggs that it is not a poem likely to appeal to Western readers, even though Pushkin gave the poem an epigraph from Byron and included in it Mazepa, a figure Byron had already written about. Whereas Byron took an incident from Mazepa's youth, Pushkin chose the moment when Mazepa declares himself the leader of the insurgent Ukraine. In 'The Captain's Daughter', as we shall come to it, and *Boris Godunov*, as we have already seen, Pushkin's interest lay more in the personality of the rebel than in the legal status of revolt. His private characters in *Poltava* are as convincing as his historical ones, particularly that of Mariya, whose infatuation with the aged Mazepa is almost monstrous in its intensity. Mazepa himself, who has no country and cannot love, takes his own sense of himself from his ability to avenge the wrongs he has suffered.

The best of the poem lies neither in the politics nor the battle. Mazepa wishes in old age to marry his god-daughter, Mariya Kochubey. In spite of the forty-five years between them, Mariya falls deeply in love with him and the pair elope. Mariya's father, in revenge for this, warns Tsar Peter of Mazepa's plans to join Charles XII and defeat the Russian army. Mazepa is an image of the foreign and the distrusted – Catholics, Jesuits, Poles – while Peter in contrast is almost a demi-god, a wise father figure to the whole nation. Soviet critics liked to distinguish the patriarchal and protective image of Peter in *Poltava* from any attempt to present him as an autocrat. For all his wisdom Peter refuses to believe in Mazepa's treachery and allows Mazepa to have Mariya's father first arrested and then executed. Hearing of her father's fate, Mariya goes out of her mind. In the last chapter Mazepa joins Charles in open war against Peter and is defeated at the battle of Poltava. The lyrical introduction may well have been addressed to Mariya, once Raevskaya.

Poltava turned out to be the first poem Pushkin had published which did not receive immediate acclaim. Perhaps a new metallic quality in his verse baffled his public. Indeed, the poem attracted hostile criticism from a hack journalist, Faddey Bulgarin, in the St Petersburg journal *The Northern Bee*. Bulgarin was a Pole who had been a liberal but was now one of Benckendorf's agents and probably the one who reported the reading of *Boris Godunov* to the Count. The quarrel that grew up between Bulgarin and Pushkin was reinforced by the *Moscow Telegraph*, whose editor, Nikolay Polevoy, described Pushkin and Vyazemsky as 'literary aristocrats'. Pushkin always tried to keep his distance from the praise of the crowd. As he wrote in 'Ezersky', 'Your work is your reward . . . .by that you breathe, but its fruit you throw to the crowd.' He was, nevertheless, hurt in an important part of himself by the hostile response. For all his championing of love with *grisettes* as '*bien plus court and bien plus commode*', he was the more in need of some emotional anchor. In Moscow he continued to drink and gamble more than ever.

It was in January 1829 that the young Gogol came up to St Petersburg, full of hero-worship for the great poet and determined to call on him, though he lost his nerve in his first attempt to knock on his door. Emboldened with a little spirits for his second attempt, he was told by Pushkin's servant that his master was resting. Gogol asked if it was true that Pushkin worked all night. 'What do you mean, *works?*' replied the servant. 'He plays cards.'[38]

Once again Pushkin retreated to the country, spending most of the time from October 1828 to early 1829 at Osipova's estate in Malinniki, where he went riding in the snow and played whist at eighty kopecks a rubber. There it was he finished the seventh chapter of *Evgeny Onegin*. Five chapters of Onegin had already been published, and Pushkin had finished writing chapter six, which ended with the death of Lensky. Now, in his maturity, he wrote chapter seven. The epigraphs all describe Moscow, yet the chapter begins in the countryside in spring. There is Lensky's grave, but Olga no longer mourns him:

> Another captured her affection
> Another with his love's perfection
> Has lulled her wretchedness to sleep.

Whatever unhappiness such betrayal may have given the ghost of Lensky, Pushkin's heroine Tatyana remains alone; she has many suitors but rejects them all. She still remembers Evgeny, even though she tries to hate him as a murderer. When a walk brings her close by his house, she cannot resist investigating. Taken by the housekeeper to see his study, she recognises a portrait of Lord Byron on the wall, which alerts her to Evgeny's mentor. The next day she asks permission to look through Evgeny's books and, as she does so, is intrigued by the lines he has marked as most important. With a flash of insight she recognises how much of Evgeny's dangerous and immoral sophistication had come straight out of the books he had been reading:

What was he then? An imitation?
An empty phantom or a joke,
A Muscovite in Harold's cloak?

This new understanding of Evgeny's posing disturbs her, but she remains under his spell. At that very moment her own future is being decided for her. The Larins have decided she is to be taken to Moscow to find a husband. Even as Tatyana prepares for the empty glitter of the season, Pushkin delights his readers with an account of the preparations the Larin servants are making for the move: the household goods for the winter season in Moscow; the mattresses, trunks, jars of jam, featherbeds, coops of chickens, pots and basins that have to be loaded up for transport. The family have to travel for a week through the snows, over bad roads 'with bedbugs and fleas at every stop', before they reach Moscow.

Its ancient domes and spires streaming
With golden crosses, ember bright
Ah friend, I too have been delighted
When all at once far off I've sighted
That splendid view of distant domes...

Pushkin writes a heartfelt tribute to Moscow's gallant recent history when Napoleon, for all his defeat of Russian armies, conquered no more than a city in defiant flames, then sends the Larin family cart trundling along Tverskaya Street to the house of Tatyana's old aunt. Once again, as so often in this brilliant poem, the intimate dialogue between aunt and mother reads as naturally as if there were no constraint of polished verse. At family dinners the daughters of Tatyana's aunt look her over and find her,

A bit provincial and affected
And somewhat pale, too thin and small
But on the whole not bad at all.

Soon Tatyana's hair is fluffed into the latest fashion and as she listens to the giddy conversations of the girls who are becoming her friends she begins to learn Moscow ways and to loathe Moscow's marriage market. Tatyana is taken to the theatre and the ballroom, and there hussars on leave look her over. Impudently, Pushkin introduces real figures, including his friends, into the world she encounters: Prince Vyazemsky himself sits down beside her. As the chapter ends, a general is looking her way in admiration even as Pushkin steers his narration towards his hero Evgeny.

Once this seventh chapter was finished, at least in draft, Pushkin left Malinniki, on 6 December, not for St Petersburg but for the winter season in Moscow and exactly that glittering matrimonial market place to which he had just consigned his heroine. For all the magnificent accomplishment of his new work Pushkin was unable to throw off his increasing depression, which he described as spleen or bile and which reached its lowest point at the end of 1829, as a poem written then reflects:

> I'm getting used, as each year goes,
> To pondering sadly to myself
> Which of the days I can suppose
> The anniversary of my death.

Perhaps it was in such a mood of hopelessness that he set off on 1 May 1829 to the Caucasus, apparently on the spur of the moment, although he must have known it would make trouble for him with Benckendorf. He had determined to visit his brother Lev in Tibilisi, and Nikolay Raevsky, who was then commanding a brigade in the Caucasus. On the way, rather unwisely, he decided to visit the famous General Ermolov, then living in retirement, who had a reputation for liberalism, and this meeting was duly reported to the police.

His four months' travel included a skirmish with a large party of Kurds. In his eagerness for action Pushkin once rode ahead of those deputed to protect him and picked up a sabre from a dead Turk as a souvenir. Pushkin enjoyed riding alongside warlike Cossacks, living in tents, eating shashlyk and drinking champagne chilled in mountain snow. Near the frontier between Georgia and Armenia he met a few Georgians with a cart on their way from Teheran. They were carrying the corpse of the writer Griboedov – who had been murdered by a mob in January – towards Tibilisi.

For all this excitement, Pushkin found military life much less glamorous than he had imagined. Erzerum fell on 27 June and revealed itself as filthy and disease-ridden and, although he valued his Turkish sword, Pushkin was glad to leave the conquered city on 21 July. On the way back to Moscow he spent a few days in Tibilisi and saw old friends from his days of southern exile in Vladikavkaz, Pyatigorsk and Kislovodsk.

After his return journey, on which he suffered further heavy gambling losses, he found himself back in Moscow in September, convinced that his restless life offered few rewards and wondering once again whether matrimony might. The woman upon whom he set his heart was a sixteen-year-old beauty, without fortune and with little interest in literature: Natalya Goncharova.

CHAPTER ELEVEN

Natalya

It was at a Moscow ball in the winter season of 1828 that Pushkin first saw Natalya Ivanovna Goncharova, then a sixteen-year-old beauty in a fluffy gown with a tiara on her head. A year later he wrote, 'When I saw her for the first time, her beauty was just being noticed in society. I loved her; my head was quite turned.'[1] This might seem a far from uncommon effect upon the susceptible Pushkin, but at a time when he was looking for a future bride it was decisive.

Perhaps just for that reason he set off for St Petersburg on 4 January 1829, staying for a few days on the way with the rakish Alexey Vulf, his one-time pupil in the pursuit of pleasure, now in Malinniki. The two young men enjoyed their usual romp together, playing cards and flirting with both provincial ladies and servant girls. Pushkin's reputation had preceded him and several of the girls thought him handsome, though they were alarmed at his long fingernails. However, Pushkin had not forgotten the beauty he had left behind in Moscow, even as he and Alexey Vulf continued the journey towards St Petersburg together, arriving there on 18 January 1829. After a week of his usual dissipated life in St Petersburg he was already complaining in letters to Vyazemsky of the lack of intelligence and gaiety in the society around him. Even in Delvig's house, where he found many of his old literary friends, he was frequently irritable and prone to take offence.

When he returned to Moscow Pushkin arranged an introduction to the Goncharov family through Count F. I. Tolstoy. In the presence of Natalya he was at first peculiarly awkward but his intention to make her his bride deepened and soon he made a definite proposal of marriage through Count Tolstoy.

It was an act of some recklessness. Natalya Ivanovna, whom Pushkin always referred to as Natasha, came from a family almost as unusual as Pushkin's own. Natasha's mother had been a lady-in-waiting at Court and a favourite not only of the Empress Elizabeth but also of Tsar Alexander himself. Natalya Ivanovna was one of the first beauties of the St Petersburg court. A cavalry guard, A. Okhodnikov, who happened to be the favourite of the Empress, fell in love with her. The Empress herself had a daughter by Okhodnikov, born in 1806, though the child died two years later. In October of 1806 an assassin attacked and fatally wounded Okhodnikov as he was coming out of the theatre. Perhaps to cover up some of the ensuing scandal, Natalya's mother was quickly married off to N. A. Goncharov, the son of factory owner Afanasy Nikolaevich Goncharov, and their wedding was attended by the whole Court. Afanasy, however, soon separated from his wife and left Russia, leaving his son Nikolay in charge of the factory. When French troops approached during the Napoleonic Wars, Afanasy returned to Russia with his French mistress Babette, whom the Goncharov family nicknamed 'the French laundress'. Babette was the cause of endless family rows and eventually Natalya's mother and her husband Nikolay Afanasevich abandoned the factory but left their daughter Natalya, who was the favourite granddaughter of Afanasy, in the care of her grandfather.

In spite of the circumstances of her marriage, Natalya's mother was happy enough with her husband until in 1814 he became ill, perhaps as a result of having fallen from a horse. He was from that time onwards both alcoholic and perhaps mad, one way or another squandering the family fortunes. On 7 January 1819 Natalya Ivanovna wrote to her father-in-law Afanasy Goncharov, 'All his disorders flow from his vast consumption of alcohol; he confessed as much to me, saying that he could drink up to seven glasses of rough wine.'[2] Her husband was now forbidden access to family funds, and from this time onwards was so impoverished that he was unable even to afford strings for his beloved violin or the sheet music he loved.

Natalya Ivanovna had once been bright and beautiful enough to attract the lover of an Empress. In her misfortune she become hard, strict, fanatically religious and domineering. Her daughter Natalya, at the age of six, was returned to the care of this harsh mother, wearing a sable coat – a luxury that suggested the life of indulgence she had enjoyed in her grandfather's house and which was altogether to be denied her under her mother's regime. She had a gentle spirit, however, and endured her mother's strictness with far less complaint than either of her other sisters.[3] While trying to present the appearance of a wealthy family, the Goncharovs were almost without resources – an incapacitated father, a fortune squandered and Natalya's mother in the throes of a religious fanaticism which meant the house was continually filled with priests and pilgrims.

The three girls were educated in French by governesses, though Natalya did have some Russian. She rode elegantly, learned how to embroider prettily and to behave with charm. Her mother's only hope for them was that they would attract wealthy husbands. Even as a young girl Natalya's beauty was remarkable and she was always surrounded by a swarm of admirers and worshippers. 'Her blooming good health was the legacy of her country upbringing in the fresh air. Strong and supple, she was unusually well-proportioned and every movement was executed with grace ... Natalya's greatest charm was her naturalness, her complete absence of affectation. Most people considered her a coquette, but this accusation is unjust. Her unusually expressive eyes, enchanting smile and appealing simplicity of manner unwittingly put everyone in thrall to her ... "Merci, Monsieur," she says, thanking an admirer for some service, and she utters the words quite simply but with such sweetness and with such an enchanting smile that the poor man is unable to sleep all night, racking his brains for some opportunity to hear once more that "Merci, Monsieur" ... It was a great mystery to me where Natalya acquired her tact and her ability to conduct herself ... without falsity. Her sisters were beautiful but one could find in them none of Natalya's refined intelligence.'[4]

To Pushkin's first proposal of marriage Natalya's mother responded evasively through Count Tolstoy. Pushkin was not surprised, nor altogether discouraged, since, as he wrote on 1 May, 'This answer is not a refusal; you still permit me to hope ... I understand the prudence and tenderness of a mother.' Pushkin understood only too well. For all his fame as a poet and his claim to aristocracy, he had neither the money nor the prospects which she must have hoped for the most beautiful of her daughters. Nor would she have found common ground with Pushkin on the exemplary virtues of the late Tsar Alexander I.

It was not, however, Natalya Ivanovna's rejection that sent Pushkin off to the Caucasus: he had decided on the trip two months earlier. There was no reply to a letter he sent to the Goncharovs but his travels did not alter Pushkin's wish to marry Natalya. He wrote a formal letter in French on 1 May 1829, renewing his offer of marriage, and allowed himself some measure of hope from her. On his return to Moscow he went directly to the Goncharovs' house, where he was received coldly by the mother and indifferently by Natalya herself. Discouraged by this, and using the same expression that he used after his rejection by Sofya Pushkina, he left Moscow for Malinniki 'with death in my heart'.

Natalya's mother had every reason to be hesitant in her response to Pushkin's offer. She had no great interest in literary fame, and wanted a wealthy and fashionable husband for her daughter. Even if she had not been so fanatically pious, she might have been anxious about Pushkin's rakish reputation. Her other daughters had so far failed to find husbands; Natalya was her one hope of a brilliant match. Several things stood in the way of it, however. It was well known among the eligible Moscow bachelors who courted and flattered her that Natalya had absolutely no dowry. The one-time fortune of the Goncharovs had been dissipated by a grandfather who ran through many millions of roubles and left debts of half a million. Moreover, Natalya's father was known to be not only a drunkard but mentally ill. Natalya's mother was imperiously bossy, vulgar and mean-spirited. It was not surprising that, for all Natalya's beauty, she had so far failed to bring any of the magnificent suitors she attracted to the point of a formal offer. Her mother calculated that she might still do so, but she did not dismiss Pushkin altogether in case she did not.

In the autumn of 1829 Pushkin renewed his acquaintance with Eka-terina Ushakova and drew a sketch in his notebooks of a severe woman whom he named 'Mama Kars' – his nickname for Natalya's mother – after a fortress in Turkish Armenia which had finally yielded to Russian force of arms. He was still far from indifferent to Ekaterina herself, who had reciprocated his feelings initially. Pushkin, when in Moscow, sometimes visited the Ushakov house as many as three times a day. Ekaterina, who was used to the company of writers and musicians, and only ten years younger than Pushkin, might indeed have made him an excellent wife. How close Pushkin came to offering her marriage is hard to establish as she burnt all her correspondence with Pushkin, apart from the album containing the celebrated Don Juan list.

Journalistic squabbling absorbed much of Pushkin's energies during the winter of 1829–30 and left him much lowered in spirits. On 7

January 1830 he once again appealed to Benckendorf for permission to leave Russia:

> Since I am not yet married or attached to the Service, I should like to make a journey either to France or Italy. However, if this may not be allowed, I should like leave to go to China with the mission that is being sent there.[5]

Benckendorf, untouched by the desperation in this letter, refused permission, mentioning that His Majesty feared such an attachment would be too expensive for Pushkin and take him away from his occupation. In any case, he added, all the diplomatic posts in the delegation to China had been filled. Humiliated or not by the bizarre grounds for this rejection, Pushkin wrote to Count Benckendorf for a pension for the widow of his old friend General Raevsky the very next day.

His request to leave Russia suggests that his attachment to Natalya Goncharova was either as yet no more deeply fixed than his earlier passions for Sophia Pushkina or Anna Olenina or that Pushkin had altogether abandoned hope of success. Indeed, on 2 February 1830 he was writing to Karolina Adamovna Sobanskaya, 'I was born to love you,' and, reflecting on that missed opportunity for happiness, rather as Tatyana was to reproach Evgeny at the close of *Evgeny Onegin*, he blames himself for not recognising it when it was near. This is a reply to a letter that Mme Sobanskaya had sent him, putting off their encounter for a day. The letter exists only in draft, and it is not clear whether it was ever sent. Pushkin concludes his draft by asking for her friendship, reminding her that her beauty will fade and that her soul will only outlive that beauty for a short time.

However, when on a visit to St Petersburg in March Pushkin heard rumours that the beautiful Natalya was about to accept the hand of the archivist Meshchersky he was galvanised into action. Guessing that her mother could little afford the expense of another Moscow season, even if she were still hopeful of finding another match for her daughter, he determined to renew his suit to 'Mama Kars'. He arrived in Moscow on 12 March, jumped from a carriage and went straight into a concert hall where he saw Natalya Goncharova herself, as beautiful as he remembered and, moreover, not yet engaged to anyone. On 5 April he called at the Goncharov house on Bolshaya Nikitskaya Street to press his suit.

It was clear that no more acceptable offer of marriage had been received. Pushkin was willing to forgo a dowry and he wrote once again in early April to repeat his proposal of marriage. It is a letter of astonishing frankness and in the light of subsequent tragic events shows a horrifying prescience:

> I felt that I played a rather ludicrous role. I was timid for the first time in my life and this timidity in a man of my age could hardly please a young person of your daughter's age ... Only habit and a long intimacy would help me to gain the affection of your daughter; in the course of time I can hope to make her become attached to me, but I shall have nothing with which to please her. If she consents to give me her hand, I shall see in this only a proof of the calm indifference of her heart ... it will be said that an unfortunate fate has prevented her from forming other connections more equal, more brilliant, more worthy of her ... Will she not have regrets? Will she not regard me as an obstacle, as a fraudulent ravisher? Will she not take an aversion to me? God is my witness that I am ready to die for her, but to have to die only to leave a dazzling widow who the next day is free to choose a new husband – this idea – this is hell.

In the same letter, Pushkin wrote plainly, too, of money:

> Let us speak of finances. I set little store on that. My fortune has been enough for me so far. Will it be enough for me once I am married? I shall not tolerate it for anything in the world that my wife should experience deprivations, that she should not be where she is invited to shine, and to amuse herself. She has the right to insist upon it. In order to satisfy her I am ready to sacrifice all the tastes, all the passions of my life, an existence that has been completely free and quite reckless. Nevertheless, will she not murmur if her position in the world is not as brilliant as the one she deserves and which I would have wished for her? Such are, in part, my anxieties. I tremble to think that you may find them only too just.[6]

It is a measure of Mama Kars's own desperation that such a letter nevertheless produced her consent. Knowing his future mother-in-law was, however, worried in addition about the surveillance he was under, Pushkin wrote to Benckendorf on 16 April 1830 explaining this anxiety and declaring that his happiness depended on a word of goodwill.

> I am marrying Mlle Goncharova, whom you must have seen in Moscow ... two objections were put to me: my finances and my relations with the government. As to the first, I was able to reply that this was satisfactory, thanks to His Majesty, who has given me the means to live worthily by my labour. As to the latter ... Mme Goncharova fears to give her daughter in

marriage to a man who would be from the outset on bad terms with the Tsar..."[7]

Benckendorf replied disingenuously, but adequately:

His Majesty the Emperor, with a completely paternal care for you, sir, has been good enough to give me, General Benckendorf, the duty, not as chief of police but as a man in whom he is good enough to put his confidence, to watch over you and to guide you with his advice; the police have never been given the order to keep you under surveillance ... What is the shadow that anyone can find in your position in this respect? I authorise you, sir, to have this letter shown to those to whom you believe you ought to show it.[8]

Some of the suspense, along with a confusion of apprehensions with which Pushkin waited for a reply to his proposal, may be guessed at from some fragmentary notes, which Pushkin described as 'translated from the French', between 12 and 13 May:

My fate is decided ... I am to be married. She whom I loved for two years, whom my eyes at first sought out everywhere, with whom a meeting seemed bliss, my God, she is almost mine. The expectation of a decisive answer was the most painful feeling of my life. The expectation of the last lingering card, remorse of conscience, the dream before a duel – all this in comparison signifies nothing.[9]

Whatever doubts Pushkin might have had about relinquishing the joys of a bachelor life vanished when a letter arrived to summon him to see his future father-in-law. He immediately took a carriage to their home, where Natalya gave him her cold, timid hand.

His proposal was accepted, and on 16 April 1830 Pushkin wrote to his parents (addressing them formally as Vy) to ask for their blessing on his marriage. His father replied with enthusiasm.

A thousand and a thousand times blessed is this day past, dear Alexander, when we received your letter. May heaven bless you and the sweet friend of your life who will give you so much happiness. I should like to write to her, but have not yet ventured to do so for fear that it would not be my place.

His mother, too, added a delighted postscript.

I would like to take you in my arms, to bless you and tell to what extent my life is bound to your happiness. Be assured that Mlle Goncharova will become as dear to me as you, my darling children.[10]

This warmth, particularly from Pushkin's mother, suggests his decision to marry had much improved his relationship with his parents. Even more surprisingly, a letter about his financial anxieties brought a helpful response. His father arranged to have his Boldino estate in Nizhny Novgorod, with 200 serfs, not as yet mortgaged, transferred to Pushkin – a transaction formally concluded on 27 June 1830. This, according to Pushkin's father, ought to give him an income of 4,000 roubles a year, which compared very favourably with his salary as a young man.

What Natalya felt towards Pushkin is a matter of much debate. No doubt Pushkin had the measure of it accurately enough: he had no delusion that she had fallen in love with him. This was common enough in marriages of the time, though Pushkin, who was hardly making a marriage of convenience, might have hoped for more. However, Natalya's frivolity, her lack of interest in literary matters and her inability to respond to his greatness as a poet seems to have weighed little with Pushkin. Annenkov, Pushkin's first reliable biographer, did not speculate about Natalya's feelings. The memoirs of Natalya's daughter by her second marriage are, above all, concerned to defend her mother's reputation. Pavel Shchegolev's *The Duel and Death of Pushkin* speaks of Natalya as having only one aim in life – the excitements of society and flirtation. Later poets have felt much indignation on Pushkin's behalf. Anna Akhmatova in particular says of Natalya, 'She did all she wanted, never taking any account of him whatsoever. She ruined him and deprived him of his spiritual tranquillity...'

Most contemporary writers agree that Natalya was a woman of extraordinary beauty and innocence, though there are dissenting voices. Pushkin's friend A. N. Vulf confided to his diary: 'I wish him happiness, but I don't know if this can be hoped for with his morals and his manner of thinking. If the law of mutual responsibility obtains, then he is going to be well and truly cuckolded. This is all the more likely because the first thing he'll do will be to debauch his wife. I hope I'm completely mistaken.'[11]

The portrait painted by V. Gau shows Natalya in her mid-thirties at the time of her second marriage, and cannot do her justice as the woman Pushkin married: Natalya was not yet eighteen when she became engaged to Pushkin on 6 May 1830. Nevertheless, it shows a woman of enchanting beauty. There is a sketch of Pushkin's own, and a water colour attributed to the fashionable oil painter Karl Bryullov, made in early 1832, which gives some idea of her young radiance, though the pale colours are too bland to give more than an impression of her. Pushkin thought of her as a Renaissance Madonna, and has her in mind in 1830 in a poem called 'Madonna', which concludes,

> My wish is granted: God has shown your face
> To me, and here now you must reign
> As an example of the purest grace.

Count Vladimir Sollogub writes of Natalya in her early youth,

In the course of my life I have seen many beautiful women who were perhaps more attractive, but I have never met a woman who presented a perfection that was almost complete, classical in both her features and in her body. She was tall, about 5'6" – therefore two or three inches taller than Pushkin – with a deliciously thin waist and marvellous bosom above which her fine head was balanced like a lily; I have never had the opportunity to contemplate such a beautiful and such a regular profile, and what colouring, what eyes, what teeth, what ears. Yes, she was a real beauty, and it was quite natural that her presence made all other women fade away, even the most charming. She always seemed reserved, almost to the point of coldness, and she talked little.[12]

There is much to pause over in this description – the distinction between beauty and attractiveness, presumably animation, for instance, and the stress on her cool manner, which Pushkin was to describe in a poem of extraordinary erotic frankness after their marriage.

For the moment Pushkin could only guess at his future bride's disposition and, though he was happy in the success of his courtship, that did not allay the anxieties the notes in his supposedly 'French translation' reveal:

I never bothered about happiness. I was able to do without it. Now I have to have happiness for two, but where am I to get it from? I am to be married; that is, I sacrifice my independence, my carefree, whimsical independence, my luxurious habits, my aimless wanderings, solitude and inconstancy ... While I am unmarried, where are my obligations? In the morning I get up when I wish, I decide to go out ... I dress carelessly if I go out as a guest,

with all possible attention if I dine in a restaurant, where I read either a
new romance or journals...'[13]

These revelatory, quasi-fictional notes have an uncannily prophetic conclusion:

> In my presence, ladies praise my choice, but behind my back they pity my
> bride. – 'Poor thing! She is so young, so innocent, and he is such a loose,
> immoral fellow.'[14]

His friends reacted to the news of his engagement with some incredulity. Vyazemsky was only convinced of the truth of it when Pushkin's
famously mean father opened a special bottle of champagne in honour
of the occasion. Once persuaded that the marriage would, indeed, take
place, Vyazemsky professed to see something appropriate in the marriage
of Russia's finest romantic poet to the first romantic beauty of the young
generation. It is a little unsettling, however, and gives a little jolt to any
idea of Vyazemsky as a friend of Pushkin who understood his inner
being, to read that Vyazemsky wrote to his wife in April 1830, 'It's hard
to believe that she will marry him or that the mother will give her
daughter to an unstable fop who derives pleasure from unhappiness.'
Elizaveta Khitrovo, no doubt a little piqued by Pushkin's commitment,
warned Pushkin acidly that she feared his poetry would suffer, and
assured him that in the long run stable happiness was monotonous and
'made a man a fat and contented fellow rather than a great poet'. To
this, Pushkin replied, 'The fact is that I am a good fellow and that I do
not ask anything better than to grow fat and be happy; the one is easier
than the other.'[15]

On 5 May 1830 Natalya wrote to her grandfather to ask him to love
Pushkin. Pushkin visited her at her grandfather's factory in May, and
both wrote verses in an album there. Even so, there were further delays
even after the formal engagement. Pushkin was plunged into prolonged
financial and petty negotiations with his future mother-in-law, a fact
attested to in a letter to P. V. Annenkov much later. Natalya was much
under her mother's influence even though she understood her mother's
character 'had been spoilt by her husband's madness and other
unpleasantness of a family nature'. At 18 she allowed her mother to
dictate cutting remarks into letters to her future husband, though 'she
always wrote a postscript after her words with tenderness, and Pushkin
understood'. Pushkin refused to yield to his future mother-in-law and

when she reminded him that he owed her respect as he was entering her family he would reply, 'It's your daughter's business. I am marrying her, not you.'

Nevertheless, he allowed himself to be bullied by her. Pushkin received absolutely no contribution towards the expenses of the wedding, though Natalya Ivanovna did mortgage her jewels and then gave Pushkin and his wife the power to redeem them. Apart from that there was no money whatever from the Goncharov estate. Moreover, Pushkin found himself acting on behalf of the Goncharov family in an attempt to persuade the St Petersburg authorities to part with 25,000 roubles to buy a huge bronze statue of Catherine II that had been in the Goncharov cellars since the eighteenth century. His attempt at persuasion was not a success, and he earned no thanks from his future father-in-law for trying.

In spite of Pushkin's accession to every demand, the wedding was postponed several times. Originally fixed for September, the ceremony had to be delayed for a further six weeks because Pushkin's uncle Vasily died in August 1830. Uncertain of his fate at the end of August, Pushkin set out for Boldino in Nizhny Novgorod to look after his newly acquired estate.

Eighteen-thirty had been a year marked not only by a frustrated courtship but also, for the first time in his literary life, by journalistic squabbling in which Pushkin's African inheritance became the subject of deliberate mockery. That he was no longer the idol of literary society had been evident for some time, but the personal attack upon him of Faddey Bulgarin, a journalist who had made a particular point of criticising authors appearing in Delvig's *Northern Flowers* and *Literary Gazette*, nevertheless took Pushkin by surprise. Bulgarin refers outrageously to Pushkin's African ancestry:

> The anecdote is told that a certain Poet ... the offspring of a mulatto man or woman, I don't remember which, began to contend that one of his ancestors was a Negro prince. In the town hall of the city, it was discovered that in antiquity there was a lawsuit between a skipper of a ship and an assistant of his for this Negro, whom each of them wished to claim as his own, and that the skipper contended that he bought the Negro for a bottle of rum. Who would have thought then that a versifier would acknowledge connection with that Negro? Vanitas Vanitatum.[16]

The allusion to his mother as mulatto stung Pushkin particularly, and he might well have challenged Bulgarin to a duel over that alone if

Bulgarin had belonged to the same class. Instead, Pushkin responded by writing 'My Genealogy'. He did not offer the poem for publication, but only allowed it to circulate in manuscript. Delvig himself advised against its publication. The main part of the poem is aimed at the newly made aristocrats at Court, whose pedigree was rarely as old as Pushkin's and whom he accused of winning their rank through toadying or equally degrading favours. In the postscript, however, Pushkin defends his great-grandfather from Bulgarin's scurrilous attack.

> Filyarin says he understands
> That my black grandad, Gannibal,
> Bought for a bottle of rum, once fell
> Into a drunk sea captain's hands.
>
> That glorious skipper set our state
> Upon its grand and mighty course
> And his great rudder took control
> Of the whole Empire by his force.
>
> My grandfather, so cheaply bought,
> The Tsar himself treated with trust
> And gave him welcome at his court.
> Black, but never again a slave.

The poem continues to list the triumphs of Gannibal's son, Ivan, at Navarino. 'My Genealogy' was a poem that signalled a disastrous change in Pushkin's situation, particularly in the society at Court. The nobility around the throne were never to forgive him for lines where he contrasts his own ancient boyar ancestry with their more recently ennobled families.

Still furious at scenes in which his future mother-in-law heaped insults upon him, Pushkin wrote to Natalya after his departure, 'Perhaps she is right and I am wrong in thinking for a moment that I was created for happiness. In any case, you are entirely free; as for me, I give you my word of honour to belong to you only, or never to marry.'[17] This offer of eternal loyalty must be offset by another letter to Pletnev in which in his unhappiness he begins to reflect on the cares of the married man and the charms of a bachelor life. Although Pushkin was frustrated by the further delay to his wedding plans, this proved to be the first of his three fruitful Boldino autumns.

CHAPTER TWELVE

Boldino

Boldino was a dirty, depressing village, little more than a row of wretched cottages and a church, surrounded by a flat plain with few trees and no meadows. 'I have spent the first month here without seeing a soul,' Pushkin wrote to Pletnev on 29 September 1830. To Natalya he wrote gloomily on 11 October that their marriage seemed to be forever receding from his grasp, while he remained isolated in a countryside of 'mud, pestilence, and conflagration ... Boldino has the air of a rock-bound island'.

Several times Pushkin tried to break through the quarantine that isolated him, but without success. Military guards were stationed on every road to prevent the movement of people carrying the infection, and Pushkin was unable to persuade them to let him through. To Vyazemsky he wrote with characteristic pungency on 5 November of his unhappiness at finding himself trapped in the wilds of Nizhny Novgorod. 'It's just like a fir cone up your arse; it went in fine, but it's rough coming out.' Yet, for all his frustration and his dislike of the poor, muddy streets through which only cows wandered, his isolation was in one way good fortune. Pushkin was writing, as he admitted in a letter to Pletnev of 9 December, as he had not written for a long time.

His genius flowed that autumn. Not only was he able to complete the final chapters of *Evgeny Onegin*, he also wrote the four brilliant 'Little Tragedies' – 'The Miserly Knight', 'Mozart and Salieri', 'The Stone Guest', 'The Feast During the Plague' – and in addition 'The Tales of Belkin' prose fiction to which generations of Russian novelists, notably

Lev Tolstoy, have acknowledged their debt. He also produced the narrative poem 'The Little House at Kolomna' and some thirty short poems.

Pushkin had taken almost the whole of his mature life to bring *Evgeny Onegin* to completion, and on the day on which he finished it he wrote:

> Kishinev 9 May 1823
> Boldino, 25 September 1830
> 7 years, four months, 167 days.

Pushkin himself had developed alongside the growth of that poem and, though the fizz of the poetry gives it a unity of feeling, it is in the chapters following the death of Lensky that we feel a range of sympathy altogether beyond Byron in *Don Juan*. Structurally, chapter eight of *Onegin* is one of the most ingenious of the book. It has an epigraph from Byron:

> Fare thee well, and if for ever,
> Still for ever, fare thee well.

That elegiac note seems at first to be explained by the way the chapter begins, not with Evgeny, as Pushkin had promised at the end of his earlier chapter, but with Pushkin's own memories of the lyceum when 'the Muse ... first lit up his student cell' and he had a sense of her presence even in the rowdy feasts of his adolescence.

> The young pursued my Muse like devils,
> While I, mid friends, was drunk with pride –
> My flighty mistress at my side.

Even as he waited in Boldino, contemplating a much-desired and still-frustrated marriage, Pushkin is able to admit that it is the writing of poetry that has given him the most constant pleasure of his life. He describes the company of the Muse during his exile in the Caucasus and Moldavia – sometimes among wild tribes, sometimes in his own garden – before leading her with great assurance into a stately ballroom in St Petersburg. There he identifies a stranger with an expression somewhere between martyred pride and spleen. It is Evgeny at 26 who,

> Without position, work or wife
> Could find no purpose to his life.

Winding a road into the story gives Pushkin an opportunity both to reflect on the course of his own life and to pay tribute to more fortunate, if less unusual people who follow less extraordinary roads and so 'at fifty are considered splendid fellows', a fate Pushkin had imagined for himself after marriage in his letter to Elizaveta Khitrovo.[1] There is an increasing melancholy in these thoughts, which even the exuberance of his verse cannot disguise.

> How sad that youth with all its power
> Was given us in vain, to burn;
> That we betrayed it every hour,
> And were deceived by it in turn;
> That all our finest aspirations
> Our brightest dreams and inspirations,
> Have withered with each passing day.

This disenchantment he shares with Evgeny who, bored with travelling, is back in St Petersburg. At a ball he sees a stately beauty who bears a resemblance to Tatyana. Amazed at her poise, he inquires from a prince standing by who she might be. He discovers she is, indeed, Tatyana and, moreover, the wife of the same prince, who leads Evgeny over to introduce him. Princess Tatyana, to his amazement, shows no sign of agitation at the sight of him. It is Evgeny who is disturbed, as much by her sophistication as anything. When he calls on her the next day she is alone but equally calm. In the evening she receives guests with the same grace and assurance. There is no sign of the rash, emotional Tatyana he remembers. Overcome with this transformation, Evgeny falls in love.

> She pays him not the least attention
> No matter what he tries to do,
> At home receives him without tension;
> In public speaks a word or two...

Frustrated by his failure to attract her interest, Onegin is reduced to writing a love letter to her in his turn, as she had once written to him. She does not answer, nor does she reply to his next missive and, when he meets her by chance, haughtily ignores him. Winter turns to spring, and Evgeny still finds himself hopelessly obsessed with a girl he had once rejected, now changed into so grand a lady. Calling on her unexpectedly one day, he finds Tatyana weeping, recognises his own letter and falls to his knees before her. At last she speaks:

> Enough. Get up. To you I owe
> A word of candid explanation.
> Onegin, do you still retain
> Some memory of that park and lane
> Where fate once willed our confrontation,
> And I so meekly heard you preach?
> It's my turn now to make a speech.

Wisely and sadly she points out that when Evgeny rejected her she had been younger, probably better-looking and had offered her whole heart. What, she wonders, has changed to make him pursue her now? Is it rank, her husband's honours, her stylish house? None of it means anything to her, and she would gladly exchange all of it for the days when, as she remembers poignantly,

> Happiness was ours ... so nearly
> It came so close.

Then, in the words that Marina Tsvetayeva responded to in tears at the age of six and which haunted her throughout her life, Tatyana admits,

> I love you. Why should I dissemble?
> But I am now another's wife
> And I'll be faithful all my life.

The frankness of her admission of continuing attachment is moving in itself. Tatyana, after all, retains the same soul. Perhaps she is a man's ideal of a woman – unhappy, proud, still beautiful, and not to be seduced. That Pushkin should propose to himself such a vision of female probity in the last few months before his own marriage shows that his poet's eye was undeceived, even as he chose so much less serious a woman.

The climax of *Evgeny Onegin* was not the only achievement of that autumn at Boldino. All five of the *Tales of Belkin* were written between 9 September and 14 October. Initially they puzzled Russian readers, who expected from prose something more like Richardson, Rousseau or Karamzin's 'Poor Liza', the tale of a nobleman's seduction and abandonment of a peasant girl, who naturally drowns herself. Pushkin's tales were, from almost every point of view, innovatory.

As for the prose itself, Ezra Pound, remarking in the twentieth century that poetry should at least have the virtues of good prose, would have admired Pushkin's delight in 'the charm of bare simplicity'. The tales are written in curt, short sentences, with few allusions of any kind, though there is often an element of parody, especially in the tale of Dunya, as we shall see. The whole collection was presented as the work of Ivan Belkin, a country squire, with 'A.P.' as no more than his editor. Moreover, Belkin himself was not supposed to be the inventor of the stories so much as a recorder of other people's accounts. None of the tales concern momentous events. Several critics, notably Pushkin's enemy Bulgarin, dismissed them out of hand as having 'not the slightest point'.

To a modern reader, they remain curiously moving. The skilful manipulation of each narrative is at once invisible and compelling. Pushkin had an instinctive understanding of the power of plot. In the second story, 'The Blizzard', for instance, Mariya and Vladimir arrange to elope. There is a terrifying blizzard and the young man, lost in the snows, takes the wrong turning through the woods. He persists in trying, with the desperation of a man in a nightmare, to find the village church at which Mariya is waiting but fails to do so. The next day Mariya falls ill and is delirious for two weeks in the care of her puzzled parents. When she recovers, her parents are so relieved they write to Vladimir and give consent to the marriage. Instead of a joyful reply, they receive a half-crazed letter. News comes first that he has rejoined his regiment and after a time that he has died in battle.

During three years of mourning the young girl receives many proposals of marriage but rejects them all. Then she is inexplicably drawn to a young colonel of 26. He confesses his love, but explains there is an insuperable barrier between them. It seems he had been lost one night in a blizzard, and arrived at a church where a pretty girl had fainted while waiting for her betrothed. The priest mistakes him for the man expected and he irresponsibly falls in with the part until he is recognised after the ceremony. Now he is tied for ever to a wife he does not know. Mariya naturally turns out to be that very girl and her own coldness to all lovers is thus explained.

In the fourth story, 'The Postmaster', a traveller stays at a well-kept inn with Dunya, the postmaster's daughter, waiting on table, and finds it easy to begin conversation. On the wall there is a painting of the Prodigal Son. As he is leaving, he asks Dunya for a kiss, and 'Many a kiss I can count ... but none has left me with a memory so sweet and lasting'.

A few years later the traveller returns to the same inn and finds it completely neglected, with the postmaster looking much older. The postmaster is at first reluctant to say what has happened to Dunya, but at last is drawn to tell the story. A handsome young hussar with a black moustache fell sick in his inn and was nursed by his daughter. When he recovered he ordered a sledge and asked Dunya to ride with him as far as the church. Dunya never returned.

Determined to find his daughter and bring her home, the postmaster sets out for St Petersburg. The young hussar is easy enough to find, but unrepentant. He gives the postmaster some money and throws him out into the street. The next day the postmaster calls on his daughter and finds her dressed in the height of fashion. She falls to the floor at seeing her father, but the postmaster is forcibly ejected once again.

So far so conventional – the ironies appear at the end of the story, which does not show the expected punishment or forgiveness of a 'prodigal daughter'. On the contrary, it is the father who takes to drink and is soon dead. Some years after this, at the same village, the traveller learns from a peasant that a lady with her children in a carriage drawn by six horses had come to visit the postmaster and that she gave him a five kopeck piece to show her his grave. Nothing very terrible seems to have become of Dunya for all the immorality of her life.

In the opening story, 'The Shot', Sylvio, a renowned marksman, irritated by an opponent's seeming indifference to death in a duel, has waited some years to take the second shot to which he was entitled. As Sylvio remarks, 'We shall see whether he faces death with the same indifference on the eve of his wedding as when he faced it eating a capful of cherries.'[2]

We cannot but remember the legend of Pushkin's behaviour in Odessa, and wonder whether, if the story was an invention, it was not one to which Pushkin contributed. Pushkin is writing the story on the verge of his own anticipated marriage and perhaps once again there is an uncanny flicker of personal premonition. It is a story with a page-turning suspense and, though it ends with a shot to a portrait rather than the planned murder, the sadism of the satisfaction remains the same.

The most remarkable of the works completed in this Boldino autumn, however, are four blank verse 'Little Tragedies', which stand among most readers' favourite works of Pushkin. They are brilliant as poetry and successful as drama in a way *Boris Godunov* was not. In *Godunov* 'the heart of Russian history can be heard', as Antony Wood puts it, but that in itself does not give the play a relevance outside Russia as the issues raised in Shakespeare's history plays resonate far outside these islands. Each of the 'Little Tragedies' focuses on a single theme: the clash between a miser and his impecunious son in *The Miserly Knight*; the envy of genius felt by mediocrity (later the theme of Shaffer's 'Amadeus') in *Mozart and Salieri*; the return of the banished Don Juan to meet the statue of the Commendator, and a carousal by desperate survivors of the Black Death in *The Feast During the Plague*.

The inspiration for three of them was drawn from the English literary tradition – one from John Wilson, one attributed to William Shenstone and the other a writer not accorded much of a place in the English canon, Barry Cornwall, with the pseudonym of Barry Proctor (1787–1874), a friend of Byron, Keats and Leigh Hunt. Cornwall's *Dramatic Scenes* were short pieces which presented the climaxes of drama without any earlier exposition. They were published in Paris in 1829 and Pushkin read them in the same year. He transmuted and altogether transcended the work he 'translated' in the last months of 1830.

As there is a strong autobiographical element in 'The Stone Guest', we may start with that, though it is neither the first to be written nor the most successful. The parallels were very clear to Pushkin. In Pushkin's drama, unlike the Mozart opera, Don Juan is a poet. More importantly, as the great twentieth-century poet Anna Akhmatova observed in 1958, Pushkin, on the eve of his marriage, is reflecting on his own life as Don Juan. Anna, the distraught heroine of Mozart's opera, was still a virgin before her encounter with Don Juan. In 'The Stone Guest' Dona Anna is a widow who had not chosen her husband but had been given to Don Alvaro by her mother because he was a wealthy man. The play opens with Don Juan's forbidden return from exile, and a glimpse of Dona Anna coming to pray at her dead husband's grave. As Pushkin was hoping to become the husband of a beautiful and much younger wife, and did not imagine she yet loved him, he cannot but have seen the resemblance of his own situation to that of Don Alvaro. Moreover, he makes the Commendator the dead husband of Dona Anna rather than her father. Pushkin broods, too, on ageing, in the voice of Don Carlos, who has taken over an earlier mistress of Don Juan's:

> You're young ... five, six years more you will be young.
> Men will gather about you six years more;
> Flatter, caress you, shower you with their gifts ...

> But when your time is past, those eyes are hollow
> Those lids are shrunk, those tresses gleam with grey
> When you're accounted old – what then?[3]

The key scenes concern Don Juan's victory over Dona Anna's scruples. Rather as in *Richard III*, Don Juan confesses that it is he who murdered her husband, but has no remorse because he loves her. In this way, though she knows his reputation as a godless libertine, he wins her consent to a late night visit. We only join the line of the Mozart opera plot as Don Juan invites the statue of Don Alvaro to dinner with them. When the statue arrives to claim him Don Juan takes the cold stone hand with a kind of relief. 'I'm glad you've come.'

Pushkin was not at this point weary of life – to write with such feverish energy hardly suggests fatigue – but he was saying farewell to the character of Don Juan he had inhabited so long, not only in the list he wrote in Ushakova's album but in his claim that his wife-to-be was his 113th love.

Anna Akhmatova commented on the French novelist Benjamin Constant's hero Adolphe, whose worldly, bored character was one of the sources of Onegin[4] and points particularly to quotations from Adolphe which found their way into the verse of 'The Stone Guest'.

'The Miserly Knight', too, has its autobiographical source. Pushkin claimed it was based on an English play by William Chenstone (presumably Shenstone), though the English author wrote no play with that title, but there is some resemblance between Pushkin's one-time situation and that of a young man who feels helpless resentment for a father who prizes gold above the well-being of his son. The Baron, for his part, has some reason to distrust a son whose credit depends on his death. When the son refuses the offer of poison from the usurer Solomon, he is the more furious because the villain has articulated a half-formed thought of his own. The most remarkable speech in the play is that of the father gloating in a trembling, near-erotic excitement over his gold. The climax of the drama comes as the avaricious old man is forced by his own liege lord to confront the anger of his son and dies helplessly clutching the keys to gold, which has no power over death.

'Mozart and Salieri', the second of the plays to be completed, deals with the rumour that Salieri on his deathbed had confessed to the crime of poisoning Mozart. The idea had been in Pushkin's mind for some time. In a letter of E. A. Baratynsky to N. L. Baratynskaya[5] there is a description of a conversation at the Karamzins between Vyazemsky and Pushkin, who had both returned from seeing the opera *Don Giovanni*. Vyazemsky grumbled that it was time for Pushkin to write 'Mozart and Salieri': 'It's perhaps not a historically accurate fact, but the drama would be marvellous.' In the same letter Baratynsky recorded that Pushkin agreed he would write the play if he lived long enough, and one of those present noted that Raphael, Mozart and Byron, all three, died at the age of 37, and Pushkin cried out, 'Is this a fateful age for geniuses? Mind you, Goethe has avoided this fate.'

In drawing the character of Mozart, he saw his own character in the composer's light-hearted love of pleasure and a good humour that took no offence at a blind fiddler scraping the tune of '*Voi che sapete*' in a tavern. He saw himself, too, in the impoverished genius, saluted as a god by Salieri, who replied, 'I'm starving though, in my divinity.' All the familiar legends about Mozart are there in addition, such as the man in black who calls to ask for a requiem, disappears without trace, yet continues to haunt the composer. Salieri's motivation is presented with some subtlety as more than merely mediocrity's envy of genius; it is a hatred of a personality incomprehensible to his own dogged spirit – just as Pushkin bewildered so many of his serious-minded contemporaries. Pushkin knew himself to be essentially good-hearted, for all his irresponsibility, and, indeed, that self-knowledge was to be amply illustrated in the years of his marriage to come, as too was the trusting nature which Salieri puzzles over in Mozart. 'Genius and evil-doing don't go together,' Mozart remarks in this play.

As we look at Pushkin's own life, for all its frivolity and the sexual habits of his age, we see a generosity of spirit which is far removed from the calculations of evil. He liked to tell the truth and, though he enjoyed the drama of his characterisation of Salieri, it troubled him that the man had perhaps been libelled. In 1832 Pushkin added a note, as if in exoneration of what he knew to be an invention. 'Salieri died eight years ago. Some German journals stated that on his deathbed he confessed to having committed a terrible crime – he had poisoned the great Mozart.'

'The Feast During the Plague' had another kind of pertinence as Pushkin was writing at a time when Boldino was cut off by cholera and he could not but reflect how easily death might sweep into his village as it had into others. It is a free translation of part of Act One, Scene Four of John Wilson's *City of the Plague* (1816; published in 1829). What makes the 'Feast' so remarkable, however, is Walsingham's song in

praise of the plague, which is Pushkin's entirely original material. This
Tsvetayeva saluted as one of the most majestic lyrics ever written and
proof that poetry itself knows no morality. It's far from clear that Pushkin
would have interpreted the speech in the same way. Indeed, his meaning
is far closer to Yeats's 'death's the mother of beauty' since the knowledge
of it intensifies the human response to the world. Pushkin himself had
every reason at this juncture to want to live, if only to marry his Natalya.

CHAPTER THIRTEEN

Marriage

When Pushkin returned to Moscow on 5 December 1830 he was still wrangling with his future mother-in-law and he even had to reassure friends and family that the engagement was still on. Then, in January 1831, he received a great blow: Delvig, his greatest friend after Ivan Pushchin, unexpectedly died. The wedding day was rearranged once more, this time for 18 February 1831, but Pushkin's own thoughts, in a letter to his friend N. I. Kriustov less than a week beforehand, were melancholy:

> I am married – or nearly married. Everything that you might be able to tell me about the advantages of bachelor life and the disadvantages of marriage, all that I have already thought over carefully ... My youth has passed noisily and fruitlessly. I have had no happiness ... *Il n'est de bonheur que dans les voies communes.* I am past thirty. At the age of thirty people usually get married ... [omission here] ... probably I shall not regret it. Moreover, I am marrying without enthusiasm and without childish infatuation. The future does not appear to me a bed of roses, but in its severe nakedness. Sadnesses will not astonish me. They have entered into my domestic calculations. Any happiness will be an uncovenanted bonus.[1]

The wedding took place at the old church of the Assumption in Bolshaya Nikitskaya Street on 18 February 1831. The night before, Pushkin listened to Nashchokin's gypsy mistress singing and wept, perhaps for Delvig's death. The loss had been a grievous one: 'No one in the world had been closer to him,' as he wrote to Pletnev on 21 January.

'I am sad, miserable. This is the first death I have wept over.'[2]

He may also, for all his delight in winning Natalya, have been weeping for the end of his bachelor life. Since his bride had no dowry Pushkin had already been forced to mortgage his estate to help with wedding expenses – it yielded the sum of 38,000 paper roubles. Of these, Natalya's trousseau immediately used 11,000, and on the very day of the wedding his mother-in-law sent to ask for money to pay for the carriage she needed. At the ceremony itself one of the wedding rings dropped on the floor and a cross and a Bible fell from the pulpit. These mishaps aroused all Pushkin's superstitious fears of ill-luck.

Nevertheless, writing to his publisher a week later, Pushkin declared himself a happy man. 'My one desire is that nothing in my present life should change – nothing better can be expected. This situation is so new for me that I seem to have been reborn.' Pushkin and his wife rented a house in the centre of Moscow on the Arbat, which had an elegant drawing room wallpapered in lilac flock flowers. According to Natalya's account, Pushkin rose early the morning after the wedding and spent the day with friends, while she spent the time weeping until he returned for dinner in the late afternoon.[3]

Society congratulated Pushkin on the end of his bachelor days, and the couple was invited everywhere. On 22 February there was a grand ball at a friend's house and then a masked ball at the Bolshoi Theatre. On 27 February, nine days after the wedding, the Pushkins themselves gave a ball which lasted till three o'clock in the morning. According to a guest, 'They entertained their guests splendidly. She is delightful, they are like turtle doves together. Everyone finds it strange that Pushkin, who has lived all his life in taverns, is suddenly managing a household. We left at three in the morning.'[4]

Perhaps 'managing' is the wrong word. Money was a problem from the outset. Of the money gained by mortgaging his estate, 10,000 roubles went to Pushkin's friend Nashchokin 'to extricate him from difficult circumstances'.[5] This may have been an act of generosity in memory of so many similar kindnesses enjoyed when Nashchokin's own fortunes were secure, or may have involved a deal with third parties. That left Pushkin only 17,000 roubles with which to settle down and set up domestic life, little enough to live on for a couple since a frugal bachelor at Pushkin's social level could hardly have managed on less than 6,000 roubles a year. None of these calculations takes into account Pushkin's substantial gambling debts. Worse, he had thought of the 11,000 roubles for his wife's trousseau as no more than a loan to his future mother-in-law, but it rapidly became clear he was not going to see any of the money returned.

Writing to his old friend Elizaveta Khitrovo on 26 March, Pushkin spoke of the 'bustle and bothers' of the previous month, and declared 'Moscow is the town of nothingness. On its gate is written: Abandon all intelligence, all ye who enter here.' Pushkin always had the habit of exaggerating everything that could excuse his failure to arrive at Khitrovo's salon and, whatever else bothered him about Moscow, he makes it clear in a letter to Pletnev that he found 'his little wife charming, and not only in outward appearance'.[6] Pushkin's own appearance, however, according to Simmons, led some Moscow wits to speak of their marriage as the wedding of 'beauty and the beast', though it is worth recalling that the outcome of that fairy tale is not an unhappy one. Many of his own friends were concerned that Natalya would miss the frivolity of Court life, while worrying that his new commitments would leave Pushkin no time to write.

Nor had his mother-in-law willingly relinquished hold on her daughter, to whom she gave advice and repeated scandalous stories about her husband's behaviour. Pushkin wrote angrily to her about this in a letter on 26 June 1832, after he and Natalya had left Moscow. 'I was being depicted to my wife as an odious man, greedy, a vile usurer etc. She was told "You are a fool to permit your husband," etc. You will admit to me that this was preaching divorce. A wife cannot with decency allow it to be said that her husband is a scoundrel and it is the duty of mine to submit to what I choose. It is not for a woman of eighteen years to govern a man of thirty two.' It was as much to escape his mother-in-law's meddling as anything else that Pushkin decided to leave Moscow, dreaming of an autumn, always his most creative period, alone with his new wife.

Barely six weeks after his wedding, on 15 May 1831, the Pushkins left Moscow for Tsarskoe Selo where they rented the less expensive dacha Kitaeva, a move arranged for them by Pletnev. There Pushkin and Natalya enjoyed five happy months and Pushkin found himself deeply and serenely in love with his wife, whose remarkable beauty he compared to the Madonna of Perugino. He retained a certain flippancy, however, on the subject of marriage: 'Don't think it will be the last stupidity I shall commit in my life.'[7]

Serious financial difficulties continued. Pushkin had always been a spendthrift and, though he took his new responsibilities seriously, Natalya's expectations exceeded anything he could provide. His Moscow creditors began to harass him and, though he delegated Nashchokin to straighten out some of his problems, he had to pawn his mother-in-law's jewels to fend off the most pressing. Pushkin was responsible for the whole expenditure of the household, Natalya was no more thrifty than himself and as poor a manager of the housekeeping as his mother had been. Pushkin treated her like a much-loved child.

There have been many indignant commentators ready to point out that Natalya had little interest in what Pushkin did to earn the money they both spent. Yet it is hardly surprising that his literary friends frightened or bored her with their obsessive talk about matters she could not understand. She took no pleasure in hearing poetry read aloud, and was well aware that some of his friends, particularly A. O. Rosset (soon Smirnova), a brilliant and attractive young maid of honour, considered her stupid. When Pushkin shut himself away in his study to work all day and far into the night, she was lonely and had little to amuse herself with. Pushkin had expected nothing else, and had only himself to blame. He remained convinced that women were insensitive to literature: 'Observe how they sing popular songs, how they distort the most natural verses, distort the measure and destroy the rhyme. Listen to their literary judgements and you will be surprised at the inappositeness and even at the stupidity of their understanding. *Exceptions are rare*' [my italics].[8] As he had not looked for a wife among these exceptions, he could hardly complain at Natalya's indifference to what he produced, even as he foolishly expected her to respect him for his work.

She had been a docile and willing daughter, and at first she did what she could to please her husband. She helped him to copy out rough drafts, and among the sheets of paper in Natalya's handwriting on the table in their oval reception room to this day are Pushkin's then as yet unpublished 'House at Kolomna' as well as fair copies of 'Secret Notes of Ekaterina II' and extracts from 'Journal of Discussion'. But she had some right to happiness herself. She hated being alone while Pushkin spent his days upstairs in his study on the mezzanine floor, which had three large windows overlooking a balcony.[9] When he came out of that study, blinking from work, Natalya turned to him for flattery and attention. He was more likely to take his composition of the day around to a literary friend. Pletnev introduced Gogol to Pushkin in June 1831, and Pushkin took particular delight in his company.

In July 1831 the royal family arrived in Tsarskoe Selo to escape a cholera epidemic raging in St Petersburg. It was then that the Tsar and Tsarina met Pushkin and his beautiful young wife in the gardens. Natalya won favour with the Emperor and Empress at once, and this at first appeared nothing but good news to Pushkin. He continued to be happy with his pretty young wife, who seemed affectionate and obedient.

However, as early as 13 July 1831, Natalya wrote to her grandfather, 'I cannot walk peacefully in the gardens as I have heard from one of the ladies in waiting that their majesties want to know the hour at which I take my walk, in order to meet me. I have now chosen to walk in more secluded spots.'[10]

Natalya clearly knew Nicholas's reputation as a womaniser and feared his interest, though she was flattered by it. On 25 July the Emperor and Empress met her in the gardens with a thousand compliments, and thereafter she was obliged 'very much against her will'[11] to appear at Court. There, inevitably, she was soon an outstanding social success.

The questions that arose about relations between Pushkin and his wife intrigued the gossips of the time long before they knew the tragic end to the story. Most of their conjectures were spiteful, and probably wrong. Professor Mikhailovna at the Moscow Pushkin museum is insistent on this point: 'Natalya loved her husband.' Certainly a wife who felt only repugnance for her husband would hardly have been as dismayed as Natalya was in June 1831 when she rushed to Vyazemsky's wife because her husband had not been home for three days. Moreover, she was as apprehensive as flattered when the Tsar showed her that he found her attractive, while Pushkin did not find the Tsar's offer of a job in any way sinister:

The Tsar has taken me into his service, not into an office or the Court or the military. No, he has given me a salary, has opened the archives to me so that I may rummage there and do nothing. Very nice of him, isn't it? He said, '*Puis qu'il est marié et qu'il n'est pas riche, il faut faire aller sa marmite.*' ('Since he is married and has little money, he must have something to keep his pot boiling.')

This Pushkin wrote to Pletnev on 22 July 1831, apparently without calculating that the salary of 5,000 roubles would be quickly consumed by the dresses Natalya needed to attend Court functions.

The following poem, more intimate than usual at that period, was probably written in 1831 or 1832 and some copies are headed, 'To my wife'.

> No, I don't enjoy the stormy ecstasies
> The wild delight and cries of maddened frenzy
> When some young Bacchante begins to writhe
> Within my serpentine embrace, who tries
> To bring on the last shudder the more quickly
> With hot caresses and quick biting kisses.
>
> Much dearer are you to me, modest love!
> When you give in to my long pleading
> Shyly cold, and unresponsive to my pleasure
> You make me the more painfully happy
> Even though you take no notice, until
> At last you find yourself roused to move
> Little by little and are brought to share
> My passion finally against your will.

Personal happiness did not preserve Pushkin from being irked by the gossip he knew his marriage had aroused. In November 1831 he sent a copy of his angry poem 'My Genealogy' to Benckendorf, with the request that it be shown to Nicholas himself, explaining the depths of his continuing resentment:

> About a year ago, in one of our journals, a satirical article was printed in which a certain man of letters was spoken of as having pretensions to noble origin, when he was only a bourgeois. It was added that his mother was a mulatto, whose father, a poor piccaninny, had been bought by a sailor for a bottle of rum. Although Peter the Great little resembled a drunken sailor, no Russian man of letters except me can count a Negro amongst his ancestors.[12]

Nicholas's reply, in his own hand, said,

> You can tell Pushkin from me that I am completely of the opinion of his late friend Delvig; abuse so low, so vile as that with which he has been regaled dishonours the one who utters it, rather than the one at whom it is directed; the only weapon against it is *contempt*, and that is what I would have shown in his place.[13]

It was not a very perceptive suggestion, however well meant, as there was no way the impoverished Pushkin, now the husband of a Court beauty, could respond to slurs with the same magnanimity.

At the end of October 1831, once the cholera had abated, the Pushkins moved back to St Petersburg and their style of life changed completely. All through the season, from November until June 1832, Natalya was out every night and Pushkin had to accompany her, though he had never been fond of either balls or dancing. Worse, he found himself disdainfully regarded by the rich and splendid, for whom his four-hundred-year-old pedigree counted little and his genius as a poet nothing. It was a situation which resembled nothing so much as the humiliation he had suffered in his childhood at dancing classes, mocked by his mother. For a time he shrugged off the unpleasantness, saddened only that it was expensive to keep up the standard of living Natalya's social position as Court favourite demanded. His finances depended on his fame as a poet and on publication, which continued to be delayed by the censorship.

Relations between the couple had not soured when Pushkin left for Moscow in December 1831. According to his friend Nashchokin, when Pushkin received a letter from Natalya he ran around the room kissing it, just as Ibrahim in *The Negro of Peter the Great* had done. Pushkin's own financial affairs, however, were in worse confusion than he feared, as he confessed to his wife, displacing a little of the blame on Nashchokin: 'Nashchokin has made a bigger muddle of his affairs than we suspected.'[14] By now Natalya was three months pregnant, and his letters show how close he felt to her, his lively concern for her health and his knowledge of her likely recklessness. 'You won't sit at home, you'll go to the Court, and before you know it you'll miscarry on the 105th step of the Tsar's staircase. My darling, my wife, my angel, look after yourself. If you go to a ball, for God's sake dance nothing but the quadrille.'[15]

Her letter to him had spoken of 'vertige' and he began to blame himself for leaving her in St Petersburg. 'Is it dizziness or sickness? Have you seen the midwife? Have they bled you? These horrors upset me so much. The more I think about it, the more I realise how stupid I was to leave you.'[16]

Pushkin was not enjoying his stay in Moscow without his wife. As he wrote to Natalya on 10 December, 'What shall I tell you of Moscow? ... Moscow is still dancing, but I have not been to any balls yet ... I dislike your Moscow.'

On 19 May 1832 Natalya gave birth to their first daughter, Maria, in a dacha outside St Petersburg, and on 22 May her grandfather, who had always adored Natalya since he had looked after her as a child, arrived in the capital to ask the Tsar for a subsidy to put his affairs straight at the factory. He gave Natalya 500 roubles for the child's first tooth, a traditional Russian gift for a newborn child. On 9 June he gave her another 100 roubles to help defray the expenses of the christening. By 8 September, however, that benevolent grandfather was dead, and Natalya's brother Dmitry, himself a ne'er-do-well, searched in vain for a deed that would establish their father (the legal heir) as unfit to run the estate. These difficulties preoccupied the Goncharovs throughout the first year of Pushkin's marriage.

On 21 September 1832 Pushkin once again set off for Moscow, still with the hope of sorting out his finances. He wrote daily to his wife, praising her for long letters and for their businesslike tone. When Natalya made an attempt to take their household in hand and wrote to Pushkin about domestic affairs, he responded with the kind of indulgent delight one reserves for children. On 25 September 1832 he wrote,

> What a clever little thing, what a sweet little thing you are! What a long letter! How sensible it is ... Conclude what terms you wish with the cook, providing only I am not to be forced, after dining at home, to have supper at my club.[17]

Natalya was perhaps not altogether pleased by the tone of his approval. On 3 October 1832 he answered a letter which must have complained of his laggardly replies:

> I shall answer your accusations point by point. One, a Russian does not change clothes on the road, but when he arrives at his destination, dirty as a pig, he goes to the baths which are our second mother. Two, letters are accepted at Moscow until 12 o'clock – and I entered the Tverskaya gates at exactly 11.[18]

Pushkin's admirers, including Akhmatova, who have found Natalya both silly and pitiless later in their marriage, did not have access to her recently discovered letters to her brother Dmitry which offer many new insights into her character. Dmitry sent his sister essential food supplies from the Goncharov estate, such as jam, pickles, game, home-spun linen and woollen socks and stockings for the children. He also sent her a young serf as a little page whom she describes in a letter of 11 March 1833 from St Petersburg: 'I have hardly seen him since he still does not have a pleasant appearance and squats on his heels by the stove in the kitchen. His fine livery will only be ready tomorrow, Sunday 12 March, when he will take his first steps into the world.' Here she resembles the foolish girl her critics imagined. In the same letter she then requests a landau, rather than the pram offered her by her mother, and asks her brother '... if possible to send it to me by Easter. And for the love of God do your best to ensure it is new and modern.'[19] The preoccupation with appearances is unmistakeable, but so, too, is the dire financial need.

The tone of Pushkin's letters to his wife, and what we can guess of hers from his replies, suggest an intimate, teasing relationship of some ease. When Pushkin did not write as frequently as she expected, Natalya often got angry with him. If her letters were not angry, he wondered. 'I expect thunder and lightning from you, for you didn't receive a letter from me before Sunday as I figured it. But you're so calm, so indulgent, so amusing that it's marvellous. What does this mean? I'm not a cuckold, am I?'[20]

By May his mother-in-law had improved her relationship with Pushkin to the point where Natalya was able to go and visit her without contention. This easing of tension brought a letter dated 14 May 1833:[21] 'Thank you with all my heart for the happiness you have offered me in leaving your wife and children with me. I am touched by the trust you show me in your letter and, taking into account the love I feel for Natalya and which you nourish for her, your trust is not in vain.' A short restrained postscript to that letter, written in French, is the only surviving note we have from Natalya to Pushkin.

Altogether, the year 1833 was unusually thin for Pushkin. Even as he made notes on his travels for his *History of Pugachev*, his notebooks show the beginnings of a story[22] about a gambler, which would turn into *The Queen of Spades*, and jottings which suggest an initial plan for *The Captain's Daughter*, which was not to be written until three years later.

Natalya gave Pushkin three further children after Marie. Alexander was born on 6 July 1834, Grigory in 1835 and Natalya in 1836. After Alexander's birth she suffered from mastitis. Pushkin preserved a good deal of his own freedom. On 7 August 1833 he received the Tsar's permission for a four-month absence to explore the Volga background of his Pugachev epic. Natalya remained at Black River in the care of her aunt Ekaterina. This was their longest separation, during which he wrote her another 16 letters, which are particularly revealing.

On 2 September he wrote from Nizhny Novgorod, 'If you are sensible, by which I mean calm and well, I shall bring you things worth 100 roubles from the country, as they say. What weather we are having! Hot days, slight frost in the morning, delightful!'²³ In another letter, written on the same day, Pushkin modifies this impression of careless pleasure by adding a passage in which his longing for her is touchingly manifest. 'The market is over and as I wandered through the empty stalls it reminded me of when the ball is over and the Goncharovs' carriage has already left. *Addio, mia bella, idol mio, mio bel tesoro, quando mi ti rivedro!'*

For all this tenderness, he was casual enough about the pressure she continued to face in his absence. In a letter to her brother Dmitry on 1 September 1833 Natalya was reduced to begging for money to see her through. At the same time she rather charmingly defends her husband against Dmitry's indignant observation that Pushkin had abandoned his wife and family without sufficient money for necessities. 'My husband left me an adequate sum of money, but I was forced to give it to the landlord of the apartment I have just rented; I did not expect I should have to pay an extra 1,600 roubles, which is why I now haven't a kopeck in my pocket. For the love of God send me something quickly...'²⁴

Dmitry was unconvinced by her excuse, and continued to berate Pushkin in his reply. Her own response has a touching dignity, and repeats her defence of her husband:

> I thank you a million times for the 500 roubles you have allowed me to take. I am committed to repaying them in the month of November. Try and be accurate, as you promised, since this is the first time I have borrowed money ... and I would be in great trouble if I were not to keep my word ... The money my husband left me would have been more than adequate until his return if I had not been forced to pay out 1,600 roubles for the apartment.²⁵

Contrary to Natalya's letters to Dmitry, Pushkin very well knew his wife needed to worry about money: 'The cook, the cabby, the druggist ... pester you for what is owed them. You don't have enough money. You're worried, you're angry with me – and it serves me right – Pugachev isn't worth it.'

During these journeys, researching the life of Pugachev, Pushkin wrote many tender letters to his wife, but the most interesting tribute to her comes in Pushkin's letter of 21 August 1833 where, having described how far the fame of Natalya's beauty has travelled, he adds at one point,

'But I love your soul even more than your face.' This comes as a surprise, but her sexual innocence and her simple Christian faith touched him. He often asked her to bless his children with the sign of the cross, as if he felt God would be more likely to pay attention to her. Some insight into what Pushkin might also have meant by her soul can be found in two erotic poems about their intimate life: the first written in 1830 about her disbelieving his vows of love; the second, already quoted, in which he describes the sexual pleasure her shy coldness gives him. He may also have hoped that the gentleness and softness of her beauty concealed the depth of his heroine Tatyana.

As his trip continued, Pushkin drove in a carriage with six horses through muddy side roads, puddles and bad weather, calling in as he passed on the estate of the Vulfs. There he stuffed himself with good country jam and lost a few roubles at whist. On the road, Pushkin encountered Sobolevsky, travelling incognito to escape from people to whom he owed money, and he joined Pushkin on the journey, agreeing to pay half the expenses. He also agreed, as Pushkin explained with complete lack of inhibition to his wife, 'Not to fart, openly or furtively, unless in his sleep and at night at that, and not after dinner'.[26]

On 26 August 1833 Pushkin was back in Moscow and called on Natalya's mother, who continued to treat him well. He was not received by her father, but reported him 'quiet enough'. He still found Moscow boring, or so he wrote to his wife, and by 2 September 1833 he was beginning to worry that he had acted stupidly in leaving her alone for so long. It was a well-founded anxiety that in his absence Natalya was beginning to care more than anything else about her growing reputation as a Court beauty. 'As for my sister-in-law,' wrote Olga, 'she is the woman most in fashion here. She is in society and they say that she is most beautiful.'[27] Pushkin did not object to her pleasure, which he felt was no more than she deserved, though he advised Natalya not to lace herself too tightly, not to sit with her legs crossed and so forth, while pregnant. He even licensed a measure of flirting, though he cautioned her against coquetting with members of the diplomatic corps. Whatever anxieties he felt, he resolutely proceeded to Simbirsk, and enjoyed the weather on the way. In his letters, however, he begins to tell stories about women who showed him attention on his travels as if deliberately to stir Natalya's jealousy: 'You will ask whether the Governor's wife is pretty. That's the trouble. She was not pretty, my angel.'[28]

When he reached the village of his friend the poet Yazykov (who was not at home) he found a four-page letter from Natalya, and scolded her for spending so much energy on it when she was sick with mastitis. In Kazan he spent an evening in the home of a 'bluestocking', whom he described as 'unendurable, with waxed teeth and dirty nails', who insisted on reading her poetry to him, took his address and threatened to visit him in St Petersburg. On his way back to Simbirsk again he was superstitiously alarmed to have a hare cross his path and was missing his wife, as a letter written on 19 September from Orenburg makes clear:

> I'm lonely for you. If I weren't ashamed to, I'd return straight to you, without having written a single line. But that's impossible, my angel. In for a penny, in for a pound – that is, I left to write: so write then, novel after novel, long poem after long poem.[29]

He continues to tease her a little by reporting on his own sexual fidelity as if it were a great merit:

> How satisfied you would be with me. I'm not paying court to the young ladies, I'm not pinching station masters' wives, I'm not coquetting with Kalmuck girls – and a few days ago I refused a Bashkir girl, notwithstanding my curiosity, very forgivable in a traveller.[30]

Pushkin was pursuing his research, in fact, both energetically and honestly. On 19 September 1833 he met Vladimir Dal, a medical man who was to become a lexicographer and a celebrated author of Cossack tales. It was he who took Pushkin around the city of Orenburg and showed him the belfry where Pugachev had tried to hoist a cannon to bombard the city. Dal also took him to visit the Cossack village of Berdy, where Pugachev had his headquarters during the six months' siege of Orenburg. There he introduced Pushkin to an old woman who had met Pugachev, and she sang him a few songs about the treasure Pugachev was supposed to have buried, sewn in a shirt and covered with a dead body. The poet talked to her eagerly for a whole morning, and when he left gave her a gold coin.

Some idea of the impression he made on the old woman can be gained from a passage in Dal's memoirs. 'We left the town but the golden coin created an upheaval. The old woman ... could not understand why a stranger should have shown such interest in a brigand and a pretender with whose name so many terrible memories were connected ... The whole thing seemed highly suspicious ... Next day they took the old woman and the gold coin to Orenburg and informed the authorities that the day before a stranger came to their town who had the following distinctive features: he was short, he had dark curly hair and a swarthy complexion, and he tried to rouse the people just as Pugachev had done by giving them gold coins. They further surmised that he was probably the anti Christ, because instead of fingernails he had claws. Pushkin laughed a lot about that.'[31]

From Boldino, Pushkin wrote to Natalya, whose letter we may guess at from his. 'Don't frighten me. Don't say you are flirting in good earnest. I'll come to you without having succeeded in writing anything and without money we shall be in real trouble.'[32] On 11 October 1833 he wrote, 'Look after the children and do not flirt with the Tsar. I am writing, I am very busy. I do not see anyone and I shall bring back lots of things.'[33]

Natalya knew her husband's passionate nature and she may have been exaggerating her successes in society in the hope of bringing him home sooner. At the same time, the suggestion that she was flirting with the Tsar deserves some comment. If Nicholas were sufficiently excited by Natalya's behaviour she might have found it difficult, indeed, to refuse him. Later in their marriage this particular suspicion, however ill-founded, was to contribute to Pushkin's misery. Present-day Russian critics may discount the possibility of such a relationship. Pushkin himself did not.

Natalya was a beautiful woman and much younger than her husband, but she had her own grounds for jealousy. At the house of Mme Karamzina, the historian's widow, and also at Mme Smirnova's, Pushkin met several clever and well-educated women. Mirsky suggests that Natalya resented his visits to Mme Smirnova. For his part, Pushkin worried not only as a jealous husband but because he knew his wife's beauty made her 'too visible, as both wife of the poet and one of the most beautiful women in Russia. The slightest false step would be pounced on immediately, and praise would turn to envious condemnation, harsh and unjust.'[34] The political dimension to his anxieties was entirely reasonable.

Husband and wife continued teasing one another at a distance, with Pushkin most apprehensive that her frivolous life endangered her health. He was very anxious when he found no letters from Natalya on arriving at Boldino, and wrote berating her about her relations with 'old (bepissed) sixty and seventy year olds'. Pushkin was generally tolerant of his wife's vanity; all the same, he lays out the limits of his tolerance:

I'm glad that you're not with child and that nothing will prevent you from distinguishing yourself at the balls now going on … I don't prevent you from coquetting, but I demand of you coldness, propriety, dignity – still not to speak of the irreproachability of conduct which is to do, not with *tone* but with what is really most important of all.[35]

The narcissism of his wife had begun, perhaps, to irritate him a little. In response to a letter in which she must have been expressing some unguarded triumph at outshining a rival, he upbraids her: 'Why should you beat her out of her admirers?' What is most remarkable about these letters to Natalya is their informal frankness. Exasperated by her pleasure in the admiration she excites, he points out, 'There is little sense in it. You rejoice that male dogs are running after you like a little bitch, with their tails like a poker, and sniffing you in the arse: that's something to rejoice over?' He even, rudely and probably unfairly, suggests that the pursuit arises as much from the appearance she gives of being willing as from her beauty. 'Where there's a trough there'll be swine. I'm not being jealous, and I know too that you won't cast prudence to the winds,' he writes, perhaps to comfort himself, but he adds, 'If, upon my return, I find that your sweet, simple, aristocratic tone has changed, I'll divorce you.' In the same letter he writes, 'You ask me what I am doing and *whether I have grown better looking* [my italics]. To begin with, I have grown a beard,' which suggests that some of her teasing was intended to be hurtful. Guessing at the resentment that lay behind it, on 6 November, in his last letter from Boldino, he pleads with her not to worry him needlessly, and adds with more tenderness than reproach, 'My dear, dear, dear wife, I am travelling along highways, living three months in the wilds, stopping in horrible Moscow, which I detest, and for what? You, you, darling, so that you should not be worried and can shine in society to your heart's content as befits a beautiful woman of your age. But, please, take care of me too. Do not add to the worries which are inseparable from a man's life, family troubles, jealousy etc, etc …'[36]

For all this fretting, nothing was further from his wishes than to resume once again the life of a solitary bachelor. Commenting on a friend's marriage, he wrote to his wife, 'He should have done it long ago. It's better setting up housekeeping for oneself than to dangle after other men's wives all one's life.'[37]

CHAPTER FOURTEEN

The Bronze Horseman

From October to November 1833 Pushkin enjoyed his last really productive literary period at Boldino. He finished his Pugachev epic, wrote a verse fairy story, *The Tale of the Dead Tsarevna*, the prose tale *Queen of Spades*, the novel *The Captain's Daughter*, a marvellous spin-off from his *History of Pugachev*, *Dubrovsky*, the unfinished but compelling story of a young, ruined landowner who takes up the life of a bandit; and his masterpiece, the narrative poem 'The Bronze Horseman'.

The great bronze statue of Peter the Great by Falconet was set up by Catherine the Great, and bears the simple inscription: 'To Peter the First from Catherine the Second.' It is one of the great European sculptures, though always a controversial one, a symbol of Peter's genius in raising St Petersburg from the swamps and treading down the swamp serpent; it is at once terrifying and splendid.

Pushkin's poem was written with great rapidity over a period of about three weeks, though a doodle of a riderless figure of Falconet's horse suggests the idea had begun to germinate in his mind rather earlier. In Mikhaylovskoe himself at the time of the great St Petersburg flood in 1824, he draws on V. N. Berkh's account of it for some of his detail, and he owes another kind of debt to the Digression from the Polish poet Mickiewicz's 'Forefather's Eve'. In Mickiewicz's poem, Konrad Wallenrod is an exile in the capital, much as Mickiewicz was himself, and describes satirically the falsities of the life he sees there. In both poems the statue of Peter the Great, cast by Falconet, is modelled on the statue of Marcus Aurelius in the Campidoglio in Rome. In Mickiewicz's poem Konrad Wallenrod meets a 'Russian bard' beside the statue, who may have been intended as Pushkin. Certainly Mickiewicz had reservations about his Russian friend and disliked recent poems which put aside the revolutionary spirit of his earlier work. It is the bard, however, who points out that, while the statue of Marcus Aurelius in Rome seems to extend a hand in protection and blessing, Peter's hand has a threatening gesture. *The Bronze Horseman* is written in a more ambivalent frame of mind. John Bayley remarks that it is 'almost as if Pushkin had said to Mickiewicz, you call that a satire on what the capital stands for? I will show you how such a thing should be done by a native who really knows.'

The Prologue, the only part of the poem published in Pushkin's lifetime, is a tribute to St Petersburg as the capital of triumphant Russian imperialism. Peter's statue not only treads down the swamp serpent but menaces the countries around Russia with a gesture at once terrifying and splendid. It is no wonder that Benckendorf allowed the Prologue's immediate publication. Pushkin, sadly, was not opposed to the oppression of Poland. Russian patriots, even Decembrists, had little sympathy for the Poles, and at the height of his misery, while in pursuit of Natalya, Pushkin had even contemplated going to fight against them. A present-day reader will savour with more pleasure the loving portrait of the streets and people of St Petersburg, even without realising that many of the details are specifically chosen to rebut Mickiewicz.

> I love the air which has no motion
> The frost of your most cruel winter
> The sledge run by the open Neva
> Girls' faces, brighter than the roses.

Mickiewicz has the St Petersburg cold *mottling* the faces of women so that they look 'as red as a lobster'.

After the Prologue, which centres on Peter, the story begins. Evgeny, a sad clerk whose pedigree was mentioned by Karamzin but whose pretensions to aristocracy are long forgotten, has nothing in the least heroic about him, as Anna Akhmatova remarked. 'All of Pushkin's contemporaries enthusiastically recognised themselves in the hero of *The Prisoner of the Caucasus*, but who would agree to recognise themselves in Evgeny from *The Bronze Horseman*?'[1]

Evgeny lies dreaming of happiness with his simple Parasha, even as the heavy rain at his poor window has begun and the floods are rising. Tsar Alexander himself is helpless against the power of the elements. Even despotism has its limits. He cannot stop the flood, but he does send out troops to help rescue the people of St Petersburg.

> The waves, like thieves, climb through the windows
> The sterns of boats smash through the glass
> And pedlars' trays have sodden covers.
> Fragments of huts, and beams and roofs
> And thrifty traders merchandise...

While the waters wreck the city, poor Evgeny sits on one of the marble lions in Peter's square, anxiously looking across the Neva to where Parasha lives with her widowed mother. As soon as it is possible he takes a boat to the place where Parasha's house once stood. There he stares around incredulously and in the most moving moment of the poem argues with himself in bewilderment:

> Here is the place where their house stands.
> Here is the willow. There was a gate.
> That has been swept away. But the house?

As he realises that he is, indeed, standing in the right place, and that Parasha has been swept away, madness rises in him and bursts out in the form of laughter. So it is he returns to confront the statue of Peter and castigates the Tsar, whose arrogant will had built a city at the mercy of the flood. These are the only words Evgeny speaks in the poem, but the bronze face responds with anger at the accusation. Seeing as much, Evgeny runs away. As he runs he imagines that the rumbling thunder of brass hooves is pursuing him. A poor creature, hounded by the anger of a Tsar, he cannot get away. His cold body is found at last on an offshore island,

> Where fisherman cook their frugal meal
> Or perhaps government clerks may take
> A boat out on a desolate Sunday.

Ironically, it was to this very island that the house of Parasha had been taken by the flood. And there, too, is Evgeny buried.

There have been innumerable interpretations of this poem. In the twentieth century V. Khodasevich sums up some of these, all existing simultaneously:

> In the first place there is the national tragedy, in the exact sense of the word. Here is embodied the clash of Peter's autocracy with the mass's genuine love of freedom. This tragedy takes on special meaning if one regards the rebellion of poor Evgeny as a protest of an individual against the coercion of the state ... The tragedy is seen in a special light when we recall that Pushkin's Peter regards Petersburg as a window to Europe ... *The Bronze Horseman* at the same time echoes the events in Poland in 1831, so that the revolt of Evgeny might symbolise the rebellion of Poland against Russia ... There is much to be said also ... for seeing in the 'Horseman' a simple tale of the destruction of the cherished hopes of a little man.

The ambiguities of *The Bronze Horseman* resonate strangely with a powerful Imperialist poem, which 'became a kind of credo of Russian Imperialism and nationalism'.[2] The year 1831 saw Field Marshal Paskevich's triumphant ending of the war in Poland, the capture of Warsaw and the end of the Polish rebellion. Pushkin's poem 'To the Slanderers of Russia' was no less than a paean of praise for Russian imperialism. There was a clamour of indignation in Western Europe about the brutality of the Tsar's suppression of the Polish uprising. To this, Pushkin wrote an angry rejoinder in 'Slanderers of Russia':

> Stop it. This is a war of Slavs between themselves,
> A domestic quarrel, one fate will decide,
> No issue for you to be involved.

Pushkin simply did not share modern liberal feelings towards Polish national aspirations. This indifference towards Polish sufferings, it should be said, was not calculated to please, even though his ability to earn money from his writing continued to depend as much on the good will of the censor as his popularity. On 6 December 1833, Pushkin wrote to Benckendorf to ask for permission from the Emperor to publish *The Bronze Horseman*. Nicholas objected, however, as Pushkin noted in his diary on 14 December after a visit to Benckendorf: 'The word *idol* was not passed by the censorship, and question marks were raised over several other points.' Pushkin was forced to break the contract he had made with his publisher for this work. As he had remarked to Nashchokin on 10 December, 'If they don't pass my *History of Pugachev* I shall have to go and live in the country.'[3]

This was an expedient he would have chosen joyfully, as he was beginning to mention more and more frequently, but the Tsar enjoyed having Natalya as an ornament at his balls and, whether or not he had a sexual interest in her, was unmistakably reluctant to allow her to depart. Scholars at Pushkinsky Dom completely dismiss any idea that the Tsar had designs of his own on Natalya, even after Pushkin's death, 'if only because he was a godfather to one of her children'. This, from both Fomichev and Vadim Stark, may well be a reaction to the Soviet insistence on seeing the Tsar's wicked hand in everything. Pushkin himself continued to be aware of the possibility, however. For all his Christian sentiments, the Tsar was well known to have a libidinous nature and several mistresses among the young ladies-in-waiting of the Court.

Whatever his motives, the Tsar raised no objections to the publication of Pushkin's *History of Pugachev*, and by 10 February 1834 Pushkin was able to write to Benckendorf that 'His Majesty has assured my fortune'. Pushkin went on to explain that he hoped to be able to use the money he realised from it to accept his uncle Vasily's inheritance, for which he needed to pay off debts of 40,000 roubles. In the same letter he asked for permission to publish the work at his own expense, and for a two-year loan of 15,000 roubles.

The Tsar gave Pushkin a loan of 20,000 roubles, which was generous, and at the same time appointed Pushkin a Kammerjunker, that is a Junior Gentleman of the Chamber, which was altogether less so. It was a rank wholly inappropriate to Pushkin's age and even insulting to someone so proud of his ancient nobility. Moreover, if Pushkin had hoped that by writing a distinguished historical book he could reproduce the central position at Alexander's Court earned by Karamzin, he must have been disappointed. Nicholas was a man much less interested in literature of any kind. It was, in addition, an appointment which carried with it the obligation to remain at Court, as Pushkin very well recognised when he wrote in his diary, 'The other day I was appointed a Junior Gentleman of the Bedchamber, which is rather unbecoming considering my age, but the Court wished that Nathalie should dance at Anichkov Palace.'

In February 1834 A. N. Vulf recorded in his diary:

I found that the poet was highly indignant with the Tsar because he had dressed him in uniform, a person who had written the history of the Pugachev rebellion. He says he is going back to the opposition. [Meaning those opposed to the Tsar's autocracy.] He set off from St Petersburg on

August 25 1834, five days before the unveiling of the Alexander column, 'so as not to attend the ceremony with the other Kammerjunkers'.[4]

The reflection that it was the Tsar's admiration of his wife's beauty which had brought him the appointment was a matter of common observation. On 7 January Pushkin noted in his diary that the Grand Duke Mikhail had congratulated him on the appointment, and that he had replied, ' "Thank you very much, Your Highness," I said, "Till now everyone laughed at me, you are the first to congratulate me." '[5]

On 17 January 1834 Pushkin records being at a ball at which the Emperor spoke to him about his *History of Pugachev*. Nicholas did not mention Pushkin's appointment as Kammerjunker, nor did Pushkin thank him. Pushkin was very well aware of the Tsar's reputation as a womaniser yet, though he had already reproached his wife for enjoying a flirtation with the Tsar, he did not yet suspect any serious danger. As a sign of this, a few days later, when Pushkin arrived at a ball in the Anichkov palace in uniform when the other guests were in evening dress, he left his wife at the ball and, instead of returning, went off to a party at his friend Saltykov's. This was not the action of a man too worried about his wife's likely behaviour. The Emperor was displeased at his departure, as Pushkin must have predicted. It would be pleasant to believe that this confidence came from the happiness he and his wife shared now that he had returned to St Petersburg.

For the most part, Pushkin was delighted to live with his Natalya again and by March 1834 he was writing to Nashchokin, 'They say that unhappiness is a good school; perhaps. But happiness is the best university. It provides the finishing touches for a soul capable of the good and the beautiful, such as yours is, my friend; such as mine is, as you know.'[6] But life in St Petersburg was not without anxieties. In the same letter he wrote more gloomily, 'This winter has been terribly full of balls. Finally, the last Sunday before Lent arrived. I thought, thank God, no more balls. My wife was at Court. Suddenly I saw her – she was not feeling well – I took her home and once there she miscarried. Now thank God she is well and will shortly visit Kaluga to see her sisters, who suffer terribly from my mother-in-law's whims.' Those balls, quite as much as worries about his wife's health, led Pushkin to write to his wife in 1834 of his longing 'to spit on St Petersburg, retire, scamper off to Boldino and there live like a lord'.[7]

Once Natalya had set off to Kaluga, Pushkin was no longer obliged to go to the Tsar's balls and could spend his days quietly working at home and then going to dine at Demuths with friends or, perhaps, playing billiards. He missed his wife, but there are some signs in his letters that she was no longer a source of unqualified happiness, nor did he any longer write to her as if to an indulged child. He was beginning to wonder whether she was looking after his children with sufficient care and was clearly irritated about her failure to run their domestic affairs – not that he himself was any better at it. Money was now a problem not only for himself but for his mother and father, who were continually pleading for help in saving what was left of their estate from falling into the hands of creditors. His sister's husband, too, was now poverty-stricken and asking for money Pushkin could not provide.

Pushkin tried to live his own life among old friends as well as he could. He frequently visited the circle around E. A. Karamzina, the widow of the celebrated historian who enjoyed the favour of Alexander I; she played an important and far from benevolent role in Pushkin's remaining years. Hers had been for more than twenty years one of the most attractive salons of St Petersburg. The guests were given strong tea, with thick cream, and bread with very fresh butter. The parties began at 10 p.m. and lasted until 1 or 2 a.m. Literary guests included Zhukovsky, Vyazemsky and the writer Lermontov, as well as some of the most intelligent foreigners and diplomats.

The true centre of the circle was by now Sofya, the daughter of the historian by his first marriage. Sofya 'like an experienced general ... arranged the big red armchairs, and between them the light straw chairs, creating comfortable groups for the guests ... I see her now, like a busy bee, fluttering from one group of guests to another, joining some, dividing up others, seizing a witty word or an anecdote, remarking on someone's nice dress, organising a party of cards for the old men ...'[8] Guests gathered every evening. On weekdays there were usually ten to fifteen of them. On Sundays there were many more in attendance, perhaps as many as sixty.

Meanwhile, Natalya spent five months, including the summer of 1834, at the Goncharov factory, at the Red House, far from the noisy looms. This was a wooden, two-storey building, which stood in a lovely park with trees, shrubs and flowerbeds. The house overlooked a lake with a little bridge and ornamental steps, its shores lined with fir trees pruned into fantastic shapes. Further off was an orangery with apricots and pineapples. The house was appointed with the most remarkable modern conveniences, including several baths.

On 20 April 1834 Pushkin wrote a rash, though engaging and far from seditious letter to his wife, which he later learned had been intercepted by the police:

> My angel wife, I am sitting out all these holidays at home. I do not intend to present myself to the new heir with greetings and congratulations; his reign lies ahead of him and he probably would not wish to see me. I have seen three Tsars: the first ordered me to remove my cap and cursed me to my nurse; the second took no pity on me; the third merely offered me protection in my mature years as page of the Court, but I would not want to replace him with a fourth, and I expect no good of him.[9]

After her miscarriage in March 1834 Natalya was spending five months in the country, recovering. Pushkin's relationship with the Tsar would have changed for the better during his wife's absence had it not been for the discovery of this letter. On 10 May he wrote in his diary,

> A few days ago I received a note from Zhukovsky. He informed me that a certain letter of mine was circulating in town and that the Emperor had spoken to him about it. I imagined that it must be some obscene poems, which the public had graciously and indulgently attributed to me. But it was not at all what I thought. The Moscow Post Office had opened a letter I had written to my wife and informed the police about it ... Fortunately, the letter was shown to Zhukovsky who explained it. Everything quietened down. The Emperor did not like me to refer to my appointment as Junior Gentleman of the Chamber without saying I was touched and grateful. I can be a subject and even a slave, but I shall not be a flunkey and clown even before the King of Heaven.[10]

On 3 June 1834 the thought that someone might be reading his correspondence with his wife still maddened him, and a letter to his wife in the country contained the following lines, plainly intended for anyone from the censorship who might be reading it: 'It is quite possible to live without political liberty, but without the sanctity of the family it is quite impossible: hard labour in Siberia is infinitely better. This is not written for you.'

These remarks were directed pointedly at the government censor, perhaps even at Nicholas himself. As if to precipitate disaster, Pushkin wrote recklessly to Natalya on 11 June, 'I am no longer angry with *him* ...' (a clear reference to the Tsar) 'He cannot be blamed for the swinishness around him. In a privy, you cannot help getting used to shit and its stench won't disgust you even though you are a gentleman. Oh, if only I could run off to where the air is fresh.'[11] Since the Tsar insisted on Pushkin remaining at Court, as he points out in a letter of 28 June 1834, 'He is to blame for everything. But God forgive him, if only he would let me go to my estate.'

There seemed to be only one way out, and that was to resign from his minor civil service post. On 25 June Pushkin wrote a formal letter of resignation to Benckendorf, pleading that family matters necessitated his presence in Moscow and the interior of the country. As a favour, he asked that permission to visit the Imperial archives should not be withdrawn. A reply came almost immediately. Benckendorf wrote on 30 June that 'His Imperial Majesty does not want to keep anyone against his will', but could not allow him further access to the archives which belonged 'solely to those enjoying the especial trust of the authorities'.[12]

Now Pushkin was at work on his (never to be finished) life of Peter the Great, still aspiring to the favoured position occupied by the historian Karamzin, and was dismayed by the unconcealed retaliation. He wrote back hastily to cancel his resignation, which he blamed on the 'petty worries' of his life, and hoped it would not be taken as a sign of ingratitude. His next letter to Benckendorf went further, suggesting he was broken-hearted at losing an all-powerful protector who had showered him with favours. Meanwhile, behind the scenes, Benckendorf reported to the Emperor that it would be much safer to keep Pushkin where he could be observed, rather than letting him leave and do what he liked as a private person. Nicholas wrote on Benckendorf's report, 'I forgive him but ask him to see you so that you can explain to him the whole senselessness of his behaviour, and that what can be forgiven to a twenty-year-old madman can't be forgiven a married man of thirty five with a family.'[13] Pushkin breathed a sigh of relief, but well understood that forgiveness was only temporary, as a diary entry of 22 July makes clear: 'I won't get away with it.'

Indeed, further responsibilities were about to descend on him. It was decided that summer that the two remaining unmarried Goncharov sisters would come to Moscow and live with the Pushkins. Ekaterina had been on the point of marrying Alexander Poivanov, but had refused him at the last moment because he was thought to have connections to the Decembrist movement. The hope was now that Natalya would be able to introduce them into society so that they could find husbands.

CHAPTER FIFTEEN

The Three Sisters

Pushkin discouraged the arrival of his sisters-in-law with good reason: he anticipated correctly that they would add considerably to the noise and bustle of a household already filled with four children and numerous servants. 'Here is my opinion,' he wrote to Natalya. 'A family ought to be alone under its own roof: husband, wife, children, are they too few? Parents, yes, when they are old, but there will be no end of trouble, and there will be no family peace.' Natalya ignored his sensible reminder that they were not rich, and his admonition, based on vivid memories of his own childhood, that 'dependence and disorder in the management of a household are terrible; and none of the pleasures of vanity can compensate for peace of mind and contentment'.[1]

He himself was hard at work, seeing his *History of the Pugachev Rebellion* through the press, and was often exasperated by descriptions of her flirtations with provincial gallants in Kaluga in the weeks she was away. She seemed altogether unaware of the efforts he was making on their joint behalf, and he was exasperated enough to reproach her. 'You work only with your feet at balls and help your husband to squander money.' Natalya remained unabashed in her determination to help find her sisters husbands, and she got her way.

On 25 August Pushkin joined Natalya at the linen factory in Kaluga, and after two weeks escorted her back to Moscow. From there he went on to Boldino, where the first snow had fallen in September. It was not the fruitful time of year that autumn usually was for him, though he did manage to write the verse fairy tale 'The Golden Cockerel'.

It was Anna Akhmatova whose independent research uncovered the influence on this tale of Washington Irving's 'Legend of the Arabian Astrologer' from his collection *The Alhambra*. The astrologer helps the Sultan; the Sultan finds a princess; the astrologer asks for the princess as his reward; the Sultan refuses, and is destroyed by the astrologer. Akhmatova looks closely at the drafts of 'The Golden Cockerel' where alterations pinpoint the allusions to Nicholas. In the line 'But it is bad to squabble with Tsars', for instance, she notes the word 'Tsars' is crossed out and the words 'the mighty' substituted as a thin disguise. The ending, too, goes through self-censorship:

> The tale's not true but there's a lesson for us,
> and a hint for *another person*.

becomes

> The tale's not true, but in it there's a hint
> a lesson for *good fellows*.

Quite apart from the problems Pushkin had with the censorship – and Akhmatova had her own reason to stress the similarity of their position with regard to censors – he was disturbed by a multitude of anxieties as he wrote that tale. She points out that by 1834 he understood that he had been 'pardoned and fettered by mercy'. And the central thrust of 'The Golden Cockerel' remains. It is an account of a ruler who does not keep his promises.

Though 1834 was not a year in which Pushkin wrote as much poetry as he usually did, he did produce his short story *The Queen of Spades* in prose, which has a surreal and icy logic far surpassing the gentler 'Tales of Belkin'. Hermann, a sober young army officer, loves cards but cannot afford to gamble. One night he hears how the Countess, an ageing beauty, once the toast of Paris, now holds the secret of three winning cards. This secret she has refused to impart to anyone, but Hermann determines to learn it. The old woman is stingy, vain, capricious and bullies her niece Lisa unmercifully. Hermann woos Lisa in order to gain access to the Countess. The narrative is stripped bare and moves forward relentlessly. Nevertheless, the details of the Countess's cosmetic preparations, or Hermann waiting outside her house with big flakes of snow falling under streetlamps, have the hypnotic clarity of a dream. Certain moments have a hallucinatory intensity – for instance, the eye of the Countess winking at Hermann from her coffin, or the moment when Hermann plays his third card, the winning ace, and sees it change before his eyes into the Queen of Spades.

The story rose from the depth of Pushkin's insight into the logic of a supernatural world, to which his own superstitious belief in signs and portents gave him ready access. In Natalya's absence he had begun to suffer from that sense of wretched isolation that had bedevilled his childhood. As he wrote to Natalya with some pathos, 'I am lonesome, and when I am lonesome my thoughts go out to you, as you cling to me when you are frightened.'

It was Pushkin who was alarmed these days. His lyric impulse seemed to have stopped flowing. How would they live if his power to produce poems and stories dried up? His parents were on the edge of bankruptcy, and his own debts seemed to multiply wherever he looked. Unable to make use of this Boldino autumn, Pushkin returned to St Petersburg in October to face a new social season. When he returned home he found that his wife's sisters had already arrived.

Ekaterina and Alexandra were by common consent less beautiful than their sister, even though they shared some of her features. Both were almost old maids by the standards of the time: Ekaterina was three years older than Natalya, a little too tall and short-sighted; Alexandra was a year younger than Natalya, but she had a pronounced squint. Both were introduced into the social round in October–November 1834, and given ball dresses by their rich aunt, Ekaterina Zagryazhskaya.

The Goncharov family, particularly Natalya's mother and brother Dmitry, had high hopes of Ekaterina being accepted as a lady-in-waiting at Court, but Pushkin was anxious about that very prospect. For Nicholas, as for most Tsars before him, maids of honour at Court had traditionally been regarded as legitimate prey – Pushkin had a horror of the scandal that might result. Nor did he want his wife to be indebted to the Tsar.

Both sisters had an allowance of 4,500 roubles from the Goncharov estate, but Pushkin's own outgoings were substantially increased as a result of their arrival. A larger apartment had to be rented to accommodate this new family, and he found he was held responsible for couturiers' bills incurred by his sisters-in-law. Domestic confusion also increased, as he had predicted, and Natalya was forced to admit in a letter to her brother Dmitry, 'We are in such an impoverished condition that there are days when I do not know how to run the house, my head goes round and round in circles.'

The sisters entered their new life uneasily, well aware of being regarded in society as mere adjuncts to their beautiful sister. On 16 October Ekaterina wrote to Dmitry from St Petersburg:

We have been to the French theatre twice, and once to the German theatre, to a party at Natalya Kirillovna's, where various people from society were introduced to us, so we hope to have partners for our first ball. We make a large number of visits, which does not amuse us very much, and people regard us rather like white bears, as the sisters of Madame Pushkina.[2]

Natalya was universally admired at Court balls. As an observer reported,

Suddenly – I shall never forget this – a lady entered, straight as a palm tree in a gown of black satin reaching to the throat (the Court was then in mourning). This was the wife of Pushkin, the first beauty of the day. Such stature and such stateliness I have never seen.[3]

On 8 December 1834, two days after attending a ball for the Tsar's nameday, however, Ekaterina wrote excitedly to Dmitry to describe the attentions paid to her by the Imperial family:[4]

So on December 6 while the ball was taking place, I was introduced to their Imperial Majesties in the study of the Empress. They were extraordinarily kind to me, and I was so shy that I found the ceremony rather long on account of the large number of questions with which they so affably showered me. A few minutes after the Empress arrived, the Emperor himself appeared. He took my hand and made various flattering remarks and finally said that if I were ever to experience difficulties in society I had only to raise my eyes and I would behold a friendly face that would always regard me with approval.[5]

The three sisters gossiped from morning to night about balls and the gentlemen who asked for their hands as dancing partners. By day Pushkin ate his meals late, and then escaped to the privacy of his study, where he remained until he went for a walk in the evening. Then he had to accompany all three sisters to their social occasions, and this gave rise to much amusement.

Natalya was three months pregnant at the ball at which Ekaterina was introduced to the Tsar, and the doctor had forbidden her to dance for fear of a miscarriage. However, in the same letter to her brother, Ekaterina reported: 'She danced a Polonaise with the Emperor. He was affable to her as ever, though he gave her rather a dressing down on account of her husband, who was said to be ill and therefore unable to don his uniform. The Emperor told her that he understood quite well the nature of this illness, and was all the more delighted that she could attend, since Pushkin should be ashamed of his absence.'[6]

Pushkin had other worries. The moment the successful publication of his *History of Pugachev* looked as if it might earn a substantial sum of money, his brother Lev and his parents turned to him for assistance. One way and another their needs and his own commitments soon swallowed up all the profits. When May came, even though his wife was on the point of giving birth, Pushkin was so depressed by the financial situation that he felt he had to run away to Mikhaylovskoe. There his old friends at Trigorskoe noticed how gloomy he seemed. As he brooded on his mounting problems, he wrote, 'But there, there in Petersburg, what misery often stifles me.'

This misery was as much due to the giggling presence of his sisters-in-law as financial pressure. They made him feel a stranger in his own home. He was away for just over a week, arriving home the day after his wife's labour on 15 May 1835. Ekaterina wrote to Dmitry to tell him that Natalya's pregnancy had ended happily. 'It happened yesterday at 6.37 in the evening. She suffered very much, but all went well, thank God, and now she feels as well as can be expected ... Your future godson is a beautiful boy, named Grigory. Pushkin, who spent eight days in Pskov, returned yesterday morning. I beg you to try and bring the shawl which you promised Tasha ... she needs it badly after her labour.'[7]

Dmitry did not attend the christening, however, though the Pushkins delayed it for him. Alexandra wrote to urge him to hurry on 20 May 1835. 'Come quick, we're waiting for you, hurry, don't make us wait. As the wealthy heir, you can bring us all your treasures.'

The childlike eagerness of this note suggests a certain charm which Pushkin may have found attractive, particularly alongside Alexandra's love of poetry and admiration of his own work. In the summer of 1835, among the sketches which illustrate the rough drafts of Pushkin's tragic poem 'The Wanderer', appear two female profiles each with a long fine nose, whose appearance is arresting for the seriousness and lyricism of their expressions. The subject of 'The Wanderer' is a family's incomprehension of a man's inner world. Since Pushkin felt himself very much in that situation, and Alexandra did at least ardently admire him as a poet, it may be significant that her face should appear among these rough drafts.[8]

How much closer they became is a matter of much dispute. Alexandra was somewhat unstable, sometimes uncontrollably cheerful, ironic and caustic, sometimes defiantly silent for days or weeks at a time. As both her father and grandmother had been mentally unbalanced, there were fears that she, too, might lose her mind. However, both Pushkin's possible attraction to his sister-in-law and her presence in the household became a matter of scandal in the following year.

Dmitry was heir to the Goncharov fortunes, but this unfortunately did not make him as wealthy a man as his sisters hoped. The Goncharov affairs had not been going well for some time, and between 1835 and 1836 they deteriorated even further. The Goncharovs had been owed 100,000 roubles for fifteen years by a merchant named Usachev. A lengthy legal process began to get under way. Between 5 and 17 August Natalya wrote to Dmitry, 'Please come as quickly as possible regarding this damned trial of Usachev ... Immediately you arrive you must see Lerkh, the lawyer, who will explain everything to you. Try to come before the departure of my husband, who must shortly leave for the country ... Come the moment you receive this letter, don't waste a moment, time is running out.'[9]

Natalya, too, had worries. She was much concerned about Sergey, her favourite brother, of whom little is known. In early summer she tried to persuade Dmitry to use his influence on the Princess Cherkasskaya to get her brother transferred to one of the regiments stationed in Moscow: 'See if it is not possible to rescue Seryozha from the mire in which he is stuck. The poor boy is pitiable to behold and has lost all his old joie de vivre.' Natalya concluded that particular letter by hoping that her brother's affairs were going well, pointing out correctly that 'so many people depend upon this'. Even while Natalya continued to take great pleasure in her life of social glitter, she was not unaware of the anxieties that beset her husband. On 14 July Pushkin refers – in a letter to Natalya's mother – to a visit Natalya made to the wife of the Finance Affairs Minister Kankrin, asking in Pushkin's name that his 30,000 rouble debt to the Treasury be annulled.

On 18 August 1835 Natalya also wrote to Dmitry to 'do her the favour of preparing 85 sheets of paper according to the pattern enclosed in this letter'. She was to continue begging for the paper Pushkin needed, and couldn't afford, for the rest of his life. On 1 October she explained to Dmitry that she had wanted to write to remind him about the paper 'but I had to see Pletnev, who has been attending to the matter in the absence of my husband'. Referring to the Usachev trial, she writes, 'I have done everything possible. Even before I received your documents I ordered copies of them to be made so they could be passed to Lerkh, whom I have asked to visit me.'[10]

There were many signs, then, that Natalya was not unfeeling about her husband's needs in 1835. In the matter of balls and Court glitter, however, the couple's interests were irreconcilable. Natalya's personal happiness derived entirely from her acknowledgement at Court, whereas even a brief smell of the country in May renewed Pushkin's desire to retire there, at least for a time. There were good arguments in favour of such a move. His living expenses had increased to about 25,000 roubles a year. His wife, three children, two sisters-in-law and his own parents, brother and sister all looked to him for financial assistance, and he was himself deeply in debt. With all these commitments in mind, he wrote to Benckendorf again, this time as respectfully and tactfully as he could, for Imperial permission to withdraw from his Court post, pleading the stringency of his financial position. 'Life in Petersburg is horribly expensive ... Three or four years of retreat in the country will place me in a position to return to Petersburg and to the occupations which I still owe to the bounty of His Majesty.'[11]

Once again his request was refused. Pushkin could certainly resign from the Service if he so wished, but the Tsar would not allow him both to remain in his service and withdraw from the Court. Pushkin's resolution faltered. His government salary was small, but he feared to lose it, and he was reluctant to abandon all access to the Imperial archives. He could hardly believe the Tsar understood his desperate situation, and wrote to Benckendorf again to explain in detail. 'During the last five years of my sojourn in St Petersburg I have contracted debts of almost sixty thousand roubles.'[12]

The Tsar was not altogether unmoved by this. He allowed Pushkin 30,000 roubles as a loan against his salary, and gave him four months' leave of absence. At this point Pushkin could have decided to give up his small government salary and retire to the country to live on his writing. This would have rid him at a stroke of his exhausting responsibilities to his sisters-in-law, who would have had no incentive to join Pushkin and his family in a village.

Pushkin did not take the opportunity. Five thousand roubles a year might not meet his expenses, still less pay off his debts, but it was at least something. The Tsar's patronage had been far less valuable than he had once imagined, but without the Tsar's favour he well knew he might not be able to publish at all. In any case, he no longer had the same faith in his own unstoppable energies. A less sensible factor in his reasoning was his desire to indulge Natalya.

On 7 September 1835 he left for Mikhaylovskoe on his own. He found little had changed there, but there was much to remind him of his own ageing. He wrote to Natalya of a family of young pines, at which he looked with vexation, 'as I sometimes look at young cavalier guards at the balls where I no longer dance'. People in the village remarked on his growing old, including an old woman whom he could hardly recognise in her own decline. He had not left his troubles behind him, and his letters to Natalya are filled with his inability to put them out of his mind and get down to writing: 'I am completely upset and write nothing, yet time flies.' Once he needed only to sit in solitude or stroll in the woods and ideas rose to his mind in a flood. His solitude now was filled with anxieties as he wrote to his wife of this opportunity to think in peace:

> But about what do I think? This is what: How shall we live? My father leaves me no patrimony; he has already squandered half of it; your estate hangs on a hair. The Tsar will not permit me to become a landowner or a journalist ... We have not a groat of sure income and certain expenses of 30,000. What will come of this God only knows. Meanwhile I am sad. If you could but kiss me, perhaps my grief would vanish.[13]

He worried, too, about failing to receive letters from his wife – she had absent-mindedly addressed them wrongly. On 29 September, however, he received two letters from her, partly speaking of Ekaterina's serious illness but evidently also recalling his previous infatuations in Mikhaylovskoe and expressing jealous fears about them as she could not make the journey to the depths of the country in autumn with the children and did not want to leave them behind. Pushkin cut short his leave of absence and returned to St Petersburg in October. His stay in Mikhaylovskoe produced little more than the intriguing prose fragment 'The Egyptian Nights', with its strange autobiographical element, having as its central figure a poet of noble lineage, who is ashamed of his own genius because it makes him seem ridiculous in high society.

When Pushkin arrived in St Petersburg he found his mother had fallen sick with a liver complaint and in October 1835 he hurried to visit her in Pavlovsk. She was terminally ill. There was gossip that Natalya had refused to take her sick mother-in-law into her home. Pushkin was incensed at the rumour, and he wrote indignantly to Praskovya Osipova that Natalya would have been quite willing to do so, 'But a cold home filled by brats and encumbered by all sorts of other people is hardly convenient for a sick person'. A letter from Pushkin's sister Olga also suggests that it was consideration for his sick mother rather than indifference that led both Pushkins to decide against inviting her into their apartment.

> His wife is pregnant again ... true, they have a large apartment, but very ill-appointed, besides she has two sisters and three children. Mother would not want it anyway. People criticise us too, of course, saying that Alexander is a cruel son and I am a hard-hearted daughter ... and father merely weeps, sighs and complains to everyone he sees.[14]

Pushkin and Natalya visited his mother often in her last illness. Of all her children, the one she had favoured least as a child was the one most concerned for her in her last sickness.

Meanwhile, financial problems remained acute. Natalya's own mother remained indifferent to her daughter's problems, and her miserliness aroused indignation from the whole family. Ekaterina's letter to Dmitry of 1 November 1835 suggests how closely she was aware of the problem. Natalya had written to her mother asking for a 200 rouble allowance. Ekaterina wrote, 'She is very angry with mother, who refused her, claiming her own strained finances. It is truly shameful that mother will do nothing to help them, this is unforgivable indifference, especially since Tasha wrote to her recently, and she [Natalya's mother] limited herself to giving advice which wasn't worth a brass kopeck and made no sense at all.'[15]

For all the financial exigencies of their life, Natalya continued to enjoy Court occasions, and by the end of 1835 her sisters were taking part in many of the society gatherings into which she introduced them. Ekaterina wrote to her old governess, Nina, on 4 December 1835, 'We are being sensible, however, and attend no more than three balls a week, more usually two.'

Towards the end of 1835 there looked to be a small window of hope – the Tsar at last agreed to Pushkin's wish to have his own journal. This was to be a quarterly modelled on the English reviews, and called *The Contemporary*. There was only one condition: that all political subjects were to be avoided. Pushkin knew he could gather about him the best writers and critics of his generation and make the magazine a voice for a real literary intelligentsia. Although his personal popularity was no longer so widespread, he was full of ideas. His notebooks were crammed with future projects, and he thought the magazine might make a useful addition to his income. He spent the first months of 1836 working on the enterprise.

Anything *The Contemporary* might make, however, was only in prospect, and their daily need for money continued to be acute. Pushkin was reduced to pawning his wife's jewels, shawls and silverware. Natalya wrote to her brother once again on 28 April 1836 to remind him of Pushkin's need for paper. 'Could you allow him a sum of 4,500 roubles a year for this? That equals the amount you allow my sisters. He will repay you at the end of the year for any he uses above this sum.'[16]

Yet all these financial pressures were minor troubles in comparison with the misery to come in 1836. Pushkin was to lose his mother, with whom he had formed a late, strong bond in the last months of her life. Indeed, before dying, Nadezhda Osipovna begged her son's forgiveness for not appreciating him enough while she was alive. She died in March 1836 and Pushkin accompanied her body to its grave in the Svyatorgorsk monastery near Mikhaylovskoe. He was about to enter his loneliest year, tormented by rumours of his wife's love for another man and mocked as a cuckold by those at Court who had always despised him.

CHAPTER SIXTEEN

D'Anthès

The Pushkins first met Baron Georges-Charles d'Anthès early in 1834. He was a French exile who had arrived in St Petersburg after the French Revolution of 1830 and since then had lived under the protection of the Dutch Ambassador, Baron Louis van Heeckeren.

D'Anthès was a man of extraordinary good looks and ready wit; he danced superbly and made a good first impression on everyone, including the Tsar and especially the Tsarina. Benckendorf's secretary, Miller, guessed the young d'Anthès must be the illegitimate son of the Dutch king, while the Dutch Ambassador himself applied to the Dutch king for permission to adopt him as a son, and subsequently (May 1836) presented him in this way to Russian society. The Tsar ordered d'Anthès to be taken into the Cavalier Guards Regiment as an officer, even though he was a foreigner, with an annual salary of 10,000 roubles – an interesting contrast to Pushkin's annual income of 5,000 roubles.

Women found d'Anthès irresistible, Natalya and her sisters among them. However, soon after her first meeting with d'Anthès Natalya suffered the miscarriage, already mentioned, in March 1834, and went off to recuperate in Kaluga for five months, only returning to society in September 1834. D'Anthès, then 23, continued to live as a gallant about town, enjoying a wild life with his fellow officers. This included a party at the house of a countess who forced her female serfs to climb posts and race on unsaddled horses without knickers for the amusement of her guests.

It was only in the autumn of 1835 that d'Anthès began to treat Natalya with more than usual gallantry, but by early 1836 his adoration of her had become the gossip of the Karamzin family and most of St Petersburg. Pushkin observed with mounting discomfort how d'Anthès exchanged glances with his wife in the ballroom, and Natalya smiled upon the handsome young officer as if enjoying his attentions. She saw in him just the kind of attractive, unintellectual man she might have married if she had had a dowry – he was handsome, lively, her own age and as much a part of the social whirl as she was.

She could not have guessed at a side of his character, well concealed from St Petersburg society, which has only recently been established with certainty. It was not only women who were seduced by d'Anthès's charm. His protector Heeckeren, too, was very much in love with him, and indulged his every whim, as a newly discovered cache of letters presented by a descendant of the Heeckeren family to Serena Vitale, a Professor at the University of Pavia, makes abundantly clear.

Baron Louis Borchard van Heeckeren was 41 when he was reputed to have first met d'Anthès at a German inn and offered him a lift in his carriage. A wealthy man, whose family was one of the oldest in Holland, Heeckeren had been a diplomat since 1815 when the Netherlands became an independent kingdom. In 1823, he was first appointed an attaché for Business Affairs at the Russian Court, and then in 1826 made Ambassador. On leave in Germany, he met Georges-Charles d'Anthès, the 21-year-old son of Baron Josef d'Anthès, 'loved him tenderly' and brought him to Russia in 1833. It is obvious that no one these days would be the least interested in the exact nature of the relationship between these two men, had it not been for d'Anthès's pursuit of Pushkin's wife, Natalya, and her own unmistakable interest in the glamorous young Frenchman.

The letters recently discovered by Serena Vitale[1] were written by d'Anthès to Heeckeren on Heeckeren's travels in Alsace to visit d'Anthès's father and in Holland to apply to the king for permission to adopt d'Anthès. They establish the passionate nature of Heeckeren's attachment to the 23-year-old Frenchman and d'Anthès's willingness to accept such a relationship, even though he already had a clandestine mistress. Most importantly, the letters give an astonishing new insight into the mind of the man to whom Natalya gave so much of her attention at Imperial balls.

In d'Anthès's first letter to Heeckeren, written from St Petersburg and dated 18 May 1835, there are phrases which go beyond simple friendship – for instance, he writes that he is 'longing for' Heeckeren. In a letter of 14 July d'Anthès reminds Heeckeren of their plan to go away to a place with a pleasant climate where they could be happy together. Here, too, there are indications of a warmth which is not exactly filial: 'Please, my precious friend, you can be sure we will be happy.'

By September 1835 d'Anthès had begun his pursuit of Natalya, but at this stage the flirtation was no more than might have been expected of a dashing young Guards officer. He makes no mention of it in his letters to Heeckeren, who had begun to demand a more intimate style of address. On 1 September 1835, writing from St Petersburg, d'Anthès rebukes him:

> My dear, you are a big baby ... Why do you want me to call you *tu*? ... When I say 'I love you', it is the same whether I say *vous* or *tu*. I am a young man and can't call you *tu* in public.

The letter continues with gossip about Prince Trubetskoy's drinking and proceeds to explain d'Anthès's difficult relations with his former mistress and her children:

> The woman is very unhappy because she lost a child [not d'Anthès's child] a few days ago, and has been told she may lose another ... With the best intentions in the world, I cannot take their place ... the last year has proved that.

D'Anthès's candour about his mistress does not extend to his wooing of Natalya, though it may be that Heeckeren had begun to hear some tale of d'Anthès's attachment because he continued to beg for reassurance of d'Anthès's affections. In a letter dated 26 November d'Anthès does, indeed, call Heeckeren '*tu*', and furthermore adds a vehement physical assertion of love, alongside further expressions of gratitude for material benefits.

> I'd like you to be here to kiss you many times, and to press you tightly against my heart. Then you would feel that my heart is beating just as strongly as yours ... You make me even richer than you are yourself, and though you deny it, I know you have many difficulties because of me, so be sure I won't betray your generosity ... Of all your presents, my favourite is the use of your carriage; without that I could visit nowhere. The condition of my heart is such that I cannot take chances with the Petersburg climate.

A little later in the letter, as he describes the brilliant festivities in honour of the architect who had designed St Isaac's Cathedral, d'Anthès betrays his own envy of wealth and power as he remarks, 'When you see how people like that live, one feels as if one is no more than rubbish.' In the margin of the same letter he scribbles a note to the effect that he has finished all relations with his mistress. In every letter he redoubles his gratitude and repeats his endearments – 'My dear, my precious. I have never loved anyone as I love you.'

No one who saw d'Anthès in the winter festivities of 1835, as he bent over Natalya's hand or looking lingeringly into her eyes, would have suspected any such relationship with the Ambassador, who supposedly wished only to adopt d'Anthès as his son. Natalya did not doubt the sincerity of his passion, and found his attentions disturbed her pleasingly. As we look at the sexual magnetism of d'Anthès's portrait her pleasure is far from surprising. The gossip mounted among the Karamzins, and even Pushkin's sister Olga wrote to her father of d'Anthès. 'His passion for Natalya was not a secret to anyone. I knew all about it when I went to St Petersburg and I also joked about it.'[2]

Although d'Anthès's own emotional commitment is always dubious, he was sufficiently overwhelmed with desire for Natalya to confess it in a letter to Heeckeren of 20 January 1836: 'The most awful thing is that I'm madly in love.' That letter was first published in 1946, but it takes on an additional force when one realises how unwelcome such a declaration must have been to Heeckeren.

> I shall not give you her name because a letter can get lost, but recall to yourself the most delicious creature in St Petersburg and you will know her name. And what is most horrible in my position is the fact that she also loves me, and that we cannot see each other, something that has been impossible so far for the husband is a man of revolting jealousy ... To love one another and not to be able to say so to each other except between two ritornellos of a dance is an awful thing ... I am telling you all this as my best friend, and because I know you will sympathise with my distress. But in God's name do not breathe a word to anyone ... you would do her harm without intending to, and I should be inconsolable ... But rest assured that I shall be prudent ... I have been so prudent up to now that the secret is known only to her and to myself ...

This letter can have left little doubt in Heeckeren's mind who the married couple in question were, since both Natalya's pre-eminent beauty and Pushkin's jealousy were common knowledge. It suggests, moreover, that

Natalya had already confessed to returning d'Anthès's love. There is an addition to the letter, not known before, in which d'Anthès, after asking for gloves and socks made of silk and wool, tries to reject Heeckeren's suggestion that d'Anthès move in with him on Heeckeren's return to St Petersburg. 'I am quite comfortable', d'Anthès writes, 'in my own flat.' However, he accepts Heeckeren's offer of new furnishing fabric with gratitude.

On 2 February 1836 d'Anthès continues to report on the progress of his courtship of Natalya, though he shows some signs of wishing to keep Heeckeren happy too.

> I have some cause for joy, because I am now admitted to her house, but I cannot see her tête à tête; it seems almost impossible though absolutely necessary ... So, my precious friend, only you can be my advisor. Because you are my best friend and I would like to be cured by the time you come back so that I won't have to think of anything but the happiness of seeing you and the happiness of being together again.

It is entirely possible that if Natalya had yielded to him, like many another had, his passion would have cooled before Heeckeren's return. That is what he wanted Heeckeren to believe and it might even have proved true.

D'Anthès continued to press for a private meeting, which Natalya refused. On 2 February 1836, however, she and d'Anthès had a long conversation in which he begged for her love and Natalya refused with nobility and dignity. D'Anthès gives an account of that meeting in a letter to Heeckeren in which he explains that they were not alone. A conversation of such intensity could hardly have been conducted on a public social occasion, however, without some agitation being visible to curious observers in the same room.

> This woman, of whom most people suspect that she has little intelligence, I do not know whether it is love that has given it to her but it is impossible to show more tact, more grace or more intelligence than she did in this conversation and it was difficult to conduct, for it was a question of nothing less than refusing to violate her duties, even for a man whom she loves and who adores her; she described her position to me with so much tact, grace and innocence that I was really defeated and I could not find a word to say in reply to her ... 'I love you as I have never loved but do not ask me for more than my heart, for all the rest does not belong to me, and I cannot be happy if I do not respect my duty.'

Tatyana refusing Onegin could have said no more; indeed, the resemblance is marked. Without wishing to minimise the nobility and dignity of Natalya's behaviour in this February meeting, however, it is perhaps worth noting that she was five months pregnant at the time. There is also some encouragement even in her rejection, though d'Anthès's vanity may have added a good deal to this account of her behaviour. He was not used to refusal.

D'Anthès's description of that meeting is given in a well-known letter of 14 February, pronouncing himself more tranquil since 'I can't see her every day and I know that nobody can enter, take her hand, embrace her waist and talk to her as I have been doing'. However, there is an addition to that letter in the new cache of discovered correspondence which is of real importance. D'Anthès continues to reassure Heeckeren of his continuing affections, and suggests that his love for Natalya is a temporary infatuation, dependent on her youth and beauty:

> You are the only one equal to her in my soul and when I'm not thinking about her I think about you. But don't be jealous, my precious, and don't turn the trust I put in you by this confession against me. You remain in my heart for ever. As for her, time will take its course and will change her, and afterwards nothing will remind me of the person I once loved so much. But as for you, my precious, every new day will remind me that without you I am nothing.

This suggests the relation between d'Anthès's physical passion and his knowledge of his own best interests. He continues to profess his love for Heeckeren, at the end of this letter: 'Goodbye, *mon cher*, be indulgent towards my new passion, for I love you from the bottom of my heart.'

Heeckeren, however, must have needed firmer assurances of the relative strength of d'Anthès's feelings for Natalya and himself. D'Anthès's letter of 5 March makes an effort to calm him.

> The Lord is my witness that at the time of my receiving your letter I had already decided to sacrifice this woman for you. Your letter was so kind and contained so much tender friendship that I did not hesitate, not for a single moment. I have now changed my conduct towards her completely. I avoid meetings with her as much as I sought them before, and talk with her without emotion as far as I can manage … That unlimited passion which was eating me up for the last six months is now behind me, and I am free to admire and worship the creature who once made my heart beat so

passionately ... Your letter was too harsh; you took the whole thing very tragically and you punished me. Yes, it was my punishment when you claimed that you amounted to nothing for me. I recognise my guilt, but my heart is innocent. How could your own heart not tell you I would never hurt you deliberately?

D'Anthès's anxiety is blatant here but, nevertheless, he defends Natalya Nikolaevna from Heeckeren's cynical charge that she would soon yield her honour to other men. There is something more than vanity in his rebuttal:

I believe there were other men who lost their heads because of her. She is certainly beautiful enough. But to believe that she would listen to them? Never. She has never loved anyone more than myself, and in the last two weeks there have been many opportunities for her to give herself to me, and what then, my friend? Never in her life. She was much stronger than I was. More than twenty times she asked me to have mercy on her and her children and her future, and she was so beautiful at those moments that if she wished me to stay away from her she would have behaved in a different way ... There is no other woman who could behave like this. Of course, there are women who talk a great deal about chastity and duty but there is no woman who has more chastity in her soul...

D'Anthès concludes his letter with the hope that when Heeckeren comes back he will find him 'completely cured'.

D'Anthès's claim that there were more than twenty occasions when, had Natalya been willing, they might have consummated their love seems an unlikely one. In any case, Natalya's pregnancy was advancing inexorably. For all her enjoyment of d'Anthès's attentions, it does not follow that she returned his passion or even spoke the words that he attributed to her. Even if her emotions were seriously engaged, she may have found the titillations of flirtation, with the occasional snatched kiss or caress, more pleasurable than granting d'Anthès her sexual favours would have been. She may even have continued to love Pushkin, and yet found it impossible to reject the excitement the young Guards officer brought her.

There is no sign that d'Anthès felt any compunction towards Pushkin. He had no sense of Pushkin's greatness as a poet, and would have been unimpressed by that, in any case. To his eyes, Pushkin was altogether unworthy to be the husband of so fine a creature.

Pushkin was well aware both of d'Anthès's pursuit and the malicious gossip it occasioned. Even if he had not been long a shrewd observer of such matters, he would have known many details of d'Anthès's manoeuvres as Natalya had the habit of sharing romantic conquests with him. This in itself would have been sufficient to torment a less passionate man, especially as she made no attempt to disguise her own pleasure in d'Anthès's flattery. Pushkin, who always maintained that his wife had never betrayed him physically, nevertheless admitted, '*Il l'a troublée.*'³

Pushkin's anger at the society that both took so much of his wife's attention from him and whispered about him falsely lay behind his quarrel with Count Sollogub, whom he challenged to a duel on the strength of a fairly harmless remark which somehow upset Natalya. Sollogub had always been an admirer of his poetry and a friend, and he was willing to produce written evidence that he had meant no offence so that the challenge was withdrawn. Pushkin knew he was behaving wildly. 'But what am I to do ... I have the misfortune to be a public man, and you know that is worse than being a public woman.'⁴

For his part, d'Anthès's obsession with Natalya reached the point where he could not write a letter to Heeckeren, as he confesses on 29 March 1836, without mentioning her. He even goes so far as to say, 'My sacrifice for you is an enormous one ... I can't conceal from you that I am still out of my mind.' This letter has a touching conclusion, which gives a rare sign of d'Anthès as a vulnerable human being. 'I'm counting the days till there is someone near me I can love. There is such a wish to love and not to be lonely. The six weeks of waiting seem to be years.'

In his letter dated April 1836 d'Anthès repeats this expression of his need:

My most dear friend, I am counting the days to your arrival. No, I'm lying. I'm counting the minutes. We'll embrace each other so tightly. We'll talk about yourself and your voyage. And I'll ask you so many questions.

Evidently, whatever earlier reluctance he had felt, he had by then agreed to move into Heeckeren's flat for in the latter part of the letter d'Anthès remarks,

One more unpleasant piece of news ... all summer we'll have builders here in our flat so I don't want to talk about the state of my heart. Because it is a subject which would never end ... nevertheless my heart feels okay and your medicine proved itself so useful I hope I am coming back to life ... in

the countryside ... because for a few moments I won't be able to see her
... Then farewell my precious friend. One kiss only to your cheeks and not
more because all the rest I want to give you when you come back.

Natalya had been in mourning for her mother-in-law for most of April
and gave birth to her fourth child, a daughter, on 23 May. She avoided
society until the end of July 1836. During this brief respite in his social
torment Pushkin found time and energy to write a beautiful sequence of
seven poems, the so-called 'Kamenny Ostrov' (Stone Island) cycle, named
after the island near St Petersburg where they spent their summer. This
sequence contains Pushkin's poetic testament – the poem 'Exegi Monumentum' (after Horace) – which every Russian schoolchild knows by
heart. Among these poems, too, is a rare lyric which shows Pushkin
drawn at this period towards the Christian religion of his upbringing.
Addressed to the 'holy fathers and unblemished women' who use prayer
to bring their souls closer to God, he confesses that lines of the prayer
of St Ephraim the Syrian, widely known to Orthodox believers, and said
traditionally on the evening of the Sunday that precedes Lent, have begun
to come frequently to his mind. He uses words from that prayer almost
verbatim in this poem:

> Lord of my life! Despondence, lethargy
> That hidden serpent, lust for authority,
> An idle tongue – keep all these things from me.
> May I, O Lord, perceive my trespasses;
> But not accuse my fellows who transgress;
> Lord grant me love, and chastity and quiet,
> And light a humble spirit in my heart.[5]

In these months Pushkin also concluded the final version of *The
Captain's Daughter*, a brilliant historical novel set in the time of Catherine
the Great, which he had begun at Boldino. It is in itself an answer to
those who claim that Pushkin had written himself out. Longer than 'The
Queen of Spades' and at first seemingly casual in structure, *The Captain's
Daughter* has an equally bony plot – the gift of a hare-skin coat to a
rogue who helps the narrator find his way to a hostelry in a blizzard, for
instance, turns out to have life-saving pertinence. The whole story can
be read at a gulp, yet scenes of the period remain etched in the reader's
imagination: the old man about to be whipped for remaining silent, who
opens his mouth to show a stump of tongue; the indignant, bossy wife

of the commander of the garrison killed by a single blow from a rebel sword. One of the few passages which reflect morally on the rapidly changing sequence of events in this tale has its own irony. The narrator remarks, witnessing a scene of torture,

> When I reflect that this happened in my lifetime and that now I have lived to see the gentle reign of the Emperor Alexander, I cannot but marvel at the rapid progress of civilisation and the spread of humane principles.

Pushkin's financial affairs remained in disarray. Since repayment of the 45,000 rouble loan from the Tsar, secured against his salary, was now due, he was no longer drawing any money from the Imperial treasury. Bills to leading costumiers for his wife's dresses mounted constantly, and some had to be paid by Natalya's aunt. His hopes for financial benefit through his magazine venture, *The Contemporary*, had not materialised. On the contrary, his debts accumulated because of it. After the death of his mother there were financial arguments with his brother-in-law Nikolay Pavlishchev, Olga's husband, about the sale of the Mikhaylovskoe estate. Most distressingly of all, he was aware that d'Anthès's public courtship was likely to begin again once his wife returned to society. No wonder that he told his friend Nashchokin, on a brief visit to stay with him and his new wife, that in St Petersburg his head went round and round as he considered what to do.

In the summer of 1836 the Pushkins and the Goncharovs rented a dacha on Kamenny Ostrov, the place of recreation for St Petersburg aristocracy which had given the title to the earlier mentioned cycle of poems. The dacha was made up of two small houses, one occupied by Pushkin and Natalya, and the other by Natalya's sisters and the children. A travelling French theatrical troupe was performing at the local theatre, and every evening the theatre forecourt was crowded with carriages. On the opposite shore a cavalry Guards regiment was stationed and among the most frequent visitors to Kamenny Ostrov was Baron Georges-Charles d'Anthès, now called Baron Van Heeckeren.

Throughout that summer there were picnics, numerous summer balls, outings and theatre visits, though Natalya was often absent, as on the picnic of 18 May, described below by Ekaterina Meshcherskaya.

> French wines poured forth into the throats of our young men, who rose

from the table more flushed and cheerful than when they sat down, especially
d'Anthès ... Finally, at ten o'clock, we tore ourselves away from the delights
of this intoxicating evening ... stopping on the way home at the dacha of
Princess Odoevskaya, where we drank tea. As for our men, they enjoyed
the 'gluhwein' with which the Princess plied them.[6]

For all the splendour of her presence at Court, observers found Natalya
equally beautiful at home, surrounded by her young children. Pushkin
preferred her so, particularly while himself melancholy and still in
mourning, as he then was, for his mother. During June and July, Natalya
was too ill to leave her room, let alone take part in the festivities attended
by St Petersburg high society when the island fell silent at the end of July.
When she had recovered from childbirth, however, Pushkin could hardly
deny her the pleasure of taking her place again on the ballroom floor.
Once there the flirtation with d'Anthès was as much a source of delighted
gossip as ever, and Pushkin had to confront new whispers behind the
hands of those who had no respect either for his genius or his claims to
aristocracy. Natalya's infatuation with d'Anthès was as clear to everyone
as d'Anthès's pursuit.

The letters between members of the Karamzin family, for all the
length of their friendship with Pushkin, show them much preferring the
beautiful Natalya and her glamorous admirer, d'Anthès, to her unhappy
husband. In a letter from Sofya Karamzina to her brother in July 1836
she writes with a kind of voyeuristic excitement: 'I walked arm in arm
with d'Anthès. He amused me with his jokes, his cheerfulness and his
amusing outbursts of emotion (as always for the lovely Natalya).'

Pushkin, in contrast, brooded on less amusing matters. In this bleak
summer of 1836 Pushkin lost his last faith in a republican democracy
for Russia modelled on the United States. He still championed the
freedom of the people but he had begun to fear the *rule* of the mob
and that summer he wrote an article on Radishchev, intended for *The
Contemporary*, in which he criticised his one-time mentor of 'Freedom'
explicitly:

How could the sensitive and ardent Radishchev not shudder at the sight of
what happened in France under the Terror? Could he hear without deep
loathing his once favourite ideas preached from the heights of the guillotine,
to the vile applause of the rabble.[7]

His disenchantment with political struggle found its way also into his poetry of this period, notably in verses labelled 'From Pindemonte' to distract the interest of the censor. They show how sceptical he had become of the 'resounding rights' which men mouthed so easily.

> All this I have to say is: *words, words, words*
> To rights of this kind I have grown averse
> I really find such freedom rather feeble:
> Subject to the sovereign or the people
> What does it matter? Let them be.[8]

Pushkin now believed only in the right to personal happiness, and wanted to be answerable to no one else for his peace of mind. He was as far from such an ideal state as ever.

Throughout the summer months Pushkin drew strength only from writing poetry. It was on 21 August 1836 that he wrote 'Exegi Monumentum', which opens,

> I've set up for myself a monument, though not in stone.
> No hands have made it, and no weeds will grow
> Along the path that leads to where the stubborn
>   Head soars above Alexander's column.
>
> I shall not wholly die. These sacred songs
> Although my dust decay, will hold my spirit.
> And I'll be known as long as any poet
>   Remains alive under the moon.

Only in the last verse of this poem does Pushkin make reference to his own treatment at the hands of the literary world, and to those who chuckled at his marital discomfiture. He does so with dignity:

> So, Muse, obey God's orders without fear,
> Forget insults, expect no laurel wreaths;
> Treat praise or slander with indifference,
>   And never argue with a fool.

Pushkin remained desperately short of money. In July 1836 Natalya had already written from Kamenny Ostrov to her brother Dmitry, 'without her husband's knowledge':

You know that I have managed without help from outside as long as I could, but my situation is now such that I consider it my duty to help my husband in his present difficulties, since it is wrong that he alone should bear the weight of maintaining his large family. I am thus obliged, dear brother, to appeal to your kindness and good heart to secure for me, with mother's help, the same allowance as my sisters receive, and if possible until January, starting from next month. I confess honestly to you that we are in such a wretched state that there are days when I do not know how to manage the house and my head spins. I do not want to bother my husband with my petty household worries, for I see how sad and depressed he is, unable to sleep at nights, and consequently in such a condition that he is unable to work or assure the means for our existence. In order for him to create, his head must be free. I am appealing to you to help me in my extreme need. My husband has given me so much evidence of his delicacy and selflessness that it is only fair that I should try to ease his situation.[9]

Natalya's letters to Dmitry in these difficult months suggest that she was far from the heartless and frivolous spirit of which she stands accused by Anna Akhmatova. In early August 1836 Natalya wrote once again to Dmitry for help.

I have just received a letter you sent me following the one in which you announced your marriage. I thank you sincerely for its contents. My husband asks me to convey to you his best wishes, and greets his new sister-in-law. He begs you to send him a supply of paper for one year, since it is running out. If you fulfil his request he promises to write a poem on the subject when your first newborn arrives.[10]

Pushkin's financial worries were not much eased by Natalya's pleas to her brother as, although Dmitry had evidently agreed to increase her allowance, he was late in sending it because of his own wedding expenses. In September 1836 Natalya wrote to him, still from Kamenny Ostrov, 'So this is how you keep your promise, my ne'er do well brother, who has not sent me my allowance by September 1? You have either forgotten, or it was impossible for you to do so, in which case I magnanimously forgive you.'[11]

Some time that autumn a new sexual element entered into d'Anthès's relations with the Pushkin family. His own most powerful desire was the conquest of Natalya, but Ekaterina, with whom d'Anthès also flirted outrageously, had also fallen madly in love with him. On 19–20 September 1836 Karamzina wrote to her brother,

On Wednesday we rested and tidied the house so as to receive many guests for the following day ... among the guests were Pushkin and his wife and the other Goncharov sisters, all three of dazzling elegance and of inexpressibly beautiful mien ... also my brothers and d'Anthès ... The after dinner hour spent in this pleasant company was all too brief; for at nine the neighbours arrived ... and the ball started in good earnest. All seemed very cheerful, to judge from their faces, apart from Alexander Pushkin who remained gloomy ... pensive and preoccupied throughout the evening. I too was infected by his melancholy. His wild, wandering and distracted stare was fixed with alarming intensity on his wife and d'Anthès, who continued joking as before, never leaving Ekaterina Goncharova's side, while throwing glances at Natalya, with whom at the end he danced a mazurka. It was distressing to behold the figure of Pushkin standing opposite them by the door, silent, pale and menacing. My God, how foolish all this is.[12]

D'Anthès continued to appear deeply infatuated with Natalya through the autumn of 1836. There may even have been an exchange of letters between them, though the only mention of such notes comes from Prince Trubetskoy, who shared accommodation with d'Anthès in the summer of 1836. His memories, however, were not set down until 1887 and are known to have some inaccuracies.

The frequent notes brought by Liza (Natalya's maid) meant nothing: in our day that was quite common ... If Nathalie had not been so impenetrably stupid, if d'Anthès had not been so spoiled, the whole thing would have come to nothing, for at that time, at least, there had been nothing much between them – handclasps, embraces, kisses, but nothing more, and in our day those things were quite usual.[13]

On 19 October Pushkin read a poem on the anniversary of the celebrations for the graduation of his *lycée* friends, and broke down in tears. He may have been remembering Delvig's death and his other close friends still in exile. He may have been grieving for the creative energy wasting under the anxieties of his daily life. As he wrote to his father, 'In the village I could work ... here I do nothing but fret myself to death.' The poem itself, a meditation on the emptiness he felt at the loss of his old comrades Pushchin and Kyukhelbecker in their exile, expressed a premonition that he would be the next to die.

Heeckeren's return at the end of May 1836 had not driven Natalya from d'Anthès's imagination, as he had once hoped would be the case. There was also an additional embarrassment for them both. When

Heeckeren returned to St Petersburg at the end of May 1836 he announced that he had successfully adopted d'Anthès as his son. Following on the research of Franz Suasso, who was granted access to an archive of letters from Van Heeckeren to the Dutch king, and of Ya. Lefkovich's recent article, however, it can be asserted with confidence that Van Heeckeren was lying.

The reasons Van Heeckeren had given to the Dutch king for his desire to adopt d'Anthès were as follows – he was 45 years old, unmarried and had for some years taken care of a young foreigner of noble blood with the full consent of his parents. Studiously withholding d'Anthès's actual age, since he knew very well that it was essential that the young man should not have reached 21, he implied that d'Anthès was still a child. Heeckeren also suggested that d'Anthès had been living with him as a son for far longer than was the case. Because the boy was a foreigner, Heeckeren asked the King to allow him to be incorporated into the Dutch nobility, as long as none of the Van Heeckeren relatives had any objection. These procedures were followed, and all 27 relatives gave their consent.

However, although d'Anthès could thereafter be considered a Dutch subject and carry Van Heeckeren's coat of arms, he could not be adopted for one further year – that is, until 5 May 1837. As Lefkovich observes, Heeckeren decided it was a long way from The Hague to St Petersburg and since no one in Russia would know about the year's delay he simply announced that he had already successfully adopted d'Anthès as a son. Heeckeren even deceived the Tsar, Nicholas I, who issued an order that the Dutch Ambassador's adopted son should henceforward be known as Baron Georges Charles Heeckeren. D'Anthès, too, must have known perfectly well that this 'adoption' had not yet taken place, but he fell in readily enough with the deception.

All d'Anthès's own emotions were at this moment focused on the seduction of Natalya. A crucial letter written on 17 October 1836 makes that plain, giving at the same time evidence both of d'Anthès's genuine involvement and an insight into the deviousness of his nature. It also establishes that a plot designed to bring Natalya to a secret rendezvous was d'Anthès's in origin.

> I wanted to talk to you in the morning but I had so little time that it proved impossible. Yesterday I spent the whole evening tête à tête with the lady who you know very well. But when I say tête à tête, I mean that I was the

only man at the reception of Princess Vyazemskaya and I talked to her for almost one hour. You can imagine what state I was in, but I gathered all my strength and played my part well enough ... and behaved as cheerfully as I could. Just pretended. Altogether I could bear it until eleven but then all my strength left me and I became so weak that I only just managed to leave the drawing room. Once outside, I started crying like a fool.

Crying and choking brought some relief. But afterwards, when I came home, I was stricken by a horrible fever. I couldn't sleep all night, and I experienced absolutely unbearable mental suffering. That's why I want to ask for your help. And I am begging you tonight to do something you have already promised to do for me. It is absolutely necessary for you to talk to her in order for me to know what to do ... I suggest you address her openly and tell her (but make sure her sister doesn't overhear this) that you have to talk to her. Then ask her whether by any chance she visited the Vyazemskys yesterday. When she answers that she did, tell her that she could do you a great favour by listening to what happened to me after I returned home. Tell it as if you witnessed it personally. You should tell her that my valet was frightened and awakened you at 2 a.m. You must tell her that you asked me many questions, but couldn't get any answers, and that you are convinced that I quarrelled with her husband and you want to prevent a disaster. (Now, in fact, her husband wasn't there.) By doing that, you will prove to her that I haven't told you about that evening at the Vyazemskys. It is very necessary that you impress her I am not frank with you about things that concern her and that you are asking only in the capacity of a father concerned about his son ... you could hint that her behaviour has led you to believe there is a closer relationship between her and myself than in fact exists ... under no circumstances should she suspect such a talk was prearranged with me. Let her see in it only the natural concern for my health ... and you should ask her to keep your words secret from everyone, especially from me. During this conversation, don't ask her to receive me ... but you could do it next time you talk to her. Beware of using any expressions which were in that letter. (*This refers to a letter of d'Anthès's to Natalya, dictated by Heeckeren, now lost.*) Once more I beg you, my dear, to help me. I give myself into your hands, because if this affair continues like this, I don't know what would happen to me. I will lose my mind ... In addition, if you could frighten her a bit, and blackmail ... (*the next words are unreadable*). Please forgive me for the unseemliness of this note, but, believe me, my head is burning as if on fire. I feel so terribly awful. If you have not enough information, please visit me in the barracks before you go off to visit the Ambassador of Bavaria. You'll find me in the quarters of the Betancourt. I kiss you...

So it was that d'Anthès tricked Natalya into a private meeting.

We shall return shortly to the odd proviso that Heeckeren should make sure Ekaterina does not overhear the conversation.

On 2 November[14] d'Anthès succeeded in bringing Natalya to a rendezvous at his friend Idalia Poletika's house in the barracks of the guard of cavalry. Idalia left as soon as Natalya arrived. She later told Vyazemskaya and her sister Alexandra that when she was left face to face alone with d'Anthès he pulled out a pistol and threatened to shoot himself unless she gave herself to him. She did not know how to get away. She wrung her hands and started to talk as loudly as possible. Fortunately Ida Poletika's daughter, then two years old, came into the room and Natalya was able to escape.[15]

According to A. P. Arapova, whose memoirs usually stress her mother's innocence and Pushkin's own moral turpitude, this interview took place much later – in January 1837. However, most recent critics now place it on 2 November.[16] Arapova excuses her mother agreeing to such a rendezvous by explaining that a letter from d'Anthès had assured Natalya he would in no way offend her honour and that he concluded the letter with a threat to his own life: 'if she refused this trivial mark of confidence he would not be able to survive the insult ...' Arapova further explains that her own governess, to whom Natalya had told the whole story, insisted that Natalya often lamented, 'the only act for which my conscience reproaches me is my agreement to that fatal rendezvous. A rendezvous for which my husband paid with his blood.'

It is not clear how many people knew about the meeting. Arapova claimed that P. P. Lanskoy was told about it by Idalia herself 'in order to be safe', but recent research by M. Yashin has established that Lanskoy was absent from St Petersburg from 19 October 1836 until February 1837, which makes this impossible. Lanskoy was to become Natalya's second husband and Arapova's own father. The other person who came to know of this meeting on 2 November, from Natalya's own lips, was Pushkin himself, though it is unlikely she would have confided the details to Pushkin as circumstantially as she did except that on 4 November he received a cruel anonymous letter.

This letter, in French, informed him he had been elected to the Most Serene Order of Cuckolds at a meeting under the Presidency of the Grand

Master, His Excellency D. L. Naryshkin, whose wife had been a mistress of Tsar Alexander 1. Twelve copies of this letter were sent to him care of his most intimate friends, among them the Karamzin family at whose house d'Anthès had first met Natalya, the Vyazemskys and Sollogub.

Pushkin's friends wanted to keep the anonymous letter secret to make it easier for Pushkin to avoid a duel. On 20 October Mme Karamzina wrote disparagingly to her son of some new contributions to Pushkin's magazine, *The Contemporary*, she had read, mentioning particularly 'an indescribable absurdity', Gogol's 'Nose'. On 7 November Alexander Karamzin wrote of his intention of having lunch with Mme Pushkina. There was no sign of any knowledge of the offensive letter, even though both knew about it very well. Sofya Karamzina was among the first to read the lampoon.

One copy of the lampoon, however, reached Pushkin. The letter was an insult which Pushkin could hardly ignore: he had responded to far less provocation all his life. In this case, as it was anonymous, it was not at first obvious how to counter it. Pushkin, already aware of d'Anthès's behaviour towards Natalya, was convinced the letter had been sent either by him or Baron Heeckeren.

Whatever else, Natalya should at this point have realised the damage she was doing, while Pushkin may have grimly recalled A. L. Davydov, Riznich, Vorontsov, Kern, Zakrevsky and other unlucky husbands to whom their wives had been unfaithful with him. His situation was similar to that of Molière, who had made so many jokes about husbands betrayed by their wives and was, nevertheless, soundly betrayed by his own.[17] Physically innocent or not, Natalya had clearly failed to safeguard her own honour so Pushkin was forced to do it for her. He sent off a challenge to d'Anthès the same evening by post.

But who was responsible for the anonymous lampoons? Pushkin was in no doubt that it was Heeckeren. As he wrote to Benckendorf, 'from looking at the paper, the style of the letter, the way in which it had been written, I recognised from the first moment that the letter was from a foreigner, from a man of high society, from a diplomat.' Yet if it *was* Heeckeren, his motivation is puzzling. Far from delighting in the possibility of the duel such a lampoon made likely, his next actions suggest a man doing his utmost to prevent it. It was he who received and opened Pushkin's challenge as d'Anthès was at the time on guard duty. His response was to appear at Pushkin's flat the following day and ask him for twenty-four hours' grace, and then a further delay of a week.

Hastening to Zhukovsky, Heeckeren even begged him to act as an intermediary in order to convey to Pushkin the astonishing proposition that the real object of d'Anthès's affections was not Natalya but Ekaterina and that, furthermore, he wished to marry her.

At this crucial point there is a letter of 6 November from d'Anthès to Heeckeren. It is two days after the insulting letter from Pushkin, but its import is veiled:

> My precious friend, thank you for your two notes. These notes calm me a little, and I needed that. I am writing these few words in order to repeat that I trust in you altogether and that any decision you make is agreeable to me, because I am already convinced that your course of action is likely to be better than mine. My god, I don't blame the woman! And I'm happy to know she is comfortable, but it was a huge carelessness on her side or madness. I don't understand it. And I don't understand what was her objective. Please send me a note tomorrow for me to know whether something new happened during the night. On top of that, you don't mention whether you saw the sister at her aunt's. How do you know that she made her confession about letters?
>
> Goodnight. I embrace you with all my heart.
>
> P.S. In all this affair, Ekaterina is a very good creature. She behaves herself wonderfully.

It is far from clear from this whether the 'huge carelessness' d'Anthès complains of is Natalya's confession to Pushkin or whether he has some other event in mind. It isn't even entirely clear whether the letters he mentions are those from himself to Natalya. In what precise way Ekaterina had proved herself a wonderful creature, we shall consider in a moment.

Pushkin responded to Zhukovsky's report of d'Anthès's interest in Ekaterina with incredulity. Heeckeren himself, however, confirmed it personally to Pushkin on 14 November at the flat of Ekaterina Zagryazhskaya. So it was that on 17 November Pushkin wrote to Sollogub, whom he had asked to be his second, to say that in view of the impending marriage between d'Anthès and his sister-in-law he would regard the challenge as not having taken place. Zhukovsky, wishing to make absolutely certain that the duel would not occur, informed the Tsar of the situation on 22 November. On 23 November Pushkin, too, had an audience with the Tsar, at which he is said to have given his word not to fight d'Anthès. If assurances were given by the Tsar in return, we do not know, but at the end of 1836 Benckendorf sent Natalya a thousand roubles 'on the occasion of the marriage of her sister, as the Tsar thought she would want to give her a wedding present'.

All St Petersburg boggled at the proposal to Ekaterina. She had for a time played the role of a chaperone when d'Anthès and Natalya met, and most people guessed she had always been in love with him herself. But that hardly explained d'Anthès's proposal. On 20 November Mme Karamzina wrote to her son, 'It's simply incredible ... the marriage, I mean ... but anything is possible in this world of impossibilities ...' D'Anthès was 'carried away by a sort of feverish gaiety and frivolity.'[18]

Sofya Karamzina, for her part, wrote,

> Natalie is very nervous and reserved, and her voice breaks when she talks of her sister's wedding. Ekaterina is wild with joy. She herself says she scarcely dares to believe her dream has come true. Society is amazed, but since the story of the letter is not known to most people it will only be the fault of Pushkin himself if, by his excitement, his enigmatic exclamations addressed to all and sundry, his manner of snubbing d'Anthès when they meet in society or demonstratively shunning him ... lead people to start guessing.[19]

According to Andronnikov, the Tsarina, too, asked, 'What is it? Magnanimity or self-sacrifice?'[20]

It seems that no one could believe d'Anthès was marrying of his own free will. There was good reason to be surprised. Ekaterina, though tall and stately, had been compared to a broomstick. She was four years older than d'Anthès, without a dowry, and an unprepossessing match for a dashing young man. With Heeckeren's protection he was a wealthy young man in expectation. Why did he not choose a beautiful heiress with connections that might have furthered his career? Being a soldier, it seems unlikely that cowardice made him reluctant to face a challenge, and the care he took in getting Pushkin to frame a letter withdrawing his challenge suggests his honour was dear to him. Nor was the duel avoided with ease. D'Anthès wrote to Pushkin, without any mention of the proposed marriage, saying,

> I desire to know why you have altered your intentions ... you should first agree, before you take back your words, that each of us must offer explanations in order that afterwards we may be able to refer to each other with esteem.[21]

He wanted to prevent Pushkin suggesting that it was cowardice which
had led to the offer of marriage. Moreover, when the two weeks Pushkin
had stipulated for a decision were up, d'Anthès sent his friend d'Archiac
to say that he remained at Pushkin's service. Pushkin had chosen Count
Sollogub – whom he had once challenged to a duel for upsetting Natalya –
as his second, and he now proposed that conditions for a duel should at
once be agreed – 'The bloodier the better.' That night Pushkin was at a
large party at the house of Count Fikelmon at which both Ekaterina and
d'Anthès were also present. Pushkin refused to allow Ekaterina to speak
to the young man, although rumours of their engagement were already
current. It was only the next day that the two seconds were able to meet
and agree a device that would satisfy Pushkin's honour, by hinting that
d'Archiac had told him in secret of the impending marriage but that
d'Anthès wished to wait until the duel was ended before making the
announcement for fear he would otherwise be taken for a coward.

In Pushkin's reply he wrote,

> I challenged Mr G Heeckeren to a duel, and he accepted without entering
> into any explanations. I ask the gentleman witnesses of this affair to be
> pleased to regard this challenge as non existent, having been informed by
> rumour that Mr George Heeckeren has decided to announce his resolve to
> marry Mlle Goncharova after the duel. I have no reason to ascribe his
> decision to any considerations unworthy of an honourable man.[22]

It is clear from the Karamzin correspondence that the names of Ekaterina and d'Anthès were publicly connected in the second half of 1836
and that for some parts of the summer of that year d'Anthès never left
Ekaterina's side. A possible reason for d'Anthès's decision – that their
relationship was already a sexual one and that Ekaterina's first child by
d'Anthès was conceived as early as mid-1836 – has been suggested by
several observers. The evidence, until recent research by Frans Suasso
and Vadim Stark, was inadequate.

On 9 November 1836 – that is, within the two weeks' grace stipulated
by Heeckeren – Ekaterina wrote to Dmitry:

> I doubt my letter today will be very cheerful, dear Dmitry, as I am not
> merely in a melancholy mood, I am sad to death. I wish to remind you that
> December 6 (Nicholas I nameday) is a day of great rejoicing here, so because
> of my position I must make various preparations for the day and absolutely
> must receive money by 1st of December, since the slightest delay would cost

me great and unpleasant inconvenience. I am happy to learn that you are happy with your lot, dear friend. As for me, my happiness is irrevocably lost. I know all too well that I shall never encounter it again on this suffering earth, and the only favour I ask of God is to put an end to this useless life of mine. Happiness for my family and death for myself ... that is what I need, that is what I pray constantly that God will grant me.[23]

Something wrong far out of the ordinary is suggested by this letter, but there is nothing to connect this directly with d'Anthès. There is now good reason to suppose that she may, indeed, have discovered herself to be pregnant. Queries about the date of the birth of Ekaterina's first child have hitherto been based on a letter from her mother which bears the date of 15 May 1837 (as first published by Shchegolev) which includes the following:

In your last letter you speak about your journey to Paris; to whom will you entrust the looking after of your little girl during the time of your absence? Will she remain in safe hands? Your separation from her must be distressing for you.[24]

This, which suggests that the child was conceived long before the marriage to d'Anthès in January 1837, was disproved by research in the Goncharov archives, by Obodovskaya and Dementev. The letter refers to a wedding which did not take place until the following year. The date of the letter should have read 15 May 1838. However, there are hints in the letters we have quoted that d'Anthès might have been saying one thing to Ekaterina and another to Natalya, hence his reluctance to have Ekaterina overhear his declaration of love as delivered by Heeckeren. New evidence suggests that this is far from fanciful. There are seven newly discovered letters between d'Anthès and Ekaterina which were written after d'Anthès's engagement to her.[25] These letters suggest relations between the two were from the outset considerably more intimate than usual between engaged couples. They establish that d'Anthès not only met Ekaterina every day at her aunt Zagryovzhskaya's apartment between noon and two p.m., as arranged, but also in his own flat, which went far beyond propriety. Most significantly, there is a letter which suggests that Ekaterina was already pregnant.

D'Anthès's first letter is interesting more for what it hints at than for what it reveals. Their behaviour had attracted unfavourable comment, but in what way it exceeded the bounds of custom is unmentioned. In the postscript, too, d'Anthès hits a note almost of subservience, which recalls letters written by d'Anthès to Heeckeren when there was something he particularly needed, as if keeping Ekaterina happy was a matter of some anxiety:

21 November 1836
My kind and good Ekaterina,
You see how the days are passing and every one of them different. Yesterday I was lazy, today I am very active, even though I have just returned from miserable duties in the Winter Palace. I complained about them to your brother Dmitry, and I don't know how I managed to spend a few hours in that horrible Field Marshall's Hall. My only consolation is that under no circumstances do I want to be displayed as a portrait there.[26] This morning I saw that lady whom you know all too well, and as always, my beloved, I complied with your commands. I announced formally that I would be very grateful if she left off negotiations which were quite useless. And if Monsieur is not clever enough to understand that, it is he who plays the fool in this whole business, and she is wasting her time, trying to explain anything to him.

One more piece of news. Yesterday evening they found our way of treating each other embarrassed everybody and was quite improper for an unmarried mademoiselle ... For my part, I can tell you I have no opinion in such matters, and intend to do whatever I like, more than ever.

Good evening, my dear Ekaterina. I hope that the performance of 'The Pirates'[27] will entertain you. Till tomorrow, I kiss your hand which you failed to give me yesterday evening before you left.
Georges

P.S. Thank you, my darling, for your kind and long letter which I have just discovered at my place. You know, I am so happy at the way I can guess your thoughts; everything you recommend in your letter has already been carried out, except for my posting a letter to le père d'Anthès and I am hurrying to finish that in time for the next post. Meanwhile, I will bring you a draft tomorrow.

Readers of d'Anthès's letters to Heeckeren will recognise the repetition of the flattering suggestion that he and Ekaterina have an almost telepathic closeness. Although Vadim Stark is clearly right in his introductory note to point out that d'Anthès does not talk of passionate love to Ekaterina, the following letter certainly offers a wholeness of affection which ignores both his own continuing commitment to Heeckeren and any attraction still felt for Natalya:

Thank you again, my kind Katherine, for everything you sent me. Upon my word it is charming, and you showed impeccable taste. I too found two pretty things. I don't know whether you approve them, but I am presenting them with all my heart.
All yours, Georges de H.

That Ekaterina might be pregnant is suggested by d'Anthès's fourth – and crucial – letter to her, written between 12 and 27 December. It is in this letter that d'Anthès makes plain that he is accustomed to receive Ekaterina alone in his room, and refers to his curiosity about the 'growth of a potato'. Whatever he intended by this 'potato', the object was something Ekaterina carried on her, with her or inside her, and it would certainly make sense to think of it as a growing child.

My kind Ekaterina,
I don't know why my health is worse than yesterday, but my recovery is delayed for some reason. I haven't asked you to come upstairs to see me this morning, because Monsieur Antoine (his servant), who always does whatever suits him, has decided to admit Karamzin. But I hope there won't be any more obstacles to prevent me seeing you, because I am very curious to look at how much the *potato* has grown since the last time.
All yours, Georges.

P.S. The Baron has just visited me, and asks me to reprimand you for not putting enough care into healing your cold.

In his fifth letter d'Anthès refers to his habit of receiving Ekaterina while undressed:

My kind Katherine,
You saw this morning that I treat you almost as a *spouse* in the most unpresentable nightwear. I feel myself, or well enough. All day I have received guests. I am very surprised at the persistence of the V's. (Vyazemsky); it looks almost like a practical joke. Young Paul V (about 16) saw that I was lying on the sofa looking almost dead but in spite of this Valuyev (Vyazemsky's son-in-law) gave me another formal invitation. I am very concerned to know what all of this could mean. In any case you should go there and tell me all about it. Farewell, goodnight, have a nice time.
All yours
Georges de H.

There is further evidence, discovered by Frans Suasso[28] and commented upon by Lefkovich,[29] to suggest that Ekaterina's first child was conceived much earlier than her marriage. There were letters between the Netherlands' Minister for Law and the King between February 1837 and February 1838 which followed d'Anthès's duel with Pushkin and his subsequent deportation from Russia. This correspondence dealt primarily with d'Anthès's citizenship and whether or not he should be excluded from the Dutch nobility. However, the crucial point is that the final decision about d'Anthès's right to retain the name of Van Heeckeren, though excluded from the Dutch nobility, was based on the fact that his wife had already given birth to 'one or even two children', who would otherwise lose their legitimacy.

Such uncertainty about the number of d'Anthès's children is odd, but would not of itself be conclusive evidence of a child conceived before marriage. However, Suasso draws our attention to a report from Heeckeren to his Minister on 2 February 1837, only three weeks after the wedding, in which he points out that his own estate is not large 'and that he has to support a family where they expect a new arrival very soon'. Ya. Lefkovich also cites a letter from Alexander Karamzin to his brother Andrey in Paris dated March 1837 and quotes the sentence, 'this person, who for so long played the role of go-between, eventually became a lover and afterwards a wife.' None of this is decisive proof, but in a letter dated 24 March 1837 to d'Anthès, then already in exile, Heeckeren speaks of Ekaterina going into 'premature labour', which would be an unusual way to describe a pregnancy of less than two and a half months.

Furthermore, the state registers in Sulz, where d'Anthès's other children are registered, show the signature of the doctor who was present at all the births, except for that of the first child, Mathilda. Suasso suggests that this was because d'Anthès's father was influential enough in Sulz to have the child's birth date registered as 19 October, whether accurate or not. Taken in relation to d'Anthès's letters, particularly that reference to the potato, Ekaterina's pregnancy does seem the likeliest explanation for d'Anthès's unexpected proposal as such a scandal would have ruined his career.

Whether or not d'Anthès had seduced Ekaterina, it is quite clear he could not be marrying her simply to safeguard the honour of Natalya. A letter from Count Benckendorf's stepdaughter makes the point succinctly. His actions were 'bound to compromise another, for who is going to

look at a mediocre painting when a Raphael Madonna is beside it? ...
d'Anthès ... that haughty young Adonis ...' Moreover, the person
most offended by the compromise was Natalya herself, who found
the engagement to her sister a humiliation, and confessed as much to
Pushkin.

The two remaining letters were written not only after d'Anthès's
marriage to Ekaterina but after the duel with Pushkin, and we shall come
to them. If, as Stark suggests, Baron Heeckeren told Pushkin about the
existing liaison with Ekaterina when he went to see him to prevent the
duel, it would add another dimension to the extremity of Pushkin's
hatred for d'Anthès. The forthcoming wedding was announced on 18
November, even though Pushkin had a bet with Sollogub that the marriage would not take place.

Some biographers have speculated that d'Anthès may have thought
that by entering Pushkin's family he would have greater ease of
access to the woman he loved. That would imply an attachment of
overpowering intensity and singleness of purpose, and it is questionable
whether d'Anthès was capable of it. Olga, Pushkin's sister, wrote from
Warsaw immediately after hearing the news of Ekaterina's impending
marriage,

> His (d'Anthès) passion for Natalya had never been a secret for anyone. I
> knew perfectly well about this when I was in St Petersburg. Believe me,
> there must be something suspicious here, some kind of misunderstanding,
> so that perhaps it would be very good if this marriage did not take place.[30]

Only one other possible motive remains to be explored for d'Anthès's
decision to marry Ekaterina, namely that d'Anthès's own strongest
attachment was to his adoptive father Heeckeren. Some light may be
thrown on this by one of d'Anthès's brother officers, Prince Alexander
Trubetskoy, who wrote,

> I do not know whether to say that he lived with Heeckeren or Heeckeren
> lived with him ... At that time buggery was widespread in high society ...
> it must be assumed that in his relations with Heeckeren he [d'Anthès] played
> only the passive role.[31]

By 'passive' one may understand the role of the beloved rather than
the lover. D'Anthès's own feelings seem tainted by financial opportunism,
yet the two men certainly remained close to the end of Heeckeren's
life. If, indeed, the attachment between them was so strong, d'Anthès's

compulsive flirting might be simply designed to cover up the fact, and a reason for selecting Ekaterina as a wife might be her willingness to go along with the fiction of d'Anthès's sexual normality in return for even a part of his affection. She would know that d'Anthès would only be pretending to be in love with her sister. Meanwhile, in a letter to Count Nesselrode, the Russian Minister for Foreign Affairs, Heeckeren had the impudence to speak of 'that elevated moral feeling which obliged my son to bind himself for life in order to save the reputation of the woman he loved'.

The reference in the anonymous lampoon to Naryshkin, whose wife was a famous mistress of Alexander I, suggests that the writer wished Pushkin to believe Natalya was involved with the Tsar. If Heeckeren were, indeed, the author, the hint at the Tsar's involvement makes complete sense. Pushkin would be unable to challenge the Tsar and would have no possible course of action other than withdrawing from society altogether, thus removing Natalya as an object of temptation. Pushkin was ready enough to believe the Tsar in love with Natalya, as he declared explicitly to Nashchokin:

> The Tsar, like any officer, runs after my wife: several times in the mornings he has deliberately ridden past her window, and at evening during the balls he asks why she always has her blinds lowered.[32]

He did not conceal his suspicions from Nicholas himself. The Tsar had warned Natalya to be careful of her reputation, and she repeated this good advice to Pushkin. Meeting Nicholas a little while after this, Pushkin thanked him for his advice. Nicholas remarked, 'Well, can you expect anything else from me?' To which Pushkin replied, 'Sire, I not only can, but I frankly confess that I have suspected you most of all of courting my wife.'[33]

Perhaps it was the recollection that Naryshkin had accepted money from Alexander I as a reward for colluding in his wife's affair with the Tsar which led Pushkin to write to the Minister of Finance, declaring his intention to repay immediately the loan he had taken from the Tsar – a gesture he could hardly have raised the funds to meet. Akhmatova argues that when, on 23 November, Pushkin met the Tsar in the Winter Palace he was persuaded that Heeckeren had sent the anonymous letters (or organised their despatch). Pushkin was asked to give his word to be silent about it, which frustrated his intention of exposing the ambassador in the eyes of Petersburg society, in return for the Tsar's promise to 'handle the matter himself'.

No one believed, as Pushkin hoped, that d'Anthès decided on marriage to avoid a duel. Zhukovsky is said to have laughed when he heard that Andrey Karamzin was trying to figure out the secret of d'Anthès's marriage. Vyazemsky describes Ekaterina at the ball on 14 January after her marriage: 'Madame Heeckeren looked happy, which made her ten years younger, and made her look like a nun who had just taken her vows or a deceived newly wed ...'

The authorship of the anonymous letter is far from solved, however. Pushkin had many enemies, including a woman, Countess Nesselrode, who remembered an insulting epigram directed at her father. Then there were two princes – I. S. Gagarin and Dolgorukov – who lived together as overt homosexuals and were connected to Heeckeren through their shared sexual tastes. This does not suggest why either of them would be likely to write the offensive letter, unless at Heeckeren's instigation.

In 1927 Shchegolev consulted a forensic handwriting expert who decided that the anonymous lampoon had been written by Prince P. B. Dolgorukov. Dolgorukov was known to have a malicious character and had once made the traditional sign of the cuckold behind Pushkin's back. In 1966, however, another expert identified more resemblance to Gagarin's handwriting. In 1987 the Russian journal *Ogonek* published an article maintaining that the handwriting belonged to neither of them. It seems unlikely that experts will settle the matter satisfactorily, not to mention that the hand that wrote the letters may not have been the instigator's.

Who, then, was responsible for it? In the Soviet period the finger has often pointed towards the Tsar but, while it is extremely likely that his secret police would have informed him of the letter's existence and he markedly failed to interfere, an autocratic ruler needs no such ingenious methods to arrange the death of one of his subjects.

The Karamzins remained socially neutral, inviting both d'Anthès and the Pushkins to their house. It was at Sofya Karamzina's birthday party that Pushkin met Sollogub and arranged to have him speak to d'Anthès's second and complete the arrangements when the fortnight's grace was up. After the birthday party the guests went on to a ball at the house of Ambassador Fikelmon. All the ladies invited to the Austrian Embassy were in mourning for Charles X but Ekaterina, as a prospective bride, wore white. On 29 November Sofya Karamzina confirms the date of d'Anthès's wedding as 10 January and observes how well appointed the apartment set aside for them would be. She goes on,

> Pushkin ... continues to behave in the most stupid and ridiculous manner. The expression on his face is tigerish, he grinds his teeth whenever he speaks of the wedding, which he is always ready to do and is very glad if he can find a new listener ... he still insists that he will not allow his wife to go to the wedding, or to receive her sister in her house after her marriage ... As for her, there is nothing quite straightforward about her behaviour ... in front of her husband she does not bow to d'Anthès, doesn't so much as glance at him, but when her husband is not here she starts her old coquetry – lowered eyelids, abstracted manner, embarrassment – and d'Anthès immediately comes and sits down opposite her, casting long looks at her and, apparently quite forgetting his betrothed, who changes countenance and is tormented by jealousy.[34]

Sofya tells this with an undisguised glee at the sheer histrionic quality of these people's pain. There is something quite unfeeling in her description of another occasion when 'Pushkin only broke his morose silence, so embarrassing for everyone, by occasional abrupt ironical exclamations, and from time to time demoniacal laughter. I assure you he was simply ridiculous.'

This, from a member of a family who had been close friends of Pushkin for nearly twenty years, suggests just that malicious pleasure in pulling a great man down to the level of smaller men which Pushkin had deprecated long ago in the biographers of Byron. Other observers witnessed Pushkin's suffering with more pity, among them Sofya's stepsister Ekaterina Meshcherskaya, who was struck by Pushkin's feverish state and convulsive movements. Mme Vyazemskaya had refused to allow d'Anthès to visit her house since October 1836 if any other carriages were outside her door. Mme Karamzina continued to reserve her pity for d'Anthès, whom she saw as forced into a loveless marriage without any advantage to himself. 'He certainly does not look like a man in love,' she observed on 9 January in the same letter in which she remarks that Pushkin looked likely to lose his bet that the marriage would not take place.

The *haut monde* who had been the butt of his poem 'My Genealogy' were equally pleased to condemn Pushkin in any way they could, and the unexpected wedding was attributed to some scandal in the Pushkin family which d'Anthès was gallantly acting to conceal. The Empress was herself very fond of d'Anthès, and Pushkin's enemies, including many who had suffered at his sharp wit, were happy to see d'Anthès as the hero of the drama.

During his own marriage Pushkin's conduct may not have been perfect but it had been on the whole conventional. He may have visited brothels, or so Arapova claims, probably at times when his wife was pregnant or sick. Natalya often pretended to be jealous of the 53-year-old Elizaveta Khitrovo, but with little enough cause. There is also a persistent rumour that he enjoyed a love affair with his sister-in-law Alexandra. She had some resemblance to Natalya, though without her love for grand society; she preferred to stay at home and take care of the household. She loved and understood Pushkin's poetry and when he needed money offered him her own possessions to pawn. She was a comfort to him as he tried to deal with demands from his brother-in-law for help in dealing with the sliding fortunes of the Goncharov estate. The evidence for a sexual element in their relationship comes from a lost chain or cross belonging to Alexandra found in Pushkin's couch in his study.

It is once again to A. P. Arapova, Natalya's daughter by her second husband, that we owe the story of the chain belonging to Alexandra which Pushkin's servants searched for everywhere before it was discovered in Pushkin's couch. Arapova, however, is a hostile witness since she both disliked her aunt and was much concerned to justify her own mother's behaviour towards Pushkin. Moreover, she related the story 71 years after the events. In Arapova's memoirs she claims that before her wedding Alexandra had a long conversation with Natalya about how best to disguise from her future husband that she wasn't a virgin. If Pushkin had been her lover, Natalya was not the most obvious person to go to for such advice.

Zhukovsky made two cryptic jottings in November 1836, one on 8 November, 'What I said (to Pushkin) about his relationships' and another, after 10 January 1837, about *'les révélations d'Alexandrine'*. These notes suggest at least he did not altogether rule out the possibility of there being some truth in the rumours. He also makes another reference to 'the story of the couch'. Neither of these allusions prove anything, but when Zhukovsky wrote to Pushkin during the November crisis – 'In this affair there is a great deal on your part also to which you have to plead guilty'[35] – he might have had Alexandra in mind. Another contemporary witness is Prince Vyazemsky's niece Sofya, who in January 1837 wrote abroad to her brother,

> Alexandra is carrying on a regular flirtation with Pushkin who is seriously in love with her, and if he is jealous over his wife on principle, then his jealousy over his sister-in-law is genuine. It's all most peculiar and my uncle Vyazemsky says that he is veiling his face and turning it away from the Pushkin household.[36]

Akhmatova, much opposed to the thought of Pushkin having an affair with Alexandra, made the very pertinent comment that Pushkin had little need to flirt publicly with Alexandra if they were sleeping together in his own house. Akhmatova accuses Arapova, the daughter of Natalya and her second husband Lanskoy, of inventing the whole Alexandra story to modify the world's ill opinion of Natalya's behaviour.

One might well be indignant that Arapova's memoirs show no sign of any appreciation of Pushkin's genius. According to Arapova, Pushkin was no more than a 'failure who had squandered all of his inheritance, an uncouth boor and vulgar libertine, the wicked husband of a long suffering, tormented victim'.[37] Arapova is wholly unfair to him as a human being, making no mention of the many tender and caring letters he wrote to his wife.

Prince Trubetskoy attributes his own knowledge of the intimacy between Pushkin and Alexandra to conversations with Idalia Poletika, who had long been a sworn enemy of Pushkin and had arranged for d'Anthès to meet Natalya alone at her house. Trubetskoy, when in his seventies, twice mentioned that he heard of Pushkin's liaison with Alexandra from Idalia Poletika, who supposedly recalled Pushkin's jealousy over Alexandra. Trubetskoy spoke of the affair as 'something more than the usual immorality', perhaps because it was a relationship which would have been regarded as incestuous at the time. An addition to the rumour comes from the grandson of one of Pushkin's closest friends, Nashchokin. When Nashchokin died in 1854 his grandson claimed to have been told there were stormy scenes between Pushkin and Natalya because of it.

Pushkin's father is quoted as saying that Alexandra seemed to grieve more than the widow on account of Pushkin's death, which may well have been the case by the summer of 1837. None of Pushkin's relatives were present at his funeral. The vision of Alexandra as the good angel in Pushkin's life is somewhat marred, however, by her preserving no token in memory of him, though he gave her a cross on his deathbed, whereas a portrait of d'Anthès hung in the dining room of Alexandra's castle until the beginning of the Second World War.

Of Natalya, Vyazemsky observes,

> She ought to have withdrawn from society and to have asked this of her husband. She did not have the character for this and once again began to find herself in the same relation with Heeckeren as before his marriage.[38]

Serena Vitale claims to defend d'Anthès from a wholesale 'demonisation of his character'. Yet the discovered letters suggest new and even more unpleasant features of his behaviour – his wheedling manner towards his protector, and his blatant flattery when gifts are showered upon him as a result. Nor can his behaviour to Ekaterina be explained in any honourable way. Serena Vitale may be right to suggest that the contemporary wish to 'sanctify' Natalya is a reaction against the antipathy felt towards her by the two greatest women poets of the twentieth century, Akhmatova and Tsvetayeva. Still, however foolish her behaviour during the last year of his life, Vitale's condemnation of Natalya is peculiarly modern, two hundred years remote from Tatyana in *Evgeny Onegin*: she blames Natalya because 'her understanding of chastity was a rather conventional one ... and for the beggarliness of her spirit ... she just provoked him with her coquetry. She continued to feed this young Frenchman with her hot Russian hors d'oeuvres, but refused to satisfy his appetite, which she caused herself.'

Vitale has no condemnation for d'Anthès 'asking the man who loves him to be the herald of his passion'. She has nothing but sympathy for d'Anthès's 'monstrous situation with the oldest Goncharov sister'. To Heeckeren, too, she seems indulgent, noting that it was d'Anthès who instructed him how to behave as he did, and that his reputation as a 'wily old fox' has to this extent been a falsification. Yet even in her own observation, Heeckeren was calculating enough:

> He understood very well that before the young man achieved his desire, he could have no peace of mind ... and after his victory, who knows? Moreover, Heeckeren had some rhetorical talent of his own when he murmured in tears, 'Give me back my son.'

As to the authorship of the anonymous letter, Vitale suggests, not very persuasively, that it could have been written by Dmitry Nesselrode, son of the Foreign Minister, whose mother once escorted Natalya to a ball which Pushkin did not want his wife to attend in his absence. She also suggests Countess Korsakovskaya as a possible author on the grounds that her remark about Pushkin's *Boris Godunov* as 'interesting for Russia' received the blistering response from Pushkin, 'In the house of your mother you, too, could be considered a beauty.' Vitale has more of a point when she asks, 'And if we are looking for enemies, why not for enemies of d'Anthès? There are not so many, but some ladies had reason to hate him, for example the "common-law spouse" whom he abandoned.'

Oddly enough, there is a letter from Heeckeren to d'Anthès, in French, dated 1 February 1837 (that is, after the fatal duel). This could be entirely duplicitous, and aimed at interception by the secret police. Still, on the surface at least, it totally exculpates d'Anthès from any knowledge of the anonymous letter, even if Heeckeren did send it:

> If you want to talk about the anonymous letter, I can tell you it was sealed badly and thinly with red sealing wax. It was a strange seal, so far as I can remember, the letter 'A' surrounded by emblems ... May the truth come out, that is my most passionate desire. Yours, heart and soul, B.d.H.

As might have been predicted, the marriage between d'Anthès and Ekaterina did nothing to allay Pushkin's torment, described by Prince Vyazemsky in a letter to Grand Duke Mikhail Pavlovich on 14 February 1837:

> The young Heeckeren (d'Anthès) continued in the presence of his own wife to emphasise his passion for Madame Pushkina. Gossip in the city was renewed and the wounding attention of society was turned with redoubled strength on the actors in the drama that was taking place before their eyes...

CHAPTER SEVENTEEN

Duel and Death

Natalya attended the Russian Orthodox marriage of her sister, but did not stay for the wedding supper. This has been put down to either pique or to Pushkin's instructions. More likely, something disgraceful was known in the family to be happening. Ekaterina's and Natalya's two brothers also both left immediately for Moscow after the wedding feast, an otherwise inexplicable piece of behaviour.

Thereafter Pushkin attempted to impose a complete ban on any contact with his new brother-in-law. He refused him admission to his flat on the Moyka when d'Anthès was making the round of calls traditionally made by newly married couples, and would have been glad to have his close friends behave in the same way. They did not. Even the Vyazemskys welcomed the newly married couple three days after the wedding, probably seeing any such refusal as a pointless exercise when the new social season would have brought the d'Anthèses and the Pushkins together.

What altogether astounds anyone aware of d'Anthès's continuing friendship with Heeckeren, and his probable seduction of Ekaterina before marriage, is that as soon as he and Natalya began to meet at balls d'Anthès resumed his courtship of her quite as openly as before his marriage. Not only did they dance together but went for long stolen walks, and people could hardly fail to notice the difference between d'Anthès's behaviour towards Natalya and the casual way he treated his own wife. Pushkin watched helplessly as the gossip was re-ignited:

'Pushkin was terribly alone at this period and his friends' behaviour lamentably slack.'[1]

D'Anthès wrote Pushkin two friendly letters in an attempt to cool the situation. The second letter Pushkin brought to the house of aunt Zagryazhskaya without opening it and, meeting Heeckeren there, asked him to return the letter to d'Anthès and say that no further correspondence would be received. Heeckeren remarked that the letter was written to Pushkin and he could not take it. Pushkin is reported to have thrown it in his face saying, 'Take it, you scoundrel!'[2]

It is uncertain how much Natalya knew about d'Anthès's duplicity. D'Anthès continued his courtship and her own vanity led her to believe he still cared for her – this she found irresistibly exciting. It is impossible to acquit her of recklessness in giving d'Anthès the encouragement she did. Continuing to flirt outrageously with d'Anthès makes her seem indifferent not only to the pain she was causing but even to the danger she was putting her husband in. Natalya well knew that Pushkin had other troubles, which her undiminished extravagance worsened month by month. Nearly everything he owned was mortgaged; he owed almost 120,000 roubles. The Court, which had always despised his lack of means, was once again chuckling to think of Natalya continuing to cheat him with the lively young guardsman. At one ball d'Anthès took the arm of his own wife and said in a loud voice, 'Come, my *legitimate* one.'

As anonymous letters began to arrive, baiting Pushkin with his wife's infidelity, he declared he would receive no post, even though so much of his pleasure had always come through correspondence. The situation had begun to make him ill, and he looked 'old, yellow, harassed'.[3] His only happiness lay in poetry. Yet he had neither ease nor peace in which to write.

The climax of his public humiliation came at a ball given by Countess Vorontsova on 23 January when d'Anthès gave all his attention to Natalya. She and Ekaterina were both served by the same chiropodist and d'Anthès punned maliciously, '*Je sais maintenant que votre cor* ('corn' shares the same sound as 'corps', body) *est plus beau que celui de ma femme.*' Natalya, with a delight which seems altogether heartless, repeated this as a poor joke to her husband. Pushkin was enraged by the hint that d'Anthès knew his wife's body and, though he continued to believe in Natalya's innocence, determined to put an end to the situation.

Pushkin pawned Alexandra's silver for the money to buy duelling pistols, and on 25 or 26 January wrote a vicious letter to Baron Heeckeren. The terms of this letter, of which Pushkin gave an immaculate copy to his second, made a duel inevitable.

Count Sollogub was in Pushkin's study on an earlier occasion when Pushkin had written an insulting letter he was persuaded not to send. At that time, Sollogub reports, 'His lips were bloodshot. At that moment he was terrifying, and only then did I really understand his African derivation.'[4] This time Pushkin kept secret what he was doing, not even telling Natalya and Zhukovsky. The Vyazemskys, too, suspected nothing and even invited the Pushkins and d'Anthèses to their house on the evening on which Pushkin wrote this letter. The writing of it seemed to release Pushkin from his morose ill spirits. Alexander Turgenev's diary records that on 28 January he found Pushkin cheerful, full of life, joking and talking with animation on a variety of subjects, as if a great load had been lifted from him. The letter itself follows:

Monsieur le Baron
Allow me to make a résumé of what has just happened. The conduct of your son has been known to me for a long time past and I could not be indifferent towards it. I confined myself to the role of observer, ready to intervene when I judged it appropriate. An incident, which at any other moment would have been extremely disagreeable to me, very fortunately rescued me from the affair. I received the anonymous letters. I saw that the moment had come and I took advantage of it. You know the rest. I made your son play a role so pitiable that my wife, astonished by so much cowardice and banality, could not prevent herself from laughing, and the feeling which she perhaps felt for this great and sublime passion was extinguished in the calmest contempt and the most well-deserved disgust.

I am obliged to admit, Monsieur le Baron, that your role has not been altogether proper. You, the representative of a crowned head, have acted paternally as the pimp of your son. It appears that all his behaviour (incidentally pretty inept) has been directed by you. It is you who probably dictated these poor jokes which he has just poured out and the bits of nonsense which he has taken part in writing. Like an obscene old woman, you would lie in wait for my wife in every corner in order to talk to her about the love of your bastard, or one who is so called, and when he was confined to his quarters by pox, you said he was dying of love for her and murmured to her, 'Give me back my son.'

You realise full well, Monsieur le Baron, that after all this I cannot endure

my family having the slightest acquaintance with yours. It was on that
condition that I had given my consent not to allow this dirty affair to have
any consequence, and not to dishonour you in the eyes of our Court and
that of the Netherlands, as I could have done and as I intended to do. I do
not care for my wife to listen to your paternal exhortations any more. I
cannot allow that your son, after his abject behaviour, should dare to
address a word to my wife, nor – still less – that he should recite regimental
puns and play the part of devotion and unhappy passion, where he is
nothing but a coward and a scoundrel. I am therefore obliged to address
myself to you, in order to ask you to put an end to all this scheming if you
wish to avoid a further scandal from which I shall certainly not shrink.[5]

Heeckeren received the insulting letter just as he was about to set off
for dinner with Count Stroganov. He was at first in something of a
quandary. The character of the letter made it impossible to ignore. If he
answered the challenge in person, which would have been difficult in
any case because of his diplomatic position, it would look as though
d'Anthès was a coward. If d'Anthès accepted, he might lose his life.
When he put the matter to Count Stroganov he was advised that d'Anthès
should make the challenge.

The letter d'Anthès then wrote to Pushkin was filled with insults in
turn:

Not recognising your handwriting or your signature, I have had recourse
to Vicomte d'Archiac, who brings this letter to you with the request to
make known to him whether the letter I am answering actually comes from
you. Its contents have gone so completely beyond all limits that I refuse to
answer all the details of this epistle. You appear to have forgotten that it
was you who retracted the challenge which you addressed to Baron George
Heeckeren and which was accepted by him ... There remains only to say
that Vicomte d'Archiac visits you in order to agree upon a place of meeting
with Baron George Heeckeren, and I add this encounter permits of no delay.
Later I will teach you to respect the dignity with which I am clothed and
which no conduct on your side must offend.[6]

Pushkin accepted the challenge at once and without paying much
attention to the contents of the letter. His only difficulty lay in finding a
second without letting the secret out among his friends, who would
certainly try once again to prevent the duel. He confided in Alexandrina,
who told no one else in the household, and in Princess Vyazemsky. But

it was Zizi (Evpraksia, the daughter of his old friend Praskovya Osipova) that he took most fully into his confidence. Zizi had come to St Petersburg to discuss some problems that surrounded the sale of the Mikhaylovskoe estate. According to her subsequent account, Pushkin had no worries about the fate of his wife and children, whom he was convinced the Tsar would look after financially.

This may have been a result of a wishful interpretation of something said to him at his meeting with the Tsar earlier in the month but, since it corresponds exactly with what then happened and combines suggestively with another teasing fragment of information, it is worth giving a little thought. A letter written by Praskovya Osipova from Trigorskoe on 16 February 1837 to Alexander Turgenev (published in 1962) suggests some vital piece of information was imparted to her daughter Evpraksia as a secret and never divulged afterwards.

'I am almost glad,' Osipova wrote to Turgenev, 'that you have not heard what he said to my daughter Evpraksia before the fatal day.' Turgenev wrote back in desperation to plead with her to let him know what this information might be, but there was no response. It is tempting, though obviously rash, to feel this might be a clue to a connection between Natalya and the Tsar so dispiriting to Pushkin that he hardly cared to go on living. There is no evidence that Natalya was the Tsar's mistress during Pushkin's lifetime, but this may hint that she became so after his death. Perhaps in reaction to the long Soviet period of impugning the Tsar at every turn, Russian scholars at Pushkinsky Dom are unwilling to countenance any such possibility.

Zizi respected Pushkin's confidence completely, and made no attempt to inform any friends who might have stopped the duel, perhaps because, to quote a letter of her husband on 28 February 1837, she could see how happy Pushkin would be to escape from those sufferings 'which tormented him terribly towards the end of his life'. For all her sympathy and warmth, Zizi's comments on Pushkin's continuing interest in her married half-sister Alexandra Ivanovna when he visited Trigorskoe some sixteen months earlier suggest that she did not see Pushkin with an uncritical eye.

Pushkin still had the problem of finding a second. At a ball on the evening of 26 January he tried to get an official of the English Embassy, Arthur C. Magenis, to act for him. The Englishman hesitated but since d'Archiac refused to discuss the matter with him, and it was thus impossible to act as an honourable second in trying to effect a reconciliation, he had a letter delivered to Pushkin's flat by hand saying he could not act for him.

On the morning of 27 January Pushkin rose at eight, wrote in his study for a time and was heard to sing in high spirits. At ten a letter arrived from d'Archiac demanding the name of his second. Fearing delay would allow the news to leak around the city, Pushkin wrote back hastily to say that he would accept any second of d'Anthès's nomination, even his 'lackey', and appear at any place of d'Anthès's choosing. 'As for the hour and place, I am entirely at his service.'

Knowing this hardly accorded with the rules of duelling, Pushkin cast about in his mind. A schoolmate from lyceum days, Konstantin Danzas, appeared at Pushkin's apartment at twelve o'clock on 27 January, most likely at Pushkin's invitation. Danzas was now a Lieutenant Colonel in the army. Still fond of his old schoolfriend, he readily undertook to be Pushkin's second when the crisis was explained to him.

The conditions of the duel were then drawn up. The two adversaries were to be twenty paces away from a notional barrier making a kind of no man's land. Both were to be armed with a pistol. When the signal was given they could fire as they advanced towards one another so long as they did not pass the barrier. Once a shot was fired neither of the two adversaries was allowed to move so that the one who fired first would meet the shot of his opponent from the same distance. Both seconds signed the document of agreement at 2.30 on the afternoon of 27 January.

To Pushkin the conditions were immaterial. Somewhere about the middle of the afternoon he wrote his last letter – to Alexandra Ishimova, a writer whom he wished to persuade to do some translations of Barry Cornwall. This began with the cool sentence, 'I am extremely sorry that it will be impossible for me to accept your invitation today.' He went on to enclose a book by the English author, in which he had marked in pencil some passages he hoped she might translate. He then washed, dressed and put on his bearskin coat, setting off by sleigh at about one o'clock in the freezing cold without reporting his destination to anyone. He drove Danzas to the French Embassy where d'Anthès's second, d'Archiac, was living, and then waited at Wolff's, a well-known pastry shop on the Nevsky Prospect, for Danzas to join him. At the moment Mme Karamzin was writing with such gloating delight about Pushkin's misery, Pushkin was waiting for Danzas, who had gone to fetch his pistols.

The meeting with d'Anthès had been arranged for five o'clock at a lonely spot near the Black River on the outskirts of St Petersburg. Danzas and Pushkin set out in a sleigh towards Trotskoi Bridge. The river Neva was frozen solid; there was a stiff wind and little light except that reflected from the snow. The shortest way lay by the forbidding Peter and Paul fortress. At Palace Quay Pushkin and Danzas recognised Natalya's carriage coming from the other direction, but Natalya did not notice her husband, perhaps because she was myopic. The general press of traffic was going towards the centre of the city but none of the friends whom they passed on the way asked why these two were driving out of town instead.

The two seconds arranged a concealed place where the fight could take place without the coachmen witnessing it. The snow was knee-deep. Pushkin sat on a mound of snow as the place was cleared and levelled in readiness. He was impatient to begin, and when the signal was given with Danzas's hat he rushed towards the barrier, marked by their seconds' capotes, to fire at his opponent. Since conversations with an historian of duelling in St Petersburg in 1997, I now understand how it was the duel went as it did. D'Anthès had no intention of giving Pushkin more than a flesh wound in the leg. He was an excellent shot, a military man, and though it was essential for the honour of his regiment that he should fight when challenged he knew Pushkin's death would be a disaster for his military career. Pushkin, on the other hand, wanted d'Anthès dead. For that reason he rushed forward to take his shot from as close to the barrier as possible. Seeing the ferocity of his opponent, d'Anthès, who had moved forward only four paces and much more slowly, was forced to fire rapidly to avoid his own death. He aimed at Pushkin's leg, but his aim was faulty and instead he hit Pushkin in the abdomen.

Pushkin was far from indifferent to his fate. He had calculated that his best chance of killing d'Anthès lay in firing from close range, hoping that, even if d'Anthès fired first, as he did, he would have him at his mercy, without his second shot. In the event, Pushkin dropped, seriously wounded by that first shot. Both seconds ran to him but Pushkin raised himself on his elbow and said, 'Wait. I have enough strength to take my shot.'

This was the courage that so impressed the mother of Marina Tsvetaeva. Not a very Christian courage to be sure, but a manly one. D'Anthès, too, showed courage. He remained exactly where he was, as the code of duelling required, sideways on to Pushkin's shot and holding a pistol upwards in his hand to protect his head and raising his other arm to protect his breast. Pushkin took his own pistol from his second and fired with a firm right hand. He knew himself to have a trained aim and, indeed, d'Anthès fell to the ground. Seeing as much and believing his adversary dead, Pushkin shouted 'Bravo' and threw his pistol aside. In fact, the bullet had gone through d'Anthès's right arm and been deflected by a button – his main injury proved to be bruised ribs. It was Pushkin who was seriously wounded, with a bullet lodged deep in his lower abdomen.

Pushkin is said to have murmured, 'It is strange. I thought it would give me pleasure to kill him but I do not feel that now.'[7] When d'Anthès's second tried to mumble reconciling words, however, Pushkin said, 'In the event it is all the same.'

Pushkin was losing a great deal of blood. The coachmen made a litter to carry him to the sleigh and they proceeded towards St Petersburg slowly as all movement was very painful. The seconds walked and d'Anthès followed in his own sledge. After a short distance they were met by a carriage sent by Heeckeren and, without saying who had sent it, d'Anthès and d'Archiac offered it to Pushkin. Danzas accepted on Pushkin's behalf and Pushkin and Danzas began to make the slow journey back to the capital. In spite of losing so much blood and being in pain, Pushkin is said to have told several stories about duels, and even joked. One anecdote, however, reminded him of the death of a friend who had been wounded in the abdomen and he suddenly seemed to realise the possible seriousness of his own wound. He then gave Danzas careful instructions about the way his injuries should be presented to his wife.

When the carriage arrived at Pushkin's apartment on the Moyka, Danzas went in and found Natalya in Alexandra's room. She looked as if she was already afraid at what his sudden arrival might mean. Danzas told her Pushkin had been wounded in a duel, but that she was not to worry as it was not serious. Hearing his words, but fearing what they disguised, she rushed to meet her husband at the entrance. There Pushkin tried to reassure her that he was not dangerously hurt, but she fainted on seeing him.

Pushkin's old valet carried the poet in his arms to his study. Pushkin asked for clean linen and then lay on the divan to wait for doctors, including Arendt, the Court physician. It was Dr Sholts, however, primarily an obstetrician, who arrived first at seven o'clock with Dr Zadler.

Pushkin asked his wife, Danzas and his publisher Pletnev, who had come on a visit, to leave the room during the examination. The doctors could not hide from him the seriousness of his wound. Pushkin knew he was continuing to lose a great deal of blood and he asked if his condition was likely to prove fatal. When they confessed it was, he thanked them and is said to have remarked calmly, 'I must put my house in order.'

There was little the doctors could do for him, though Zadler went in search of instruments and Sholts applied a new compress. When he was asked whether he wanted to see his close friends, he looked around the books in his study and said, 'Farewell, friends.'

When Arendt, the Tsar's physician, arrived he examined the wound and told Pushkin there was little hope of recovery. Ice packs were put on his abdomen and Arendt then departed to report Pushkin's condition to the Tsar. Pushkin asked him to beg the Tsar not to prosecute his second, Danzas, for taking part in the duel. When Spassky, Pushkin's family physician, arrived, Pushkin asked him not to give his wife any false hopes as she was not a dissembler, and added, with unparalleled generosity of spirit, 'Poor thing, she suffers in innocence and she may suffer still more in the opinion of other people.'[8] Although accounts of so many of his words vary, all agree that his first words to Natalya when she appeared were 'Do not worry. You are not guilty in this matter.'

The news of Pushkin's duel and wound spread rapidly and soon there were crowds of admirers begging for information. The numbers were so great that Danzas was obliged to send for police reinforcements outside the house. Pushkin was much loved, and many of those who had come to inquire about him did so in tears. An old man who kept a shop next to the house exclaimed in astonishment, 'Why, I remember once how a Field Marshall died, but it was not like this.'[9] There was a stream of friends – Zhukovsky, the Vyazemskys, A. I. Turgenev and aunt Zagryazhskaya among others. Pushkin received them all calmly, refusing to allow Natalya into his room, however, as he did not wish her to see him suffer. When asked what it was that had touched the hearts of so many people, Zhukovsky answered by referring to one of Pushkin's Little Tragedies, 'Mozart and Salieri': 'In general, genius is good.'

When, at midnight, Dr Arendt returned from the Tsar, he is said to have brought a personal note from Nicholas, which read: 'If God does not permit us to see thee any more in this world, I send thee my farewell and the last advice: Die as a Christian. About your [in the second person] wife and children, do not worry: I will take care of them.'[10]

Pushkin asked to keep the pencilled letter, but Arendt had been ordered to bring it back to the Tsar. There is no written evidence to support this apocryphal story but, as has already been mentioned, the Tsar did, indeed, make provision for Natalya and the children.

Although there was a brief improvement in Pushkin's condition the following day, towards evening gangrene set in and the pain returned. He said goodbye to his closest friends one by one, and regretted that he was unable to say farewell to Ivan Pushchin. At about two o'clock he sent for Natalya, asking for cloudberries. On her knees, she fed him cloudberry preserve with a spoon. Zhukovsky stood at the head of the bed and Turgenev at his side. Pushkin began to hallucinate, dreaming of climbing to the top of his own bookcases and getting dizzy there. Suddenly, as if awaking from a sleep, he opened his eyes wide and said, 'Life is ended. It is hard to breathe. Something is weighing me down.'[11]

Natalya returned to the room at the very moment Pushkin died and threw herself sobbing at his side, calling, 'Pushkin, Pushkin, are you living?' Pushkin died at a quarter to three.

After everyone else had gone, Zhukovsky remained, looking at the calm, dead face of his friend and trying to fathom the purity of his thoughtful expression. 'At that precise moment it may be said that I saw death itself, divinely mysterious, death without its veil. What a stamp it placed on his face ... I swear to you I have never seen on his face an expression of such profound, sublime and triumphal thought. Such was the end of our Pushkin.'[12]

EPILOGUE

The Imperial authorities, who had taken no trouble to prevent the duel that led to Pushkin's death, were seriously alarmed at the widespread signs of popular grief. In the secret archives of the Third Department, indeed, a document has survived, compiled by Kashintsev, an officer of the Tsar's secret police. This report speaks of 'too much attention being paid of a kind only suitable for people who had displayed exceptional merit, whereas the principal part of this poet's work, as everyone admits, is both freethinking and immoral'.[1] Kashintsev refused to allow the Simonov Archimandrite to be approached with a request for a full-scale memorial service, or even to have Professor Pogodin read a tribute in Pushkin's honour. Black borders around newspaper announcements of Pushkin's death were forbidden, and the author of one of the obituaries that appeared on 30 January was reprimanded by the censor for the extravagance of his praise. 'Was Pushkin a Commander, a Minister or a Statesman?'

The Requiem Mass, to which Natalya Nikolaevna had already issued invitations, was to have been held at St Isaac's Cathedral on 1 February at 11 a.m. At the last moment it was transferred to another, smaller church near Pushkin's apartment. Nevertheless, a long line of mourners filed past his coffin, including noble friends such as Vyazemsky and Zhukovsky and people from every part of society, some openly in tears, some dressed in sheepskin coats or rags, and many students, even though the University had been expressly forbidden to interrupt its courses so that they might attend the requiem.

Pushkin was to be buried at Mikhaylovskoe. Benckendorf, after a meeting with the Tsar, ordered the Governor of the province of Pskov not to allow any ceremony at the burial other than the rites customary for any member of the nobility. A. I. Turgenev was given the task of escorting Pushkin's body to Mikhaylovskoe. The few mourners there included Praskovya Osipova and Pushkin's faithful old servant Nikita

Kozlov. For all Zhukovsky's pleas, the Tsar was adamant that no monument should be erected to the memory of Alexander Sergeevich Pushkin.

Perhaps the most moving of all the many letters which speak of personal grief at the death of Pushkin was that of Evgeny Baratynsky, the only poet of a stature in the least comparable to Pushkin, who writes of sharing his grief with Pushkin's father and hearing the old man declare, 'It only remains for me to pray to God that I should not lose my memory, so that I should not forget him.'[2]

Among closer friends, it was Gogol who expressed loss with the most pain:

> All that brought joy to my life, all that gave me the greatest pleasure, vanished with him ... I did not write a single line without imagining him standing before me. What would he say of it? What would he notice? What would make him laugh?[3]

In the weeks following Pushkin's death, manuscript copies of Mikhail Lermontov's poem 'Death of a Poet' began to circulate in St Petersburg. Lermontov, a 22-year-old hussar, and a genius of the next generation, not only condemned the foreign murderer of a Russian poet in his poem but also denounced those at Court who had taken no action to prevent the tragedy.

> A greedy crowd lurking behind the throne,
> Hangmen of freedom, genius and fame,
> You hide behind the shelter of the law
> Though truth and justice stand before you plain.
> In God's court, you accomplices in crime,
> Another judgement threatens. He will wait,
> Nor is He moved by any golden bait.
> He knows your thoughts and actions in good time.
> None of your petty slanders then will touch
> His heart, nor whisper do you good,
> Nor change the sentence of that final Judge.
> No shame wipe off the murdered poet's blood.

Nicholas was incensed at the implication of Court involvement and, after a medical examination to establish whether Lermontov was quite sane, had him exiled to a dragoon regiment in the Caucasus.

In the higher echelons of the aristocracy fewer people grieved for Pushkin, and there were even those ready to lament the fate of d'Anthès.

Provided all the proper conditions of private combat were observed, participants in duels were not usually punished. Both Heeckeren and d'Anthès, who had seen Pushkin mainly in court circles where he had seemed unimpressive, were astonished at the popular rage that followed his death. Neither read Russian or had grasped the extent of Pushkin's importance as a national figure. In spite of Heeckeren's diplomatic influence, and to the indignation of his friends, d'Anthès was immediately arrested and brought before a court-martial. There he was initially condemned to death, though the Tsar ordered the sentence to be commuted to life imprisonment.

We now have a letter from d'Anthès[4] dated between 18 February and 21 March 1837. This letter was written from prison to his wife Ekaterina. It is marked by self-pity rather than regret, still less remorse:

> My good friend, you always like to do as you wish. That's how you manage to get what you asked for.[5] I knew in advance they would not allow you to come and see me. The commander stated that very clearly. And you can't hope to see me without permission, because the officer who was on guard yesterday would be arrested for allowing you to come to the guard room. The room in which I am kept is surrounded by spies, who know everything I am doing; for example, this morning the Commander of the Grenadier regiment came to reprimand the officer I mentioned, and then afterwards the Commander of the Peter and Paul fortress appeared with the same task. So you see, my dear friend, we must abandon hope any tricks will work. I think it was useless for the Baron to present his own appeal inside your letter. He should present the request in his own name, and, of course, in that case the Commander could not refuse him ... I embrace you both with all my heart.
> Georges
>
> P.S. If you can please send me newspapers.

Before d'Anthès was deported from Russia on 19 March he was allowed a final meeting with both Heeckeren and Ekaterina, as the following letter, written between 18 February and 24 March, makes plain:

> Madame La Baronesse de Heeckeren
> I hope, my good and excellent friend, that you will sleep well tonight and wait patiently for our meeting tomorrow. I talked to the Commander, and your visit has been allowed. But you must write a note to his wife in the

morning, and indicate which persons will escort you. He told me that you could bring anybody you want. I embrace you as much as I love you, which means very strongly.

Georges

D'Anthès added a postscript for Baron Heeckeren:

To the Baron, my kind friend, now I hope you are no longer so worried about me. And I embrace you as I embrace Katherine.

Baron Van Heeckeren was forced to give up his position as Ambassador and leave St Petersburg, taking with him the customary jewelled tobacco pouch from the Tsar as a sign of *congé*. His diplomatic career, however, suffered little more than a short break and he was appointed Ambassador to Vienna three years later.

After the Ministerial deliberations we have already discussed, d'Anthès was adopted formally as Van Heeckeren's heir and continued to live in apparent contentment with Ekaterina, with whom he had several children. Ekaterina died young, but d'Anthès lived on for a further sixty years.

As for Natalya, she withdrew to the country, as Pushkin had requested, for two years, returning to the Court only at the Tsar's particular request. The Tsar showed Natalya remarkable kindness in her widowhood. He made her a direct payment of 10,000 roubles, paid off all the debts on Pushkin's estate and appointed both of Pushkin's sons as pages to his Court with an allowance of 1,500 roubles to each for their education.

On her return to Court, Natalya had lost little of her beauty and the Tsar ordered a portrait to be painted of her in the dress she wore for the costume ball she attended in 1839. In 1844 she married P. P. Lanskoy, a Major General of the Life Guards. It will be remembered that Lanskoy was a friend of d'Anthès. Nicholas much approved of the match and, indeed, Lanskoy's career advanced very swiftly after the marriage; the Tsar was a frequent visitor at the family home. Natalya had three further children by Lanskoy, and the Tsar was godfather to the first.

Altogether, those who had brought Pushkin's early death upon him suffered little harm as a result, although there were those eager to avenge his death: the Polish poet Mickiewicz, for instance, sent an open challenge to d'Anthès. Those who loved Pushkin could only remember what he had written in his poem for André Chenier:

Soon I shall die. Companions of my spirit,
Keep safely, each of you, a manuscript;
And, faithful band, in more propitious times
Foregather now and then to read my lines;
Carefully listen, then say, 'This is he;
This is his voice.' And from eternity
I'll come to you unseen, and seated near
I'll listen with you...[6]

For Pushkin's victory over the ill-natured and untalented courtiers who had made his last year so miserable with their heartless mockery, it was necessary to wait rather longer than the twenty years of Nicholas I's increasingly repressive reign. In the immediate aftermath of Pushkin's death literary critics, concerned above all with the 'social content' of literature, turned against what they saw as his aristocratic frivolity and aestheticism.

The first posthumous edition of Pushkin's work, published between 1838 and 1841, was censored and incomplete, and there was little chance of correcting the distortions for many years. The Revolutions of 1848, which rocked the rest of Europe, aroused such terror in St Petersburg that all repressive measures were redoubled. As P. Annenkov, Pushkin's first sensitive and scrupulous biographer, put it, 'People live now as though in hiding. The streets and everywhere else are ruled by the police, officials and amateur informers.'

Nevertheless, Pushkin's posthumous reputation was quietly being made. The first serious assessment of Pushkin in relation to the development of Russian literature was that of the great critic Vissarion Belinsky in 1844, who gave an account of *Evgeny Onegin* as an 'encyclopedia of Russian life'. Nikolay Gogol, who had already written in 1834, 'in his works, as if in a dictionary, are contained all the wealth, strength and flexibility of our language,' wrote warmly in 1852 of his debts to Pushkin's encouragement, admitting proudly that he owed the plots of his two best-known works – 'Dead Souls' and 'The Inspector General' – to Pushkin's casual generosity.

However much 'realist critics', notably Dmitry Pisarev, disputed Belinsky's claim for Pushkin's central importance, his place as a cultural icon was becoming assured. P. Annenkov (the biographer mentioned above) whose brother had been in the same regiment as Natalya's husband General Lanskoy, gained access to Pushkin's manuscripts when Natalya and Lanskoy wanted to bring out a new edition of the poet's work. Encouraged by Vyazemsky, Annenkov began assembling the materials for a life of the poet, drawing memoirs from Pushkin's father, sister and younger brother, Danzas, P. V. Nashchokin and Pletnev, and suggesting to Anna Petrovna Kern that she should write her own recollections.

His *Materialy* of 1853 give a marvellous picture of Pushkin's poetry and personality. There was much that could not be included, naturally – for instance, any reference to Pushkin's friendship with the Decembrists, his own exile in the south, or – as Natalya was still alive – of the circumstances which led to the fatal duel. However, in addition to the *Materialy*, Annenkov prepared a new and fuller collection of Pushkin's work which came out in six volumes between 1853 and 1855. In 1857 Annenkov made use of the more relaxed censorship conditions under the new Tsar Alexander II to add a further volume.

On 19 October 1869 a committee was formed to renew the question of a monument to Pushkin, and in April 1871 Alexander II personally supported the project. The Russian sculptor Opekushin was given the commission, and a statue in Pushkin's honour was unveiled in Moscow on 5 June 1880 during a public holiday lasting three days. Hundreds of thousands of Russians converged on the ceremony, and Turgenev (not Pushkin's friend A. I. Turgenev but the celebrated writer) gave a measured address, placing him among the immortals, though below Homer and Shakespeare. His speech made little impact on the vast crowd. It was a matter of some sadness to Turgenev that Lev Tolstoy, who had expressed so much admiration for Pushkin, particularly his *Tales of Belkin*, earlier in his life, had come by 1880 to distrust all literature, including his own, as a distraction from the truths of Christian Revelation. He therefore refused to attend the ceremony.

It was Dostoevsky who, on 8 June, gave a speech which earned the crowd's ovation. There are some ironies in this as Dostoevsky's tribute projected his own Slavophile image on to the poet he praised, and grotesquely misrepresented him as a nationalist and Christian prophet leading Russia against the forces of the secular West.

Turgenev had misread not only the mood of the assembled crowd but also the peculiar status the Russian people were ready to accord their poet, which was to have an almost religious fervour, however surprising that might have been to Pushkin himself.

Barely a year after these events the government, in reaction to the assassination of Alexander II, put a halt to any celebration of the fiftieth anniversary of Pushkin's death. What they had not thought to prevent, however, was the sale of his books. At one well-known St Petersburg bookshop, where the entire stock of Pushkin's work was sold out by midday, there were riots.[7]

In the West, where his work has generally been received with less enthusiasm, Pushkin's fame spread first through the use composers made of his stories. Ironically, Pushkin, who had once declared he would not be a librettist even to Rossini, was seized upon by some of the most important Russian writers of opera. Mikhail Glinka's opera *Ruslan and Lyudmila* had its first performance in St Petersburg as early as 1842. There were at least four attempts to base an opera on *Boris Godunov*, two by Modest Mussorgsky and two by Rimsky Korsakov. Mussorgsky's first version of 1869 was rejected by the committee of Imperial theatres, but in January 1874 another, much cut version was performed successfully and has since been played widely.

It was Peter Ilyich Tchaikovsky who did most to make Pushkin's work popular. His *Evgeny Onegin* was first performed publicly in Moscow in 1881, went to London the year afterwards and subsequently to Milan, New York and all the opera houses of the world. His *Mazepa* (based on Pushkin's *Poltava*) was first performed in 1884, while his *Queen of Spades* received in 1890 a first performance in La Scala, Milan. Rimsky Korsakov's *Tsar Saltan*, first performed in Moscow on 3 November 1900, has been performed in opera houses as far away as Buenos Aires. Rimsky Korsakov's last opera, *The Golden Cockerel*, however, was not performed until after his death; the censor evidently judged that its message remained dangerous.

By the celebrations of 1899 the literary avant garde, under the influence of Symbolism and particularly the poet Valery Bryusov, renewed the struggle to restore Pushkin's most important works from the distortions and cuts made by the censorship. A fashion developed among poets for essays called 'My Pushkin', in which poets defined themselves by their own readings of their great predecessor.

With the Revolution in 1917 it might have been expected that the Bolsheviks would follow the iconoclastic Futurists in wishing to jettison Pushkin along with Dostoevsky and Tolstoy as having no relevance to the twentieth century. For all the Bolshevik desire to promote proletarian art, however, they chose instead to present him as a noble victim of the Tsar, emphasising his friends among the Decembrists, his love for folk lore and his peasant nanny. Lunacharsky, the Commisar for the Arts, in an unfinished essay on Pushkin, even made a plea for considering class origin irrelevant to excellence. Alexander Blok, whose celebrated poem, 'The Twelve', shows Christ himself riding with the Revolution, wrote memorably, 'The gloomy names of Emperors, generals, inventors of weapons of murder, the torturers and the martyrs of life. And next to them – this one bright name: Pushkin.'

There were ironies in the changing Pushkin myth as it was to grow in the Soviet years. Extravagant celebrations took place in 1937 to mark the first centenary of Pushkin's death, even though it was the grimmest year of Stalin's purges of the intelligentsia. Nevertheless, as writers like Evgenia Ginzburg attest, Pushkin's poetry accompanied all of those who went into Stalin's Gulag. One of Pushkin's poems, 'The Prophet', essentially a rendering of Isaiah, speaks of the poet as one whose lips God touches with the fire of truth. Pushkin remained a powerful image of truth-telling throughout the Soviet era.

Anna Akhmatova saw herself as a poet in this tradition, particularly in poems which could not even be written down under Stalin. Her intuitions have been mentioned at several points in this book, and she expressed particular indignation at Natalya Goncharova's unworthiness as a mate for one of the finest minds of the day. Herself an acknowledged beauty, Akhmatova particularly condemned Natalya's vanity and self-deception. Marina Tsvetaeva, Akhmatova's only equal as a woman poet of the twentieth century, saw Pushkin in her own idiosyncratic way as quintessentially an outsider. She recalls visiting the Pushkin monument in Moscow where he seemed 'A black giant among white children ... The Russian poet – is a Negro – is a Negro and the poet – was struck down'. A Goncharova, she observed contemptuously, was no more than an instrument for the poet's destruction by a society in which he was always an alien.

Pushkin has remained an iconic figure, even after the collapse of the Soviet Union, though the younger generation in post-Soviet Russia is rethinking its relationship to 'the educated Western gentry who left a legacy of independence and dignity to the embattled intellectuals of the Soviet period, but whose scorn for commerce, its politics of palace rebellion, and its lack of participation in the liberal professions may have left a more negative heritage for the Russia which finds itself trying to develop a market economy, modern professions, and a parliamentary democracy'.[8]

The hold Pushkin has maintained for so long on the Russian imagination lies exactly in the area where art and ethics meet. For all his impatience with didactic poetry, art does have an ethical function for Pushkin. As Caryl Emerson of Princeton University explains in her essay on 'Pushkin as Critic',[9] 'It was a practising ground for the virtues – and especially those virtues that enable a creative attitude towards work: curiosity, precision, discipline, good humour in the face of disappointment, gratitude.' Perhaps it is not surprising that precision and grace should have enduring appeal in a country where life has commonly been inchoate and brutal.

All the figures so much more important than Pushkin during his short life now find themselves minor figures in 'The Age of Pushkin', as Anna Akhmatova observed in 1961, some five years before her own death. 'All the beauties, ladies in waiting, mistresses of the salons, Dames of the Order of St Catherine, members of the Imperial Court, ministers, aides-de-camp, gradually began to be referred to as contemporaries of Pushkin, and at length have been simply laid to rest (with their dates of birth and death garbled) in the indexes to editions of Pushkin's works.'[10]

NOTES

INTRODUCTION

1 The biographies still to be found in libraries are also unsatisfactory, though there is a short book by the excellent critic D. S. Mirsky (1926) and a scholarly work by Ernest Simmons (Harvard, 1937) which remain useful. Henry Troyat's *Pouchkine* (1946, in English translation 1950) has many intriguing details, but is written like a popular novel with freely invented dialogue. David Magarshack's *Pushkin: A biography* (1967) includes later research, but has neither notes nor references. The most recent biographer, Robin Edmonds (1994), deliberately avoids any attempt to make Pushkin's poetry accessible to the non-Russian speaking reader, but is very useful on the diplomatic and historical context of Pushkin's life.

2 Frans Suasso, *Dichter, Dame, Diplomat* (Leiden, 1988)

3 This continues work begun by Abram Efros in 1933, and by T. G. Tsyavlovskaya in *Risunki Pushkina*, Moscow, 1983

4 Chapter 1, verse 50

5 The poem was not published until 1829.

6 A. P. Kern, *Vospominaniya, dnevniki, perepiska*, Moscow, 1974

7 See Vickery: 'Odessa: Watershed Year', David Bethea ed., *Pushkin Today*, Indianapolis, 1993

8 A. D. P. Briggs, *Alexander Pushkin* (Croom Helm, 1982)

9 Ibid.

CHAPTER ONE *Imperial Russia*

1 Edmonds, p. 15

CHAPTER TWO *Childhood*

1 Pushkin Vol VII, p. 74

2 *Pushkin v vospominaniyakh ego sovremennikov*, Moscow, 1956, p. 30

3 According to Ivan Liprandi, a friend of Pushkin's from Bessarabia

4 *Pushkin v vospominaniyakh ego sovremennikov*, Moscow, 1956, p. 3

5 Yury Lotman, *Pushkin: biography of the writer. Articles and notes, 1960–1990, 'Evgeny Onegin': commentary* (St Petersburg, 1995), p. 28

6 'Zapiski, M. A. Korfa', in Ya. K. Grot, *Pushkin ego v vospominaniyakh litseysksie tovarischchi*, p. 250

7 'A journey from Moscow to Petersburg', cited Magarshack, p. 20

8 *Letopis'zhizni i tvorchestva, A. S. Pushkina 1799–1826*, ed. M. A. Tsyavlovskaya 2nd edn, Leningrad, 1991

9 P. K. Guber, *Don Zhuansky Spisok Pushkina* (Moscow, 1990)

10 Troyat, *Pouchkine*, p. 43

11 Tsyavlovskaya, op. cit., p. 28

12 Folio 42, Pushkinsky Dom Notebook 836

13 'Russky Pelam', IV, 702–703

14 Tsyavlovskaya, op. cit., p. 35

15 Molodost A. S. 'Pushkina po razkazam ego mladsshogo brata' in L. N. Mailkov, *Pushkin: biograficheskie istoriko-literaturnye ocherki*, St Petersburg, 1899

16 Simmons, *Pushkin*, p. 31

17 Simmons, op. cit., p. 32

18 Simmons, op. cit., p. 32 quoting an unnamed friend

19 In 'Rodoslovnaya Pushkinov i Gannibalov', *Polnoe Sobranie Sochineniy*, 4th ed. (Moscow, 1934) VI, p. 382

20 Simmons, op. cit., p. 12

21 See J. Thomas Shaw, David Bethea, op. cit.

22 Onegin, Vol. III, p. 438

CHAPTER THREE *Schooldays*

1 Ivan Pushchin, *Zapiski o Pushkine i pisma*, ed. S. Straykh, (Moscow, 1956) in Cathy Porter's translation, p. 44

2 Pushchin, op. cit., p. 44

3 Lotman, op. cit., p. 26

4 Lotman, op. cit., p. 29

5 Lotman, op. cit., p. 29

6 P. K. Guber, Moscow, 1990

7 Lotman, p. 330

8 *Pushkin v vospominaniyakh ego sovremennikov*

9 Pushchin, p. 53

10 Pushchin, p. 55

11 Ibid.
12 Simmons, op. cit., p. 44
13 'K Galichu', I, p. 112
14 '19 Oktyabrya 1825'
15 Pushkin, Vol. I, p. 79
16 Wolff, facing p. 46
17 Verse 2, Chapter 8, trans. Charles Johnston
18 *Pushkin v vospominaniyakh ego sovremennikov*, 1956, p. 22
19 Shaw, Vol. I, p. 59
20 Trans. Jill Higgs
21 His Don Juan list
22 Pushchin, op. cit., p. 63
23 Told by K. A. Shtorkh in *Russkaya Starina* (1879) XXV, 378-9
24 Quoted in Guber, op. cit.
25 Quoted in Guber, op. cit.
26 Trans. Antony Wood
27 Trans. Jill Higgs
28 Pushchin, op. cit., p. 65
29 Simmons, p. 64

CHAPTER FOUR *Dissipations*

1 Simmons, p. 68
2 L. S. Pushkin 'Biographical information about A. S. Pushkin until 1826' in *Pushkin v. vospominaniyakh sovremennikov*, ed. D. Golin, Moscow, 1974
3 Prince V. M. Volkonsky, I, p. 528
4 Quoted Simmons, p. 79
5 Baron Korf, op. cit.
6 'Iz zapisnoi knizhki, 1820 1822' VI, p. 374
7 Zernov, 1945, p. 57
8 Mirsky, p. 29
9 'Moi zamechaniya o russkom teatre' VI, pp. 7-13
10 Vyazemsky, *Sobranie sochineniy* (St Petersburg, 1893)
11 Shaw, Vol. I, p. 64
12 L. S. Pushkin, 'Biographical information about A. S. Pushkin until 1826' in *Pushkin v. vospominaniyakh sovremennikov*, ed. D. Golin, Moscow, 1974
13 Simmons, p. 92
14 Pushchin, p. 69
15 Pushchin, p. 70
16 Ibid., p. 71

17 *Sobranie sochineniy,* St Petersburg 1893, p. 515

18 Simmons, p. 96

19 Alan Palmer, *Alexander* I, p. 23

20 Pushkinsky Dom, no. 829

21 N. Glinka, 'Udalenie Pushkina iz Peterburga', *Russkye Arkhiv,* 1866, p. 918

22 Simmons, p. 96

CHAPTER FIVE *To The south*

 1 Quoted in Simmons, op. cit., p. 100

 2 I. P. Liprandi, Russky Archiv, 1866, pp. 1412–16

 3 *Russky Vestnik,* St Petersburg, 1841, no. 1

 4 *Russky Arkhiv,* 1863, p. 900

 5 Letter to his brother, 24 Sept. 1820 Shaw, *Letters,* Vol. I, p. 75

 6 Rudykovsky, op. cit.

 7 Fomachev, p. 52, commenting on PD 834

 8 Pushkin's father in a memoir written after Pushkin's death always maintained Pushkin had had the basis for doing so since his childhood.

 9 M. N. Volkonskaya, *Zapiski,* 2nd edn, Moscow, 1921, p. 62

10 Guber, op. cit., p. 52

11 Quoted in Magarshack, *Pushkin,* p. 99

CHAPTER SIX *Kishinev*

 1 Trans. Jill Higgs

 2 Quoted in Simmons, p. 121

 3 Briggs, p. 137

 4 Yakushkin, *Zapiski,* p. 49

 5 *Perepiska,* No. 99, I, p. 137

 6 Tsyavlovsky, *Letopis,* op. cit., pp. 292–3

 7 A. Raspovov, 'Vstrecha s A. S. Pushkinym', *Russkaya Starina* (1876) XV, p. 464

 8 Tsyavlovskaya, op. cit., p. 155

 9 Shaw, op. cit., Vol. II, p. 88

10 Shaw, op. cit., Vol. I, p. 105

11 Shaw, op. cit., Vol. I, p. 110

12 Tsyavlovskaya, p. 70–71

13 Shaw, op. cit., Vol. I, p. 92

14 Soviet editors, notoriously uneasy about explicit sexual references, did, nevertheless, print this poem, cf. A. D. P. Briggs, p. 136.

15 Trans. D. M. Thomas, Pushkin, *The Bronze Horseman and other poems*

16 Trans. D. M. Thomas

17 Shaw, op. cit., Vol. I, p. 111

18 Simmons, quoted p. 126

19 Simmons, p. 130

20 P. I. Bartenev, 'K Biografii v Pushkina, *Russky Arkhiv*, 1866, p. 1133

21 Ibid.

22 Simmons, p. 128

23 V. P. Gorchakov, 'Iz dnevnika ob. A. S. Pushkine', *Moskvityanin* (1850), No. 2, pp. 152–3

24 Ibid.

25 Guber, op. cit. (Pushkin may, however, have learnt this song from the waitress Marionilla at the Green Inn.)

26 Guber, op. cit., p. 68

27 Shaw, op. cit., Vol. I, p. 79

28 Edmonds, p. 75

29 Ibid.

30 Wolff, p. 47

31 Shaw, op. cit., Vol. I, p. 95

32 Shaw, Vol. I, p. 103

33 Ibid.

34 Shaw, Vol. I, p. 135

35 Draft quoted in Tatyana Wolff, p. 61

36 Shaw, Vol. II, p. 77

37 Tatyana Wolff, p. 43

CHAPTER SEVEN *Odessa: July 1823–July 1824*

1   F. F. Vigel *Zapiski*, ed. S. Ya Shtraykh, Moscow, 1928 II, pp. 204–5

2   Shaw, Vol. I, p. 140

3   Shaw, Vol. I, p. 136

4   Ibid.

5   Henri Troyat, *Pushkin*, tr. Amphoux, p. 78

6   Guber, p. 75

7   Ibid.

8   L. S. Pushkin, op. cit.

9   Guber, p. 65

10 Guber, p. 76

11 Guber, p. 77

12 Magarshack, p. 139

13 Guber, p. 87

14 Trans. Antony Wood

15 Quoted in Simmons, p. 176

16 Quoted in Simmons, p. 178

17 Magarshack, p. 173

18 Trans. Antony Wood

19 Kozlov was a mediocre contemporary writer.

20 Shaw, Vol. 1, p. 152

21 *Perepiska*, no. 65, 1, 95

22 Shaw, Vol. 1, p. 153

23 Shaw, Vol. 1, p. 162

24 Shaw, Vol. 1, p. 155

25 Shaw, Vol. 1, p. 161

26 Quoted in Magarshack

27 *Perepiska*, No. 70, 1, p. 103

28 Simmons, p. 180

29 Magarshack, p. 154

30 Translations from *Evgeny Onegin* are taken from James E. Falen (World Classics, Oxford University Press, 1997).

CHAPTER EIGHT *Mikhaylovskoe 1824–6*

1 Mirsky, p. 81

2 Magarshack, p. 160

3 Shaw, Vol. 1, p. 183

4 Shaw, Vol. 1, p. 190

5 *Perepiska*, No. 108, 1, pp. 147–8

6 *Perepiska*, No. 269, 1, p. 388

7 Shaw, Vol. 1, p.308

8 Mirsky, p. 83

9 Ibid.

10 Mirsky, p. 84

11 I. I. Pushchin, op. cit.

12 Pushchin, *Zapiski*, op. cit.

13 Trans. A. D. P. Briggs

14 Magarshack, p. 182

15 Ibid.

16 Magarshack, p. 184

17 Magarshack, p. 185

18 Kern, op. cit.

19 Kern, op. cit.

20 Shaw, op. cit., Vol. I, p. 194

21 Mirsky, p. 87

22 'Vospominanya A. P. Markavoy-Vinogradskoy', in L. N. Mailkov, *Pushkin*, p. 233

23 Kern, op. cit.

24 Shaw, Vol. I, p. 233

25 A. P. Kern, op. cit.

26 Shaw, Vol. I, p. 233

27 Shaw, Vol. I, p. 225

28 Shaw, Vol. I, p. 263

29 Tsyavlovsky, op. cit., p. 99

30 Tsyavlovsky, op. cit., p. 459

31 Shaw, Vol. I, p. 209

32 Stanza 32 in Nabokov

33 Trans. Jill Higgs

34 Quoted in Simmons, p. 237

35 Shaw, Vol. I, p. 228

36 Shaw, Vol. I, p. 242

37 Shaw, Vol. I, p. 248

38 Ibid.

39 Shaw, Vol. I, p. 194

40 Shaw, Vol. I, p. 267

41 Cited in Klyuchevsky, *Sochinenya*, Vol. v, p. 254

42 Shaw, Vol. I, p. 303

43 Shaw, Vol. I, p. 303

44 Shaw, Vol. I, p. 311

45 Shaw, Vol. I, p. 311

46 PD 836

47 Quoted in Simmons, p. 248

CHAPTER NINE *Pushkin and the Tsar*

1 Simmons, p. 220

2 Simmons, op. cit.

3 Trans. by A. D. P. Briggs

4 M. P. Pogodin, *Russky Arkhiv*, 1865, p. 97

5 Yury Lotman, op. cit., p. 366

6 *Russky Arkhiv*, 1865, Sub. 1248–9

7 Mirsky, p. 101

8 Eidelman 1985, p. 193, 'Secretnaya audienciya' *Novy Mir*, pp. 190–217
9 Gertzen Kilokol, 1 Marta 1860, list 64, p. 534
10 N. I. Lorer *Zapiski moego vremeni*, and Veresaev, *Pushkin v zhizni* (5th edn) Akademya, Moscow, 1932, cited in Simmons, p. 253
11 Davydov, MS, op. cit.
12 Lotman, op. cit., p. 367
13 T. G. Tsyavlovskaya, *Risunki Pushkina* (Pushkin's Drawings) ed. Moscow, 1986
14 Shaw, Vol. II, p. 338

CHAPTER TEN *Moscow*

1 I remember walking through Moscow alongside Yevtushenko in the 1970s and experiencing the same phenomenon.
2 *Perepiska* no. 273, IU, p. 374
3 B. L. Modzalevsky, 'Pushkin pod taynym nadzorom', p. 33, cited in Simmons, p. 260
4 A. N. Muravyov, *Acquaintance with Russian Poets*, Kiev 1871, pp. 11–13
5 Quoted in Simmons, p. 263
6 By, among others, Blagoy 1967, Tomashevsky 1977, Makagonenko 1985
7 See George J. Gutsche, 'Pushkin and Nicholas: the problem of "Stanzas" ', an article included in David Bethea's 'Pushkin Today', 1993, Indiana University Press.
8 Ibid.
9 For other parallels see Gutsche, p. 191
10 Guber, p. 180
11 Other accounts suggest golden hair.
12 Shaw, Vol. II, p. 336
13 Modzalevsky, op. cit., p. 64
14 Simmons, p. 270
15 Edwards, p. 120
16 Quoted in Simmons, p. 298
17 Mirsky, p. 110
18 Kern, op. cit., p. 46
19 Kern, op. cit., p. 260
20 Kern, ibid.
21 Simmons translates this in the future tense.
22 Mirsky 109
23 In an article for A. D. P. Briggs, *Why Pushkin?*, seen in MS

24 Anna Olenina, *Dnevnik Anny Alekseevny Oleninoy*, ed. Olga Oom (Paris, 1936) pp. 10–11
25 Pushkin's own note, cf. Wolff, p. 210
26 Korf, op. cit., p. 120
27 Trans. Jill Higgs
28 Kern, op. cit., p. 43
29 Kern, op. cit., p. 44
30 Tsyavlovskaya, op. cit., pp. 266
31 Kern, op. cit., p. 45
32 Trans. Antony Wood
33 Wolff, p. 216
34 Quoted in Simmons, p. 296
35 Ibid.
36 PD 837
37 John Bayley, *Pushkin: A Comparative Commentary* (Cambridge, 1971)
38 Annenkov, *Materialy*, p. 369

CHAPTER ELEVEN *Natalya*
 1 P. V. Annenkov, *Materialy*, p. 369
 2 I. Obodovskaya and M. Dementyev, *Natalya Nikolaevna Pushkina po epistolyarnym materialam*, Moscow, 1985, p. 31
 3 Ibid., p. 35
 4 Memoirs of Natalya Eropkina in Obodovskaya, op. cit., pp. 40–41
 5 Shaw, Vol. II, p. 371
 6 April 1830, Shaw, Vol. II, p. 405
 7 Shaw, Vol. II, p. 407
 8 Cited in Veresaev, *Pushkin v zhizni*, p. 212
 9 Quoted in Simmons, p. 320
10 Obodovskaya, op. cit., pp. 50–51
11 Quoted in Simmons, p. 332
12 Quoted in Robin Edmonds, p. 132
13 Annenkov, *Materialy*, Chapter XXI
14 Ibid.
15 Shaw, Vol. II, p. 415
16 Veresaev, op. cit., p. 21
17 Shaw, Vol. II, p. 426

CHAPTER TWELVE *Boldino*

1 Shaw, Vol. II, p. 433
2 All quotations from *Tales of Belkin* are taken from Gillon Aitkens's translation (Vintage, 1993).
3 Trans. Antony Wood in *Alexander Pushkin: Mozart and Salieri, Little Tragedies* (Angel Books, 1982)
4 Akhmatova, p. 181
5 E. A. Baratynsky, *Sochineniya* publ. 1881, pp. 510–11

CHAPTER THIRTEEN *Marriage*

1 Letter to N. I. Krivstov, 10 Feb. 1831. Shaw, Vol. II, p. 458
2 See letter to Pletnev, Shaw, Vol. II, p. 455
3 Obodovskaya, op. cit., p. 59
4 Obodovskaya, op. cit., p. 60
5 Edmonds, p. 138
6 Quoted in Edmonds, p. 141
7 *Russky Arkhiv*, 1902, III, 482
8 Obryvki iz pisem, mysli i zamechaniya, V.22
9 Obodovskaya, p. 63
10 Obodovskaya, p. 65
11 Ibid. 65
12 Shaw, Vol. II, p. 536
13 A paraphrase of this note is cited in Shaw, Vol. II, p. 578.
14 Pushkin's letter of 16 December 1831, Shaw, Vol. II, p. 539
15 Shaw, Vol. II, p. 539
16 Ibid.
17 Shaw, Vol. II, p. 557
18 Shaw, Vol. II, p. 561
19 Obodovskaya, p. 52
20 Shaw, Vol. II, p. 560
21 Obodovskaya, p. 84
22 PD 842
23 Shaw, Vol. III, p. 608
24 Obodovskaya, p. 96
25 Obodovskaya, p. 97
26 Shaw, Vol. III, p. 604
27 Quoted in Simmons, op. cit.
28 Shaw, Vol. III, p. 607
29 Shaw, Vol. III, p. 611

30 Ibid.

31 *Perepiska*, No. 1083, pp. 88–389

32 Shaw, Vol. III, p. 613

33 Shaw, Vol. III, p. 615

34 Obodovskaya, p. 103

35 Shaw, Vol. III, p. 615

36 Shaw, Vol. III, p. 619

37 Shaw, Vol. III, p. 614

CHAPTER FOURTEEN *The Bronze Horseman*

1 Akhmatova, p. 201

2 Mirsky, p. 193

3 Shaw, Vol. III, p. 622

4 Quoted in Magarshack, op. cit.

5 Ibid.

6 Shaw, Vol. III, p. 636

7 Ibid.

8 *I. I. Panaev, Literaturnye Vospominaniya*, Academia, L. 1928, pp. 143–4

9 Shaw, Vol. III, p. 643

10 Magarshack, p. 277

11 Shaw, Vol. III, p. 660

12 Magarshack, p. 278

13 Ibid.

CHAPTER FIFTEEN *The three sisters*

1 *Perepiska*, no. 856, III, p. 154

2 Obodovskaya and Dementev, p. 125

3 *Russky Arkhiv* (1878) I, p. 442

4 Obodovskaya, p. 130

5 Ibid.

6 Obodovskaya, p. 131

7 Obodovskaya, p. 133

8 *Risunki Pushkina*, ed. T. G. Tsyavlovskaya, Moscow, 1986

9 Obodovskaya, p. 155

10 Obodovskaya, p. 159

11 Shaw, Vol. III, p. 713

12 Shaw, Vol. III, p. 717

13 Shaw, Vol. III, p. 725

14 Obodovskaya, p. 179

15 Ibid.
16 Ibid.

CHAPTER SIXTEEN *D'Anthès*

1 All the quotations of letters from d'Anthès to Heeckeren, unless otherwise
   indicated, are taken from Serena Vitale, Vadim Stark, M. I. Pisareva, S. V.
   Slivanskaya, *Letters of Georges d'Anthès to Baron Heeckeren*, 'Zvezda' (St
   Petersburg, 1995, No. 9). Their dates are cited in the text.
2 Obodovskaya, p. 176
3 *Russky arkhiv*, 1901, III, p. 619
4 V. A. Sollogub, 'Zapiska': in B. L. Modzalevsky, *Pushkin* (Leningrad, 1929)
5 Trans. Antony Wood
6 Obodovskaya, p. 182
7 Pushkin, VI: 215, cited in Davydov, op. cit.
8 Trans. Antony Wood
9 Obodovskaya, pp. 165–6
10 Obodovskaya, p. 169
11 Obodovskaya, p. 167
12 Shchegolev, *Duel'l i Smert' Pushkina: issledovaniya i materialy* (Kniga,
   Moscow, 1987)
13 Shchegolev, pp. 421–2
14 S. L. Abramovich, *Pushkin v 1836 godu*, Nauka, Leningrad, 1989
15 Vickery, p. 102
16 Abramovich, 1836, Nauka Leningrad, 1989
17 Guber, p. 183
18 Andronnikov, pp. 69–70
19 Andronnikov, p. 70
20 Andronnikov, p. 71
21 P. E. Shchegolev, Moscow, 1928, p. 98
22 Shaw, Vol. III, p. 804
23 Obodovskaya, p. 185–6
24 Cited in Shchegolev
25 All letters between d'Anthès and Ekaterina derive from Serena Vitale, V. P.
   Stark, M. I. Pisareva, S. V. Slivinskaya ('Zvezda', St Petersburg, No. 8,
   1997). These were written in French, first published in Italian by Serena
   Vitale; here they are translated from the Russian of Vadim Stark by Alla
   Gelich.
26 Vitale comments that the hall he mentions was decorated by portraits of
   Russian field marshals.

27 The opera of Bellini

28 Frans Suasso, *Dichter, Dame, Diplomate* (London, 1988)

29 Ya. Lefkovich, 'Papers from the Netherlands Archives', (St Petersburg, *The Pushkin Journal*, 2–3, 1994–1995) pp. 19–32

30 Arapova, in 'Novoe vremya', 1907, no. 114413, p. 6

31 Shchegolev, p. 400

32 Shaw, Vol. III

33 Quoted in Simmons, p. 393

34 *Pushkin v pismakh Karamzinykh*, pp. 148 and 288

35 Quoted in Simmons, p. 394

36 Cited in Shchegolev, p. 284

37 Ibid.

38 Ibid.

CHAPTER SEVENTEEN *Duel and death*

1 Akhmatova, p. 231

2 Shchegolev, *Duel' i Smert' Pushkina*, p. 48

3 Simmons, p. 404

4 Sollogub *Vospominaniya*, p. 186

5 Shaw, Vol. III, pp. 817–18

6 Quoted in Simmons, p. 410

7 Shchegolev, 'Duel' i Smert' ', pp. 153–4

8 Shchegolev, p. 202

9 Ammosov, 'Posledni dni', p. 38

10 Shchegolev, p. 183

11 Shchegolev, p. 194

12 Shchegolev, pp. 194–5

EPILOGUE

1 I am indebted for this to a radio programme written by N. S. Nechaevaya and A. S. Frumkina, recently broadcast from Moscow and translated by Tatyana Wolff

2 Moscow broadcast transcript, translated by Tatyana Wolff

3 Quotation supplied by Tatyana Wolff

4 Vitale, op. cit.

5 This suggests Ekaterina had managed to have a letter delivered to d'Anthès

6 Trans. Antony Wood

7 Robin Edmonds, p. 237

8 William Todd III, 'Pushkin and Society: Post 1966 perspectives'; MS to

appear in David Bethea's forthcoming *Proceedings of the Wisconsin Pushkin Conference*

9 Caryl Emerson, 'Pushkin as Critic', from David Bethea (ed.) *Proceedings of the Wisconsin Pushkin Conference*

10 Anna Akhmatova, op. cit., p. 148

SELECT BIBLIOGRAPHY

S. L. Abramovich, *Pushkin: Posledniy god* (Sovetsky pisatel', Moscow, 1991)

Gillon Aitken, trans., *The complete prose tales of Alexandr Pushkin* (Vintage, 1993)

Anna Akhmatova, *Complete Prose* (Ardis)

Pavel Annenkov, *Materialy dlya biografii A. S. Pushkina* (Sovremennik, Moscow, 1984)

Walter Arndt, *Pushkin Threefold* (London, 1972)

John Bayley, *Pushkin: A Comparative Commentary* (Cambridge University Press, 1971)

David Bethea, ed., *Pushkin Today* (Indiana University Press, 1993)

A. D. P. Briggs, *Pushkin: A Critical Study* (London, 1983)

A. D. P. Briggs, *Eugene Onegin* (C.U.P., 1992)

A. D. P. Briggs, *Selected Poems of Pushkin* (Everyman, 1997)

S. L. Davydov, 'The Evolution of Pushkin's Political Thought'. MS from David Bethea's *Proceedings of Pushkin Conference*, Wisconsin

Fyodor Dostoevsky, *The Pushkin Speech* (trans. S. Koteliansky) (London, 1960)

Robin Edmonds, *Pushkin* (London, 1994)

Nathan Eidelman, *Conspiracy Against the Tsar: A Portrait of the Decembrists*, trans. Cynthia Carlisle (Progress Publishers, Moscow, 1985)

N. Ya. Eidelman, *Pushkin i Decabristi*, 1979

Caryl Emerson, 'Pushkin as Critic', MS from David Bethea's *Proceedings of Pushkin Conference*, Wisconsin

James E. Falen, *Evgeny Onegin* (Oxford University Press, 1996)

John Fennell, *Pushkin Selected Verse* (Bristol Classical Press, 1991)

S. A. Fomichev, *Grafici Pushkina* (Pushkinsky Dom, St Petersburg, 1993)

M. O. Gershenson, *Mudrost Pushkina* (Moscow, 1919)

P. K. Guber, *Don-Zhuansky Spisok Pushkina* (Moscow, 1990)

George Gutsche, 'Pushkin and Nicholas: The problem of "Stanzas" ', David Bethea, *Pushkin Today* (Indiana University Press, 1993)

Charles Johnson, *Evgeny Onegin* (Penguin)

A. P. Kern, *Vospominaniya o Pushkine* (Sovetskaya Rossiya, Moscow, 1988)

V. V. Kunin, *Posledniy god zhizni Pushkina* (Pravda, Moscow, 1988)

Ya. Lefkovich, *Papers from the Netherlands Archives* (St Petersburg, The Pushkin Journal, 2–3 (1994–1995) pp. 19–32

Dmitry Likhachev and Sergey Fomichev, *Introduction to the Working Notebooks of Alexander Pushkin* (London, St Petersburg, 1995)

Yu. Lotman, *Pushkin: Biografiya pisatelya: stat'i zametki 1850–1990: Yevgeniy, Kommentariy* (St Petersburg, 1995)

David Magarshack, *Pushkin: A biography* (London, 1967)

Jonathan Miller, ed., *The Don Giovanni Book: Myths of Seduction and Betrayal* (Faber and Faber, 1990)

Professor William Mills Todd III, 'Pushkin and Society: Post 1966 Perspectives', MS David Bethea's *Proceedings of Pushkin Conference*, Wisconsin

D. S. Mirsky, *Pushkin* (London, 1926)

Vladimir Nabokov, *Eugene Onegin*, 4 vols (Princeton University Press, 1975)

P. Obodovskaya and M. Dementyev, *Natalya Nikolaevna Pushkina po epistolarnym materialam*, 2nd edn (Sovetskaya Rossiya, Moscow, 1987; translations Cathy Porter)

Dmitry Obolensky, *The Penguin Book of Russian Verse* (London, 1965)

Alexander Pushkin and his time in the Fine Arts of the first half of the nineteenth century (Leningrad, Khudozhnik RSFSR 1987)

Alan Palmer, *Alexander I* (London, 1974)

I. I. Pushchin, *Zapiski o Pushkine* (Moscow, 1925; translations Cathy Porter)

Burton Raffel, *Russian Poetry under the Tsars* (State University New York Press, Albany, 1971)

J. Thomas Shaw, trans. and ed., *The Letters of Alexander Pushkin*, 3 vols (Indiana University Press and University of Pennsylvania Press, 1963)

J. Thomas Shaw, 'Pushkin on his African Heritage: Publications during his lifetime,' from *Pushkin Today*, ed. David Bethea (Indiana University Press, 1993)

P. E. Shchegolev, *Duel' i smert' Pushkina: issledovaniya i materialy*, 4th ed. (Kniga, Moscow, 1987)

Ernest Simmons, *Pushkin* (Oxford University Press, London, 1937)

Andrey Sinyavsky, *Strolls with Pushkin* (Yale, 1993)

V. P. Stark, *Pisma Zheorzha D'antesa k Ekaterine Goncharovoi* ('Zvezda' Magazine, St Petersburg No. 8, 1997)

Frans Suasso, *Dichter, Dame, Diplomat* (Leiden, 1988)

D. M. Thomas, *The Bronze Horseman and other poems* (Penguin 1982)

Marina Tsvetaeva, 'My Pushkin' (*Selected Prose*, trans. Janet King, Ardis)

M. A. Tsyavlovsky, *Letopis' zhizni i tvorchestva A. S. Pushkina 1799–1826*, 2nd edn (Nauka, Leningrad, 1991)

T. G. Tsyavlovskaya, *Risunki Pushkina* (Iskustvo, Moscow, 1970)

Walter Vickery, *Alexander Pushkin* (Boston, 1970)

Walter Vickery, 'Odessa: Watershed Year' in *Pushkin Today*, ed. David Bethea (Indiana University Press, 1993)

Walter Vickery, *Pushkin: Death of a poet* (Indiana University Press, 1979)

V. V. Veresaev, *Pushkin v zhizni: Sistematicheskiy svod podlinnykh svidetel'stv sovremennikov* 2 vols (Moscow, 1836)

Serena Vitale, *Il Bottone di Pushkin* (Adelphi Edizioni, Milano, 1995, 149)

Serena Vitale, V. P. Stark, M. I. Pisareva, S. V. Slivinskaya, *Letters of Georges D'Anthès to Baron Heeckeren 1835–1836*) ('Zvezda', Petersburg, 1995, no. 9)

Serena Vitale, V. P. Stark, M. I. Pisareva, S. V. Slivinskaya, *Letters from Georges D'Anthès to Ekaterina Goncharova 1836–1837* ('Zvezda', St Petersburg, no. 8, 1997)

Hugh Seton-Watson, *The Russian Empire, 1801–1917* (Oxford, 1967)

Solomon Volkov, *St Petersburg: A Cultural History*, trans. Antonina Bouis (London, 1996)

Solomon Volkov, *Mir Pushhkina* (Molodaya gvardiya, Moscow, 1989)

Pavel Vyazemsky, *Sobranie sochineniy* (St Petersburg, 1893)

'*Mozart and Salieri: The Little Tragedies*', translated with an introduction by A. W. (Angel Books, 1982)

Tatyana Wolff, *Pushkin on Literature* (Athlone Press, London and Stanford University Press, California, 1986; first published Methuen, 1971; revised Athlone Press, London, and North Western University Press, Evanston, 1998)

INDEX